1993

N o L

DIONYSIUS I
WAR-LORD OF SICILY

Frontispiece: Syracuse: Silver decadrachm, late 5th century

DIONYSIUS I

WAR-LORD OF SICILY

Brian Caven

YALE UNIVERSITY PRESS
NEW HAVEN AND LONDON 1990

Set in Linotron Goudy Old Style by Best-set Typesetters Ltd, Hong Kong; printed and bound by The Bath Press, Great Britain.

ISBN 0–300–04507–7

LC NUMBER 89–50651

CONTENTS

CONTENTS

ILLUSTRATIONS

Plates

ILLUSTRATIONS

Maps and Plans

Text Figure

FOREWORD

This monograph on the career of the tyrant Dionysius I of Syracuse was originally conceived, a good many years ago, as part of a much larger work on the history of tyranny in Sicily, from Phalaris in the early sixth century to Hieron II in the second half of the third. Unfortunately, the over-conscientiousness of the cleaners employed at that time by Birkbeck College led to the incineration of a great part of my research material, just as I was about to commence writing in earnest. What appears here rests upon that section of my notes – *de bonis quod restat reliquiarum* – that somehow escaped the holocaust and upon the all-embracing scholarship of K. F. Stroheker's *Dionysius I*. I desire, notwithstanding, to express my gratitude to Birkbeck, and in particular to Robert Swainson, lately Clerk to the Governors, for giving me accommodation in College after my retirement as a teacher, and to the Department of Classics there (now, alas, swept away upon the foul tide of rationalization) and to its late Head, Dr R. G. Mayer, and to Miss Betty Dove, its Secretary, for all their kindness.

I wish to acknowledge a grant from the Central Research Fund of the University of London, which, with help from the American Institute for Foreign Study, enabled me to visit Sicily and southern Italy. I wish also to thank those colleagues and friends who assisted me with advice, encouragement and sympathy: Dr Michael Trapp, who helped me with my Greek, Dr A. W. Johnston who put me right about the cities of Sicily, Dr M. J. Price of the British Museum Coins and Medals Department, who gave me invaluable assistance in the selection of coins for illustration, Dr A. F. Tatham, of King's College, and P. K. Clark, of the Royal Geographical Society, who found me maps of South Italy and Gela, Merle Abbott, of the Birkbeck College Geography Department, J. W. Kay and E. Else, of the College's Printing Unit, who helped me to produce the maps that appear in this book, the late Dr J. R. Bray (whose untimely death was such a grievous blow to scholarship), Judith Higgens, of the Institute of Archaeology, and Eleanore Harries and my wife, Jane, who read the proofs.

Lastly, but by no means least, let me express my thanks to my editor,

FOREWORD

Catharine Carver, who preserved me, in the teeth of a determined resistance, from countless errors of style, spelling and punctuation, and to Yale University Press, in the person of Robert Baldock, for its helpfulness, good humour and patience.

Brian Caven

Birkbeck College, London

The most important dates of the period covered by this book:

c. 485–478 BC	Tyranny at Syracuse of Gelon, son of Deinomenes, tyrant of Gela.
480	Battle of Himera, conclusion of a peace of seventy years' duration between the Sicilian Greeks and Carthage.
466/5	End of the Deinomenid tyranny at Syracuse, introduction of *politeia*.
431	Outbreak of Peloponnesian War in Greece.
? 430	Birth of Dionysius, son of Hermocritus.
427–424	First Athenian expedition to Sicily.
415–413	The great Athenian expedition to Sicily.
412	Reforms of Diocles – *politeia* replaced by democracy at Syracuse.
409	Exile of Hermocrates. Hannibal's invasion of Sicily, destruction of Selinus and Himera.
408–407	Return to Sicily, campaign and death of Hermocrates.
406	First Punic War, fall of Acragas.
405	Dionysius elected *Stratēgos Autokrator*. Battle of Gela. Peace of Himilco.
404	Surrender of Athens – end of the Peloponnesian War – beginning of the 'Hegemony of Sparta'. The Great Revolt at Syracuse.
403	End of the Great Revolt, Dionysius' tyranny firmly established.
403–399	Dionysius makes himself ruler (*archōn*) of eastern Sicily.
397	Second Punic War. Capture of Motya.
396	Himilco in Sicily, battle of Catane, siege of Syracuse.
395	Overthrow of Himilco.
394	Outbreak of the Corinthian War in Greece. Battle of Cnidus.

392	Mago in eastern Sicily. Dionysius makes peace with Carthage.
390–387	Dionysius extends his power to southern Italy.
389	Defeat of the Thurians by the Lucanians, disgrace of Leptines. Battle of the Eleporus. Dionysius makes peace with the Italiots.
388–387	Siege and fall of Rhegium. Plato visits Syracuse.
387/6	Dionysius sends naval assistance to Sparta. The King's Peace, end of the Corinthian War.
? 386	The conspiracy and exile of Leptines. Dionysius' operations in the Adriatic.
384	Sack of Pyrgi.
383/2–? 375	Third Punic War. Surrender of Croton, battles of Cabala and Cronium. Dionysius makes peace with Carthage (the Halycus line).
378	Renewal of general warfare in Greece.
377	Formation of the second Athenian League.
371	Battle of Leuctra, end of the 'Spartan Hegemony'.
369, 368	Dionysius sends aid to Sparta.
368	Athenian citizenship bestowed on Dionysius. Fourth Punic War. Truce between Dionysius and Carthage.
367	Dionysius' victory at the Lenaea. Treaty between Dionysius and Athens. (Spring) Death of Dionysius.

INTRODUCTION

The subject of the book and the sources

Perhaps no other of the great men of antiquity has so just a cause of complaint against History as Dionysius, son of Hermocritus. Misty, legendary characters like Theseus, Lycurgus, Romulus and Numa, ephemeral statesmen and soldiers such as Phocion, Pelopidas, Flamininus and Lucullus, attracted the attention of Nepos and Plutarch, with the result that their lives and careers have survived in copious, albeit often inaccurate or purely imaginative, detail. But ancient biography, if it was to be acceptable, had to be positively exemplary, it had to portray Virtue; and Dionysius, for thirty-eight years tyrant of Syracuse, at the time of his death lord of all Sicily except for parts of the Carthaginian province, because he had seized and continued to hold power illegally, and because he ruled for his own benefit, primarily, and not for the benefit of his subjects, could not be allowed to embody any of the virtues that would justify his being made the subject of a biography. It is true that the obscure second-century AD writer Amyntianus tacked a pair of *Lives*, one of them Dionysius', on to the *Lives* of Plutarch; but the fact that the parallel Roman life was that of the despotic Emperor Domitian suggests that Dionysius, too, was intended to serve as an awful warning. Amyntianus' *Life* – poor stuff, if it was anything like his life of Alexander – has been lost anyway.[1] There was indeed plenty of contemporary material available to a biographer, for, apart from the 'standard' histories of the period, Hermeias of Methymne's history of Sicily covered most of Dionysius' 'reign', and, more importantly, there were the four books of Philistus, the companion, adviser and, with one disastrous lapse, the lifelong supporter of the tyrant. Philistus, however, had been stigmatized as a 'lover of tyranny', and although his merits as a historian were recognized in the Rome of Cicero, his predilection for tyranny made him unacceptable as a source for biographers of the late Republic and early Empire.[2]

In fact, we owe almost all our knowledge of Dionysius' career to Diodorus of Agyrium – Diodorus Siculus – who lived and worked at

1

Rome between (approximately) 60 and 30 BC, produced a Universal History in forty books and has been justly described as 'only as valuable as his authorities'.[3] Debate continues among scholars over the question of Diodorus' sources for the period with which this book is concerned; but I see no good reason to dissent from the widely accepted opinion that for his Books XIII to XV he used as the basis of his narrative a historian of the fourth century, Ephorus of Cyme, who was a pupil of Isocrates and wrote a Universal History in thirty books. Stroheker, however, is among those who believe that Diodorus 'changed horses' for his Sicilian chapters and followed not Ephorus but a somewhat later historian, Timaeus, who was the accepted authority on Western Greek matters. Stroheker takes the view that Timaeus' personal experiences had prejudiced him against Dionysius, and that this prejudice shows through the narrative of Diodorus.[4] It is quite true that Timaeus' ancestors had suffered at the hands of Dionysius, who had destroyed their city, Naxos, and expelled its inhabitants. Timaeus' father had collected the exiles and led them to Tauromenium (in the vicinity of Naxos) in about 358, made himself master of the city and (according to his dutiful son) proved a model ruler. In 317, however, the city was seized by Agathocles and Timaeus fled to Athens. Tyranny and tyrants had, for almost two centuries, enjoyed an unsavoury reputation with Athenian intellectuals, and the Academy and the Peripatetics with whom Timaeus associated were particularly hostile to the memory of the Dionysii. That Timaeus displayed a bitter animosity towards Philistus (who died before Timaeus was born) was recognized by Antiquity, and we may be reasonably certain that he rejected Philistus' philo-tyrannical interpretation of Dionysius' 'reign'.[5]

Stroheker takes the view that Timaeus relied upon Philistus for his facts, but reacted violently against the latter's ardent approval of the monarchy; but he suggests that Philistus none the less sometimes shows through Timaeus; for instance, in the vivid passages describing the fortification of Epipolae, the preparations for the second Punic War, the plague and the battle by the Great Habour. The Thucydidean flavour of these passages (Philistus was an avowed admirer of Thucydides and also an eye-witness of the events themselves), as well as the favourable light in which they present the tyrant, do indeed stamp them as Philistian. But we are entitled to ask if it is likely – if indeed it is conceivable – that Timaeus, who according to Stroheker hated the memory of Dionysius, and who certainly disapproved most strongly of Philistus, esteeming himself the superior, as a writer of history, of both Philistus and Thucydides, should have borrowed from his 'enemy' these vivid descriptions of events, utterly at variance with his own sympathies and style? And the same objection holds good if we suppose that Timaeus used as his source not Philistus but Ephorus, who had himself incorporated passages of pure Philistus in his history.

If, however, it is unlikely that Philistus would have been permitted to 'show through' Timaeus, what evidence is there that Timaeus shows through Diodorus? Stroheker suggests that Timaeus' bitter animosity towards Dionysius can be detected in the hostile bias of Diodorus; but can we be quite certain that Timaeus did, in fact, display such animosity? It is true that he was nicknamed in antiquity, 'Epitimaios' (Censorious), but this was on account of the strictures that he levelled against other historians.[6] No doubt he attacked and 'corrected' Philistus' partisan estimate of Dionysius' motives and policies, and no doubt he expressed the conventional view of tyrants and tyranny; but it is, I believe, significant that Polybius, in his lengthy attack on Timaeus, accuses him of showing inordinate animosity only towards Agathocles, not towards Dionysius.[7] Stroheker has characterized the long and bitter tirade against Dionysius in Book XIV by a certain Theodorus as 'pure Timaeus'; and it cannot be asserted that it is not, for it certainly conforms to Polybius' strictures on Timaeus' inserted speeches. On the other hand, Diodorus tells us that he has occasionally permitted himself the luxury of a piece of rhetoric (*rhetorikoi logoi*),[8] and it may be that the 'Theodorus' harangue is an original composition of the Agyriate. I give my reasons for supposing that Timaeus is probably not responsible for it in Chapter 7; but even if Stroheker is right and the speech is pure Timaeus, it still does not prove that Diodorus based his Sicilian sections on Timaeus, but only that he was prepared to transpose or paraphrase excerpts from Timaeus' work into his own History.

There are, indeed, certain passages in Diodorus which may be adduced in support of the view that he did *not* follow Timaeus. His brief notice of the pacification of Greek Sicily in 424 suggests a source that was neither Timaeus nor Thucydides, and he followed Thucydides and Philistus in stating that in 413 the Athenian generals were put to death by the victorious Syracusans, not given the opportunity of committing suicide, as Timaeus asserts. His account of Plato's adventures in Sicily in 387 is not what might have been expected had Timaeus been his source; he states, in contradiction of Timaeus, that Philistus was pardoned by Dionysius the Elder; and his description of the death of Dionysius owes nothing to Timaeus'.[9] But, indeed, there was probably no good reason why Diodorus should have felt it to be necessary to switch from Ephorus to Timaeus; for if Philistus provided the basic *factual* material for both historians, there would have been little significant difference between their narratives. Ephorus would have been no more sympathetic towards Philistus' philotyrannism than Timaeus, and as an Italiot he would have had his own reasons, apart from those supplied by the intellectual consensus of his day, for disliking Dionysius. Nor, indeed, is Diodorus' History conspicuously biased against Dionysius *in general*, although there are several distinct passages which are; against which may be set those sections which are positively laudatory. Dionysius must have been something of an embarrassment to this moral and god-fearing historian, whose purpose was to instruct and edify his readers, providing vicarious experience to guide their conduct.[10] Dionysius had great achievements to his name, but he was, by Diodorus' time, established as the model of The Tyrant and accordingly was by definition *bad*. He could not be allowed to possess Virtue (*arete*), and the denigratory tradition, backed as it was by the august authority of Plato and the Academy, was accepted by Diodorus (and by Antiquity in general) as the true picture, although the historian's honesty compelled him occasionally to acknowledge that there was another side to the story.

I believe that we may assume that Diodorus was a well-to-do, well-educated man, and he can hardly have been unaware how a historian was supposed to set about his task. It may be assumed that he had read Polybius' twelfth book (indeed, he deprecates, although without naming Polybius, the Achaean's bitter polemic against Timaeus), and he knew that a historian has first to collect his material and then to sift it, comparing one statement with another, and choosing what he intends to use, being guided above all by the desire to attain to the truth.[11] But Diodorus was not a scholar in the modern understanding of the term. He did not aim to 'push back the frontiers of knowledge', but rather to provide the educated classes of the Roman Empire with a reasonably accurate map of the territory enclosed by the existing frontiers. However, had Diodorus confined himself to the simple abridgement of his basic authorities he would hardly have taken thirty years to write his forty books. Now, as an educated Sicilian he must have been familiar since boyhood with Timaeus' history and probably with Philistus' as well; and when he came to collect his material he can hardly have omitted to refresh his memory of these works and also of the considerable quantity of other literature that bore directly or indirectly upon the history of his native land. This would have included the works of historians other than those mentioned above, essays, *memorabilia*, collections of anecdotes and of speeches and letters, genuine or (perhaps more often) spurious: everything, in short, that came under the heading of *hypomnēmata*. We may reasonably assume that Diodorus, like Pliny, never read anything without taking notes; and so I believe that we may fairly postulate his possession of a collection of well-filled notebooks, containing material that could be used to supplement, and where he deemed it necessary, to correct his basic authorities.

For the period of the 'reign' of Dionysius, Diodorus' chosen authority was, I believe, Ephorus. As I have said above, there was probably little difference in essentials between the latter and Timaeus, whose importance as a historian, and whose originality in all likelihood, lay in the periods of Timoleon and Agathocles (whom Polybius accuses him of over-praising and libelling, respectively) and in the history of early Italy and Rome).[12] We know, however, that Diodorus respected Timaeus as a chronologist, and when he came to compose the Sicilian sections of his work he would have been able to make use of Timaeus' expertise in this field and also to draw upon his own notebooks for interesting items not mentioned by Ephorus, as well as discrepant figures for the Punic armies and casualties and for the Greek forces in the Gela campaign (Timaeus regularly discounted Ephorus' figures, either because he followed a different source or, as I believe to be more likely, by simple guesswork). If Stroheker is right, Diodorus also found among his notes on Timaeus the long and undistinguished speech of 'Theodorus'; but this I believe to be either an original composition of Diodorus – perhaps one dating from his student days? – or something that he found in a collection of rhetorical exercises (may there be any significance in the fact that a contemporary of Diodorus' was a highly thought-of rhetorician named Theodorus of Gadara?)[13] Diodorus never cites Philistus by name, but he was probably familiar with his writings from his student days, and Philistus' books were in the bookshops of Rome. From Philistus, then, he transcribed on to his tablets, and from these produced his versions of, the striking descriptions of the walling of Epipolae and of the rearming of Syracuse, together with the eulogistic picture of the dynast himself, of the plague that struck the camp of Himilco and of the battle on the shores of the Great Harbour. Perhaps from anecdotal sources whose interest was mainly literary he took his accounts of Dionysius' literary activity and of the dynast's death.

It was not Diodorus' express purpose to denigrate the memory of Dionysius, who was, it must be remembered, already established in the minds of the reading public as the arch-tyrant and therefore by definition a villain. Diodorus, however, had found among his notes the dictum of Polybius, that a historian should repeat the good as well as the bad about his subject;[14] but as no one had produced a balanced portrait of Dionysius up to that time (for Philistus' was regarded as unacceptably partisan), and as he lacked the literary skill to do so himself, he was content to introduce all undigested into his narrative – itself inevitably biased against the tyrant – the laudatory passages from Philistus which portray Dionysius as the popular national leader and an organizer of genius, as well as the denigratory tirade of 'Theodorus' and the anecdotes that present the tyrant as a foolish poetaster and a paranoiac. No attempt was made to reconcile this conflicting material or to arrive at a self-consistent representation of Dionysius, as potentate, soldier or man. In the eyes of Diodorus he is a tyrant, simply, and the definitive picture of The Tyrant had been established almost four centuries earlier. Such a one could be of no particular interest to a civilized reader.

This book represents an attempt to put matters right, to get behind the 'malice of Plato' and of the Academy, the conventional bias of Diodorus and the resultant slighting of Dionysius on the part of History, and to present a glimpse of the personality of the romantic who spent his life in the pursuit of glory, of the war-lord who was arguably the finest soldier produced by Greece (excluding the Macedonians), who built up the most powerful State in Hellas (and one of the richest), who was regarded by Isocrates as one who might be persuaded to assume the mantle of *hegemon* of the Greeks, who won the prize for Tragedy at the Lenaean Festival at Athens, and who died in his bed at the height of his power, lord of the greater part of Sicily and for thirty-eight years tyrant of Syracuse.

Because of the unsatisfactory nature of the historical tradition, the serious limitations of Diodorus' method (to say nothing of the breakdown of our text at one of the most important points of Dionysius' career), the lack of interest in Western Greek affairs shown by Xenophon and the confusion (due to over-compression) of the few notices in Justin; because of the general tendentiousness as well as inexactness of the anecdotal tradition; and because of the extensive areas of ignorance through which the historian of classical Sicily must tread his way (for instance, the loss of the Aristotelian *Constitution of the Syracusans*[15] has left us very much in the dark about Syracusan State and society, and earthquakes have rendered the very shape of Syracuse itself debatable); for these reasons I have found myself obliged to strike a subjective note and to fall back upon conjecture and hypothesis more often than a respectable historian cares to do. It will, I foresee, be objected that such expressions as 'I believe', 'I would conjecture', 'must have' and, above all, 'probably', appear in this book unconscionably often. Yet, as Polybius says, the function of History is to discover the causes of events, and if our ancient authorities do not supply them, or if they supply what appear to be false or tendentious explanations of the causes, it becomes necessary to attempt to make good their deficiencies. In doing this I have tried not to go beyond what our sources warrant; I have availed myself of the scholarship of those modern historians who have dealt most competently with the subject; and I have allowed myself to be guided by what I have learnt from more than half a century's study of Greek and the Greeks and from four years' experience of soldiering and war. And if it be objected that Dionysius seems generally to have been given the benefit of the doubt, I reply that, after twenty-three and a half centuries of denigration, it is high time that the scales of Justice were restored to a more level plane.

CHAPTER ONE

The historical background, down to 411

On the 27th of August 413, an eclipse of the moon occurred which certainly affected the subsequent course of Greek history. An Athenian expeditionary force comprising over 40,000 men, which, even before its reinforcement, had been reckoned to be 'the costliest and most splendid that had sailed from a single city with a Greek force up to that time', had, since the preceding summer, been besieging Syracuse, with almost daily diminishing hope of success after the arrival of the Spartan Gylippus to assume command of the defences. Now, beaten on land and knowing that, while disease and despondency were eating away their own strength, the enemy was growing steadily stronger and more confident, the Athenians were preparing so far to cut their losses as to withdraw by sea up the coast, to a base that would give a freedom of movement by land and sea denied them by their present positions on the western shore of the Great Harbour. Nicias, the general with whom the decision rested, to whose irresolution (he was, be it said, a sick man) the failure of the enterprise was in large measure due, took the eclipse to be a sign from Heaven, countermanded the order to move and so gave the enemy (warned by deserters of his intention) the opportunity, first, to defeat his ships in the Great Harbour, and then to cover the roads and fords that he would have to use in a retirement by land.

The frequent clashes with Syracusan hoplites at the road-blocks, the unremitting attacks from high ground or close cover of the Sicilian cavalry and javelin men on the march, lack of food and water, the division of their forces, desertions and a final breakdown of discipline, brought about the surrender of what was left of the once splendid force: hardly more than 7,000 beaten men. Thousands had been captured on the march and not declared to the authorities; thousands (probably) had managed to slip away or became lost, especially during the nights, and escaped to Athens' ally, Catane; many more thousands had been killed on the roads and at the attempted crossing of the river Assinarus. The prisoners were herded into the quarries of Syracuse; the generals, against the wishes of Gylippus, were put to death; and the rest were eventually

7

1 Syracuse: Ortygia with Plemmyrium in the background

either ransomed or sold (many of the better-educated, to Syracusans with a passion for Attic culture and Euripides), or else rotted to death in that insalubrious place. But for many days they must have provided the Syracusans with a show, an ocular demonstration of the truth of the ancient saying, that the arrogant are hated by gods and men.[1]

Among the crowd of men, women and children who flocked to the edge of the Quarries to gape (and probably to jeer) at the crestfallen Athenians, at whose hands they had so narrowly escaped enslavement, was, we may be sure, a certain large red-haired and freckled young fellow, on the threshold of manhood. It is difficult, knowing what we do know of him, to imagine that this fearless youth, with his irrepressible desire for fame and glory, played merely a spectator's part when the fates of Syracuse and Athens were being decided in the bloody fighting in the Great Harbour and on the roads behind the city. He may have been just old enough, in such a crisis of his city's affairs, to take his place in the phalanx; or perhaps he was one of the boys, below military age, who put out in wherries to support the Syracusan galleys. We shall never know the truth, since virtually all the biographical material connected with Dionysius has been lost; that is, if it ever existed, since Philistus, the imitator of Thucydides, would not have wasted his ink on such matters. However, the utter destruction which Dionysius had witnessed of the

8

great armament sent to conquer Sicily by the most powerful and the most arrogant city in the world – something so much in keeping with the Greek conception of the tragic peripeteia – must have had a profound effect upon his mind.

It can hardly have escaped this very intelligent young man that what, more than any other single factor, had brought the Athenians – so often so close to victory – to eventual ruin had been the inadequacy of their leaders. Starting with three generals, all with different ideas of the way in which the campaign should be conducted, they had, before very long, found themselves under the command of one sick man, whose prestige, the product of a reputation for personal integrity, great wealth and long political activity, neutralized the influence of the colleagues sent to assist him, and whose dilatoriness wasted his splendid opportunities. Nor was it only the Athenian leadership that had shown up badly in the war. Syracuse had, on the eve of the Athenian invasion, been riven by bitter social and political animosities, and although she had had at her disposal a notable leader in Hermocrates, she had refused to put her full trust in him; and it was not until the arrival of the Spartan Gylippus to take charge of the defence that the Syracusans ceased to think of capitulation.[2]

It seems to me likely that Dionysius had already begun to share the opinion held by many influential Athenians and Syracusans alike, that Athens' failure and his own city's near-disaster were both the products of their similar political systems: that democracy was incompatible with effective leadership. Of the seven generals that Athens had sent to Sicily in the course of the war, three had, in 425, been punished by the Demos with exile or heavy fine, not for military incompetence but for failing to prevent the Sicilians from bringing to an end the internecine war that benefited nobody except Athens: that is to say, for failing to achieve something that was beyond their power to achieve.[3] In the campaign that had just come to disaster, Alcibiades had been driven by political intrigue and the suspicions of the Demos into exile; Lamachus, perhaps Athens' best 'fighting general', had lacked the political weight to impose his strategy, militarily the best conceived, upon his colleagues at the outset; and Demosthenes, a good soldier and possessed of ample moral courage, was unable, even with the support of a colleague, to persuade Nicias to brave the wrath of the Assembly, to risk the fate that had befallen Pythodorus and his colleagues in 425 and to abandon an enterprise that had degenerated into a futile reinforcement of failure.[4]

At Athens it was the very completeness of the triumph of radical democracy that militated against the effective conduct of a protracted war; at Syracuse, it was rather a continuing political disunity. Athenian democracy owed its many very real merits to its relatively slow and almost bloodless growth, from the beginning of the sixth century to near the middle of the fifth. The old aristocracy had not been a ruling caste alien to the mass of the people, as in the Dorian cities and the colonies; racial homogeneity was celebrated, by the late fifth century, in the myth of Attic autochthony. During the sixth century, as a result of the reforms of Solon and the acceptance of the ideals which inform his poetry and which had become a part of the young Athenian's education, the Athenian people acquired a common national identity and became, by the end of the century, a unified Demos. National unity was reinforced by the 'myth of democratic opposition to tyranny' (after the overthrow of the Peisistratids), and confirmed in the common struggle against the Persian Empire. The Persian Wars united the Athenians behind their aristocratic leaders who continued, down to the radical 'revolution' of 462, to dominate a constitution which reflected the character of the hoplite society of the turn of the century but which was falling out of touch with the age of naval imperialism and the emergence as a political factor of the landless element, entrenched in the city and the Piraeus. The 'revolution' of 462 did not, however, represent a rising of the lower classes against the aristocracy; rather was it the outcome of a struggle for political power between rival aristocratic factions, the faction 'in opposition' following the example of Cleisthenes and claiming to 'take the Demos into partnership'. By abolishing the political power of the Areopagus in the name of political equality they gave constitutional expression to the idea of *demokratia* – that all power (*kratos*) should be vested in the Demos: that is, in the Popular Assembly – and by so doing, sealed the political fate of their own order.

The reformers would appear to have triumphed less because the mass of the people, who were peasant farmers and more concerned with wresting a living from the poor soil of Attica than with constitutional questions, desired change, than because a fervent nationalism, reflecting the spectacular growth of Athenian maritime power and influence since the Persian Wars, had developed among them. This was given direction and impulse by the proposal of the 'Opposition', that Athens should take advantage of Sparta's domestic troubles to wrest from her the hegemony of Greece. Although her attempt to dethrone Sparta ended in failure, Athens emerged from the first Peloponnesian War with her maritime empire not only intact but even more firmly under her control; and during the long 'reign' of Pericles, when the whole community, landed proprietors and landless alike, was reaping the rewards of a moderate exploitation of empire, the dispute between the 'Little Attic-ers', who might also be seen as the critics of democracy, and the Imperialists, identified with the champions of the popular interest, was limited to political sniping.

As long as Pericles lived, he preserved the appearance of national unity; of which indeed he himself, in his person and in his unique position in the state, was a symbol. Member of the old aristocracy but also the principal proponent of the maritime imperialism upon which radical democracy depended for survival, patron of the most advanced intellectual movements and at the same time *prostatēs tou demou* (champion of the People), he bridged the ancient division between the classes. On his death, however, the struggle for control of the Assembly was reopened; and with no one statesman having the stature and authority of Pericles, the aristocratic *prostatēs* was succeeded by the *demagōgos* (demagogue), the persuasive politician who prided himself on being a Man of the People'. Since 431 Athens had been at war with the Peloponnesians, and the demagogues, the self-appointed watch-dogs of the democracy, on occasion made political capital out of the real or imputed shortcomings of the military commanders. As these were elected from the upper class – which was also, generally speaking, the section of the community least enamoured of the war – a certain amount of class feeling was reawakened. To outward appearances the unity of the Demos appeared to be intact. The Assembly tolerated no serious criticism of its basic policies, and so opposition to the continuation of the war, to the exploitation of the allies and to the wishes of the 'maritime mob' (*nautikos ochlos*) came to be characterized as hostility to democracy itself, Demos and democracy being regarded as identical, and therefore as unpatriotic and even treasonable. As a result, those men who disapproved of the way that things were going either disguised their real sentiments or withdrew from the political field.

For a brief space, when Alcibiades, the ward of Pericles, entered public life, it looked as if the old notion of an aristocratic *prostatēs* of a united Demos might be revived; but the deficiencies of his character and the malignity of his enemies proved his ruin.

In 411, as a result of the Sicilian disaster, the revolt of the allies and the departure of the scratch fleet to Samos, the middle class was won over to the idea of establishing a *politeia* of the kind later to be preferred by Aristotle; of a return, that is, to something not very different from the hoplite constitution of Solon – the *patrios politeia* (ancestral constitution) – involving the political disfranchisement, although not the exclusion from civil rights, of the landless. This constitution, described by the aristocratic Thucydides as 'the best in my time', was in fact stillborn. Radical democracy was restored by Alcibiades and the fleet, and an attempt was made by means of an amnesty to re-establish the shattered unity of the people. But the second rejection of Alcibiades and the infamous trial and condemnation of the generals after the victory of Arginusae, with its sinister affirmation of the right of the Assembly to disregard the laws, bespoke both the breakdown of political responsibility and the subservience of the board of generals to the whim of the Assembly. Athens, indeed, had to go through a period of deep distrust, military humiliation, tyranny and civil war before national unity was finally restored – although to the exclusion of many of the intelligentsia – at the end of the century.

The political history of Syracuse was very different from that of Athens. The first decade of the fifth century, when Athens' feet were firmly set upon the road to radical democracy, saw Syracuse a narrow aristocracy, ruled by the founding families, the *Gāmoroi* (sharers of the soil). These were, in 485, driven out of the city and its territory by an alliance of the Demos and the serfs, the Cyllyrians. Solon had preserved the aristocrats of Attica from a similar fate, almost a century earlier; and the Syracusan nobles were restored to their estates not by compromise and covenant, as seems to have been the case at, for instance, Syracuse's metropolis, Corinth, but by foreign military intervention. Gelon, the aristocratic tyrant of Gela, seized the long hoped-for opportunity of making himself master of Syracuse, espoused the cause of the *Gāmoroi* and occupied the city. He gave the exiles back their lands and their social predominance, but took up residence in Syracuse, making it the capital of a great territorial 'kingdom' in eastern Sicily.[5]

Gelon, however, and his brother Hieron who succeeded to his power, were not Syracusan national leaders, as, for instance, Peisistratus and his sons had been national leaders of the Athenians. Gelon enlarged the city by transplanting the whole or part of the populations of other cities to Syracuse and by enfranchising over 10,000 mercenaries, many (if not most) of whom must have been native Sicels, barbarians. He thus did violence to the basic principles of the *polis*, both by the destruction of free political communities and by the contempt he displayed for the exclusiveness of the *polis*, regarded as a national family. Thus, whereas Peisistratus at Athens, and even the Cypselids at Corinth, had encouraged the development of a unified people, Gelon and Hieron did the opposite, in their desire to enlarge the hoplite class without at the same time increasing its political influence. They further mongrelized an already heterogeneous population by introducing discordant and mutually hostile elements; for the tyrants, aristocrats themselves, were profoundly contemptuous of the common people.

In 466/5 the Syracusans rose in revolt, doubtless under the leadership of members of the old ruling class, augmented by 'new' families that had risen to wealth and influence under the tyrants, and with the aid of both Greeks and barbarians defeated the mercenaries of Thrasybulus, the last of the Deinomenid tyrants, and drove him into exile. In place of the tyranny they established what Aristotle describes as a *politeia*: a mixed constitution containing oligarchic and democratic elements. The survivors and descendants of the people transferred by Gelon from Gela and Camarina returned to their former homes (Megara and Euboea had been fully incorporated into the territory of Syracuse); but the survivors of Gelon's enfranchised mercenaries – some 7,000 in number – remained and under the new laws were excluded from holding any office.[6]

Apart from the statement above, Aristotle tells us nothing about the constitution or, indeed, the structure of society, and any attempt to arrive at a picture of fifth-century Syracuse from the few scattered hints let fall by ancient writers must be almost wholly conjectural. Syracuse was a Dorian colony and it is reasonable to assume that the form of her society and her institutions reflected the Dorian pattern. The earliest settlers seem to have reduced to serfdom the natives whose lands, adjacent to the foundation, they had seized (these were the Cyllyrioi mentioned by Herodotus); and we need not doubt that, in early times, the *polītai* – those who owned the *polis* and enjoyed political rights – lived *in* the city and had their land worked and their flocks herded by serfs, slaves and free labourers. The question is, did this situation change with the growth of the State, the admission of numerous new settlers and the incorporation into its territory of neighbouring communities, such as Casmenae, Acrae, Megara and Euboea? There are passages in both Thucydides and Diodorus which might be taken to indicate that, by the end of the century, at least a sizable part of the hoplite class – the class, that is, that enjoyed political rights in a *politeia* – lived in the countryside, like the majority of Athenian citizens before the Peloponnesian War.[7] Moreover there is mention, in the military narrative, of strongpoints which seem to correspond to villages.

However, these passages are far from conclusive, since the men described as 'being brought in from the countryside' could well be city residents engaged in supervising the harvesting, as well as poor peasants, landless field-workers and herdsmen and the like, who would be employed as skirmishers: the villages being their homes. When Dionysius decided to build the north wall of Epipolae, he mobilized the ochlos – the masses – from the countryside, and they amounted to well over 60,000 able-bodied men. Obviously these fellows were not yeomen, since the whole hoplite force of the city in 415 apparently amounted to only about double that of the Athenians: namely, to something like 10,000 men.[8] On the other hand there is nothing in the narrative to suggest that they were not freemen: probably, like the work-force of Athens, they were a mixture of free and unfree. In the latter category, although many were, no doubt, slaves, many (I believe) belonged to the ancient class of serfs – a class for which Greek has no special word – for I do not find convincing the view of some historians, that the serf class had disappeared before the end of the fifth century. The account given by Polyaenus of the suppression of a 'slave' revolt during the siege of Syracuse would bear out the idea that these 'slaves' were in fact serfs.[9] As regards the urban character of the hoplite class, the story of the disarming of the Demos by

Dionysius, after the Great Revolt, only makes sense if we suppose that the hoplites were normally resident in the city and went out to their farms on agriculturally important occasions, such as the harvest. It is significant, too, that when the Syracusan Demos, and later Dionysius, depopulated cities (such as Leontini and, in Italy, Caulonia and Hipponium) the citizens were removed to Syracuse and there enfranchised: which probably indicates what was done in the case of the earlier incorporated communities. It appears to me probable, therefore, that all landowners of hoplite census (and above, of course) resided in, or close to, the city.

I would conjecture that all those possessing political rights were distributed over five tribes (phylai), the 'Old' Citizens, who enjoyed full political rights, composing the three Dorian tribes, the 'new' Citizens, who were debarred from holding office, being enrolled in the others. All tribe members might attend meetings of the Assembly. We never hear any mention of a Council (boulē), but there must have been some body intermediate between the executive officers and the Assembly, if only for the purpose of putting in order the business to be laid before the latter. Perhaps the system found in the Boeotian cities (whose pattern of society seems to have resembled that at Syracuse) may offer a pointer to that of the Syracusans. In Boeotia, the whole full-citizen body composed four Councils (boulai), each of which sat in turn as a probouleutic committee to an assembly of the other three. We are not told how this assembly was styled (perhaps a synod?); but a writer of Diodorus' time would almost certainly have called it an ecclesia: which is the word used by both Thucydides and Diodorus to describe the Assembly of the Syracusans. If a similar system was employed at Syracuse, it would perhaps explain the non-appearance of a permanent Council in the literary tradition. At Syracuse the composition of the Council (whatever its nature) may have been related to the tribes (the Boeotians do not appear to have employed the tribal system).[10] There was a board of fifteen generals (strategoi), to which was attached a minimum-age limit and, we may assume, a census qualification.[11] There will also have been civil officers (archontes?), to whose selection similar rules applied. Both these groups of officers were chosen by direct election, from members of the three Dorian tribes, by the Assembly of all citizens with political rights.

Thus the very factors – written laws (these seem to have been the work of a nomothetes of the archaic period, probably a Corinthian, named Diocles),[12] tyranny, revolt against tyranny and democratic reform – which at Athens had contributed to the creation of a united and harmonious people, at Syracuse served to perpetuate disunity and disharmony. We are told that a general recall of exiles and a reapportionment of land (gēs anadasmos) throughout Greek Sicily followed upon the dissolution of the great kingdoms. Exiles returning to Syracuse would have demanded the restoration of their properties: a demand which, whether acceded to or rejected, could only produce bitterness and resentment. There was bloody civil war before the disfranchised ex-mercenaries, who had taken up arms to recover their lost political rights, were brought under control. We are not told specifically that the survivors were expelled from the country and we may conjecture that they remained, a disgruntled element with racial, social and, no doubt in some cases, economic grievances to brood over. An élite corps of 600, drawn, presumably, from the 'best' families, was honoured by the State for the part that it had played in putting down the rising; and for the next decade a large group of rich and powerful families within the privileged full-citizen class dominated the political life of the city. [13]

Diodorus states that the period following the overthrow of the tyrants was one of great and growing prosperity in Sicily, owing to the cessation of internecine warfare. In fact, there had been rather less fighting in Sicily in the era of the tyrants than there had been in metropolitan Greece, although several cities had been depopulated and there had been a brief, albeit bloody, war between Hieron and Thrasydaeus of Acragas. Certainly, after the fall of the tyrannies the various empty cities were repopulated and throve, so that it could be claimed that the prosperity of the island (which was undoubtedly very great) was now more widely shared; and the *poleis*, whose development had been impeded by the rise of the powerful 'kingdoms', flourished in the brief period of general peace – a peace that probably did not embrace Syracuse's relations with her Sicel neighbours in eastern and south-eastern Sicily.

That Syracuse's internal condition was less than truly happy is shown by the fact that, in the '50s, one Tyndarides gathered a following among the poor, armed them and prepared to set himself up as tyrant, but was forestalled and killed by the 'respectable' elements (*hoi chariestatoi*). As, however, it was felt that the constitution was still under threat, the Syracusans, in 454, introduced their own version, *Petalism*, of the Athenian institution of *ostracism*, which the Athenians had employed most recently in 461 to bring about the removal of Cimon, the leader of the pro-Spartan (and anti-radical) 'party'. The result at Syracuse, we are told, was to drive the 'respectable' men out of public life and turn politics over to the 'baser' elements. [14] Divested of its aristocratic bias, this probably means that, as Syracuse once more began to extend her sway over the indigenous Sicels, and their tribute started to flow again into her treasury, so that political power and patronage acquired an additional attractiveness, the members of the old ruling class, who regarded the government of the city as something that belonged to them by right, were forced to contend for power against ambitious 'new' men; and many of them either were sent into exile or else retired from the contest, rather than run the risk of falling victims to the new *petalism*.

The situation had features in common with that at Athens, both back in the '80s when (as seems probable) Themistocles was using *ostracism* to remove aristocratic obstacles from his upward path, and in the '60s, when the dominant 'conservative' faction was being opposed, and was finally overthrown, by the 'radicals'. An important difference was that in Attica national unity was, after Marathon, already too strong to be seriously shaken by 'party' politics; whereas at Syracuse the rift between the very large ruling class and the Demos had never been properly closed. The bitterness of the struggle for power soon destroyed what harmony there was – the product of the need to close ranks in the face of armed insurrection – and aristocracy and Demos remained estranged. Rhetoric, the scientific study of the art of forensic speaking, had, we are told, been invented (by Corax) in order to deal with the oubreak of litigation in the cities that followed upon the restoration of freedom. Even in Homeric society the ability to be 'a speaker of words' had been highly valued, and the new science was quickly applied to politics. In divided Syracuse, demagogues and informers flourished. However, *petalism* itself, perhaps as a result of a recovery of confidence on the part of the upper class, was abolished after a few years.[15]

Two elements of confusion were introduced into Sicilian affairs in the late '60s and the '50s by the rise of Ducetius as a national leader of the Sicels, and by the recrudescence of the former rivalry between Syracuse and Acragas for the hegemony of Sicily. Ducetius set himself to unite the Sicels (Hybla stood aloof) into a confederation (*koinon, synteleia*), and plainly entertained the ambition of raising this to a level at least of equality with the combined might of the Greek cities. When, however, he began to liberate Sicel towns that were under Greek domination, he came into conflict with both Acragas and his quondam ally, Syracuse, and inflicted a defeat upon them which led to the execution of the Syracusan general, Bolcon, for treason: an indication of the strength of political feeling. However, Ducetius was totally defeated, in 451, by joint Syracusan and Acragantine action; and, having thrown himself upon the mercy of Syracuse, was spared – through the exertions of the 'respectable' men – and sent into exile at Corinth.

Relations between the two leading Greek cities, already strained, broke down when Ducetius returned to Sicily and, with the assistance of the ruler of Herbita, founded the Graeco-Sicel city of Calacte on the north coast. Acragas clearly suspected that he had taken this action with the connivance of Syracuse, and that it was directed ultimately against herself. War followed, in which the allies of both parties joined. It was perhaps now (448) that Leontini, together with Rhegium in southern Italy, made a treaty with Athens: a treaty which, renewed in 433/2, played its part in bringing down the Athenian Empire. The Acragantines marched north against the new settlement, in the summer of 446, and were decisively defeated on the Himera River. The peace which brought the war to a close apparently recognized Syracuse's hegemony of the Sicilian Greeks, the Siceliots, for whom another period of tranquillity and prosperity followed. During this time, Syracuse completed her subjugation of the indigenous Sicels of eastern Sicily, so that she now controlled the whole region east of a line from the Hyrminius River to Calacte, apart from the north-eastern corner of the island and the Chalcidian cities on the east coast.[16]

The war against Acragas had the effect (as is so often the case) of at least temporarily reuniting the discordant Syracusan body politic. Successful military leadership enhanced the prestige and authority of the governing class (it was probably now that *petalism* was abolished); and the increased tribute from the Sicels – and perhaps some confiscated land as well – must have served at least to assuage the city's social and economic problems. Diodorus notes, under the year 439, that Syracuse built 100 ships, doubled the number of her cavalry (from 600 to 1,200), improved her infantry and increased the tribute of the Sicels; and that all this was done with the intention of gaining control, by stages, of the whole of Sicily and establishing an empire in the West to rival that ruled by Athens in the East.[17] As Diodorus' next mention of Sicilian affairs is under the year 427, we may reasonably conjecture (knowing Diodorus' literary method) that this 'programme' was in fact spread over the next ten years; perhaps the doubling of the cavalry – reflecting the restored predominance of the class from which the *Hippeis* were drawn – belongs to 439, and the other adjustments followed; Syracuse not being ,in fact, ready to embark upon the subjugation of her neighbours until after the outbreak of the Peloponnesian War.

By the spring of 433, the war-clouds were perceptibly gathering over western Hellas. Corinth, after lengthy preparation, was ready to avenge her defeat in 435 by her other great, but notoriously unfilial, colony in the West, Corcyra. The latter, in alarm, negotiated an alliance with Athens, who then, it would seem, renewed her earlier treaties with Rhegium and Leontini. In the light of Athens' subsequent policy towards the Siceliots, and also of the dictum attributed, no doubt correctly, to Pericles, that the sea was her domain, it would be rash to discount Thucydides' suggestion that she was already contemplating the extension of her *thalattocracy* to the waters of Magna Graecia and Sicily. At all events, Syracuse, the acknowledged *hegemon* of the Dorian cities of Sicily, brought her allies (with the exception of Camarina) into line with the Peloponnesians, in the war that broke out in the spring of 431.[18]

The causes of the Peloponnesian War were many, some openly proclaimed, others – prominent among them resentment, jealousy and FEAR – unacknowledged; but it was with the avowed purpose of breaking up Athens' maritime empire and 'liberating' the Hellenes that the cities

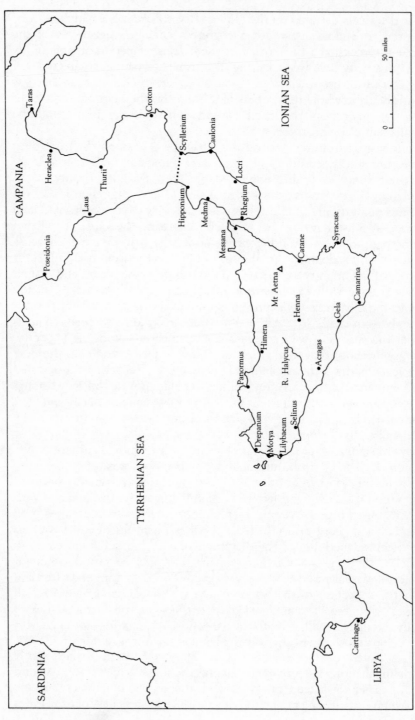

SARDINIA

TYRRHENIAN SEA

CAMPANIA

Taras

Poseidonia

Laus

Heraclea

Thurii

Croton

Scylletium

Caulonia

Hipponium

Medma

Locri

Rhegium

Messana

Catane

Syracuse

IONIAN SEA

Mt Aetna

Henna

Camarina

Gela

Acragas

Himera

Panormus

R. Halycus

Selinus

Drepanum

Motya

Lilybaeum

LIBYA

Carthage

50 miles

0

A CARTHAGE, SICILY AND MAGNA GRAECIA

of the so-called Peloponnesian League, together with Athens' ancient enemy, Thebes, went to war. Athens accepted the challenge because she had no practicable alternative; for the truth was that the exploitation, however moderate, of her 'allies' provided the economic basis of the radical democracy. And so the cities of metropolitan Greece and the Aegean (apart from those of Achaea and the Arogolid) were ranged against each other, the continental powers (plus Corinth) against the maritime. Since the nucleus of the opposition to Athens was provided by the Dorian cities of the Peloponnese and the Isthmus (with the important exception of Argos, irreconcilably hostile towards Sparta), the confrontation could be interpreted – and, for the purpose of war propaganda, *was* interpreted – as one of Dorian against Ionian; with the further implication that the Dorians, the 'master race' of the Peloponnese, before whom, in post-epic days, the Ionians had fled to Attica and Asia or had declined into an inferior status, were necessarily the superior in arms. This polarization along racial lines was not taken too seriously in the East, if only because it was patently incomplete: the Boeotians, for instance, were not Dorians, nor the Corcyraeans Ionians. But it certainly suited the Syracusans' book to see the struggle in those terms, since to do so was to justify the assault that they were contemplating upon the independence of the Chalcidic (Ionian) cities of the east coast, the subjugation of which would give them ownership of the whole of eastern Sicily, south of Messana. The Chalcidic cities, naturally, played the Ionian card for all it was worth, in their efforts to obtain military assistance from Athens.[19]

Dionysius was born not long after the outbreak of the Peloponnesian War, in, or about, 430. His father's name is given by all our sources as Hermocrates, but Beloch was surely correct when he suggested that it was in fact Hermocritus; a name which is attested as that of a son of Dionysius and which became confused with that of the famous Syracusan statesman and soldier to whose faction Dionysius belonged and whose daughter he married. Isocrates speaks rather slightingly of Dionysius' lineage; he belonged 'well down the social scale' (*pollostos tōi genei*); but this need mean no more than that his family did not belong either to the old aristocracy or to the very rich. Cicero, who had read his Philistus, uses the words *bonus* and *honestus* to describe Dionysius' parentage and social position (although admitting that there is another side to the story): terms which, if they had been applied to a Roman, would imply at least equestrian status. We may therefore, I believe, assume that he came of well-to-do but undistinguished stock.[20] Philistus – oddly, one might think, for a man who was a pupil of sophists and an admirer of Thucydides – recalled that Dionysius' mother, before her confinement, dreamt that she had given birth to a satyr child: a dream which the Galeotae of Hybla, the most revered (non-Greek) interpreters of omens in Sicily, explained as a sign that her son would be the most famous man in Greece and would enjoy lasting good fortune. Stroheker is of the opinion that Philistus tells this story in order to put Dionysius into the class of extraordinary mortals, and this may be so. However, since we do not know the context of the passage, we cannot exclude the possibility that he told it in order to provide a psychological explanation of the development of Dionysius' character and ambition. It would also, perhaps, account for the name that his father chose for him, satyrs being associated with Dionysus. Cicero (to whom we owe Philistus' anecdote) also implies that Dionysius enjoyed an upbringing and education and a circle of acquaintances in keeping with his respectable social position.[21]

The momentous but remote events of the Peloponnesian War must have impinged only slightly upon the mind of the growing boy. The Siceliots limited their participation in it to the export of grain to the Peloponnese, thus easing the manpower problems of cities like Corinth, and presumably contributing to the survival of yearly devastated Megara. No doubt Leontini's treaty with Athens was denounced at Syracuse and may have afforded a pretext for the latter's attack upon the Chalcidic city, whose rich plain – some of the best land in Sicily – was greatly coveted by the Syracusans to whom it had belonged during the period of the tyranny. By the summer of 427 the war had come to involve most of the Greek cities, although there is no evidence of any very serious fighting except between Syracuse and Leontini, the latter being reduced to such straits that she sent her foremost rhetorician, Gorgias, at the head of an embassy to Athens, to ask for the implementation of the treaty of 433/2. The Athenians could by now feel that their darkest hours were past. They had survived the plague, defeated the attempt of Mytilene to leave the Empire and strikingly demonstrated their mastery of the seas. Pericles' restraining influence upon the exuberance of his countrymen had been removed by his death; and it was no bad policy to keep the Siceliots occupied in their own island and, by securing the command of the Ionian Sea, to prevent the shipment of grain to their enemies. But Thucydides, a member of the Athenian 'official' class and aware of what was being thought and said in the city in 427, tells us that the Athenians were already in the mood to look for an opportunity to bring Sicily under their control.[22]

Accordingly, in the late summer of 427, the Athenians based a fleet of 20 ships at Rhegium, which, under a democratic regime, had taken the side of the Chalcidic cities. This force was too small to make a decisive impact upon the course of the war in Sicily, and the Athenians were persuaded by their allies to despatch larger forces in 425. These, however, were diverted to take part in important operations around Pylos and Corcyra and achieved nothing of importance in the Sicilian theatre, either in 425 or in the following year. However, Leontini survived and Camarina seems to have captured Morgantina, thus perhaps relieving the pressure upon the Chalcidic city. It was in the course of the summer of 424, following the cessation of hostilities between Gela and Camarina, according to Thucydides and Timaeus or between Syracuse and Leontini, according to Diodorus (whose ultimate source may have been Philistus), that the Siceliots held a peace conference at Gela.[23] We now meet for the first time, in the pages of Thucydides, a Syracusan whose character and political ideals were destined to exert a powerful influence on the imagination and career of the young Dionysius: Hermocrates, son of Hermon. To have been sent to Gela as the delegate of his city, Hermocrates must already have achieved distinction, and presumably distinction as a military commander. He must, therefore, in 424 have been over thirty years of age, and a member of the governing class. Indeed, he is regularly identified by Thucydides with the *oligoi* (the few), who are also the faction tainted with militarism. Hermocrates is described as being well informed, second to none in intelligence (*synesis*), experienced in war and of conspicuous courage. At a later date, in the great war against Athens, he was to display foresight, strategic ability and steadfastness in time of crisis. Xenophon praises his diligence, enthusiasm and accessibility as a commander. He was regarded as an outstanding planner and speaker. Indeed, both historians give us the impression of a man who, but for the malignity of his enemies, might have played a role at Syracuse similar to that which Pericles had played at Athens: that of an aristocratic leader of a free people, a true *prostatēs tou demou*.[24]

At Gela, Hermocrates' good sense and eloquence prevailed upon the other delegates to agree to a general peace, more or less on the basis of *uti possidetis*; and the Athenians, deprived of their allies and their bases in the West, had no alternative but to accept it, for which failure to carry out the wishes of the Demos their generals were punished on their return home. Hermocrates had stood forward as the champion of the idea of 'Sicily for the Sicilians'. Admitting, in effect, that war is 'the pursuit of politics by other means', and that Syracuse was not prepared to renounce the use of force as a means of imposing her hegemony on others, he called upon the Sicilian Greeks to come to terms *for the present*, in order to get the Athenians – the interlopers – out of the island. Their sole purpose in being there, he said, was to subjugate the Sicilians and bring them into their empire. There was no mention of Carthage, and there is no good reason to suppose that in 424 Hermocrates entertained any idea of breaking the solemnly sworn peace with the Phoenicians and attacking their cities in the far west of the island. Indeed, in a later book, Thucydides makes Hermocrates suggest that, in face of Athenian intervention, Carthage's interests coincided with those of the Siceliots.[25]

Syracuse's failure to subdue the Chalcidic cities must have been damaging to the authority of her governing class and correspondingly heartening to their political adversaries. Peasants did not like long and inconclusive wars and withdrew their support from leaders who failed to produce the promised results. It is true that soon afterwards Leontini fell for a short time under Syracusan control, but when the Chalcidic city broke free Syracuse found herself involved in a desultory war with that section of the populace which refused to accept the incorporation of their territory (and aristocracy) into the Syracusan State. An attempt by the Athenians to rouse the other Sicilians by diplomatic means to make war on Syracuse came to nothing, although a subsequently useful contact was established with the native Sicels.[26]

In 416, during the uneasy lull in the Peloponnesian War known as the period of the Peace of Nicias, Athens was offered another and more tempting opportunity of establishing herself in Sicily; this came through a new flare-up in the mutual hostility of Selinus and the Elymian city of Segesta, uneasy neighbours in the far west of the island. Segesta, hard pressed, appealed for assistance, first to Acragas and to Syracuse, and then to Carthage, but without avail. She then sent ambassadors to Athens, with which she had, in 427, renewed a defensive alliance concluded in the '50s. In the spring of 415, the Athenians, in a fit of national insanity, decided to send a large armament to Sicily, in spite of the fact that Amphipolis, her most important possession in the northern Aegean, was still unrecovered, that hostilities continued in central Greece and that Sparta, her prestige restored as a result of a victory over Argos and her allies (including Athens) in 418, was already meditating the renewal of her offensive operations against Attica.[27]

Hermocrates, in the pages of Thucydides, comes forward to warn his fellow countrymen against the Athenians, who are planning to crush Syracuse as a preliminary step to the subjugation of all Sicily. He calls again for a pan-Sicilian alliance against them, an alliance to include Carthage, which he (like Alcibiades, later in the same book) represents as threatened by Athenian sea power. Consistently with his daring and aggressive character, he urges the Syracusans not to wait for the Athenians but to establish themselves at friendly Taras and contest the passage of the Ionian Sea with them. At least, he says, let the Syracusans open their eyes to their peril and make the necessary preparations to meet it. However, Hermocrates and his friends were still out of favour, and his call to arms was stigmatized by his opponents as alarmism, designed to put power into the hands of himself and the warmongers.[28] None the less, the city – at first merely provisionally but later, with the Athenian fleet at Rhegium, in grim earnest – put itself into a state of preparedness, and Hermocrates' credit with his fellow citizens was largely restored when his warnings proved so well founded. According to Diodorus, Hermocrates was elected one of three generals with full executive authority (*autokratores*), when the Athenians were known to be at Rhegium; but Thucydides, whose account is, I believe, to be preferred, says that this step was taken at the end of the summer, after the Syracusans had suffered defeat in a pitched battle before the walls of the city. Once again Hermocrates displayed his exceptional powers of leadership, urging the members of the Assembly to learn wisdom from their defeat, to improve their training and discipline, to enlarge the phalanx by providing shields for those who could not afford them and, most importantly, to entrust the absolute discretion of command to a small college of generals in place of the present cumbersome board of fifteen. His advice was followed, and he was himself elected one of the three who would come into office in the summer of the next year (414). Infected by his energy, the Syracusans built a new wall to enclose the Temenites district of the city, stationed outposts to defend Megara and the temple of Olympian Zeus and raided Catane, which had become the Athenians' base. Hermocrates himself was sent to Camarina, to stiffen that city's wavering allegiance, and he there reiterated his theme of 'the common good of Sicily' and the need to combine against an external foe.[29]

However, the year 414 started so badly for the Syracusans that Hermocrates was obliged to adopt the policy of declining battle; there was also a serious revolt of the slaves, which was broken by Hermocrates by an astute – if thoroughly dishonourable – trick. No doubt he did not consider binding an agreement made with the unfree. As the leader of the insurgents bore rather an aristocratic name and is described as a friend of a member of the governing class, we may perhaps conjecture that they – or many of them – were serfs, the descendants of the people called Cyllyrians by Herodotus. Before the summer was over the Athenians were so completely in command of the situation that Hermocrates and his two fellow generals were dismissed from office and negotiations for peace were opened with Nicias. Fortunately, Gylippus and his Corinthian colleagues arrived with reinforcements from the Peloponnese and from western Sicily just in time to prevent the Syracusans from throwing up the sponge. Although Timaeus preserved a tradition that Gylippus was not well received initially at Syracuse, the newcomer not only provided the *professional* military expertise that the Syracusans, including Hermocrates, lacked, but also, being both a Spartan and a man outside the political rivalries of the citizens, he was able to give the city the unity of command that had so far been wanting. It was to him that Philistus, no doubt an admirer of Hermocrates, gave the chief credit for Syracuse's victory.[30] Hermocrates, who was not re-elected to the generalship in 413, may be presumed to have swallowed his chagrin and co-operated loyally with the Spartan; and he certainly gave him his full support in the Assembly over the proposal to challenge the Athenians at

sea, a proposal that ultimately ensured their defeat; and it was Hermocrates who tricked Nicias into delaying his retreat into the interior, after
the last, fatal, naval battle. In the debate on the treatment to be meted
out to the Athenian prisoners, Diodorus and Plutarch portray Hermocrates as the proponent of generosity, opposed by one Diocles, the most
influential of the demagogues; Thucydides mentions only Gylippus'
wish to spare the lives of the Athenian generals and take them back to
Sparta.[31]

Hermocrates certainly emerged from the war as one of his country's
heroes and a proper object for the admiration of the impressionable
young Dionysius, then (in late September 413) just entering manhood.
However, Hermocrates made a fatal error of political tactics – or perhaps
it would be more fair to say that his generosity of spirit momentarily
blinded him to his political interests. During the winter of 413/12
all Hellas was in a ferment, in anticipation of the overthrow of the
Athenian Empire. The Peloponnesians set about building a fleet of 100
ships, and before the spring the revolt of Athens' subjects had begun, and
contact had been made with the Persian satraps of Lydia and Phrygia.
We may assume that embassies went back and forth between Sparta and
Syracuse. Hermocrates persuaded his countrymen to repay the debt that
they owed to the Peloponnesians by sending an expeditionary force to
the Aegean, to assist in the destruction of the Athenian Empire, thus
crowning their achievement in destroying the Athenian armada before
Syracuse.

Not that the city could afford to give the whole of her attention to the
Aegean. War continued with Catane, in which the Cataneans – reinforced by refugees from Nicias' army and, during 412/11, probably also by
a formidable force of Libyan and Campanian mercenaries originally hired
to help the Athenians – acquitted themselves well, and with Naxos and
Leontini as well as with the numerous Sicel towns that had espoused the
Athenian cause.[32] In fact, what with a measure of disagreement at first
among the allies over their immediate objective, and a spirited naval
counter-offensive on the part of the Athenians which immobilized a
large part of the Peloponnesian fleet in the Saronic Gulf, the main
expedition sent to liberate Athens' subjects was delayed until the late
summer of 412, after the conclusion of the shameful treaty between the
Lacedaemonians and Persia. By that time the Athenians had recovered
from their first shock of horror and dismay and were taking energetic
steps to contain the revolt of their subjects. Hermocrates prevailed on his
countrymen to send a strong squadron – 20 ships and 2 from Selinus –
under three generals, of whom he was one. This fleet sailed about
midsummer, after the new board of generals came into office, and on
arrival brought the strength of the combined fleet collected for the relief
of Miletus up to 55 galleys.[33]

The Great Siege had had a significant effect upon the balance of political power at Syracuse. Indeed, much the same factors as had contributed to the triumph of radical democracy at Athens had been present – albeit not in the same chronological order – at Syracuse. The whole population had been concentrated within the walls, exposed to a common peril and pledged to a common effort. The military importance of the landless urban population and the poorer farmers had been made manifest, and with it went a new enlargement of their political aspirations and effectiveness. And now the leader of the 'conservative' faction had departed from the city (as Cimon and his friends had departed from Athens in 462, to assist the Spartans in Messenia) at a time when the opponents of 'oligarchy' were strong and had found an effective leader in Diocles.

It seems quite clear that this Diocles has become thoroughly confused, in the pages of Diodorus, with a lawgiver (*nomothetēs*) of the archaic period of the same name, probably a Corinthian and worshipped as a hero at Syracuse. The Laws of Diocles were written in so archaic a style that they twice required reinterpretation, once in the time of Timoleon (the late '40s of the fourth century) and again under Hieron II; which would hardly have been the case with statutes drawn up towards the end of the fifth century. It seems to me probable that the confusion existed in the anecdotal material with which Diodorus occasionally enlivens his narrative. The Laws of Diocles will have enjoyed the same dignity and authority at Syracuse that the Laws of Solon did at Athens; and when Timoleon reformed the constitution, both the archaic laws and the statutes introduced by the Diocles of 412 must have been the subject of considerable discussion and even controversy. Probably the confusion of the two men entered the historical and anecdotal tradition about that time.[34]

In the late summer of 412, Diocles carried a bill through the Assembly to set up a body of lawgivers, which should include himself, to revise the constitution. Aristotle tells us that the result of this revision was to change the constitution from a *politeia* to a democracy; so it clearly did more than just exchange direct election for election by lot in the selection of the civil magistrates, which is all that Diodorus specifies. The essential difference between *politeia* and democracy is that under the former only those of a certain (usually, hoplite) census enjoyed full political rights, whereas under the latter every member of the Demos did. At Syracuse the matter was complicated by the restriction of the right to hold office to the 'old' citizens, whom I have taken to be the members of the old Dorian *phylae*. Now, presumably, both the 'old citizen' and the hoplite-census qualifications were abolished. The military commands remained elective (as they were at Athens, which provided the pattern for classical democracy), but both they and the civil offices were presumably thrown open to all tribe members. One might have expected a probouleutic Council of the Attic pattern to have been set up, but there is no indication of such an institution in any of our sources. Freedom of speech (*isēgoria*), the hallmark of democratic liberty, seems to have been established, but without the provision of an effective safeguard against the taking of snap decisions by the Assembly. One result of this 'revolution' (the counterpart of the Athenian 'revolution' of 462) was to give Diocles temporarily a Periclean position in Syracusan politics.[35]

In 411, hostilities against the Chalcidic cities were stepped up, and Leontini was taken – if it had not been taken the previous summer. Apparently no change was made in the Aegean command: Diocles and his faction would not want Hermocrates and his friends back until the new constitution was firmly rooted. The Syracusan contingent had gained the reputation of being the most energetic and also the most independent-spirited section of the allied force; and Hermocrates, who had come east to fight for Greek liberty, fell foul of Tissaphernes, the astute satrap of Lydia, and went from Miletus to Sparta to complain of his duplicity. He was back, however, in time to command the right wing of the Peloponnesian fleet in the battle of the Hellespont, in which the Athenians won a clear victory over the allies, drove the Syracusans to flight and captured one of their ships, so laying the bogy of Syracusan naval superiority. Athens, in 411, had undergone a revolution of her own, but one of an oligarchic character which ultimately produced a *politeia*, praised by Thucydides. This, however, had been dissolved when the new regime lost the command of the Saronic Gulf and of the vital island of Euboea. The fleet at its base on Samos had remained loyal to democracy – had, indeed, been the democracy in exile – so that the victory in the Hellespont had been a victory for radical democracy as well as for the city.[36]

CHAPTER TWO

The Punic invasion of 410

But while the attention of the Syracusans was directed towards their domestic affairs, the harassment of their Chalcidic neighbours and the progress of their Aegean squadron, events were taking shape in the extreme west of Sicily which were to affect cataclysmicly the lives and history of all the peoples of the island. The annihilation of the Athenian expeditionary force had left the Segestans, who had brought the Athenians into the island, in a worse situation than they had been in 416; for now Selinus had moral indignation and the sympathy of most of Sicily on her side. Accordingly, Segesta abandoned the disputed frontier district without a fight. Selinus, however, as she had done before, demanded in addition the surrender of a large portion of her neighbour's rightful territory; and Segesta, knowing that she would receive no help from fellow Greeks, appealed once more to Carthage, the protector of her neighbours and ancient allies, the Phoenicians of Motya. This time – perhaps at the very time that, in the remote eastern Aegean, the Spartans were signing away the liberty of the Greeks of Asia and the islands to the Great King – the Segestans offered to put their city under the suzerainty of Carthage.[1]

This offer placed the government of Carthage in a serious quandary. It is probable that one of the clauses of the solemn treaty of 480 required her to 'do the Greek cities no harm', and in 416 she had, very properly, refused to listen to Segesta's plea for assistance. She had also remained neutral in the struggle between Athens and Syracuse, although Athens certainly, and Syracuse possibly, sought her alliance. It is true that, probably in the summer of 413, she had allowed Athens' Siceliot allies to hire 5,000 Libyan mercenaries and had, perhaps, also assisted them to hire 800 Campanians. These troops had arrived too late to help the Athenians, but they may well have played an important part in beating off Syracuse's attacks upon the Chalcidic cities: they had by now returned to Africa. However, although Carthage's action could be regarded by Syracuse as 'an unfriendly act', if could hardly be seen as openly interventionist, or as evidence of a fundamental change of Carthaginian policy towards the Greeks.[2]

2   Selinus: north-east corner of the walls of the acropolis

Carthage had had plenty to occupy her, militarily, since her shattering defeat by Gelon in 480 and her consequent withdrawal from Sicily. She had consolidated her hold upon Sardinia, her principal granary, and she had waged wars against the Nomads of the Interior, against the Mauri (in order to make secure the all-important trade routes to Spain and West Africa) and against the Libyans, to whom she had hitherto been content to pay a rent for the site of the city and whom she now reduced to subjection. These successful wars had been fought under leaders of the warlike Magonid dynasty, who are described, I believe accurately, by Diodorus as constitutional monarchs (*basileis kata nomous*): kings. Like the constitutional kings of Lacedaemon, they were, subject to certain statutory restraints, the most influential men in the state.[3] The reigning king of Carthage in 411 was Hannibal, whose father Gisgo was the son of the Hamilcar, general of the Carthaginians, who perished at Himera in 480. Perhaps because he had been involved in his father's defeat but had failed to share his legendary self-immolation, Gisgo had been exiled and had ended his days at Selinus, which in that disastrous war had been Carthage's ally. Hannibal, now an old man, nourished a burning desire to avenge his grandfather's death and the disgrace of his father by a spectacular victory over the Greeks. In an aristocratic society such as the Carthaginian, the influence of a powerful man of strong personality, guided though he might be by motives wholly personal and by his

28

passions, could sway the minds of the Councillors, provided that they were not positively prejudiced against his policy. Hannibal persuaded the Council to accept Segesta's offer of allegiance and by doing so committed his city to a struggle with the Greeks which was to continue until the advent of Rome upon the Sicilian scene.[4]

The Carthaginians were indeed faced by something of a dilemma; rather as Athens had been when offered the Corcyraean alliance in 433, and as Rome was to be, in 264, when appealed to for assistance by the Mamertines. They could reject Segesta's offer and watch the rich and populous – and therefore powerful – city of Selinus crush her Elymian neighbour and establish a formidable power in the proximity of their ally (probably, subject ally) Motya. Selinus was an ally of Syracuse; the Carthaginians can hardly have been unaware of Syracuse's ambition to become the overlord of Greek Sicily at least; and by defeating the Athenians, the Syracusans had emerged as a potential (perhaps exaggerated) threat to Carthage's maritime supremacy in the west: a threat with which conclusions might, at some perhaps by no means remote date, have to be tried. On the other hand, if western Sicily were included within her own empire, Carthage's command of the western Mediterranean, south of waters in which her allies, the Etruscans, were masters, would be complete. Defeated by Segesta with Carthaginian aid, Selinus could be forced to become an ally of Carthage; the minor Powers, like Elymian Eryx, would quickly fall into line, and the western Mediterranean would be (apart from the Etruscan and Massiliot spheres of influence) a Carthaginian lake.

Against these arguments in favour of a policy of defensive imperialism in western Sicily, the Carthaginians had to take into account the very real danger of their becoming involved in a war with the rest of the Siceliots. Selinus was an ally of Syracuse, which, moreover, by absorbing Selinus' metropolis, Megara, had succeeded to the latter's metropolitan role. Selinus had aided Syracuse in the recent war, and at the present time had two ships serving with the Syracusan squadron in the Aegean. If Carthage attacked her, Syracuse was bound to come to her aid, and many if not all of the other Siceliots, and perhaps even some of their Italian allies, could be expected to respond to a call for a common Hellenic effort against the barbarian. On the other hand, it probably seemed to many Councillors that the present circumstances offered the best opportunity that they were likely to get of establishing Carthaginian control over western Sicily *without* having to fight the Greek Powers east of Selinus. With Acragas, Carthage enjoyed good relations and a flourishing trade; Acragas would be unlikely to move against her without the assurance of Syracusan support. Syracuse (as the Carthaginians must have known) had been having her domestic troubles, her governing class must be sorely disgruntled, her best-known leader, together with one-fifth of her navy, was campaigning in the Aegean, and she was currently involved in a protracted conflict with the Chalcidic cities. If a clash with Syracuse could be avoided, and if the solemn peace which Carthage had sworn with Syracuse – but not with Selinus, which had then been her ally – could be preserved, Carthage could round off her empire at comparatively little cost to herself, and peace could return to western Sicily.

Accordingly, Hannibal proceeded to neutralize Syracuse by diplomacy. As the friend of Segesta, he quite properly, together with the Segestans, asked Syracuse to arbitrate between the two disputants; presumably suppressing the fact that his own city had already decided to accept Segesta as a subject ally and to support her with force of arms if necessary. The result of his proposal was what he had foreseen. Selinus, no doubt also unaware of the altered situation in western Sicily, refused to accept arbitration; and Syracuse, with matters nearer home engrossing her attention and believing that her ally was perfectly capable of holding her own against the Segestans, refused to interfere. Carthage now felt that she was at liberty to give limited, but decisive, assistance to Segesta.[5]

In the summer of 410, the Carthaginians shipped to Sicily (no doubt through Motya) the 5,800 Libyans and Campanians, who, as said above, had probably been mainly responsible for the successful resistance of the Chalcidians to Syracusan assaults, and who must have returned to Africa at the close of the previous campaigning season. With this truly formidable reinforcement, the Segestans fell upon the men of Selinus, who, contemptuous of their hitherto weaker opponents, were carelessly pillaging the border region, and routed them with heavy loss. Selinus was now the city in peril, for the Segestans and their auxiliaries could maintain a prolonged campaign against her, and if the Carthaginian navy were to be brought in to mount a blockade of her port, her position would become desperate. She therefore appealed to Syracuse for assistance, an appeal to which Syracuse could not turn a deaf ear. Knowing that Selinus was invoking the aid of the strongest city in Sicily, the Segestans reminded Carthage of her new obligations towards them; and Carthage, whose government had known all along that war with Syracuse might in the end be unavoidable, but who could tell themselves that now they were acting to defend an ally and therefore were not breaking their oaths, began to make preparations for a major war in the following summer: a war in which Carthage would find herself opposed by a coalition of the chief Greek cities.[6]

At this time, the Carthaginians, more realistic than the Athenians, did not look beyond the establishment of a permanent province at the western end of the island, the infliction upon the Greeks of a salutary defeat that should make amends for their own humiliation two generations earlier, and the imposition upon them of a treaty of the kind that their grandfathers had been obliged to accept at Greek hands. They had some reason to hope that the Siceliots would fail to present a united front against them. Acragas had remained neutral in the war with Athens and the pro-Syracusan faction in the city had been expelled. In addition, her enormous wealth, undiminished by any lengthy war since Theron's day, and the luxurious style of living of her aristocracy derived largely, nowadays, from her export of olive oil and wine to the Phoenician cities of Libya, and there was likely to be little enthusiasm among her leading citizens for war with her best customer.[7] The Chalcidic cities were still being harassed by Syracuse; and at Syracuse itself there was division and bitterness.

During the summer, the Athenians annihilated the allied fleet at Cyzicus, the Syracusans only saving their ships from capture by burning them. Hermocrates' enemies at home seized their opportunity to destroy him, and he and his fellow generals were sentenced *in absentia* to exile, the charge against them being perhaps the one familiar to Athenian generals, that of failing to carry out the orders of the People; and we may suspect that the slanders against Hermocrates put about by Tissaphernes had found ready ears at Syracuse. Opposition to the wily satrap's policy could have been interpreted as treason towards the cause of the alliance. Hermocrates and his colleagues protested their loyalty to the city and the Demos and surrendered their command to the men sent out to succeed them, most of the trierarchs pledging themselves to work for the restoration of their civic rights on their return home.[8] Hermocrates, still pursued by the malevolence of Tissaphernes, betook himself to the court of Tissaphernes' rival, Pharnabazus, who received him as a friend and supplied him with funds with which he began to collect mercenaries and build ships, in order to be able to bring pressure to bear on the Syracusans to reinstate him in his rights. Xenophon states that Hermocrates was still in the Levant in the summer of 408, when he accompanied envoys of the various powers to the court of the Great King; but this cannot be correct, for it was in the summer of 408 that he was killed in the approaches to the agora of Syracuse.[9]

The Carthaginians entrusted the command in the coming war in Sicily to Hannibal, and he spent the intervening period in putting together an army of Iberian mercenaries, the toughest fighting men from the cities of Libya (by which I take Diodorus to mean the Phoenician cities) and citizen levies from Carthage itself. He also built or requisitioned transports and warships. The size of his army can only be a matter of conjecture, since the figures given by the earliest historians – 204,000 by Ephorus and 100,000 by Timaeus – are not useful even as pointers.[10] It may well be that Ephorus' figures, both here and later, derive from

Philistus; and if this is so we must suppose either that the latter was misinformed or that he deliberately inflated the Punic numbers, not only to excuse the defeats and enhance the final triumph of the Greeks, but also in order to make it appear that the hosts which assailed Sicily in Dionysius' day did not fall *too* far short, in point of numbers, of those which Gelon was said to have overthrown. Timaeus' more modest estimates probably represent 'corrections' of Ephorus rather than figures taken from a source other than Philistus. Even if Carthage could have raised, and Hannibal controlled, ten or twenty myriads of warriors, such vast numbers were not required by the task in hand. Hannibal was coming to Sicily to capture two cities, not to conquer the island. He knew that he would be reinforced by the soldiers of Segesta and the Phoenician cities and probably by some thousands of Sicans, the indigenous inhabitants of western Sicily, and as a good Carthaginian he would not want to spend more of the city's money than he had to.

Some indication of the likely size of the Carthaginian armies in this and later wars may be given by the fact that a force landed in Sicily in 345 was said to have consisted of 50,000–60,000 infantry; that the army defeated by Timoleon on the Crimisus (in the raising of which the city made a special effort) was said to have amounted to some 80,000 men – which may well represent an exaggeration on the part of Timaeus, designed to enhance the glory of Timoleon – and that in 262, when faced by two Roman consular armies, Carthage put 56,000 men into the field. But whatever may have been the size of the army that was being prepared during the winter and spring of 410/9, such reports of it as may have found their way to Sicily do not appear to have alarmed the Siceliots unduly; and even the Selinuntians, on whom the first blow must fall, did not take the elementary precaution of repairing their dilapidated walls.[11]

When the campaigning season of 409 opened, Selinus sent cavalry patrols into the western extremity of the island to watch for the coming of the enemy; and so her horsemen witnessed the arrival in the bay of Lilybaeum, in the territory of Motya, of Hannibal's expeditionary force, convoyed by 60 warships. These were hauled out of the water, thus advertising the fact that the expedition was not directed against Syracuse (which could not have been attacked with any real prospect of success without the assistance of naval forces), and also, no doubt, so that the crews could be employed as light infantry. Hannibal made his base camp at the site of the future city of Lilybaeum, and was there joined by the augmented forces of Segesta (which can hardly have totalled less than 8,000 men) and by the contingents of the Phoenician cities. When he marched against Selinus, with all his preparations for the intended siege complete, Hannibal had perhaps between 40,000 and 50,000 men.[12]

When they learnt of the arrival at Lilybaeum of the Carthaginian armament, the people of Selinus debated the question of submission or resistance; for Selinus was an ancient ally of Carthage, with which she no doubt enjoyed (like Acragas) a lucrative trade, and a prominent citizen, Empedion, urged his countryment not to go to war against Hannibal. Knowing, however, that submission would entail not only their being obliged to accept the status of a tributary ally of Carthage (which to a Greek would constitute enslavement) but also the surrender of territory to Segesta, and having confidence in the strength of their defences and in the loyalty of their allies, particularly the Syracusans, the Selinuntians voted for resistance, and sent messages to their allies asking for assistance.[13] When he had put his army in order, Hannibal marched along the coast, took the small Selinuntian trading colony of Mazara, and then advanced on Selinus itself. No doubt he first gave the citizens the opportunity of accepting terms (neither Carthage nor he had any quarrel with Selinus), and when his offer was rejected he divided his army so as to assault the city on both sides.

Selinus occupied a strong natural position; but now for the first time Greeks encountered modern siege methods, which the enemy had probably introduced from Phoenicia; a branch of warfare in which they lagged far behind the Phoenicians. On all sides the fortifications were battered with iron-tipped rams, while archers and slingers (perhaps this is the first appearance in recorded history of the famous slingers from the Balearic Islands), posted on tall siege-towers, swept the walls of their defenders. Then waves of mercenaries, carried away by the prospect of loot, their attacks spearheaded by the terrible warriors of Campania ('the Koreans of the Ancient World') hurled themselves into the breaches opened by the rams. The city almost fell to the first assault, and only the desperate heroism of the defenders threw back the Campanians. Urgent pleas for immediate assistance were sent to Acragas (over 50 miles distant), to Gela (almost as far again) and to Syracuse (more than 150 miles away). But even if Selinus' allies had been in a state of readiness, help could not have arrived from Syracuse in less than about twenty days, and the others were in no mind to encounter Hannibal without the support of Syracuse's field army.[14]

Up till now, Syracuse had not, apparently, taken the Carthaginian threat to Selinus very seriously. Selinus was a large, populous, well-sited city, and no fifth-century Greek would have expected such a place to fall except by starvation or treachery. That spring, Syracuse had sent five ships to reinforce her Aegean squadron, and she also seems to have sent five ships to the Peloponnese to assist the Lacedaemonian 'home fleet' (unless, of course, these two groups of ships are in fact one and the same, the vessels proceeding to the Aegean after completing their operations in the Pylos area). Moreover, hostilities continued against the Chalcidians.[15] However, when the latest messages arrived from Selinus the Syracusans responded vigorously enough. They made peace (or perhaps merely a truce) with the Chalcidians and put in hand thorough preparations for a major campaign. They also sent an advance force to Acragas, consisting of 3,000 select men (*epilektoi*): those on the hoplite roll who were prepared to take the field at short notice (as on the present occasion) or to make up a task force comprising a portion only of the whole field army. This body was under the command of Diocles, at that time the leading man in the city.[16]

Hannibal, however, had not come to Selinus to invest it with pampered citizen militiamen but to storm it with expendable mercenaries. At dawn on the second day the assault was recommenced and was maintained, against furious resistance and with savage street fighting, for nine days before the last Selinuntian stand in the agora was broken and the unhappy city given up to massacre and plunder. Of the men of the city, some 16,000 dead were counted, 5,000 were taken alive and 2,600 escaped to the shelter and hospitality of Acragas. Those women and children who had fled for refuge to the temples, and presumably such slaves as escaped the slaughter, were spared for sale in Libyan markets.

In response to representations from the Greeks, Hannibal now agreed to allow the refugees to return to their city (whose walls he demolished) on condition that tribute was paid to Carthage. By this politic move, he deprived the allies of Selinus of the services of a small army of good fighting men, and no doubt hoped, by earning the gratitude of the Selinuntians, to give a measure of security, without cost to his city, to this corner of the new province. I consider it likely, in spite of the words that Diodorus (or rather, his source) puts into his mouth, that Hannibal also followed contemporary Greek practice and permitted the 5,000 prisoners of war to ransom themselves and resume their civic rights. No doubt many of the women and children also benefited from his liberality, which may be explained by the related facts that Selinus had been the ally of his grandfather, had sheltered his father's exile and had, at the present time, no quarrel with Carthage. Moreover, he had apparently quieted the fears of the other Siceliots. Acragas made no move to mobilize her forces and no more troops came from either Gela or Syracuse to join Diocles, who had reached Acragas shortly after the fall of Selinus.[17]

In less than a month Hannibal had effected the purpose for which his city had sent him to Sicily: there remained the matter of the exaction of vengeance for the defeat and death of his grandfather and the disgrace of his father. Leaving Selinus he marched north-east across the island to the little city of Himera, on the north coast. He put his army, probably amounting, after the heavy losses incurred before Selinus, to about 40,000 men, into camp on high ground to the south of the city, and with the assistance of some 20,000 Sicans and Sicels (to whom it must have seemed that the Carthaginians had come to break the age-old domination of the Greeks) he repeated the tactics that had proved so sucessful at Selinus, employing in addition fire and sap. Once again only the desperate courage of the defenders still kept his mercenaries outside the walls at nightfall of the first day of the fighting. Diocles, who had left Acragas when news of Hannibal's march reached him and, with his force augmented to 4,000 men (clearly the southern Siceliots did not regard what happened to Himera as being any great concern of theirs), then arrived at Himera and assumed command of the defence.[18]

The hoplite was at his most formidable in pitched battle against light infantry, rather than in defending (or attacking) fortifications; and so it was decided to try the effect of a sortie. Accordingly, the next morning 10,000 Greeks broke out of the city and, with the advantage of complete surprise, at first carried all before them. Then Hannibal counter-attacked from his main camp, caught them in the disorder of pursuit (where the light infantryman was superior to the heavy) and routed them with the loss of nearly a third of their number. When the fighting was over, 25 Greek ships arrived at the port. According to Diodorus, these were the vessels of the Syracusan Aegean squadron, which had been equipped with new ships by Pharnabazus after the the disaster of Cyzicus. It is not really possible to reconcile this statement with the chronology of Xenophon's account of the war in the Aegean, even making allowance for Xenophon's occasional unreliability in this field. If (as Diodorus implies) Hannibal opened his campaign in the spring of 409, it was probably not yet midsummer. But Xenophon's narrative strongly suggests that the Syracusan ships were in the neighbourhood of Ephesus towards the *end* of the campaigning season, and states categorically that the Selinuntian galleys serving with them were still there after the news arrived of the fall of their city. Moreover, four of the Syracusan ships were captured by the Athenians that same summer. It is most unlikely that the Syracusans would had recalled their fleet before the urgent summons came from Selinus. The shortest distance over the open sea from Syracuse to Ephesus is more than 700 miles; and there would hardly have been time for a message to reach the ships and for them to make their way back to Sicily and still to have carried out the operations in the Aegean detailed by Xenophon. It seems to me better to reject Diodorus' (that is to say, his source's) identification of these vessels with those of Hermocrates' late command, and to assume that they had been sent directly from Syracuse.[19]

A rumour of the sort familiar in time of war now spread through Himera, to the effect that the Syracusans were marching in full force, with their allies, to the relief of the city and that Hannibal, informed of their approach, was planning to bring up his ships from Motya and make a dash by sea with his best troops against a Syracuse denuded of its defenders. Diocles and the commanders of the fleet, remembering how the Athenians, in 415, had exploited the march of the Syracusan field army to Catane to effect an unopposed landing in the neighbourhood of the city, decided that their first duty was to the defence of their fatherland. They therefore ordered the indignant but helpless Himerans to evacuate their city by sea, in two stages; and the first batch of refugees, mostly women and children, sailing under cover of darkness were put ashore somewhere beyond the borders of Himera: perhaps on the edge of the territory of Messana. Diocles himself, with perhaps 1,000 Himerans and their wives and children, set off by land for Syracuse.[20]

Next morning the Carthaginians renewed their attacks upon the walls of Himera, which were heroically resisted, the defenders only succumbing to the relentless onslaughts of the Iberians on the second day, when the galleys, returning to pick them up in their turn, were already in sight of the city. The inevitable massacre and sack followed. The women and children were distributed as slaves among the soldiery, but the men – some 3,000 in number – were solemnly sacrificed to the shade of Hamilcar on the spot where tradition said that he had met his death. The city itself was razed to the ground. Then Hannibal, having completed his work and satisfied public and private desire for vengeance, dismissed his Sicilian auxiliaries and also the Campanians (much to their disgust); and, after putting garrisons into the cities of what was thenceforth to be regarded as a Carthaginian dominion, returned with his expeditionary force to Carthage, where his arrival was celebrated as a personal, family and national triumph.[21]

There is good reason to suppose that a substantial majority at least of the Council was satisfied with the gains that Carthage had made as the result of this war. Possession of western Sicily enabled her to exclude the Greeks (the only trade rivals she had any cause to fear) from the southern waters of the western Mediterranean. The nearest free Greek city to Selinus was Heraclea, some 30 miles distant, and Acragas, the nearest major Power, was more than 20 miles beyond that. On the northern coast there was now a gap of about the same size between Solus and the nearest Greek settlement, the militarily insignificant Cephaloedium. This gap indeed was narrowed when, probably in 407, Carthage established a colony at Thermae, seven miles to the west of the site of Himera, in order to utilize the territory of the vanished city. The survivors of the destruction of Himera settled at Thermae, which became wholly Hellenized and, from being the easternmost Carthaginian city, replaced Himera (by which name it was often referred to) as the westernmost Greek.[22]

Western Sicily did not become a province in the Roman sense of the word, in that there was no governor and no provincial administration. The Greeks called it the Epicraty (*Epikrateia*) – possession – of Carthage.

It was a region within which the Phoenician, Elymian and Greek cities were her subject allies and the Sican communities either subject or free allies; its eastern frontier lay along a notional line running from the eastern boundary of Selinus to that of Himera. Carthage now had all that she needed to make her maritime empire secure. She did not need any additional territory or any more alien subjects, who would have to be held down by mercenary garrisons: a source of potential unrest and a drain upon the city's fincances. It would have seemed much more profitable to merchant aristocrats, accustomed to balance profit against cost, to restore friendly commercial relations with the Greeks (upon whom they relied for many of their imported luxuries) than to embark upon the uncharted waters of the conquest of all Sicily. Indeed, with the establishment of the Epicraty, Carthage had taken the first major step towards joining the Hellenic world.

It is quite clear that the Greek cities did not regard Hannibal's expedition as having any other than a limited object. Only Syracuse, the ally of Selinus and indebted to her, made any serious military preparations to resist him. The Greeks must, of course, have been both shocked and alarmed by the speed with which he stormed Selinus: it was their first experience of modern warfare. Yet Hannibal's treatment of the citizens was less brutal than Sparta's treatment of the Plataeans or Athens' of the people of Melos.[23] Moreover, if (as is probable) Selinus had been a party to the treaty of 480, it was as an ally of Carthage; so that the latter, by attacking her now, broke at most only some clause referring to the Greek cities in general. But Himera was another matter. Himera had been part of the empire of Theron of Acragas, one of the signatories of the treaty, and the destruction of this city, which had (as far as we know) given no offence to Carthage, and the ritual sacrifice of its survivors, must have had a more profound effect. It was, indeed, a serious error of policy, if Carthage wished to renew her friendly relations with the Siceliots; but old Hannibal had been too obsessed with the notion of revenge to allow his mind to dwell on the probable consequences of his act of barbarity. For the Siceliots could not fail to be aware that the tide of barbarism was rising on all sides, and that Hellenism was under threat in Italy, in Asia and now in Sicily itself. Carthage was only a day's sail from the western tip of the island, and now she had established a military presence there. Only eighteen months earlier she had probably been generally regarded by the Siceliots as a remote barbarian city, once humbled by their forefathers and with no special stake in Sicilian affairs. Now she had assumed the appearance of a near and deadly threat to their liberties if not to their very existences.

However, it is most unlikely that the disunited and mutually distrustful Siceliots would have made any concerted move against the Epicraty: indeed, no formal state of war existed between any of them and

Carthage. But for the intrusion into the affairs of western Sicily of the restless daring of Hermocrates, pre-war normality would probably have been restored to the relations of Greeks and Phoenicians, at all events for the time being. However, once established in Sicily, Carthage would have found it difficult in the long run not to be drawn into the conflicts and rivalries of the Greek cities and thus into collision with one or other of the major Powers, and so into an attempt to bring the whole island under her control.

CHAPTER THREE

The Second Carthaginian invasion, down to the fall of Acragas

In the late summer of 409, when the minds of the Siceliots were still in a state of turmoil, Hermocrates, the one man who might have been able, had he enjoyed the leadership of his city, to inspire and direct a Panhellenic movement, arrived on the scene. His friend Pharnabazus had provided him with the means of acquiring a private force of 5 ships and 1,000 soldiers. Diodorus says that he collected this little armament at Messana, but Beloch's suggestion, that he brought it with him from the satrapy (where shipbuilding material and fighting-men were readily available), is more likely to be correct. He arrived at Messana and from there opened communications with his friends in Syracuse, for the purpose of getting his sentence of exile revoked. However, the last thing that Diocles wanted, after his poor showing at Himera, was to see Hermocrates back in the city and demanding, as a matter of Panhellenic principle, that energetic military action be taken in order to liberate Himera and Selinus. He would be afraid, too, that Hermocrates, with the backing of at least a substantial section of the aristocracy, would use his influence, and probably the covert threat of his private army, to reverse the 'reforms' of 412. Consequently he saw to it that Hermocrates' request was turned down.

Hermocrates now recruited some 1,000 Himeran exiles and marched across Sicily to Selinus, which he seized. He fortified one of the quarters of the city (probably in the region of the so-called North Gate) and sent out a call to all Selinuntians and any others prepared to support his crusade against the Carthaginians to join him. In this way he put together a very respectable army of some 6,000 first-rate soldiers. Using Selinus as his base, he spent the rest of the campaigning season attacking and harrying Carthage's allies, inflicting serious defeats upon the forces of Motya and Panormus.[2] Hermocrates can hardly have failed to realize that his activities were certain to provoke a violent Carthaginian reaction. The imperial city could not stand idly by and watch all the fruits of Hannibal's triumphant campaign being wrested from her. We must, therefore, I believe, assume that Hermocrates now saw in Carthage the

3 Panormus (Ziz). Copy of Syracusan silver tetradrachm (2 shekel), 400–390: (above) head of Arethusa/Tanit; (below) chariot, with legend, ZIZ (Panormus)

threat both to the freedom of the Hellenes and to the ambitions of Syracuse that, fifteen years earlier, he had seen in Athens. For, with Carthage established in western Sicily, not only would Selinus be permanently lost to the Siceliot nation but there would also be the danger that, in any conflict with Syracuse (for instance, over the question of the hegemony of the Siceliots), Acragas, with her lucrative trading connection with Carthage – now her neighbour in Sicily – might be tempted to seek Punic aid and alliance, as Segesta had done with such spectacular success. If Sicily was to be safe for Hellenism, Carthage must be driven out of the island. This could be done only by the kind of pan-Siceliot alliance that had defeated her in 480, under Gelon's leadership. His, Hermocrates', recent exploits had demonstrated that the Epicraty was vulnerable and that, under a proper leader, Greeks were superior in war to barbarians. Under *his* leadership, Syracuse could mount a crusade for the liberation of Sicily that would also set the seal upon her own hegemony of the Siceliots.

The recall from exile of Hermocrates became a topic of major interest in the Syracusan Assembly; yet Diodorus must be wrong when he tells us that 'the Demos clearly wished to have him back'; for if that had been the case, his friends could have had a bill passed in favour of his recall.[3] Although there must have been a number of people of all classes who regarded Hermocrates' conduct – the stirring up of the Carthaginians after they were safely back in Libya – as wholly irresponsible, it is likely that most Syracusans felt their spirits raised by the news of his achievements. National pride, stimulated by the victory over the Athenians and kept high by the gallantry, even in defeat, of their fleet in the Aegean, had received a severe blow at Himera. Hermocrates' campaign had done much to restore that pride, but it also gave rise to serious apprehension. Men were saying publicly (especially the young men) that here was the national leader, the *hegemon*, for whom the city and all Sicily were looking: a second Gelon. But Gelon, like Hermocrates a member of the old ruling class of his city, had been no friend to democracy and had made himself tyrant. Was it not all too likely that Hermocrates would, either as a prelude to, or in the wake of, a triumphant campaign against the Carthaginians, reverse the enactments of Diocles and either restore the *politeia* or even set himself up as tyrant?

That there was a strong body of opinion in the city, comprising the greater part of the Quality, that would have welcomed the overthrow of the radical democracy we need not doubt. Equally certainly, however, they would have strenuously opposed the establishment of a tyranny, the very antithesis of *politeia*. But there must already have existed a small but determined faction that welcomed the idea of monarchy; some from selfish, some from unselfish motives, believing that in the rule of one man lay the city's only hope of safety, some, no doubt, from a mixture of the two. They saw Syracuse as a society divided and leaderless, a state of affairs that had very nearly proved fatal in the war with Athens. Did not Homer himself say, 'a multiplicity of leaders is no good thing: let there be one leader'? But in the famous debate 'recorded' by Herodotus (which formulated basic constitutional theory for Antiquity), it was noted that the popular leader who put down faction and restored national unity before very long assumed the monarchy. If, therefore, Hermocrates returned and united the nation, he could not help becoming tyrant. The same debate also enumerated the objections to tyranny. A monarch is unaccountable (*aneuthynos*); he is full of hubris and envy; he listens to (but despises.) calumniators and flatterers; above all, he changes the laws, he violates women, he puts people to death without trial. But those who championed Hermocrates' cause knew that *he* would in no way conform to this pattern. He had, many times, given proof of his patriotism, his love for his fellow citizens, his magnanimity, his self-abnegation and his readiness to listen to advice: he would be a ruler in the tradition of Gelon. To this faction Dionysius belonged.[4]

Dionysius was by now in his early twenties and we may assume that he followed the fashion of the well-to-do young men of the period, frequenting the gymnasia, attending the lectures of sophists and practising the rhetorical skills that they taught him in argument and debate with his companions. More or less a contemporary of his was the wealthy Philistus, whose father may have borne the patrician-sounding name of Archōnides. We are told that Philistus was a disciple of Euenus of Paros, and it is tempting to conjecture that the two young men may have been 'class-mates'. Certainly they both emerge into the light of history as political associates with a common belief in the virtue of monarchy, although they were later to discover that each saw it as a means to a different end: Dionysius, that of personal fame, Philistus that of national security and sound, because authoritative, government. Possessed of a conviction of the great destiny foretold by the Galeotae (belief in omens was in no way inconsistent with a 'rational' education), and also of a restless energy that brooked no restraint or delay in the fulfilment of that destiny, Dionysius was the very type of the Young-men-in-a-hurry said by Thucydides to have regarded Hermocrates as their leader, even before the Athenian invasion (although Thucydides may well have had Dionysius and his friends in mind when he wrote this passage).[5]

Dionysius must have been greatly shocked by the Demos' treatment of Hermocrates and he certainly became an active member of the political club (*hetairia*) whose members were pledged to the task of bringing about the restoration of Hermocrates to his civic rights (and of his colleagues to theirs); making speeches in public in support of these aims, and no doubt singing songs in private in praise of aristocracy and, latterly, of monarchy, and in disparagement of Diocles and fellows of his kidney. Although some of these extremists were no doubt wholly patriotic (like Philistus), none can have failed to appreciate the fact that men who help a tyrant to power may expect to be rewarded for their loyalty. Some of the *hetairoi* would have been impoverished aristocrats who hoped to benefit not only from the proceeds of war and imperialism but also from the confiscations of property and forced sales that usually followed a successful *coup d'état* (Aristotle ascribes this motive to Hipparinus, a few years later). Dionysius, an ardent and impetuous young man with a poet's vision of the glory that would attend the regeneration of Syracuse and victory over the barbarian – a glory in which the followers of the leader would share – would also have seen in that glory a set-off against his own relative obscurity, and a means of accelerating his rise to a position of authority in the State. Nor is he likely to have lost sight of the fact that it was as Master-of-Horse to the tyrant Hippocrates of Gela that the great Gelon had been able to succeed to the monarchy.[6]

There was, then, a faction in favour of recalling Hermocrates, and by no means a negligible one (it will have included most of the trierarchs who had served in the Aegean and who returned to Syracuse at the end of the year); but it formed a minority in the Assembly. We may be sure also that Diocles, with his political career at stake, and his supporters lost no opportunity of spreading the word that Hermocrates was a danger to the city, a war monger and a man who wished to exploit the perilous international situation that he had himself created in order to overthrow the democracy.

Informed by over-sanguine friends in the city that public opinion was beginning to swing in his favour, Hermocrates, in the spring of 408, made what he hoped would prove to be a winning throw. He marched to Himera and he collected the bones of the Syracusans who had fallen in the rout, whose bodies Diocles had left unclaimed and unburied on the field of battle: an offence to the deepest and strongest feelings of the Greeks. Hermocrates brought the remains with all due ceremony to Syracuse, he himself halting at the frontier. His action, as he had expected, provoked a political crisis. It was proposed that the fallen should be given a public funeral, and Diocles, who knew that the occasion would be used by Hermocrates' friends to point the contrast between his own pusillanimity and contempt for sacred custom and the gallantry and patriotism of the exiled Hermocrates, opposed the motion. He lost the vote and with it the last shreds of popular favour. He was sent into exile and is heard of no more. Yet even so the Demos was not prepared to readmit Hermocrates and he had no option but to return to Selinus.[7]

It must now have become clear to him that he had nothing to hope for from a reliance on constitutional measures, and that the democracy was not going to accept him as a Periclean *prostatēs*. Society was too sharply divided and the Demos, now all-powerful, was too suspicious, too ready to doubt the good intentions of any aristocrat, too ready to listen to the envious and self-interested defamations uttered by the popular orators, for any man to achieve a Periclean position. The same had become true of Athenian society, as Alcibiades was to discover to his cost the following year. Indeed, the reports of the abortive attempt made by a section of the Athenian governing class, in 411, to replace the radical democracy by a *politeia* must have increased considerably the suspiciousness of the Demos at Syracuse and strengthened the hand of Hermocrates' enemies. If Hermocrates was to return from the wilderness, it would have to be by the use of force; and if he was to rule at Syracuse, it could now only be as the head of an aristocratic faction or as a tyrant.

The most determined of Hermocrates' friends at Syracuse now decided to risk a *coup d'état*, and laid their plans for him to seize the city. He was to march by the southern coast road to Syracuse, where his friends would admit him, by night, by the Achradine Gate. With the forces at his disposal he should have no difficulty in making himself master of the city. Accordingly, when he received the word from his friends, Hermocrates set out from Selinus with 3,000 men. Rightly appreciating that speed was essential to achieve the surprise upon which the success of his venture depended, when he arrived at the last stage of his march the leader pressed ahead with such rapidity that only a small portion of his army (probably the horsemen) could keep up with him; and so he reached the rendezvous with only a handful of men. His friends had loyally performed their part of the undertaking and, Dionysius among them, had occupied the gate. If Hermocrates had gone at once to the agora, where the citizens would assemble once the alarm had been given, he might perhaps have avoided disaster; for he could have disarmed them or won them over as they straggled in, sleepy, bewildered and leaderless. Unhappily, he chose to wait at the gate for the remainder of his force to come up, and this gave the people time to gather, under arms, in the agora and for some kind of command to be established. Diodorus' narrative (which must go back ultimately to Philistus) suggests that Hermocrates realized his mistake and went forward towards the agora with what men he had; but the delay proved fatal and he and his party were overwhelmed by numbers and the majority slain.[8] The survivors who fell into the hands of the authorities were tried and exiled.

Dionysius, who was severely wounded in the fighting, managed like several of his companions to reach a friendly house and was given out as dead by his family. What we are not told by our sources is how he subsequently recovered his civic rights, was re-enrolled in the muster-roll of hoplites and even held minor office. It seems to me that the explanation probably lies in the report of 'some writers' that one Heloris, a member of the aristocracy, was Dionysius' adoptive father. In an age in which verbal testimony played, to a large extent, the role enjoyed today by written records, it would not have been very difficult for an influential man to adopt a young man who had not yet made his mark in public life and cause his name to be entered upon the various lists without exciting remark.[9]

The death of Hermocrates and the consequent cessation of the attacks upon the Epicraty did not improve the international situation. In 409, Carthage had been taking steps merely to establish her dominion over the western – the mainly non-Hellenic – corner of the island, and had endeavoured to avoid embroilment with the major Greek Powers. It is likely that Syracuse's triumph over the Athenians had given the Carthaginians an exaggerated idea of her naval and military strength and political stability. That idea must now have been sharply revised. The Syracusans had not exactly distinguished themselves in the fighting around Himera, and the attempted coup of Hermocrates would have suggested that all was not well politically. But Hermocrates' military operations had demonstrated the vulnerability of the Epicraty. An army roughly equivalent in size to that of a middling Greek city had made itself master of the open country; at that rate, it would not be long before Selinus was restored and the security of Carthage's allies put in jeopardy. Carthage was now faced with the alternatives of either setting up permanent garrisons in the Epicraty – an expensive, unproductive and possibly even dangerous expedient – or of extending her dominion over the whole island.

Accordingly, Carthage decided on a war of conquest in Sicily and took the first step by founding the new city of Thermae in 407, pushing the frontier of the Epicraty eastwards to the borders of Cephaloedium. Preparations for war on a much larger scale than in 409 were begun and old Hannibal was asked to take command; but in view of his great age he was given Himilco son of Hanno – probably his first cousin – to assist and, if necessary, succeed him.[10] Either late in 407 or early in 406, the Carthaginians sent an embassy to Athens, which was, of course, still at war with Syracuse. Athens' affairs, in 407, were at a critical stage. Cyrus, the younger son of Darius, had come down to the coast of Asia Minor as the Great King's viceroy, and was co-operating energetically with the Spartan admiral, Lysander, to wrest from Athens her command of the Aegean; and Alcibiades, Athens' generalissimo in 408, had fallen from favour and gone into exile. Carthage would have been anxious to ensure that Athens did not come to terms with her enemies (as she could have done, with advantage to herself, after the battle of Cyzicus), and so leave Corinth and Sparta free to assist the Siceliots. Athens' vaunted Hellenism was not strong enough to permit her at this juncture to throw away the opportunity of putting difficulties in the way of the Syracusans, and so she sent an embassy to Sicily in the summer of 406, and an understanding was reached with the Carthaginian generals.[11]

During 407 Carthage's recruiting agents and ambassadors were busy, hiring mercenaries in Iberia and the Balearics and demanding contingents from her allies in Libya, Numidia and Mauretania. The invasion force was also to include levies of subject native Libyans and her own citizens. Once again our sources are not very helpful about the size of the army. Ephorus put it at 300,000 (the same number as that given for Hamilcar's host in 480), and Timaeus at something over 120,000. Perhaps half Timaeus' figure is a realistic estimate. A fleet of 90 triremes is acceptable enough, although Diodorus' '1,000 transports' would appear to be based on Timaeus' figure for the army to be transported.[12]

A rumour of Carthage's intentions could hardly have failed to reach the Siceliots, and Syracuse took it seriously enough to send in the early spring of 406, first, a strong protest to Carthage, and secondly, a fleet of 40 ships into the waters of western Sicily, probably basing them on Selinus, clearly for the purpose of destroying at sea any expeditionary force that Carthage might send to Sicily. About the beginning of April, the Carthaginians, their preparations complete, sent an advance force of 40 ships across the Sicilian Channel and these were engaged by the Syracusans off Drepanum and defeated in a lengthy battle, 15 being sunk and the remainder apparently taking refuge in the Aegates Islands. When the report of the action reached Carthage, Hannibal put to sea with the rest of the fleet and presumably joined forces with the vessels defeated in the sea battle, thus bringing his command up to 75 vessels and outnumbering the Syracusans by nearly two to one. We hear no more of the Greek fleet and must assume that it retired to Syracuse, allowing Hannibal to transport his huge army to Sicily without interference. We are told that he left 40 of his ships at Motya and Panormus, and it may be that, because of the size of his armament, he landed it in two divisions (as he later moved and camped) at these two ports.[13]

When it became evident to the Siceliots that Carthage really meant business, Syracuse, assuming the hegemony of the Greeks, took energetic steps to encourage a united resistance to the common enemy, and sent envoys also to those South Italian states that were well- disposed towards her, and to Sparta, to ask for their assistance. It was clear that the storm must fall first upon Acragas, for Hannibal could not march towards the Straits by the northern route leaving such a powerful enemy behind him. The Acragantini, although they might have made terms with the barbarian, decided to resist and to bring their huge population – estimated by Antiquity at 200,000, of whom 20,000 were citizens (that is, presumably, adult male citizens) – as well as their gathered crops and possessions within the circuit of their walls.

So when Hannibal appeared before the city and offered the citizens the choice between active alliance with Carthage and friendly neutrality, his proposal was rejected. To make an alliance with the barbarian against fellow Greeks with whom they were on friendly terms was unthinkable to the Acragantines; and after the sack of Selinus and the even more barbaric treatment of Himera, both in time of solemn peace, no Greek city could feel secure in a land dominated by Carthage. Brought face to face with the threat of subjugation, however mild, by a people whose language, customs and gods were wholly alien to their own, the Acragantines preferred to stand by their allies, to arm all men of military age and to defend their walls. They were not without useful auxiliaries. They had taken into their service a Spartan soldier of fortune, Dexippus, who had, I believe, served under Hermocrates and who had brought from Gela (through which Hermocrates had passed on his last, fatal journey) 1,500 mercenaries and also the 800 Campanians discarded by Hannibal after the Himera campaign. These crack troops held the Hill of Athena, commanding the steep north-east approach to the city.[14]

Hannibal split his army, positioning the Iberians and a portion of his Libyan levies on the hills to the east of the city, and the rest of his host, in a fortified camp, in the plain near the south-west corner of the defences, where the assault was launched, using mounds, siege-towers and engines. But the defenders, for all the luxuriousness of their way of living, fought well; and plague – the result, said the soothsayers, of the destruction of the tombs and especially of the tomb of Theron, for the sake of their materials – struck the besiegers. Among the many that it carried off was old Hannibal, so that the sole command devolved upon Himilco, who at once halted the demolitions and took measures (including human sacrifice) to placate the offended spirits. Although a less determined and aggressive soldier than his cousin, he continued to prosecute the siege with vigour.[15]

The Syracusans had been waiting for the arrival of the contingents from Messana and from their Italiot allies before marching to the relief of Acragas. Now they moved out, advancing through the territories of Camarina and Gela and adding the men of those cities to their host, as well as troops from the Sicel communities of the interior. Diodorus gives their numbers as over 30,000 foot and no less than 5,000 horse; but I believe that the figure for the foot soldiers may refer only to men on the hoplite rolls, whose numbers would be accurately recorded, and that perhaps a considerable number of light-armed skirmishers, drawn from the poorer classes, should always be added to the totals given us of Greek citizen armies. Thirty Syracusan ships covered the seaward flank of their march. The 'senior' general and therefore the effective commander-in-chief of the expeditionary force was one Daphnaeus; and Dionysius was acting as adjutant (*grammateus*) to the board of generals.[16]

Himilco moved the division that had been covering the eastern approaches to Acragas down into the plain to meet the advancing Greek army. In the ensuing battle the two sides were probably pretty evenly matched in point of numbers; indeed, the Greeks may have been the more numerous, and they had the decided advantage of fighting as hoplites against light infantry. The Carthaginian division was routed after a stubborn fight, with the loss of over 6,000 men, and fell back on the main camp. But Daphnaeus (whose leadership, if Polyaenus is to be trusted, had contributed to the victory) knew that Himilco had another army in reserve; and he would have remembered how, after just such a victory before Himera, the Greeks had been overwhelmed by a counter-attack. So he halted the pursuit, and a similar prudence restrained the Acragantine generals from launching the sortie demanded by their men against the flank of the defeated enemy as they retreated past the southern walls of the city.[17]

Daphnaeus now occupied the upper camp abandoned by the beaten Carthaginian division, and to this the Acragantine field army as well as Dexippus and his men made their way; and there a tumultuous multinational assembly was held, in which the indignation of the besieged against the supineness of their generals, who were rumoured (no doubt quite falsely) to have been bribed by the enemy, became inflamed to such a pitch that four out of the five were stoned to death. No doubt the tension between governing class and demos, found almost everywhere in the Greek world, lay at the root of this outrage. But the Greek hoplite had been brought up to believe that wars should be settled quickly by pitched battle (*agōn*), and excessive caution on the part of a general, when it appeared to the rank and file that the opportunity of a clear-cut victory was being offered, was frequently interpreted as cowardice or corruption. On the present occasion, although a Hannibal or a Scipio with seasoned troops might have achieved a spectacular success, a sortie by an inexperienced citizen militia could itself have been taken in the flank from Himilco's lines and, with Daphnaeus' men over a mile away, across the river, have resulted in disaster and even in the capture of the city.[18]

The Greeks now went over to the offensive against the besieger, a fact which suggests that, after losses by plague and battle, Himilco's forces did not greatly outnumber the combined armies opposed to them. His camp was too strongly fortified to be taken by assault and so Daphnaeus fell back on blockade, which he maintained throughout the heat of the summer; with the result that by the time the campaigning season came to an end the invaders found themselves reduced to serious straits, with mutiny and mass desertions threatening. However, Himilco learnt that the Syracusans were sending a large consignment of grain by sea to provision Acragas, whose inhabitants had not been exercising economy in their consumption of food. He brought up the 40 ships that he had left at Motya and Panormus and, achieving complete surprise, intercepted the inadequately protected convoy, sank or drove ashore the escorting warships and captured the freighters. Once again the roles were reversed and Himilco became the besieger.[19] The Campanians in the Greek camp, professionals and expert judges of the way the wind blew, promptly deserted to the enemy, and before very long Acragas' store of food was exhausted. The Italiots, who had made no plans for a winter campaign and who had the sea between them and home, now withdrew from the camp and marched away to the Straits. Dexippus was rumoured to have counselled this move, bribed to that end by the enemy: a story which, if it proves nothing else, shows how firmly the Spartans' reputation for venality was rooted in the Greek tradition. The position at Acragas had become hopeless and it was agreed by the Acragantine generals and the allied commanders that the city must be abandoned.[20]

The evacuation was carried out by night, in mid-December. The huge mass of men, women and children, leaving behind those whom old age, infirmity or sickness rendered immobile, made its unhappy way to Gela, some 40 miles to the east, escorted by the soldiers. Himilco occupied the abandoned city at daybreak. Almost all those who had remained behind were butchered and the houses and temples were plundered. The booty from this great city, one of the wealthiest, most civilized and most luxurious in the Hellenic world, included a great haul of paintings and works of sculpture (among the latter the bronze bull which passed in local legend for the instrument of torture of the infamous tyrant Phalaris), the best of which Himilco sent back to Carthage. There, their effect upon the taste of the upper class was comparable to that exerted upon Roman aristocratic taste by the spoils of Syracuse, almost two hundred years later, and Hellenic influences began to affect the native Phoenician strains.[21]

Himilco probably sent his ships back to Carthage and installed his army in winter quarters in Acragas. The refugees from that city were eventually settled at Leontini by the Syracusans. Many other Siceliots took refuge at Syracuse, and others sent their families and their movable possessions for safety to Italy, although the people of Gela, despite the fact that they would be the first objective of Himilco's offensive in the coming spring, decided to put their trust in their gods, in the loyalty of their allies and in the strength of their fortified hill-top site, and remained where they were. They were reinforced by Dexippus and his company, left behind by Daphnaeus. The citizens of Camarina, too, decided not to leave their town.[22]

CHAPTER FOUR

Dionysius' accession to power

When Dionysius marched home from Gela with the army, having gained a reputation for outstanding bravery in the fighting against Himilco, his mind was already made up: he was going to make himself tyrant – master (*despotēs*) – of Syracuse. He was going to take into his own hands, not indeed the day-to-day management of the city's domestic affairs, but the non-accountable direction of her foreign polity, the overall command of her armed forces and the disposal of her resources, human, material and economic. He was going to do this, first (and this was the ostensible motive), because he believed that only if the conduct of the war were put in the hands of one man, answerable to no one for his policy and his actions, could the city escape disaster; and, secondly (the motive that came to light later), because the tyranny would offer him the opportunity, not merely of adding his name to the list of great Sicilian war-leaders, from Phalaris through Hippocrates to Theron and Gelon, but of standing out as the most illustrious of them all, as the man – surely destined to be accorded the status and honours of a hero – who liberated Greek Sicily and expelled the Carthaginians from the island of Heracles.

Three important conditions needed to be satisfied if a tyranny was to be established *from within*, in a Greek *polis*. First, the *polis* itself must be in an unhealthy state, its natural resistance to despotism impaired by serious faction (*stasis*), to such an extent that national unity could be said to have wholly broken down. Secondly, there must be standing ready to avail himself of the opportunity offered by circumstances a man not only possessed *of* the gift of leadership but also possessed *by* an irrepressible lust for power (either as an end in itself, or as a means to an end) and by a total conviction, communicable to others, of his unique ability and therefore of his logical *right* to assume and sustain the responsibility of monarchy. Such a man, a supreme egoist, must appear in his own and his followers' eyes as a Man of Destiny. Thirdly, this Man must have at his disposal, or be able to call upon at need, the force (*bia*) necessary to overcome the residual powers of resistance of society.

The *polis* of Syracuse in 406 was not healthy but it was not sick unto

50

death. The old governing class had withdrawn, as a class, from the contest for the leadership of the Assembly, which was being exercised by men who (whatever their social origins) identified themselves with the common people, and sustained their influence by criticizing and attacking the generals and the class from which the generals were still drawn; so that mutual resentment, embittered by contempt on the one hand and suspicion and envy on the other, informed the relations of aristocracy and Demos. This unhappy state of affairs deprived the city of the services of many of those citizens best equipped to serve it, and rendered such men as were prepared to undertake the generalship insecure, nervous of taking resolute action because apprehensive of the consequences of even partial failure. Yet the democracy was firmly established and ready and able to defend itself, as the failure of Hermocrates' attempted coup had shown. The aristocrats, rich, numerous and conscious of their identity as a class apart from, and above, the common people though they were, and with a formidable military force at their disposal in the Corps of Knights, had none the less refused to rise in support of Hermocrates, a man of their own caste and a war-leader of proven worth. There was no likelihood that they would support a coup against the State on the part of the obscure and youthful Dionysius: particularly with the barbarian almost at the gates of the city.[1]

The situation at Syracuse, then, although it might be said to be crying out for the appearance of a national leader in the Periclean mould, a man acceptable to all classes who could evoke and embody in himself a real sentiment of national unity, was not propitious to the success of an attempt to subvert the democracy. The second of the three conditions was certainly satisfied by the personality of Dionysius. However, when we come to the third condition, the possession by the aspirant to monarchy of the force sufficient to put him in power and keep him there, we see that of all the tyrants about whose rise we have any reliable information or can form a reliable conjecture, none, with the possible exception of Polycrates of Samos, started his career with fewer material resources than Dionysius. Where a *polis* was ripe for subversion (as in the great majority of cases it was), the oldest and the most common course was to champion the Demos against the aristocracy. The second was to seize power with the aid of a strong *hetairia* or a private army. This seems to have been the method favoured in Sicily and it was also employed by Peisistratus, in his first coup, and by Polycrates. The third course was to take over the city with the aid of foreign auxiliaries. It was thus that Peisistratus finally established himself, and thus that Gelon, commanding the troops of his native Gela, had become master of Syracuse. In none of the known cases was the overthorw of a stable democracy involved. Peisistratus took over the management of the *politeia* set up by Solon, but Attic society was deeply divided still, and a large part of the free inhabitants supported him. Polycrates subverted some form of democracy with, according to Herodotus, the help of only fifteen hoplites, but that regime can hardly have been a stable one; and the same may be said of the popular regime ousted by Gelon with the support of the Syracusan aristocracy. The fate of Hermocrates had shown that the Syracusan Demos was not going to surrender tamely to any *hetairia* or small private army. So Dionysius, with an astute grasp of the requirements and the possibilities of the situation, resolved to persuade the people of Syracuse to provide him with a private army *within* the city walls, with which he would make himself their master; borrowing, student of history that he was, something from Peisistratus and something from native Sicilian practice.[2]

The only resources that Dionysius possessed initially were the *hetairia* whose existence I have assumed (for although it is nowhere specifically attested by our authorities, without the aid of a certain number of associates he could not possibly have carried out his plan), the wealth of Philistus, his own reputation for personal courage in the field and the exceptional personal qualities of which he was, over the next thirty-eight years, to give such striking proof. To these qualities even the uniformly hostile tradition that we possess bears grudging testimony. Polybius tells us that Scipio Africanus (who probably knew of Dionysius through Timaeus, since he links his name with that of Agathocles) reckoned him to be 'a most efficient man and a man of the utmost daring tempered with prudence'. Nepos acquits him of four of the stock failings of the tyrant: lust, luxuriousness, avarice and greed (except, of course, for power). Other natural attributes may readily be deduced from an examination of his actions.[3] His physical courage has already been noted, and to this should be added the self-confidence and tenacity of purpose that we may, in part at least, attribute to his belief in his destined greatness. His mental powers were impressive. He was far-sighted (with one important reservation), shrewd and calculating. To effect his purpose, there were no means, no duplicity or guile, that he would scruple to employ. He had immense organizing ability, and – perhaps the most important thing of all in a would-be monarch (and in an established monarch) – he had the gift of inspiring others with his own enthusiasm and his own confidence in himself: the gift of leadership. These qualities were complemented by a rhetorical ability that was no doubt the product both of sophistic training and natural aptitude. Of his failings, the most serious that need to be mentioned here were a consequence of his intensely introverted character: secretiveness, a tendency towards over-optimism (which displayed itself, in terms of military cliché, as a tendency to 'despise his enemy'), together with the despondency which follows the frustration of over-high expectation, and an insensitiveness to the feelings and probable reactions of others.

On the debit side must be set his youth, especially in an age and in a society where youth was politically suspect.[4] At only twenty-four he must have been the youngest man ever to aspire to the sole rule of a Greek city. He had held no important office (we are quite ignorant of the nature and duties of the *grammateus* to the generals, but the position can hardly have been one of any real authority). Moreover, he did not belong to the old nobility, and so must have appeared to the Quality as an upstart. Of course, what appears to be the most unfavourable circumstance was that the regime which he was proposing to subvert was, with all its shortcomings, firmly established and would have the support, however grudging in many cases, of the majority of the population in any conflict with a would-be tyrant. However, this factor could be turned to the advantage of the conspirators, as it helped them to disguise their real purpose. For they intended to appear as men, bent not on overthrowing the democracy – in contemporary language, on 'changing the laws' – but on securing the appointment of a military supremo whose role it would be to defend Syracuse *and* the democracy. They intended to aim their appeal not at any disaffected section of the populace – which would be to proclaim a revolutionary purpose and alert the ever-suspicious Demos to their true intentions – but at the patriotic sentiment of the whole people. They were going to come forward as the defenders of Syracusan freedom, not as its enemies. And this being so, they had a most powerful ally, albeit an unconscious one, outside the walls of the city in Himilco and the menace of enslavement, or worse, at the hands of the barbarian.

It is clear that, whatever contingency plans Dionysius and his friends may have made before the winter of 406/5, they cannot have worked out the details or taken the final decision to act until after the failure of the Acragas campaign. If Daphnaeus had succeeded in raising the siege, which he seems to have come close to doing, he would have been the hero of the hour at Syracuse, and if anyone had been elevated to the standing of national leader (*hegemon*) it would have been he. As it was, the course of events had been entirely in their favour. The cry of 'treachery' had been raised at the disorderly assembly of the allies, and it was raised again when the Acragantines gathered at Syracuse; and there was a general outcry against the supineness of the Syracusan commanders. At a meeting of the Assembly, held probably in early January 405, it became clear that in the present crisis, perhaps the most serious in her history, Syracuse was to all intents and purposes leaderless. There was neither an aristocrat of the stature of Hermocrates, nor a demagogue with sufficient influence, to dominate the meeting and propose a practicable plan for survival.[5] Finally Dionysius, who had drawn twelfth place in the list of speakers, stood up: it was regarded by his friends as a happy omen that the letter M (which stood for the numeral twelve) is the initial letter of the word Monarchy (*mounarchia*)! He moved that the generals should be deemed to have betrayed their trust and should be dealt with by the Assembly in much the same way as the Athenians, in the previous October, had dealt with *their* generals (who had, indeed, won a vital battle, not lost a campaign), and be condemned out of hand.[6]

The presiding authorities (Diodorus says the *archontes*; but Thucydides uses the same term when he plainly means the generals, so we cannot tell whether civil officials or generals presided) tried to silence Dionysius by fining him; Diodorus says, for inflammatory language, but it may have been for making an illegal proposal. Philistus, obviously playing a pre-arranged part (although this is not noted by Diodorus), now came forward and undertook to pay any fines that the speaker might incur. Accordingly, Dionysius went on, not only to accuse Daphnaeus and his colleagues of corruption but to implicate the governing class as a whole, raising the familiar demagogic cry, Democracy is in danger! He urged the people the choose their generals on the grounds, not of their social and political influence (*tous dunatōtatous*), but of their loyalty to the Demos; their humility not their haughtiness, should be the criterion. He must, I believe, have proposed specifically that the property *and age* qualifications be waived. His words were in tune with the prejudices and emotions of his hearers, and we can hardly doubt that the other conspirators played their part by applauding. The Assembly dismissed the board of generals and replaced it by a new one, presumably composed of middle-class nonentities, but including Dionysius himself.[7]

With the first step towards monarchy successfully accomplished, Dionysius set himself to get rid of his colleagues and to enlarge his personal following. He caused a rumour to be spread (here, too, his *hetairia* will have been invaluable), to the effect that the other generals were secretly negotiating with the enemy (many people must have remembered how prominent Syracusans had had secret dealings with Nicias), and he pointedly distanced himself from them, so that he could not be suspected or accused of complicity. Not surprisingly, the notabilities reciprocated his ill will and lost no opportunity of attacking him; and no doubt this was represented as proof of their hatred of the People who had put its trust in him. A fine atmosphere of distrust and fear was thus created, which dominated the frequent meetings of the Assembly. Dionysius successfully carried a proposal to recall the political exiles, meaning, of course, the friends of Hermocrates; his colleagues not daring to offer any opposition. The exiles, all or most of them his former comrades in arms, were expected to attach themselves to their deliverer.[8]

With the approach of spring, the people of Gela sent to Syracuse to ask for military assistance. Gela was in a state of unrest, no doubt the outcome of long-standing grievances on the part of the Demos against the governing class, brought to a head by the events of the previous winter and by fear of the imminent Carthaginian attack upon the town. The government (unaware of what had taken place at Syracuse) probably hoped that the advent of Syracusan troops would restore public confidence; but Dionysius had had himself appointed to lead the Syracusan contingent – 2,000 foot and 400 horse – his colleagues being very glad to see the back of him. At a meeting of the Gelôan Assembly, Dionysius 'accused' the leading citizens, presumably implicating them in the 'treason' of the deposed Syracusan generals. Diodorus says that Dionysius 'condemned them, put them to death and confiscated their property'. This must mean that his presence and that of his army gave local demagogues the confidence to take quasi-judicial action against their notables. Diodorus does not expressly say that the victims included the Geloan generals; but his language implies that the regime had been oligarchic and it is therefore to be presumed that they did, that elections were held under Dionysius' aegis and that new generals were appointed. The proceeds of the confiscations enabled the Geloans to pay Dexippus' mercenaries their arrears and won their loyalty for Dionysius – at the cost, however, of their captain's good will, for Dexippus rejected Dionysius' overtures to attach himself to his cause. While the Syracusans were at Gela, a herald arrived from Himilco with proposals for the ransoming of his prisoners of war: proposals which Dionysius rejected, although he was extremely grateful for the embassy.[9]

The Geloan Demos looked upon Dionysius as its liberator and sent envoys to Syracuse to tell its allies how pleased it was with him. And so, having strengthened his following at the expense of the unfortunate Geloan upper classes, and having secured some invaluable ammunition to use against his colleagues, Dionysius returned with his men to Syracuse; replying to the protests of the Geloans with an undertaking to come back soon with a bigger army. When he re-entered Syracuse, he found the city en fête (perhaps a festival of Dionysus was being celebrated: a good omen for the young man named after him), the play had just come to an end and the people were leaving the theatre. Naturally the citizens crowded around the troops and asked for news from what would soon become the war-front. Dionysius replied that Syracuse had more dangerous enemies within her walls than outside; while the citizens kept holiday, the generals were embezzling the funds, leaving the soldiers unpaid and neglecting to make any preparations for the coming war. Himilco, he said, had sent a herald to ask him to remain inactive (since he would not actively co-operate with the Carthaginians), as most of his colleagues had undertaken to do. For this reason, he (Dionysius) had returned to the city to hand in his resignation.[10]

Dionysius' words spread like wildfire through the city. At a meeting of the Assembly on the following day, at which he repeated his allegations against his colleagues, it was proposed – probably by Hipparinus – that

Dionysius should be appointed General Plenipotentiary at once, without waiting for the regular elections. It was as General Plenipotentiary, the people were told, that Gelon had overthrown the Carthaginians at Himera – a story invented, I believe, by Dionysius' friends and now put into circulation for the first time.[11] The motion was carried, and Dionysius was appointed, presumably (we are not told otherwise) upon the customary terms, under which he would hold office until the summer of 404. General Plenipotentiary was not the same thing as *sole* general; and I believe that we may assume that, when Dionysius' 'traitorous' colleagues had been dismissed, other men (perhaps not a full board of fifteen – if indeed the board still numbered fifteen) were elected in their places. According to the Academic tradition, one of these was Hipparinus; was Heloris another – he is described later as a soldier of experience? Dionysius' first public act was to have the pay for military service doubled, as he had promised to do, at Gela, when he secured Dexippus' men their arrears. There would, he said, be no difficulty in finding the money; perhaps he was thinking of the property of the generals, which would be confiscated by the State on their conviction for treason.[12]

His next move was said to have been suggested by the first coup of Peisistratus. He ordered all Syracusans liable to military service, up to the age of forty, to muster at Leontini under arms and with rations for thirty days. Leontini was full of refugees from Acragas, the majority of whom were bitterly hostile to the 'oligarchs' who were supposed to have betrayed them, and were prepared to give their support to anyone who promised them the chance of recovering their city and their lands. But there were other reasons as well for the march to Leontini. From the military point of view it was a sound move to hold the muster there. The twenty-odd miles march would be a useful preliminary to a short period of intensive training in an area where food was plentiful (the Plain of Catania is the garden of Sicily), where the Acragantine and other allied contingents could easily be combined with the Syracusan, and from which the war-front could be reached by a shorter march than from Syracuse itself. I consider it highly likely that Daphnaeus too had made Leontini his forward base camp in the earlier campaign. But Dionysius had another reason for taking the Syracusan army to Leontini. He wanted to separate the 'young men' – those whose prejudices and emotions were most susceptible to patriotic oratory and demagogy – from their more sober, less hasty elders. At the same time, since the Greeks (unlike the Romans) held that where the Demos was, there was the State, the removal of the Syracusan army to Leontini would enable him to hold what could be represented as an assembly of the people under extraordinary conditions and at a distance from his most determined critics. Diodorus (whose narrative derives of course from a tradition hostile to Dionysius) says that Dionysius hoped that most of the Syracusans would

4 Leontini: entrance to the acropolis

not join the muster. If this is anything more than a malicious comment it may suggest that in fact the upper-class citizens, and especially the Knights, absented themselves and so played into Dionysius' hands.[13]

Dionysius rode out to Leontini. He nearly lost his horse while fording a swollen river, but received a heartening portent when a swarm of bees settled in the animal's mane, foretelling the successful outcome of his plans. He laid out his camp in the vicinity of the town. After nightfall there was shouting and confusion and the General fled from the camp to the acropolis, where watch-fires were lighted and to which his most reliable supporters made their way. Next morning an assembly was convened and Dionysius carried a proposal to give himself a bodyguard of 600 soldiers, to be chosen by him. Diodorus says that he selected over 1,000 men of great daring but small means, and provided them with 'costly arms' – but there is some ground for supposing that his bodyguard did in fact number 600 and was composed of light infantrymen. Perhaps he gave them the 'costly arms' (swords and light shields?) on his return to Syracuse. He now ordered Dexippus to bring his command from Gela, and on its arrival he attached the mercenaries to himself and packed Dexippus off to Sparta. He also re-officered the Syracusan army with men whom he felt he could trust, among them many of the restored exiles who had joined him.[14]

Dionysius now marched the army back to Syracuse and set up his headquarters in the naval arsenal at Lakkios, on the Little Harbour, to the east of the causeway that joined Ortygia (Quail Island, the oldest settlement) to the mainland. Diodorus says that he now 'openly proclaimed himself tyrant', but I doubt if he put it quite as crudely as that. He may very well have issued a proclamation (like that of Peisistratus, after his final seizure of power) that he took upon himself in the present crisis the direction of all public business; but if he did, his position was still constitutional, even though it must have become clear to everyone that, if he called upon his bodyguard and the mercenaries to support him, it would take a civil war to depose him. Dionysius' position was still very different from that of either Peisistratus or Gelon, both of whom had been aristocrats of the archaic age who had seized power at the head of an army. Dionysius was a middle-class citizen and he belonged to the 'classical' – the political – age. He was the generalissimo chosen by the city to lead her army – in which the cavalry and hoplites outnumbered his guards and mercenaries by more than 5 to 1 – against her enemies. There was as yet no good reason to suppose that Syracuse was entering upon a thirty-eight-year period of autocratic rule.[15]

Among the returned exiles had probably been Hermocrates' brother-in-law, Polyxenus. He now married Dionysius' sister Theste, and it was probably he who gave Hermocrates' daughter, his niece, to Dionysius in marriage, thus attaching the latter more firmly to the following of Hermocrates and bringing him into the circle of the aristocracy. Dionysius summoned a meeting of the Assembly and impeached the two public figures whom he most wanted out of the way, Daphnaeus and Demarchus. (Probably this was the Demarchus sent out, with others, to take over the Aegean squadron from Hermocrates and his colleagues, and so considered a strong democrat. He was, no doubt, one of the generals deposed earlier in the year.) Both men were condemned to death, and a passage in Polyaenus suggests that the other generals fled or were sent into exile. It is, of course, not impossible that these men *had* in fact been in communication with Himilco; not for the purpose of betraying the city, but in the hope of securing acceptable terms for a negotiated peace.[16]

CHAPTER FIVE

The battle of Gela and the Peace of Himilco

At the beginning of the summer of 405, Himilco, having completed the destruction of Acragas and made his preparations for the forthcoming campaign, moved his army against Gela. Gela was a Dorian city, founded in 688 by colonists from Rhodes and Crete and itself the metropolis of Acragas. It was built on a long, low hill running parallel to the coast, and took its name from the river Gela (or Gelas) which ran – torrentially in winter, according to Ovid – into the sea a short distance to the east of the town. The acropolis occupied the eastern end of the ridge. Gela, which commanded a fertile, wheat-growing plain, enjoyed great prosperity and a correspondingly high level of culture in the fifth century. Aeschylus was buried there, beneath an epitaph of, perhaps, his own composing.[1]

Himilco brought no warships with him, for the Gulf of Gela is very exposed and a fleet would have been of little use in an attack upon a city whose seaward flank is composed of steep cliffs. Clearly, after his experience before Acragas, he did not anticipate being free to embark upon the siege of Syracuse before the next campaigning season. He first ravaged the territory of Gela and then that of its neighbour, Camarina, so both provisioning his own army and depriving the Greeks of sustenance, and then marched into the coastal plain of Gela and laid siege to the city. He took the normal precaution of a general intending to conduct a lengthy siege, far from his base and with a powerful enemy force expected to arrive in the vicinity, and fortified his camp with a ditch and a strong palisade. If we take into consideration Himilco's commissarial problems, the lie of the land and the subsequent course of events, we need have no doubt about the *approximate* position of the Carthaginian camp. Himilco had a huge number of mouths to feed (there were no doubt many servants and camp-followers, in addition to the fighting-men), and his provisions had to come by land from central and western Sicily and also by sea. He had, therefore, to choose a position where he could keep open his lines of communication. Moreover, Gela being built along the top of a hill, the only place where siege-towers could be used effectively against its fortifications was at its western end,

5   Gela: Silver tetradrachm, 410–405: (above) River-God Gelas with corn grain; (below) chariot with eagle above

where the road climbed a steep slope up the Gate of Acragas. Not that this was a weak point, as the approach to the gate was flanked by fortified spurs of the hill.[2]

The only difficulty in the way of the acceptance of the obvious, that Himilco laid out his camp opposite the western end of the city, is presented by the customary translation of the narrative of Diodorus. Himilco (he says) *epi Gelan poreutheis para ton homonumon potamon tei polei katestratopedeusen*. This is usually rendered as: 'having marched against Gela, he camped along the river of the same name as the city'. Now the river Gela flows across the plain from NNE to SSW, and empties into the sea close to the *eastern* end of the city, at the site of the ancient port. Since Diodorus' narrative makes it quite clear that the Siceliots camped near the eastern end, ingenious efforts have had to be made by modern historians to make topographical and military sense of what Diodorus' words *have been taken* to mean. The most drastic of these efforts involved the identification of ancient Gela, not with the modern city of that name (formerly Terranova), but with Licata (which is in fact the ancient Phintiades). Less extreme was to postulate the existence in classical times of an 'ancient course' of the river, running roughly from east to west across the plain and falling into the sea to the west of the city. No traces, however, of this course can be discovered, even by aerial photography, and the hypothesis is unsatisfactory from a military point of view as well. There are, however, two easy ways out of the difficulty. We can either cite the judgement of Polybius, that neither Ephorus nor Timaeus could give a satisfactory account of a land-battle, and simply assume that Diodorus (an armchair warrior, like them) had 'got it all wrong'; or we can translate Diodorus' sentence as, 'he marched along the river of the same name as the city and encamped'. There is no good reason why the words should not be so translated, and an army coming from the direction of Camarina would, if it took the direct road, follow the line of the river, for, at any rate, a short distance.

Himilco, then, laid out a linear camp – what could more properly be described as lines – opposite the western end of the city, probably running from SW to NE, with its right flank resting on the sea-shore and its left 'in the air'. Since the Greeks would have been expected to camp near the mouth of the river, so as to maintain close contact with the Geloans, Himilco's lines would be fronting their camp, with the city ridge and the whole extent of the flat plain between them. Greek warfare being what it was, he did not have to worry (as a present-day commander would) about the possibility of his left flank's being turned by a surprise attack. He brought up his siege engines against the west end of the city, their operation covered by the forces on either flank: the Campanians on the seaward side, the Libyans to the north.[3]

Putting their trust in Dionysius' promise to bring strong forces to assist them, the Geloans made ready their defences, their women-folk gallantly refusing to be evacuated with their children to Syracuse. Himilco launched relays of assault forces against the city, in the area of the Acragantine Gate, and the citizens resisted equally fiercely; the women and children working with the men to rebuild, during the night, the portions of wall breached during the day. The Geloans also patrolled the countryside vigorously and used their knowledge of the locality to harass the Carthaginian forage-parties, bringing back numerous prisoners. Morale remained high in Gela, while they waited for the coming of their allies.[4]

Dionysius had not forgotten his promise to the people of Gela, nor had he been idle; but he could not expect to see his allies or mobilize his countrymen until after the harvest was in. It was therefore probably about midsummer when he took the field, with a force of 50,000 men, 'according to some': a phrase which may mean that Ephorus offered no figure and that Diodorus drew upon Philistus directly. Timaeus gave Dionysius' strength as 30,000 foot and 1,000 horse, supported by a fleet of 50 ships, and, as I have suggested above, the figure of 30,000 may not have taken into account the light-armed. This army included contingents from Italy (from Syracuse' ancient ally Locri, certainly, and perhaps from Rhegium, which would be imperilled by a Carthaginian conquest of eastern Sicily). Timaeus allows Dionysius slightly fewer foot soldiers than Daphnaeus had, and, if Diodorus' text is sound, no less than 4,000 fewer cavalry.

There are various ways of explaining this discrepancy, none of them satisfactory. That the horse-owning elements dissociated themselves from the war because of their disapproval of Dionysius is an absurd conjecture, for if anyone had a cause of grievance against him it was the Knights of Syracuse, and they were certainly there; and even if the reforms of Diocles had reduced their number to the old figure of 600 (which is possible, but, I believe, unlikely), we should still have to suppose that the rest of Sicily (less the Geloans) *and* the Italiots contributed at the most 300 lances: for at least 100 of the mercenaries were mounted. Perhaps this time the Italiots did not bring their horses? Perhaps the Sicels, looking on the Carthaginians as liberators, did not join the muster? But these explanations would imply that the Italiots, the Geloans and the Sicels had provided four-fifths of Daphnaeus' cavalry, which is equally absurd. It seems to me that the only possible explanation is that, in the transmission of Diodorus' text, the word or the symbol for either 3,000 or 4,000 (which are the sort of figures that we should expect) has become corrupted. We may recall Polybius' remark that admission of the possibility of scribal error is to be preferred to the acceptance of nonsense![5]

Arrived at Gela, Dionysius pitched his camp at the mouth of the river, probably on the eastern bank. He sent out his light infantry to assist the Geloans in cutting up Himilco's foraging parties, while his cavalry, who may have been stationed further upstream, ranged far afield. The ships were given the task of preventing supplies from reaching Himilco by sea. This skirmishing continued for some three weeks, by the end of which time Dionysius was forced to accept the fact that he was not going to starve Himilco into raising the siege. The Carthaginian had stocked his larder with the plunder of the territories of two cities and it is clear that he was able to bring in food from western Sicily, despite the attentions of the Syracusan cavalry. With an army very largely composed of mercenaries and Libyan conscripts, he could remain in the field as long as supplies and the prospect of loot held out. Moreover, his natural caution had been reinforced by the lessons of the previous year: that his light infantry was extremely fragile when pitted against a hoplite phalanx, and that the Greeks would not maintain a campaign through the winter. Time was on his side. He did not have to offer battle, although he could not refuse it if the enemy offered, for fear of damaging the morale of his army and risking desertions, especially on the part of the notoriously volatile Campanians.[6]

There was probably no serious shortage of food in the Greek camp or in the city, despite Himilco's having ravaged the plain. Supplies could be brought in without difficulty both by road and by sea. On the other hand, Greek citizen armies did not like protracted campaigns for a variety of reasons, of which the intense heat of a Sicilian summer will not have been the least cogent. The Greeks wanted a decision by battle in the Greek manner – and then to go home to their neglected farms. It is a reasonable assumption that there was by now considerable, and increasing, agitation in Dionysius' camp, and particularly from his Italiot allies, for decisive action.

Dionysius had come to Gela to raise the siege, and if he could not starve or wear Himilco out of his lines he would have to fight him. But Dionysius' predicament was complicated by political considerations. To go all-out for victory without counting the cost (as Himilco could do, if he had to); to fight a pitched battle against an army that outnumbered his own by the ratio of, perhaps five to three; to pit militiamen against Iberian and Campanian professionals; was to gamble not merely with the safety of Gela and the lives of his soldiers but with his own political future and, indeed, his very life. But Dionysius was not a gambler by temperament, and consideration of the fate of Gela would not have been allowed to deflect his gaze from the grandiose vision of the future. Committed as he was by circumstances and the demands of his army to a pitched battle, he addressed himself to the task of planning it with an eye as much to the avoidance of disaster as to the achievement of victory.

Let us consider first of all, Diodorus' account of the battle of Gela, an

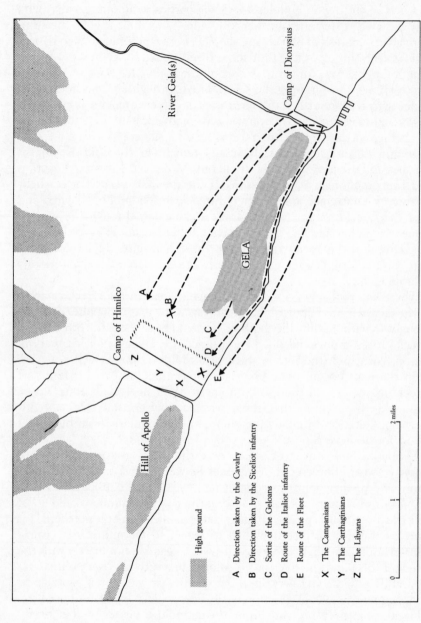

River Gela(s)

Camp of Dionysius

GELA

Camp of Himilco

Z Y X

Hill of Apollo

A
X B
C
D
E

High ground

A Direction taken by the Cavalry
B Direction taken by the Siceliot infantry
C Sortie of the Geloans
D Route of the Italiot infantry
E Route of the Fleet
X The Campanians
Y The Carthaginians
Z The Libyans

0   1   2 miles

B THE BATTLE OF GELA

account which I assume follows that given by Ephorus. Although Ephorus must have had before him the narrative of Philistus (who either was present, himself, as one of Dionysius' advisers or certainly heard the General's own description of the action), he seems to have allowed his own account to be coloured by his sympathy with the Italiots and by his feeling that although Dionysius' Italian auxiliaries did all that was asked of them, they were left in the lurch by the Sicilians. It is, after all, not impossible that Ephorus actually met and talked with veterans of the campaign. Diodorus' narrative is as follows.

Dionysius divided his infantry into three parts. He made up one division of the Siceliots, whom he ordered to advance on the stockade, keeping the city on their left. He formed the second division of [Italian] allies and ordered them to march quickly along the beach, keeping the city on their right. He himself with the corps of mercenaries proceeded through the city towards the area where the Carthaginian siege-engines were sited. And he ordered the cavalry to cross the river when they saw that the infantry had marched and to ride over the plain and to join in the fighting if they saw that their own side was having the best of it, and, if they saw them being worsted, to cover the hard-pressed. He ordered the shipboard forces to sail in against the enemy encampment, synchronizing their attack with that of the Italiots.

The fleet carried out its orders punctually. The Carthaginians rushed to the threatened sector, endeavouring to repel the men disembarking from the ships; for, indeed, they had left unfortified the whole part of the camp that lay along the shore line. At this juncture, the Italiots, having completed their march along the seashore, launched their assault upon the Carthaginian encampment: they found that most [of the enemy] had gone to deal with the threat from the ships. They routed the forces left behind in this sector and broke into the camp. When this happened, the Carthaginians turned about with the bulk of their forces and, after a long struggle, with difficulty drove out those who had forced their way inside the trench. The Italiots, overwhelmed in their withdrawal by the mass of the barbarians, since they received no support, were driven on to the sharp stakes of the palisade. The Siceliots, who were marching across the plain, were behind time, and the mercenaries with Dionysius were making their way with difficulty through the streets of the city and were unable to move as quickly as they had planned. The Geloans made a limited sally in support of the Italiots, for a short distance, but they were chary of abandoning the defence of their walls. As a result, they arrived too late to be of assistance. The Iberians and Campanians serving with the Carthaginians pressed hard upon the Greeks from

Italy and killed over a thousand of them. But as the men on the ships held off the pursuers with arrows, the rest [of the Italiots] got safely to the cover of the city.

In the other sector, the Siceliots fought it out with the Libyans who came out to engage them, killed many of them and pursued the rest into the encampment. But when the Iberians and Campanians, as well as the Carthaginian division, came to the support of the Libyans, they withdrew to the city, having lost about 600 men. When the cavalry saw that their own side had been defeated they also withdrew, under heavy pressure, to the city. When Dionysius had with difficulty traversed the city and realized that his army was beaten, he retired within the walls.[7]

Diodorus' narrative is clear, concise, consistent and, up to a point, intelligible; but, reading it, we are reminded again of Polybius' criticism of armchair historians: that they are incapable of giving a satisfactory account of a battle. Diodorus fails, of course, to tell us many of the details that we should expect of a modern writer. For instance, we are not told where, precisely, Dionysius' camp was situated (that it was on the eastern bank of the river is only conjecture), what the strengths of the individual Greek and Punic corps were, what was the distance between the western end of the city and Himilco's lines, or the time of day at which the attack was launched. But the most serious omission is that we are not told what Dionysius' *plan of attack* was. That there *was* a plan we cannot doubt; unless, of course, we are content to accept the conclusion that a youthful, inexperienced and over-sanguine commander, confronted by an enemy substantially superior in numbers and occupying a fortified position, simply committed himself and his army to Fate and the gods and ordered a general advance on a wide front, failing to appreciate that the hill of Gela (close to which he was encamped!) must split his forces, put his left wing, his centre and his right wing out of touch with each other throughout the operation, and deprive his army of his own overall command. Such ineptitude, such ignorance of – or contempt for – the fundamental rules of warfare seem to be inconsistent with what we know of the character and gifts of Dionysius, who was not the person to disregard the advice of his counsellors and whom one would expect to come to grief through over-cleverness rather than through crass stupidity.

Stroheker, indeed, credits Dionysius with a rational, a 'modern' (that is, a sophistic rather than a traditional) approach to military problems. He believes that in planning this, his first, battle Dionysius broke with tradition; that his intention was to make an all-out attack upon Himilco's lines, abandoning the principle of the phalanx that had dominated Greek military thinking since the mid-seventh century and using the terrain and the element of surprise (something generally neglected by Greek commanders) in order to split the enemy's defences by a combined assault of horse, foot and ships.

Stroheker is certainly right to recognize the innovatory nature of Dionysius' plan for the battle, but he does less than justice to the leader's common sense and appreciation of the realities. It is true that Dionysius was a very young man who (as far as we know) had never held an independent command before his present command of some 50,000 men (including the Geloans and the fleet); but he had a good, trained mind, an interest in history and first-hand experience, under Daphnaeus, of Greek warfare. He must have had some insight into the nature of the problems that beset a commander of Greek troops, and he also had his War Council, composed of his friends, some of whom were older and probably much more experienced than he. It can hardly have escaped him and his advisers that the hoplite – and his army consisted mainly of hoplites – was only formidable when massed in a phalanx; and that a phalanx, the essence of which is the shield-wall, cannot assault even a field fortification and maintain its front unbroken: even the Spartans, who had developed the phalanx to its limit, acknowledged their inadequacy as besiegers. No sensible man would throw hoplites, peasants trained only to fight in the phalanx, against a trench and palisade defended by superior numbers of disciplined, seasoned and determined light infantrymen. The hard military fact was that Dionysius could not hope to storm Himilco's camp without first inflicting a clear defeat on him *in the field*; and to defeat him in the field he must employ the traditional phalanx, simply because all but a handful of his soldiers understood no other formation or mode of fighting.[8]

Because the ground between the two camps was split by the hill of Gela, it was only on the wide plain north of the city that an army could be deployed for battle. If Dionysius offered battle there, Himilco could array against him an equal or superior number of seasoned troops, while holding in reserve a force sufficient both to contain the Geloans, should they attempt a sortie, and to take the Greek phalanx in the flank, either during the *agōn* or (as had happened at Himera) when it was disrupted by victory. All this was fully appreciated by Dionysius and his War Council, who judged the plain of Gela to be 'unsuitable for a decisive engagement'.[9] The terrain, then, and the limitations of the human resources at his disposal dictated Dionysius' tactics, forcing him to produce a plan of battle that was original, daring, even brilliant in conception. But we need have little doubt that, had the configuration of the land been other than it was, he would have settled for a straightforward agōnal hoplite battle.

It is true that there was one part of Himilco's lines against which a frontal assault might enjoy initial success. At their southern tip the beach was left open and un-staked, presumably to facilitate the running in of supplies, and this fact will have been reported by the fleet. A surprise landing here might create such confusion in the area that hoplites advancing along the beach would be able to force their way into the camp. But the narrowness of the front precluded the use of more than a portion of the army, and once the attackers were inside, the balance of advantage would swing back in favour of the defenders. Militiamen could not form a phalanx in a matter of moments, and they would be assailed while still in disorder by Himilco's storm-troops, the dreaded Iberians and Campanians.

Dionysius needed a victory, and he wanted it to be a spectacular one. But at the same time he had to make provision to extricate himself, his guards and, if possible, the Syracusan troops from a possible catastrophe. Himilco's camp could not be taken by a frontal assault, and a victory over the Libyans in the northern sector, even if he managed to extricate his men from Himilco's counter-attack, would not by itself win the campaign. Daphnaeus had inflicted a resounding defeat on them, the previous summer, and had none the less been forced to abandon Acragas.

In order to get to grips with the Libyan division of Himilco's army, the Greek infantry must cross the plain in full view of the enemy, thus affording him ample time to make his own dispositions for battle; but it would hardly have escaped Dionysius' notice that the enemy would not be able to tell, through the great cloud of dust rising from the parched – and scorched – countryside, and with the morning sun shining in his eyes, whether the advancing columns comprised 30,000, 25,000, or 20,000 men. Knowing that he enjoyed a substantial superiority in numbers, and being experienced in the methods of Greek generals, Himilco could be expected to assume that Dionysius was at last offering battle with his entire army, and his attention would be concentrated upon this sector of his front. He would send out his Libyans to confront the phalanx and would prepare to strike its flank with his best troops, from the centre and the right. But this stroke could be prevented by an attack by sea and land, delivered by a portion of the Greek infantry supported by the ships, upon the southern extremity of Himilco's lines, *to coincide with the arrival of the main body* in front of the Carthaginian left. In this attack, surprise *could* be achieved, since the enemy would be used to seeing the fleet rowing past the southern end of their camp and would not be put on the alert by its appearance; and the cliffs on the seaward side of Gela would screen the approach of an infantry column until it was within striking distance of the palisade. Neither wing of Himilco's army would be able to reinforce the other, and if the men of the phalanx succeeded in driving the beaten Libyans back from the palisade (to which they would flee), there was the possibility of overwhelming the Carthaginian troops of the centre, where Himilco himself would be standing, and of achieving the rout of the whole army.

What role are we to assign to Dionysius himself in this plan? First and foremost, he must be in overall command, and he must *be seen* to be in command, of the allied army. It was for that purpose that he had been elected General Plenipotentiary; and besides, nothing demoralizes soldiers more quickly than the suspicion that no one is in charge. The obvious place for him to position himself was in, or near, the centre. From the high ground at the west end of the city he would be able to follow with his own eyes, and through the eyes of observers posted on the walls, the progress both of his right wing across the open plain and of his left wing and the ships. Since Himilco would be in a position to reinforce either of his wings from the other or from the centre, if the enemy permitted him to do so, whereas the interposition of the city prevented Dionysius from doing likewise, the proper co-ordination of the two attacks on Himilco's lines was vital to the success of the whole operation. From the west end of the city Dionysius could overlook the whole battlefield and could give the signal for the assault to the infantry of the left wing and the ships, as soon as he saw that his phalanx was ready to engage the enemy on the right. Moreover, from the centre he could himself lead a surprise attack, debouching from the city gate with his best troops, the mercenaries, against the centre of Himilco's position, overrun his siege works and take in flank or rear either the Ibero-Campanian division struggling with the men of the Greek left wing, or the Carthaginian citizen troops preparing to reinforce one of their own wings. Himilco's army would be split, and if the gods were exceptionally propitious, Himilco himself might be killed – or, better still, captured – and the battle, the campaign and perhaps the war won at a stroke. And even if the prime object of the operation – the total defeat of the enemy and the capture of his camp with all its booty – were not achieved, Himilco might well be dealt a sufficiently serious blow, by the destruction of his siege equipment and the rout of at least a part of his army, to force him to raise the siege of Gela and retire to Acragas.

Perhaps not the least of the merits of the plan with which I have credited Dionysius (believing him to have a strong grasp of the realities of the situation), was that the only troops who would find it difficult to disengage, if things went wrong, and who would thus be exposed to serious danger, were those assaulting the seaward end of Himilco's lines. Prudently, therefore, he entrusted this sector to the Italiot auxiliaries; who indeed had held the left wing of Daphnaeus' army the previous summer.[10]

Let us now see if we can arrive at an acceptable reconstruction of the events of the day of the battle. First thing in the morning, as soon as the men had breakfasted, the Siceliots moved out of camp and began their march across the plain, to the north of the city. They must have numbered something over 20,000, and advanced in several columns, for Dionysius will have heeded old Nestor's advice:

Divide up the men according to nationality,

and the men of each city will have marched and stood in line together, under their own generals. We do not know whom Dionysius put in command on the right; perhaps it was his adoptive father, Heloris, whom we find (in a later book) described as a man with a reputation for military leadership. The Siceliots would have to march about three miles before deploying to engage the enemy. The Italiots, numbering 7,000–8,000 men, advanced along the beach, probably in a single column in order to avail themselves of the cover afforded by the run of the cliffs. Their leader would have been one of their own generals, and they would have had a shorter march to their start-line for the assault than the Siceliots. From there, on a signal from the commander-in-chief, they would proceed as quickly as possible towards the palisade, deploying into line as they approached it. The men of Gela would, on Dionysius' command, issue from their gates and sally-ports and support the attack of the Italiots. The fleet no doubt kept close inshore, probably within hailing distance of the soldiers. On the extreme right of the whole Greek advance, the cavalry, perhaps augmented by Gela's 500 horsemen, rode out on to the plain, covering the right flank of the Siceliots.[11] Having spoken words of encouragement (as Greek generals were expected to do) to his army and seen it on its way, Dionysius led his own small but formidable body of men – about 2,000 strong – through the Harbour Gate of the city and up its eastern slope.

The head of the Italiot column, advancing briskly along the beach, would be at its start-line in less than an hour; but by that time the much greater mass of Siceliot infantry, progressing slowly over cultivated land, crossed by water channels and obstructed by the ruins of farm buildings and the stumps of olive and fruit trees, would not be very far out on the plain. The narrow streets of Gela were filled with all the confusion of early morning in a town in which water must be drawn from the public wells or cisterns and the day's food purchased in the markets, with the men gathering under arms in the agora for the planned sortie, or already moving towards the western end of the town. Dionysius and his men found it impossible to make headway.

Time passed, and the Italiots, huddled under the cliffs at the western end of the city and apparently undetected by the barbarians, whose attention will have been directed towards the plain to the north, were becoming increasingly impatient. No soldiers, even war-hardened professionals, relish waiting for the order to attack; and the Italiots had painful memories of their last encounter with the enemy, when they had come close to defeat. No doubt their generals were eager to retrieve their cities' military reputation in the eyes of their allies; but their natural distrust of all Sicilians must have been increased by the continued failure of orders to reach them from the commander-in-chief. At last, despairing of receiving the order to advance, and fearful of the effect of further waiting upon the morale of their men (and having, perhaps, received confused and misleading reports of the progress of their allies from the watchers on the hill above), the Italiot generals decided to attack, and communicated their decision to the ships. Or perhaps it was the admiral of the fleet, observing that the enemy holding the seaward end of the camp were not on the alert, who decided to act on his own initiative; and the infantry, seeing the fleet going in to attack the beach, moved forward to support them. The Geloans, who may have had some idea that things were not going according to plan and who had a natural reluctance to leave their fortifications without the express command of Dionysius (whom they regarded as their leader), began to file out of the city and fall into line when they saw, from the high ground at the western end of the city, that the Italiots were actually storming the palisade.

Events now followed the course described by Diodorus. The landing force, composed mainly of light infantry, including many archers, seems to have put up a good fight before being forced back to the ships; but as a result of the failure of the Geloans to give their allies close support, the best troops in Himilco's camp had only the Italiots to deal with, instead of the very much larger body of men that the plan envisaged. Following the costly rout of the Italiots, the Geloans poured back into their city and effectively precluded any chance that Dionysius and his brigade might have had of taking part in the battle, which by then was lost anyway. How premature had been the attack on the Greek left is shown by the fact that Himilco's Ibero-Campanian division had time to repel the landing force, regroup, and 'in a long struggle' (whose length may, of course, have been exaggerated by the indignant Italiots) defeat the men from Magna Graecia, pursue them beyond the stockade, regroup again and march perhaps three-quarters of a mile to the support of the Libyans, and still arrive before the Greeks could break into the camp. Himilco had probably held back the troops of his centre until he was assured of the safety of his own right wing. The alacrity with which the Siceliots retired is shown by the relative smallness of their casualties (perhaps 3 per cent, compared with perhaps 14 per cent in the case of the Italiots).

I have endeavoured to reconstruct Dionysius' plan of battle on the basis of what Diodorus tells us actually happened, and on the assumption (which appears to me to be warranted by everything that we know about the man) that he would not have thrown his army against a strongly entrenched enemy who enjoyed a considerable superiority in numbers without a plan: and that he would have given himself a prominent role in it. Now the operation, as described by Diodorus, envisaged a *co-ordinated* assault by all four divisions of the combined force ('the Siceliots. . .came *too late*'); and if such an operation was to have any real chance of success, one (at least) of two sets of conditions must be satisfied. Either the commander-in-chief must be in visual contact with *all* the corps of his army, at any rate during the final stages of the advance, and must be able to control their movements by some reliable means of communication; or else he and his corps commanders must have practical experience (preferably through working together) in the handling of large bodies of troops, and, at the critical stage of the operation, no corps should be out of sight of the rest of the army. As things turned out, none of these conditions was met, although I believe that Dionysius' plan was intended to take care of the first set.

Given the circumstances, the plan itself – the plan of a young theorist without any experience of independent command – would, but for one fatal flaw, have been a good one. That flaw was the general's decision to march with his division through the streets of Gela. He was no stranger to the city and he ought to have foreseen the possibility (to put it no higher) of a hold-up on the morning of the battle. Whatever the plan was, Dionysius' presence on the field of battle was essential to its success, both from the army's point of view and from Dionysius' own, and nothing should have been allowed to prevent it. But Dionysius clearly felt that the commander-in-chief should see his army out of its camp, and he may have judged that if he stationed his guards and mercenaries at the western end of the town, they would impede the sortie of the Geloan infantry. Yet, flawed as it was, the plan bespoke the most ambitious application of the intellect to a military problem hitherto attempted by any general. No amount of good luck (an indispensable element in any military operation, however meticulously planned) could have given Dionysius victory at Gela; yet the battle may fairly claim to be a landmark in the history of ancient warfare.

Tactically, the result of the battle was a defeat, merely, not a disaster. The Greeks had probably killed more of the enemy than they had themselves lost, and we are told that the army was in the mood to meet the enemy again. Strategically, however, it was a disaster. At the Council of War which Dionysius called immediately after the battle, his friends were of the unanimous opinion that the terrain was unsuitable for fighting a decisive engagement. On the other hand, he could not remain where he was indefinitely. He had an army of almost 30,000 men (and, no doubt, a number of non-combatants) and a populous city to feed; and with the approach of autumn, the Bay of Gela would become a perilous place for shipping, and winter would render the roads across the hills difficult or impassable. Moreover he could not expect his Italiot allies to agree to serve a winter campaign, especially after the severe handling they had received in the battle. If Himilco could not be defeated then

Gela would have to be given up; and it was clearly better to carry out the withdrawal sooner rather than later, while the weather was still good and privation had not had a chance to weaken troops or civilians.[12]

Accordingly, Dionysius sent a herald to Himilco to negotiate, for the following day, the customary truce in order to take up the dead; and as soon as darkness fell, he began the evacuation of the townspeople. At midnight he put his army on the move towards Camarina, leaving 2,000 light infantry to keep watch-fires burning throughout the night, so as to hide from the enemy the fact that town and camp had been abandoned. The next day, when they perceived that the enemy had departed, the Carthaginians occupied Gela and plundered it. Although Camarina was strongly walled and protected on its west side by a marsh, it could no more be defended through the winter than Gela could; and so Dionysius ordered its inhabitants too to flee to Syracuse. Once again the roads of Sicily were thronged with a pathetic herd of refugees: old men, invalids (apart from the unhappy wretches without relatives or friends to help them, who had to be left behind to the tender mercies of the barbarian), women and children, driven by terror of Himilco's approach and the memory of the butchery at Selinus and Acragas and the holocaust at Himera.[13]

The Italiots, who would have returned home at the close of the campaigning season anyway, now set off by the most direct route to the Straits, and the Siceliots began their retreat to Syracuse. Dionysius' popularity must have been at a very low ebb. He had brought about the deposition and execution of Syracuse's leaders, and had created for himself a position which was only a short step removed from open tyranny, on the grounds that those leaders had betrayed their trust and abandoned a Greek city to the barbarians. But Dionysius' leadership had proved more disastrous, not less. He had achieved less than Daphnaeus in the field, he had given up *two* important towns, and, like Diocles in 409, he had left his dead unburied. There is no reason to suppose that Diodorus (or Ephorus) has exaggerated the resentment and suspicion voiced by the retreating army; but Dionysius was still the general in command and, despite the mutterings, open revolt against his leadership was confined to the Syracusan cavalry, who regarded him as a threat to the liberty of Syracuse and a demagogic enemy of their class, and who owed him a mortal grudge for the destruction of Daphnaeus. They would have liked to make an end of him there and then, on the march, but his mercenaries remained loyal to the man who looked after them; and so the Knights rode off to Syracuse, to which the news of the disaster had not yet come. They were admitted by the unsuspecting guards to the dockyard area, where they plundered Dionysius' house and so maltreated his wife, Hermocrates' daughter, that she killed herself. This piece of wanton brutality was, I suspect, due less to a kind of warped bravado (as

Diodorus suggests) – for they did not believe that Dionysius would now dare to return to the city – than to an outburst of bitter resentment against one who had, in their eyes, betrayed her caste by marrying the 'tyrant' and, perhaps, by attempting to defend his house.[14]

Dionysius now showed how energetically and decisively he could act in a crisis. Taking with him such men as he felt he could trust, and giving orders to those left in charge of the army to follow by forced marches, he raced ahead and arrived before the city at midnight with 100 horsemen and 600 light infantrymen, the latter presumably his bodyguard. He found the Achradine Gate closed but not guarded, and he proceeded to burn it down. By the time that this was done and the way into the city clear, the rest of his party had come up and – no doubt with vivid memories of the last occasion on which he had been involved in just such an adventure – he went at once to the agora, where his enemies were gathering to resist him. This time there were no burghers hastening to the spot under arms to support them, and they were taken completely by surprise by Dionysius' arrival. The leaders of the faction had already reached the agora, and these were surrounded and shot down. Dionysius then scoured the city, breaking into the houses of those known to be hostile towards him, killing any that showed fight and driving the remainder from the city. Those of the Corps of Knights (and, presumably, others of their class) who survived the killing fled to the town of Aetna, some 35 miles distant, and seized it. At daybreak the rest of the Greek army arrived and found the city quiet and the General in control. The men of Gela and Camarina, who were resentful of Dionysius' abandonment of their cities, moved off to join the great refugee camp at Leontini, and the Syracusans dispersed to their homes.[15]

There occurs at this point in Diodorus' narrative one of those exasperating lacunae in the text which beset the historian of this period. Himilco certainly advanced to Camarina, and there, apparently, his army was visited by plague, which carried off half his men. The historicity of this plague has been questioned; but if we take into account the facts that Himilco's army was largely composed of fairly primitive tribesmen, that he was campaigning through the heat of the Sicilian summer, that the environs of Camarina are marshy and that knowledge of hygiene and medicine is unlikely to have been very advanced in his camp, the likelihood of such a visitation becomes apparent.[16] However, Himilco could well have felt that he had done enough to entitle him to regard the war as now won. Carthage was mistress of Sicily, apart from the eastern corners of the island. Syracuse had been humiliated and virtually isolated: she certainly posed no threat to the security of the Epicraty. But Syracuse's army was still intact, her fleet was ready for service and her fortifications had defied the assaults of the Athenians for two years. She was not likely to be stormed like Selinus and she would not be tamely given up as the other Greek cities had been. It was too late in the year to lay siege to the city, especially without the support of a fleet, and by the following summer Syracuse's situation would have improved. Carthage's 'ally', Athens, had lost her fleet and her empire at a blow; she was blockaded by her victorious enemies by land and sea, and must capitulate before very long. The Peloponnesians would then be free to send help to their kin in Sicily.[17] And if the effects of the plague were anything like as serious as our authorities make out, Himilco would require not only a fleet but also substantial reinforcements in soldiers, if he was going to lay Syracuse under siege in the spring of 404.

Dionysius also wanted peace. He had been forced by circumstances to challenge Himilco before Gela, but the events of the last five years must have convinced him that a large Carthaginian mercenary army – an army, that is, composed of men who were not only professional soldiers but were also men whose death, so far from being a matter of grief to their employers, represented a financial saving – could not be driven off the field by a motley force made up mainly of Siceliot and Italiot militiamen, inferior in numbers to the enemy. If Carthage was to be decisively defeated, a large army was needed of which the nucleus must be a substantial body of disciplined professional soldiers, preferably Greeks. Such a force would take time and, above all, money to put together. In addition, Syracuse's cavalry had to be reconstructed. Gelon and his ally Theron had been able to destroy Hamilcar and his army at Himera in 480 because they had at their disposal the resources, human and economic, of extensive territorial kingdoms. Before a serious attempt could be made to drive the Carthaginians out of Sicily, Dionysius must build up an empire (*archē*) like that of Gelon. At present, the Greek cities of eastern Sicily, apart from Leontini, were independent of Syracuse, and her Sicel allies and subjects, of whom the latter provided her most important source of revenue, had thrown off their allegiance and embraced the Carthaginian alliance when the Syracusans withdrew into their own territory.[18] The Sicels must be brought back under Syracuse's sway, and her hegemony over the Greek cities restored, before any attempt could be made to reverse the verdict of the present war.

Nor can Dionysius have been really happy about his own position. It was true that he had got rid of most of those who might stir up, and provide the leadership for, a popular revolt against his authority, and his guards and mercenaries could easily suppress any popular disturbance before it could develop into an organized rising. But, with the temper of the citizens and the displaced allies what it was, and with a large section of the nation and that the most influential in a state of armed secession only a day's ride away to the north, he probably felt that he could not risk summoning an Assembly and calling the people to arms, as he would have to do if he allowed the war to continue. Nor would he have forgotten that when the Peloponnesians sent aid to Syracuse before they took over the command of the defence. So when Himilco sent a herald to Syracuse to propose the conclusion of a peace agreement, he found Dionysius happy to come to terms.

The terms required by Himilco were: that the Phoenician cities (described by Diodorus as colonies of Carthage), and the Elymi and the Sicans of western Sicily should belong to Carthage; and that the Greek cities taken by Carthage should be restored to their owners, who were to leave them unwalled and were to pay tribute to Carthage. Leontini (restored to its own people) and Messana, as well as the Sicel communities, were to be independent (*autonomoi*). Catane and Naxos, which had probably taken no part in the war, seem not to have been specifically mentioned: a diplomatic oversight on Carthage's part, since their omission from the treaty left Dionysius at liberty to attack them. There were also the customary clauses relating to the repatriation of prisoners and the handing back of captured ships. Diodorus says that Dionysius was specifically recognized as the ruler of Syracuse; but this, I believe, is no more than an inference drawn from the fact that Dionysius took the oath as Head of State, which he was by election. The treaty was probably sworn to by other representative bodies on both sides; but it does not appear to have been accorded the solemnity of the treaty of 480.[19]

This treaty gave Carthage virtually everything that she had gone to war in 406 to gain. She had forced the Greeks to recognize the fact of the Epicraty, and by her suzerainty over Camarina and (probably) by the foundation of a colony at Halaesa, on the north coast of the island, she had advanced her sphere of influence to within 50 miles of Syracuse in the south and 70 miles of the Straits in the north. She had not embarked on the war either to acquire additional territory or to extirpate Hellenism, although Hellenism certainly declined within the borders of the Epicraty. Segesta (which had already become largely hellenized) ceased to strike money, and so did its ancient rival Selinus, which became increasingly punicized. The purpose of the Carthaginians in going to war had been to make secure the eastern frontier of their maritime empire; and they must have felt sure that the inhabitants of the Greek cities of Sicily would not forget in a hurry what happened to those so foolish as to defy the might of Carthage. They believed that the Greeks would be content with their tributary status as the price of their recovering their lands and cities, and the tribute, especially that of Acragas, would be a welcome accession to the Carthaginian treasury. Syracuse, the only Greek Power from which Carthage had anything to fear, was now isolated and her hegemony discredited. Stripped of her tributary Sicel subjects and her Greek allies, she posed no threat to the Epicraty; and the 'liberated' peoples would realize that it was to their own interest to prevent her from re-establishing her 'empire'. Indeed, Carthage as the guarantor of the autonomy of the Siceliots and of the native Sicels, could have set herself up as the arbiter of Sicilian affairs.

Having concluded the treaty and stationed a strong force of Campanian mercenaries in the Epicraty to protect it from any repetition of the marauding attacks that had followed Hannibal's withdrawal, Himilco took his army back to Libya, and with it the plague, which spread and ravaged Carthage and her possessions.[21] This visitation, which incapacitated Carthage from engaging in serious military commitments abroad, and also rendered her service unattractive to the hireling tribes of Europe, must be regarded as contributing to the failure of the treaty to bring lasting peace to Sicily. But a more important factor – one, indeed, ultimately fatal to Carthage and her empire – was the chronic failure of the Carthaginians to acquaint themselves with the national character of the people they were concerned with. The Greeks with whom the merchant princes of Carthage had dealings were, for the most part stateless traders, and the Carthaginians judged all Greeks by the standard of these and of their own Phoenician and Liby-Phoenician allies. They failed to appreciate the Greek passion for 'autonomy', of which the imposition of tribute constituted a derogation that amounted to 'enslavement'. Himilco, anxious on his own account to extricate himself from Sicilian affairs, was oblivious of the fact that the cry of 'Liberty' has an emotional appeal that takes little account of reason or expediency. But the alternative to relying on Sicilian good sense to preserve the peace was to accept the need to maintain a large army of occupation in Sicily; and such a measure was, on economic grounds, wholly unacceptable to a Carthaginian. What Carthage wanted was a swift return to normality; to a condition of peace and tranquillity in which her trade could flourish and expand, its monopoly in the southern portion of the western Mediterranean secured by the distant menace of the Carthaginian navy.

Dionysius was probably neither greatly surprised nor greatly disappointed by the outcome of his first crossing of swords with the Carthaginians (he had no intention of abiding by the terms of the treaty anyway). For all his visions of Homeric glory and of out-Geloning Gelon, Dionysius was a man of the sophistic 'enlightenment', a man of reason and expediency. The first and all-important step towards the realization of his vision was to secure his monarchical position at Syracuse, and the second, to build an empire that would provide him with the resources to meet Carthage on something like equal terms. His situation was, in fact, a precarious one. Syracuse had been stripped of all her possessions and forced to sign a much more humiliating peace than either Diocles or Daphnaeus could in all probability have secured. With the ending of hostilities, the need for a General Plenipotentiary disappeared; and by continuing to hold the title (as he must have done, for we hear no word of his having abdicated it) he advertised the fact – already fully appreciated, no doubt, by the citizens – that he intended to remain in control of the city. He still needed the title, for he was not yet in a position to defy the whole people, nor was he a Gelon, a great nobleman, a priest of the Goddess, moving in the last twilight of the aristocratic era with all the tradition-hallowed standing of one descended from heroic ancestors, and with the personal prestige of the greatest soldier of his age.[22]

Dionysius' first task was to secure himself from the kind of attack that had led to the death of his wife. Perhaps under the pretext of making safe the naval arsenal that fronted on to the harbour of Lakkios, he had a wall built across the isthmus, strengthened by towers and pierced by a fivefold gate, so cutting off the whole of 'the island', Ortygia, the Old Town of Syracuse, from the rest of the city. In this area (the language of Diodorus should mean, on the mainland side of the wall) he undertook the construction of basilicas and capacious stoas. Within the wall he built a fortress palace that embraced the arsenal, which could accommodate 60 ships and was approachable from the sea through an opening only one ship wide. In this way he provided himself with a conspicuous, permanent headquarters, which was also a secure place of refuge in case of a revolt of the people, where he could hold out for as long as he could man ships to run, or break, a blockade. How he met the cost of this building programme we do not know. We are told that he borrowed the treasures of the temples, and those of Athena and Apollo on Ortygia were at his disposal. But he must have acquired a fair amount of booty when he evacuated Gela and Camarina (would he not have made himself responsible for the removal and safeguarding of their treasuries?) and when he sacked the houses of the Notables.[23]

Plato and the Academy accused Dionysius of driving 'the best elements' out of the city; and it seems to me likely that a very large part of the upper class had indeed fled from Syracuse, following the failure of the Knights' attempted coup against him. Their departure left vacant most of the best houses in the city (including most of those on Ortygia) and also a very great deal of good agricultural land. Diodorus says that Dionysius 'selected the choicest portion of the land and made a gift of it to his friends and to those appointed to positions of authority, and the remainder he distributed equally among aliens and citizens, including under the title of citizens manumitted slaves, whom he styled New Citizens. And he shared out the houses among the lower orders, apart from those on the Island. These he presented to his friends and to the mercenaries'.[24] Diodorus' statement would imply that Dionysius put through a full-scale redistribution of land (gēs anadasmos), the terror of Greek landowning societies; but I believe that we may safely say that this was not the case. Even if Dionysius had had the force at his disposal to evict thousands of small landowners, all of them in possession of their arms, from the soil, he had no reason to wish to do so. He was a war-lord in the making, not a social reformer or revolutionary. He had not been put in power as the result of a rising of the landless against the landowners, and although he had not scrupled to exploit class suspicion, it had been that of the hoplite class against the governing class. He did not have the 10,000 disbanded mercenaries to satisfy that Gelon had, he did not depend upon the landless elements for political support and he had no quarrel with the 'middle class' – upon whose good will, indeed, as the men who composed the hoplite phalanx, he must depend if he was to be able to prosecute his designs. However, if we take 'the land' in the first clause above to mean 'the land *left vacant*', the difficulty disappears. It is not to be expected that ancient writers would trouble themselves over such a distinction: it was, after all, in the nature of tyrants to ride roughshod over the rights of citizens. Among the 'slaves' mentioned in the passage quoted above we should, I believe, include serfs, some of whom were, perhaps, employed as light infantry (as the Spartans employed their helots) and were now rewarded. The new owners of the best houses and land would provide the new élite, from whom the reconstituted Corps of Knights could be recruited.

CHAPTER SIX

The Great Revolt and Dionysius' preparations for the second Punic War

By the summer of 404, Dionysius had put Syracuse's house in order, had strengthened his following (as he believed) among all classes, and now expected his fellow citizens to continue to accept him as their national leader and to support his policy – which was the traditional policy of the city – of reimposing Syracuse's dominion over the Sicels. But his insensitivity (which I have noticed above) to the possible response of others to what he regarded as reasonable and acceptable, led him to fail completely to gauge the depth of the resentment that had been building up against him in the breasts of his countrymen since the previous summer. Since no elections for the generalship had been held, the citizens could now have no possible doubt about Dionysius' intentions, and they felt (and not without reason) that they had been most cynically tricked into setting up as tyrant over themselves a man who had not only failed disastrously as a soldier, but who had banished many of their fellow citizens, defiled the body politic with aliens and slaves and distributed among them the property of true citizens. And there were still a good many well-to-do men in the land who had ties of kinship or friendship with the exiles.

In the summer of 404, Dionysius, who mistook the quiescence of the Syracusans for evidence of a general acceptance of his rule, prepared to attack the important Sicel town of Herbessus, close to Syracuse's western borders. He called the people to arms, perhaps ordering them to muster near the border; so that for the first time since the retreat from Camarina the Syracusans were assembled in a body, and under arms, in their camp before Herbessus. They were under the command of one Doricus, appointed by Dionysius; the latter would appear to have pitched his tent among those of his guards and mercenaries, apart from the militia lines. Before long mutiny was in the air, and the soldiers, gathering in groups, were openly expressing regret at their failure to support the revolt of the Knights. Tactful handling of this explosive situation by the officers might perhaps have averted the catastrophe, but Doricus resorted to violence and was killed by the hoplites. The deed had been unpremeditated, the troops were scattered about the camp, and the critical period, when the tyrant might perhaps have been fallen upon unawares and slain was occupied by the group of men who felt that they had now committed themselves irrevocably to revolt in raising a general mutiny and sending a message to Aetna to recall the exiles.[1]

Dionysius was taken wholly by surprise by the mutiny; but he realized that if he could reach the security of his fortress he could still survive, and he fled at once to Ortygia. The mutineers chose as their generals the men (clearly well-to-do citizens) whose action had precipitated the revolt, and, having been joined by the Knights from Aetna, marched back to the city and occupied the heights of Epipolae, so cutting Dionysius off from communication with the interior of Sicily. The Syracusans sent to the Straits Powers to enlist their naval aid, and 80 ships came from Messana and Rhegium. There is no evidence, however, that the Chalcidic cities (who had no more reason to trust the Demos than the tyrant) took any part in the affair. Syracuse's metropolis, Corinth, was notorious for her detestation of tyranny, and her assistance, and probably that of Sparta too, was sought.[2] Athens had surrendered in the spring of 404, and Corinth was at liberty to take an active interest in Sicilian affairs. She sent one Nicoteles, presumably with a small force, to take command of the revolutionaries. A price was put upon the tyrant's head, citizenship offered to deserters from his camp and vigorous attacks launched on the defences of the Island.

Blockaded by land and sea, his fortifications under constant attack and his mercenaries beginning to desert in numbers, Dionysius, perhaps for the only time in his career, was reduced to despair. Philistus, who was present at the meeting of the tyrant's council, has recorded how he talked wildly of ending his brief 'reign' in a blaze of glory; for tyranny, in a long-remembered aphorism of Heloris, 'is a noble winding-sheet'. His other friends demurred. Polyxenus urged him to ride through the besiegers' lines to the Epicraty, and win over the Campanian garrison. Somebody else advised him to remain in Ortygia and see the siege to an end. 'A tyrant, he said, 'should not leave his realm unless dragged by the leg.' This, the wisest, counsel prevailed, and it was agreed that an attempt should be made to purchase at any price the assistance of the Campanians. I think (on the basis of a rather curious anecdote of Polyaenus) that Dionysius also sent his brother Leptines to the Peloponnese to hire mercenaries and to confer with the Lacedaemonians, to counteract the embassy of his opponents.[3] It was at the end of this summer that Lysander returned to Sparta, having 'liberated' the Greeks and set up the system of *harmosts* (military governors) which effectively replaced Athenian rule of the Aegean by Lacedaemonian. Lysander would have been inclined to look favourably upon a man like Dionysius; but, this apart, it may well have seemed good to the Ephors and to the Gerousia, in the hour of total victory in Greece, to support the party at Syracuse which was opposed by Corinth, the most independent and the most critical of Sparta's allies, to whom (and to Thebes) they had recently given offence by refusing to acquiesce in the destruction of Athens. And so it was decided to send one of their leading men, named Aretas (or perhaps, less probably, Aristos), to Syracuse, ostensibly to co-operate with Nicoteles but in fact to ensure the defeat of the 'republicans'.[4]

During the winter of 404/3, Dionysius opened negotiations with the citizens and obtained an agreement from them by which he would be permitted to leave Ortygia with five ships; an agreement which he had no intention of honouring if he could help it, but which might prove his salvation if all else failed. The citizens relaxed their vigilance and the Knights, the most inveterate of Dionysius' enemies, were relieved of their military duties ('horsemen are of little use in a siege') and seem to have returned to Aetna. With the coming of spring, the greater part of the hoplites drifted away to look after their farms. Bored with a life of inactivity in the Epicraty, and eager for the promised reward, the Campanians, 1,200 mounted men, arrived at Agyrium, some 50 miles to the north-west of Syracuse. They deposited their baggage in the care of the friendly tyrant Agyris and made a dash on Syracuse, where they achieved complete surprise and cut their way through to Ortygia. A further reinforcement of 300 mercenaries came in by sea, probably from the Peloponnese.[5]

Aretas probably arrived in Sicily in the spring. He held a secret conference with Dionysius and then proceeded to the 'republican' camp, where he set himself to undermine the authority of Nicoteles (who was said to have been a drunkard). Probably the *stasis* mentioned by Diodorus, between those who wished to continue the siege and those who wanted to abandon it and Syracuse, reflects the struggle for the leadership between the two men: a struggle which ended with the death of Nicoteles, whether after some form of trial or by simple murder we are not told. No doubt informed by Aretas of the state of things in the city, Dionysius led a sortie into the Neapolis district, which routed the citizens with little bloodshed, since Dionysius (like Peisistratus at Pallene) intervened to prevent a massacre of the fugitives. The defeated hoplites fled into the country and subsequently more than 7,000 of them – that is to say, the greater part of Syracuse's field army – withdrew to Aetna. However, the tyrant had no use for an empty city and deserted fields, and so he offered the exiles reconciliation (*dialuesthai*), which those who had left their families behind – probably the great majority – accepted, leaving the irreconcilables to constitute a centre of opposition to Dionysius.[6]

A central feature of the reconciliation must, beyond any doubt, have been a clear-cut statement of the political relationship between the dynast and the *polis* of the Syracusans. Since monarchy (the rule of one man) was, by its nature, incompatible with *polis* (rule and be ruled in turn), and since magistracy had, over many years, been divested of power (*kratos*), it was impossible for an autocrat to be integrated into a Greek political society by investing him with an office, in the way which the survival of offices with *imperium* was to make possible at Rome. Dionysius' position would not be one whit more acceptable because he held the office of General Plenipotentiary. Moreover, Dionysius is not styled 'general' in any of the three extant Athenian decrees relating to him, nor is there any mention of the generalship in the account of the succession of his son to his power. I believe, therefore, that he did not bother to have himself reinvested with the extra-ordinary office which had lapsed the previous summer. We are told that he had studied the methods of Peisistratus, the outstanding example of the 'good tyrant' of antiquity; and he perhaps knew that Peisistratus held no office at Athens, only ensuring that someone he could trust always held the Archonship (Presidency).[7]

Peisistratus, however, had been a man of peace, who had seized power (leaving aside his private motives) in order to impose on the Athenians the *eunomia* (social harmony) that Solon had preached but failed to achieve. Dionysius was a man of war, and he had not made himself master of Syracuse in order to waste his time on political and social problems. He wanted a stable, law-abiding, prosperous and above all acquiescent Syracuse, which would be able to supply him with the sinews of war on demand. Let the Syracusans accept him as their War-lord, their *Hegemon* (leader), in effect surrendering to him the control of their foreign policy, and they could be as autonomous as they liked on their own side of the cross-wall; even retaining the basic elements of freedom, the right to accept or reject their Leader's request to make war and pay taxes, and the right (as far as we know) to administer their own laws. Physically as well as constitutionally Dionysius stood outside the *polis* of the Syracusans; he was a Power in his own right, with his seat in Ortygia. Yet he retained his rights as a Syracusan citizen, and as *hegemon* he was no doubt accorded certain privileges, such as the right of summoning the Assembly, or of having it summoned for him. Established in Ortygia, the oldest and most venerable part of the city, Dionysius could claim (as Peisistratus did, from his palace on the Acropolis of Athens) to be the protégé of Athena, the Guardian Goddess of cities; for her temple was in his keeping. This may not have been a small or unimportant matter where the mass of the people was concerned. With tranquillity restored, the Syracusans turned their attention to the getting in of the harvest (the narrative of Diodorus here as elsewhere implies that the majority of the farmers lived *in* the city), and the tyrant took advantage of their absence to visit their homes and impound their shields.[8]

Dionysius was too well acquainted with the lawless proclivities of

Campanians to retain the 1,200 horsemen in his service, and accordingly he dismissed them with the promised reward. Anticipating the behaviour, more than a century later, of another party of Campanians, the Mamertines, they seized by treachery the Sican town of Entella in western Sicily, slew all the men of military age and made themselves masters of their wives, their properties and their city.[9] Dionysius probably spent the rest of 403 in strengthening his position at Syracuse and in making preparations for the resumption of his interrupted campaign against his Sicel and Greek neighbours in eastern Sicily. He built a second wall around the fortress-palace complex and constructed new warships. He also enlisted a large number of mercenaries, who, with the temporary cessation of hostilities in Greece, were now readily available. It would, however, appear from Diodorus that his 'new model' army included a considerable number of Campanians, presumably recruited by his agents in their homeland. It was perhaps during the latter part of this year that Lysander, whose political influence both at Sparta and throughout the Aegean area was beginning to wane, visited Syracuse as an envoy. Sparta would have been anxious to cement firmly the good understanding with Dionysius of which Aretas had laid the foundations.[10]

Clearly, Dionysius' first major task must be to disembarrass himself of the irreconcilables congregated at Aetna; and against that town, in the summer of 402, he led a strong army. The place fell and the exiles fled to Rhegium. On his return march from Aetna, he made a demonstration against Leontini; but when the citizens, tenacious of their precarious freedom, refused to submit he withdrew, ravaging their territory. It is impossible to be precise about the chronology of the series of campaigns that follows, since Diodorus (true to his habit) lumps them together under the year 403/2; but it is probably best to assume that they were spread over the years 402–400. Dionysius first turned his attention to the Sicels. We are given specific information about his dealings with only two communities, both of which succeeded in preserving their independence; but Plutarch says that Philistus omitted from his History many of Dionysius' 'crimes against the barbarians'; and if Ephorus used Philistus as a source, this silence on the latter's part may be responsible for our lack of information regarding the subjugation of the Sicels: for subjugated they undoubtedly were.

At Henna, one of the strongest and most important of the Hellenized Sicel towns and the centre of the important cult of Demeter and Kore, Dionysius aided the townspeople to overthrow their recently installed tyrant, Aeimnestus (whose coup Dionysius had himself instigated, in the expectation that he would prove a pliant tool), but he did not attempt to seize the place for himself. We may, however, assume that he concluded

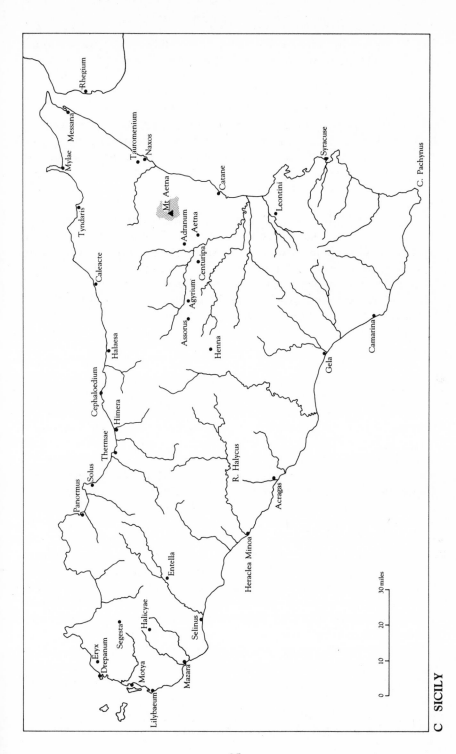

Rhegium

Mylae Messana

Tauromenium
Naxos

Tyndaris

Catane

Mt Aetna
Adranum
Aetna

Leontini

Syracuse

C. Pachynus

Caleacte

Centuripa
Agyrium
Assorus

Halaesa

Henna

Cephaloedium

Gela

Himera
Thermae

Camarina

R. Halycus

Solus
Panormus

Acragas

Heraclea Minoa

Entella

Halicyae

Segesta

Selinus

Eryx
Drepanum

Motya

Mazara

Lilybaeum

0   10   20   30 miles

C SICILY

85

a pact of friendship with the Hennans. He failed in an attempt to capture the city of Herbita, whose population had been augmented by refugees from other Sicel towns and whose chief magistrate, Archonides, had further strengthened his city's defences with numerous mercenaries. However, it is a reasonable assumption that the peace which Dionysius concluded with Herbita brought the city into a friendly relationship with himself, if not into an alliance. To ease the overcrowding of his city, Archonides led the refugees and many of Herbita's poorest inhabitants to Halaesa, where the Carthaginians appear to have established a colony in 405. This had already fallen into decline and was ready to receive the Herbitans.[11]

Having established his suzerainty over the Sicels, and so provided himself with a regular source of revenue, Dionysius turned his arms against the Chalcidian cities of the coast: Catane, Naxos and Leontini. These cities had been incorporated in Hieron's empire but had recovered their independence on the fall of the Syracusan tyranny. Naxos and Catane had been on Athens' side in the war of 415–413, and had remained neutral in the war between the Greeks and the Carthaginians. Leontini, having been absorbed again by Syracuse, had only recovered its freedom under the Peace of Himilco.

Dionysius took the field with an army of 17,000 men (if Polyaenus is to be trusted). This seems to me rather too large a number to have been made up wholly of mercenaries, at this time, and it may be that another anecdote of Polyaenus, which describes how Dionysius rearmed the citizens 'to meet an enemy threat', subsequently disarming them again 'after the battle', refers in fact to the campaign against the Chalcidians. The subjugation of these cities had long been an aim of Syracuse's foreign policy, and would therefore have the support of the People; and if Dionysius now had in his service some 10,000 mercenaries, he would have been in a position to ensure the good behaviour of the citizens and to disarm them without fear of a mutiny. His task was rendered easy by the perfidy of the leading men in the threatened cities. Arcesilaus, the general of the Catanians, betrayed Catane to him and Procles betrayed Naxos. Dionysius had clearly decided upon a 'permanent solution' of the Chalcidic problem and treated both cities with exemplary harshness. They were given up to the soldiery to be plundered and the inhabitants (apart from those who had favoured Dionysius' cause) were sold: the customary treatment meted out in the fifth century to peoples who rejected an initial summons to surrender. Naxos, the oldest Greek settlement in Sicily and the metropolis of the other Chalcidic cities, was destroyed (apart, probably, from its temples) and its territory was made over to the neighbouring Sicels. Catane was later given to the Campanian veterans and formed a valuable outpost of Dionysius' power.[12]

Dionysius now led his whole army against Leontini. This time the

Leontines, completely isolated and cowed by the disaster that had befallen their kin, offered no resistance and allowed themselves to be removed once again to Syracuse and reincorporated in the Syracusan community. Nothing is said about the city (which seems to have been left intact) and the territory; but since the latter comprised some of the best land in Sicily, which can hardly have been left uncultivated, and since the Leontines (now Syracusan citizens) had to have a means of livelihood, it is best to assume that the landowners remained in possession of their fields, working them by means of slaves or perhaps renting them to long-established Syracusans, and that the proletariat either took service with Dionysius or joined the colony which he established at Adranum (named after the reputed father of the twin gods, the Paliki), on the northern edge of the Plain of Catane, in 400/399.[13]

Syracuse was now the only Greek city, apart from Adranum, on the eastern seaboard of Sicily south of Messana. But the remorseless advance of Dionysius' power, and the planting of his colonies at Catane and Adranum, had alarmed the rulers of the Straits cities, who could see in him another Gelon – and one, moreover, whom they had already offended by giving support to the insurgents in the Great Revolt. In addition, most of the Syracusan exiles (and many, probably, from the Chalcidic cities) were residing at Rhegium; and these continually impressed upon their hosts the necessity of destroying Dionysius before his power became irresistible and before the new fortifications being constructed at Syracuse rendered him militarily unassailable. They promised (as is wont to be the way of political refugees) the support of the disaffected people of Syracuse.[14]

It was probably in the summer of 399 that Rhegium (after sounding out the government of Messana) sent 6,000 infantry, 600 horse and 50 ships across to Sicily and called upon the Messanians to join them in a crusade against the tyrant. The generals of Messana called out their city's forces, without, however, consulting the People; and a formidable combined force of 10,000 infantry, 1,000 cavalry and 80 ships moved southwards to liberate Syracuse and restore the Chalcidic cities. But Dionysius had friends among the Messanians, and at the end of the first day's march one Laomedon harangued his compatriots and called on them not to begin a causeless war against the dynast. As a result the Messanians abandoned their generals and marched home, leaving the men of Rhegium no alternative but to follow their example. Dionysius, preferring to encounter the 'liberators' at a distance from Syracuse, where their approach might have provoked a popular insurrection, had advanced to the frontier, perhaps to the river Symaethus. We do not know his strength, but if he had anything like the 17,000 men that (according to Polyaenus) he led against the Chalcidian cities, he could have faced the invaders with confidence – provided the Syracusans proved loyal. On the other hand, it seems to me very likely that he would not have ventured to rearm the citizens against an invader who was coming to liberate them, and that he confronted his enemies with his mercenaries only (perhaps 10,000 men); in which case it was perhaps just as well for him that the Straits army turned back when it did. On the return home of their soldiers, the cities sent envoys to Dionysius to make their peace with him, and peace was concluded.[15]

Dionysius now felt strong enough to begin to make preparations for the realization of his Grand Design, the conquest of the Epicraty and the unification of all Sicily under his rule. A crusade against the barbarian would be very much in harmony with the sentiments of the Hellenic world, throughout which barbarism was visibly on the advance. In central and southern Italy the Greek cities were already falling before the encroachment of the Sabelli, and in Asia, following the collapse of Athenian sea power, the satraps were fighting to restore their Master's ancient suzerainty over the Hellenes. If Dionysius was going to beat the Carthaginians out of Sicily, he needed to be able to mobilize the manpower of the Greek cities, and he could feel confident that the tributary status imposed upon them by the Peace of Himilco would ensure their support for a crusade that offered a reasonable prospect of success. First, however, he had to secure the loyal support of his own people, not just their passive acquiescence in his rule. They must be persuaded to see in him their *Hegemon*, their national leader, not their tyrant. But before Dionysius could ask the Syracusans to follow him in his proposed assault upon the Epicraty, he had to be able to guarantee their safety and the safety of their families, in the event of their being driven out of the field, as Pericles, more than half a century earlier, had guaranteed that of the Athenians. Syracuse, which had come within an ace of falling to the siege technique of the Athenians, must be made impregnable against attack by the far more formidable skills of the Carthaginians; and must, in addition, have her access to the resources of the outside world secured by her command of the sea.

Two lessons of the Great Siege and of the Great Revolt had been that the command of the heights of Epipolae and command of the sea were all-important factors in the defence of the city. Dionysius' version of the Athenian Long Walls was a wall, impregnable against contemporary siege methods, that would eventually encompass the whole plateau, and, in conjunction with the existing city walls, would provide a system of more than 16½ miles of fortifications. The north wall, 30 *stades* (about 3¼ miles) long and running from the sea in the region of Trogilus to the key point at Euryalus, was the first section to be built, probably in the spring of 401, and it was finished in twenty days. The scheme was completed by 398/7, with the building of the south wall, running

6 Syracuse: Epipolae, from Euryalus

south-east from Euryalus, over the south-west spurs of the Temenites heights, to enclose Neapolis and Achradina.[16]

The following is a free translation of the account of the building of the north wall given by Diodorus, which patently derives from that of Dionysius' apologist, Philistus, himself one of the 'friends' – that is, privy councillors – mentioned. The tone of the piece, so laudatory of Dionysius, so strikingly free from anti-tyrannical invective, forbids us to see in it, with Stroheker, 'Philistus showing through Timaeus'. It derives, I have no doubt, directly from Philistus.

He [Dionysius] saw that the area called Epipolae naturally commands the city of Syracuse. Accordingly he consulted his master builders and, in the light of their advice, decided that he should fortify that part of Epipolae where today the wall adjoining the Six Gates still stands. This side of the plateau faces north and is precipitous throughout its length and is so rugged as to be almost inaccessible from the interior. As he wanted the construction of the wall to be completed quickly, he gathered everyone in from the countryside, selected the fittest for the work in hand, to the number of about 60,000, and distributed them along the line of the wall. He put a master builder in charge of each *stade* [a little under 200 yards] of the wall, and to each *plethron* [about 100 feet] a builder with 200 of the unskilled to work under his direction. Apart from these, a great host of workers was engaged in quarrying the rough stone, which 6,000 pairs of oxen dragged to the site. The immense size of the labour force, such universal keenness to

89

see the work completed, presented an astonishing spectacle. For in order to evoke an enthusiastic response from the mass of the workers, Dionysius offered large rewards to those who finished their sections first, graded according to status: master builder, builder, workman. He personally attended to the work, along with his friends, during the whole period; he visited every section and lent a hand to anyone who had run into difficulty. He laid aside completely the dignity of his position as ruler [*archē*] and put himself on a level with the commonalty; he faced up to the heaviest tasks and endured the same toil and hardship as the rest, so that a great competitiveness was aroused and some men even added part of the night to the labours of the day, so great an enthusiasm had taken possession of the masses. And for this reason, the wall, against all expectation, reached completion in twenty days. Its total length was 30 *stades*, and its height was in proportion. There were tall towers at frequent intervals and it was constructed of squarehewn stones four feet long, precisely fitted together, so that the combination of the wall and the natural strength of the position rendered the former impregnable.[17]

Dionysius, a student of history, must have been acquainted with the manner in which the whole population of Athens had turned out to build the city wall, after the retreat of the Persians, and will have appreciated the tremendous impulse towards a feeling of national unity which such an undertaking would give, which could be carried over into the projected war against Carthage. The accounts of the building of the north wall and of the preparations for the war which Diodorus took from Philistus were intended by the latter to show the dynast not only as a superb organizer but also as the *leader* of his people, calling forth their patriotic enthusiasm and at the same time appealing to their self-interest. He could not be described as a 'king' (*basileus*), for kingship belonged only in the heroic past, among primitive peoples and barbarians, and in a unique form at Sparta. Since we do not know how closely the language of Diodorus has followed that of Philistus, we cannot tell whether or not the phrase 'dignity of his *archē*' above goes back to Philistus. If *archē* is Diodorus' word, he is probably using it quite generally, with the meaning of 'rule'; but if it is Philistus', although the same thing may be true, he *may* have in mind the title that Dionysius approved for himself: that of *Archōn* (ruler) of Sicily. But it was not as their *ruler* but as their Leader (*hegemon*) that Dionysius shared in the labours of his people.[18]

When completed, the fortification of Epipolae served a threefold purpose. It made Syracuse virtually impregnable on the landward side, it provided an extensive, elevated (and therefore healthy) refuge for the country people in a national emergency and it offered the means of delivering an attack upon the flank of an enemy operating against the city from positions on the lower Anapus plain. A parallel has been drawn above between Dionysius' fortifications and Pericles' Long Walls at Athens. But there was a fundamental difference between the rationale of the one and the other. The Long Walls were only one element in an imperial plan, other elements of which were (apart from the leadership and statecraft of Pericles himself) the maintenance of what amounted to a fully professional navy and the political influence of the proletariat – an excessive influence, in the eyes of conservative Greeks – which supplied a large part of the oarsmen. The Athenian Empire was a maritime empire, and provided that the navy remained undefeated the Athenians could (in theory, at least) remain within the safety of their walls indefinitely, since both their supply of food and raw materials and their revenues were assured. The withdrawal of the people from the soil of Attica within their fortress was a positive action, an affirmation of the indispensability of their empire, upon which the survival of Periclean democracy depended. But Dionysius' empire was a territorial empire, and his retirement into the fortress of Syracuse would be an admission of defeat and an acknowledgement that his empire *and its revenues* were already lost. The Syracusans could hold out in their city only as long as their reserves of silver and the readiness of Dionysius' soldiers to continue to serve on credit lasted. Pericles' walls guarded the rear of a far-flung maritime empire: they were an essential part of the grand design of a democratic city-statesman – and a sailor. Dionysius' wall enclosed a military base, and it represented the thinking of a soldier; of one who appreciates the necessity of preparing a strong camp in his rear, in case his army should be driven off the field.

With his retreat as secure as he could make it, Dionysius began his preparations for the assault upon the Epicraty. For this he needed every man and ship that he could raise. Carthage had been weakened by plague, Diodorus tells us; and, despite Maurin's arguments, I see no good reason to reject the statement, for it helps to explain both Carthage's failure to make even a protest at Dionysius' flagrant violations of the Treaty of Himilco and the initial feebleness of her response to his attack. The plague apart, however, militarism, rampant at Carthage for a century and a half, was dying out with the decline of the Magonids.[19] Himilco the king was not by nature an adventurer, and was probably content to rest on his laurels. Moreover, the Carthaginians could tell themselves that neither the fortification of Syracuse – essentially a defensive move – nor even the reconstitution and extension of her territorial empire, which faced eastwards, directly threatened the Epicraty. The relative ease and the completeness of their triumph over the Greek cities must have given the rulers of Carthage a feeling of security, especially as most of those cities were now tributary subjects. Carthage

7 Syracusan gold 20 drachma (100 litra), early 390s: (above) head of Arethusa; (below) Heracles fighting the Nemean lion (Sicily was the Island of Heracles, and the lion was native to classical Libya)

desired peace, and peaceful, profitable trade, with the Greeks; and no doubt she told herself that Dionysius, who needed her tacit support to maintain his position, wanted peace also. Our own age has demonstrated how potent wishful thinking on the part of a nation and its rulers can be; and how effectively a people or a government can deceive itself, even in the face of discrepant evidence, about the intentions of a foreign Power. This same blinking of the unwelcome facts of imperial defence was in the end to cost Carthage her empire.[20]

The initiative rested with Dionysius; he could strike when he judged that the time was ripe, and he could make sure that his preparations were complete and his plan of campaign fully considered before he struck. Dionysius had, with the conquest of eastern Sicily, restored both the prestige of the city that he presided over and, no doubt, the self-esteem of its citizens, who could hardly fail to acclaim the achievements of *their* tyrant; achievements which brought considerable economic benefit to Syracuse, negatively by making the tyrant economically self-sufficing and positively by providing him with funds to spend on public works. Dionysius had made Syracuse impregnable, and under his aegis the city was enjoying a period of peace and stability and of great prosperity. He was deservedly popular and now felt secure enough to seek to enlist his fellow citizens in the great crusade, ostensibly to liberate the Hellenes from barbarian domination, in fact to make himself lord of all Sicily and the greatest Greek of his, or any other, age. The time had come to rearm the Syracusans and to take his place once more at their head, not as tyrant but as Leader.

Diodorus, in a lengthy passage deriving again from Philistus, gives us a picture of Dionysius, the very personification of Syracusan nationalism, moving freely about among an enthusiastic people, the accepted Leader of a nation in the grip of a righteous war-fever.

Therefore he at once mobilized by decree the skilled tradesmen from the communities subject to his rule, and also attracted others from Italy and Greece and even from the Carthaginian province, by the offer of high wages. It was his intention to prepare a huge arsenal of weapons and every kind of missile, and in addition to construct both triremes and quinqueremes, although no example of the latter type had hitherto been built. When a large body of skilled tradesmen had been got together, he divided them into groups according to their various skills, and put a leading citizen in charge of each group, promising large bounties to the arms producers. Because his mercenary force was a medley of many nations, he distributed among the working parties patterns of the various sorts of equipment peculiar to the different races; for he was anxious to fit out every soldier with the arms of his own people, judging that so equipped his army would strike consternation into the foe, and that in battle all those who were fighting together would make the most effective use of the equipment to which they were accustomed. As the people of Syracuse enthusiastically supported Dionysius' policy, the preparation of the weapons developed into an intense rivalry. Every space was crammed with workmen, the vestibules and rear porches of the temples as well as the gymnasia and the porticoes around the agora. And apart from public places, great quantities of equipment were manufactured in the most distinguished private houses.

It is a fact that artillery was now invented at Syracuse, since the best tradesmen had been brought together from every quarter. Their keenness had been whetted both by the lavishness of their wages and by the number of special rewards offered to those who were judged the most productive. Apart from this, Dionysius made a daily round of his work force, chatted amiably with the men and rewarded the most zealous with gifts and invitations to his table. Therefore the tradesmen became intensely competitive, and invented novel missile weapons and other engines of war of great potential value. He also put in hand the construction of triremes and quinqueremes, being the first person to think of building the latter type of ship. For he had heard that the trireme had been first built at Corinth, and was eager to build ships of a larger size in the city founded as a colony by Corinth.

When he had got permission to export timber from Italy, Dionysius sent half his woodcutters to the slopes of Aetna, then well covered with fir and pine, and half to Italy; and he prepared teams of oxen to bring the timber down to the sea, and ships and crews to tow the rafts as quickly as possible to Syracuse. When he had collected enough wood, he began the simultaneous construction of over 200 ships and the refitting of the existing 110. He also began to build, at great cost, 160 ship-houses around the shore of what is today called the Great Harbour. The majority of these accommodated two ships each; and he set about repairing those already standing, 150 in number.

The spectacle of such a quantity of arms and ships being prepared in one place was quite staggering. For when an onlooker considered the energy being expended on the ships, he supposed that the whole of Sicily was engaged on the task; but when he mingled with those making arms and engines of war, he imagined that the entire organization of labour was directed solely to them. However, with the unsurpassable zeal that was expended in both these directions, 140,000 shields and as many side-arms and helmets were manufactured, as well as 14,000 corselets of every design and of the most expert workmanship. It was Dionysius' purpose to issue these last to his cavalry and to the infantry officers and to his bodyguard. Catapults of every kind were constructed, and a great quantity of the other kinds of missile weapon. Citizens supplied the bow and stern officers as well as the rowers for half the warships that were fitted out; for the remainder, Dionysius hired foreigners. When he was satisfied that the naval and armaments programmes had reached completion, Dionysius gave his attention to the recruitment of soldiers; for he judged it to be to his advantage not to hire these far in advance, in order to avoid heavy expense.[21]

Here again, as in the account of the building of the north wall of Epipolae, Philistus presents his hero to us not only as the inspiration and director of a highly emotional national war effort but also as a master of organization. He involved the whole of Syracuse and her gods in the preparation for his crusade. He laid the technical skills of Italy, Greece and the Epicraty under contribution (there must have been many unemployed shipwrights available in the dismantled Piraeus). By this time, Dionysius had had plenty of experience in the waging of war and the conducting of sieges, and he knew, at any rate in general terms, what he wanted of these men; which was, military engines that were at least as good as, and preferably better than, those of the Carthaginians. He wanted missile weapons that would outrange the bows of the archers defending city walls or firing from the decks of ships, and the answer to his demand was the catapult. According to Hero of Alexandria, the earliest catapults were developed from the hand bow; they were called belly bows (*gastraphetai*) because the operator pressed his belly against the rear end of the 'stock' when bending the weapon. They were the ancestors of the crossbows of the Middle Ages and fired a bolt to a significantly greater distance than the hand bow could reach. It may well be that by the time Dionysius was ready to take the field, modifications of the original design had been introduced, incorporating the winch (for bending the bow) and the stand (to give it greater stability and accuracy) that were features of the developed catapult.[22]

Dionysius also wanted ships that would enable his new navy to defeat the experienced sailors of Carthage. The Phoenician cities of the Epicraty were seaports and to take them he must achieve at least local command of the sea, and the Carthaginian navy, which, like that of Athens, was largely manned by citizens, could be mobilized at very short notice. In their great struggle against the Athenians, the Syracusans had sought to neutralize the superior skill and experience of their adversaries by modifying the build of their ships. What Dionysius now asked his shipwrights to design were ships that would give victory to raw and unpractised seamen over men who could probably defeat merely numerical superiority, on the high seas and not just in the confined waters of a harbour. The answer was the 'fiver' (*pentēris*), usually known by its Latin name, quinquereme.[23]

95

It is a reasonably safe assumption that the design of these earliest 'fivers' derived directly from that of the trireme, involving a relatively small increase in the size and strength of the hull, in order to accommodate a double-banking of the two upper tiers of oars, thus giving (very roughly) five times the oarage of a penteconter (50 oars), from which the trireme (three times the oarage) had developed. That the fiver *was* invented at this time, and at Syracuse, I can see no good reason to doubt. The account in Diodorus of the arming of Syracuse is patently almost pure Philistus, and the invention of the 'fiver' is mentioned twice. On the other hand, I do not believe that Wesseling's conjectural reading of *tetrēreis* (quadriremes or 'fours') for the *triēreis* (triremes) of Diodorus' text is defensible. It has been urged, against the invention of the fiver by Dionysius' designers, that the type is not heard of again until the latter half of the century. This silence, however, can be readily explained, first, by the apparent ineffectualness in battle of the new ships; secondly, by the difficulty and the cost of finding the large crews that they required; and thirdly, by the fact that we do not know whether or not Dionysius included fivers in the great fleets that he employed in his later wars.[24] However, I do find it difficult to accept the manuscript reading *triēreis* in Diodorus 14.58.2, from which it would appear that in 396 the greater part of Dionysius' 180 ships were fivers. I consider it most unlikely that very many fivers were built at this time, for, quite apart from the technical problems involved, it would hardly escape the notice of the dynast and his advisers that a huge fleet composed largely of fivers would require a very great increase in the number of rowers over that required by a fleet of triremes, and that Syracuse possessed neither the *nautikos ochlos* (the nautical rabble) nor the multitude of maritime allies that had enabled Athens to man great fleets for one campaign after another. On two occasions in the war with Carthage we hear of a crack squadron of 30 ships. It is true that on one occasion these are called triremes; but Greek writers regularly used that word to denote, simply, warship (much as nineteenth-century writers used 'ironclad' to denote battleship); and it seems to me likely that these 30 ships were the fivers.

Even if some of the preparations for war described by Diodorus were begun before 399 (such, for instance, as the repair and construction of the ship-houses), it is unlikely that all was ready before the summer of 398; indeed, we have a hint that the new fivers were only coming into service in the early summer of 397.[25] And there were still the mercenaries to recruit. I believe, therefore, that we should follow Diodorus' chronology and date the opening of the war to the summer of 397, and not, with Beloch, followed by Berve and Stroheker, to the summer of 398.[26] Dionysius sent his recruiting agents to Greece, where the continuing (although insecure) state of peace made unemployed fighting men plentiful. Lysander was once again enjoying great influence at Sparta (which had recently brought recalcitrant Elis to heel), and this year secured the succession of Agesilaus to the Eurypontid throne, left empty by the death of Agis II. The Spartans, in the fabric of whose vaunted *eunomia* dangerous cracks were already becoming visible (it was to be rudely shaken, the following year, by the Conspiracy of Cinadon), must have been very happy to avail themselves of the social safety-valve provided by their friend's request for recruiting facilities and readily granted them. Dionysius also overhauled the military organization of Syracuse (almost disused since the Great Revolt); allotting the physically fit to their regiments and giving notice of levy to the communities under his rule. Another of his concerns was the provision of native and foreign rowers for the fleet (who must have amounted to over 40,000 men) and the appropriation of several hundred transports.[27]

The statement of Diodorus, that Dionysius expected the war to be a long one, probably goes back to Philistus. The cities of the Epicraty were strong, and would have to be reduced by regular siege – perhaps by starvation, for Dionysius could not squander men in storming parties as the Carthaginians could. Nor would his citizen soldiers serve through the winter. And there were the Carthaginians to be reckoned with. He must have been thinking in terms of at least three years of campaigning, before the Epicraty could be brought completely under his rule. Where he seems to have displayed a culpable carelessness was in his failure to anticipate the magnitude of Carthage's eventual response. The explanation may be that the reports reaching Syracuse of the plague that had struck her had seriously exaggerated its effects. Certainly, in view of Carthage's reliance on European mercenaries to supply the best part of her expeditionary forces, Dionysius could confidently expect not to encounter her army in Sicily in 397; but the course of events strongly suggests that he was wholly taken by surprise by the strength of her counter-offensive in 396. Since Carthage was only a day's sail from western Sicily and had many Greeks resident in the city, it would not appear to have been a very difficult matter to obtain up-to-date information about her intentions and preparations. Perhaps, however, Himilco (who did understand the importance of denying information to the enemy) had taken precautions to inhibit all communication between Libya and Sicily during the period of his preparation.[28]

CHAPTER SEVEN

The second Punic War

Before he could venture to strip his dominions of reliable fighting-men for the invasion of the Epicraty, Dionysius had to secure them against a possible repetition of the invasion of 399 by the cities of the Straits. Messana, indeed, was not unfriendly, but at Rhegium the Syracusan and other exiles still exerted a powerful influence against him. Messana was now won over to his side by a gift of territory, formerly the property of Naxos. To the Rhegines he proposed a more intimate alliance, asking for a wife from among the well-born maidens of the city. In return, he promised to do all he could to enlarge their power and their territory (at present narrow and confined); perhaps at the expense of Medma or Hipponium. The Rhegines discussed the offer seriously but decided to reject it, although probably not in the highly insulting terms put about by sources hostile to the tyrant.[1]

Unable to secure her friendship, Dionysius could, at any rate, render Rhegium harmless. Accordingly, he now approached Locri, an ancient ally of Syracuse and a friend of earlier tyrants, which bordered on Rhegium to the east and inhibited her expansion. The Locrians accepted Dionysius' proposal and offered him Doris, the daughter of their leading citizen, for a wife. We do not know whether the laws of Syracuse (as amended by Diocles) discouraged citizens from marrying outside the citizen body (as they did at, for instance, Athens and Sparta); but in any event, Dionysius' marriage of political convenience with a Locrian lady would have tended to emphasize the schism between tyrant and city which, especially at the present juncture, he was very anxious to minimize. Accordingly, he betrothed himself also to Aristomache, the daughter of Hipparinus, who had been an associate and counsellor of his from the beginning, and who is described as Syracuse's leading citizen. Although bigamy was a violation of Greek customary social morality, Dionysius (although he could not style himself a king) could point to the double marriage forced upon King Anaxandridas of Sparta in the sixth century, by the Ephors and the Gerousia, as a sort of precedent for his conduct. Just as the union between the dynast and Doris symbolized the union between him and Locri, so his marriage with Aristomache symbolized the union between *hegemon* and city. It is possible that this

98

exaltation of the house of Hipparinus gave mortal offence to Dionysius' adoptive father, Heloris; for the next that we hear of this nobleman is as the leader of the exiles at Rhegium. Another possibility, of course, is that he (and perhaps others) rejected Dionysius' militarism and broke with him over the unprovoked attack upon the Epicraty.[2]

All this diplomatic activity, along with preparation for the war, occupied the late summer and autumn of 398. In the early summer of 397, Dionysius sent to Locri the first quinquereme to be completed – I believe that we know her name: the *Boubaris* – resplendent with gold and silver fittings, to convey his foreign bride to Ortygia. Aristomache travelled from her home to the citadel in a chariot drawn by four white horses – a quadriga, such as appeared on the coins of Syracuse. A double marriage was celebrated, and citizens and soldiers were entertained at public banquets: another sign of the reconciliation between the dynast and his countrymen. In order to show that neither wife had any grounds for supposing that she was more legitimate than the other, Dionysius slept with them by turns; and it was Doris who had the distinction of being the first to provide him with an heir (scandal said, through the machinations of her mother).[3]

By now the mercenaries had arrived at Syracuse; and so, a few days after the wedding, Dionysius convened the Assembly and proposed that the city declare war on Carthage, on the grounds that she constituted a permanent threat to Hellenic freedom. The Syracusans responded to his call to arms with enthusiasm. Apart from specific grievances against the Carthaginians, they were no doubt moved by genuine Panhellenic sentiment, such as had inspired Gorgias of Leontini, and Hermocrates. Panhellenism was much in the air at this time: Syracuse's ally, Sparta, was fighting in Asia to liberate the Greeks there from the barbarian yoke that she had herself contributed to putting upon them. A wave of anti-Carthaginian feeling, sanctioned if not actually inspired by Dionysius, swept Syracuse and spread to the other cities of the island. The houses and ships of the numerous wealthy Carthaginian merchants were plundered, and their owners were subjected to every kind of violence and outrage, in reprisal for the brutality which their countrymen had displayed at Selinus, Himera and Acragas. It is worth nothing that apparently no reprisals were taken against Greeks living at Carthage, either then or later. On the heels of this widespread eruption of war fever, his military preparations being now complete, Dionysius sent an ultimatum (which he knew would be rejected) in the form of a letter to the Carthaginian Senate, demanding the liberation of the Greek cities as the condition of continuing peace.[4]

The Carthaginians, weakened by plague, must have told themselves that Dionysius' massive war preparations, of which they can hardly have failed to hear reports, were not directed against themselves, and had taken no steps to prepare for war. There was apparently a body of opinion in the Senate that would have avoided war even now: after all, Dionysius was demanding, at this stage, no more than the liberation of the *Greek* cities. But there were others who saw that acceptance of his ultimatum would bring his power to within easy striking distance of the Phoenician cities, and would damage, perhaps fatally, their own city's prestige. And the loss of the Epicraty might be only the prelude to an attack upon Carthage herself. The Senate being divided in opinion, the ultimatum was referred to the Assembly of the people, which rejected it. Members of the Senate were sent with ample funds to raise troops in Spain for service in the following year, and old Himilco, again appointed to the supreme command, set in motion the cumbrous machinery for raising the levies of Carthage's Libyan allies and subjects and mobilized the navy for immediate service.[5]

By midsummer (after the gathering in of the harvest) Dionysius was ready to march, by the south coastal road, towards Motya, the richest and most powerful city of the Epicraty, which commanded the Bay of Lilybaeum, whose shores provided the most readily accessible and convenient bridgehead for a Carthaginian invasion of Sicily. On his march he incorporated into his army, and armed, the levies of Camarina, Gela, Acragas and Selinus, as well as a contingent from Thermae-Himeraeae. According to Diodorus, the force that arrived in front of Motya, comprising Syracusans, Siceliots, Sicels and mercenaries, amounted to 80,000 foot and over, 3,000 horse. We would expect this total to have derived from Philistus, but it looks both impossibly large and absurdly ill balanced. In the campaigns of 406 and 405, the united Siceliot foot forces (probably including a contingent from Messana), plus a strong force of Italiots, had amounted to about 30,000; and for the autumn campaign of 396, Dionysius had 30,000 infantry. His mercenaries probably numbered about 10,000, some of them no doubt horsemen. If therefore the figure of 80,000 is accepted it must be taken to include the crews of the ships, who could be used as light infantrymen in siege operations. Perhaps, then, we should allow Dionysius a field army of about 40,000 infantry and something over 3,000 cavalry; which would give a weak ratio of horse to foot but still a much better one than Diodorus'. Rather less than 200 warships (there had clearly been manning problems) under the command of the dynast's brother, Leptines, and 500 transports accompanied the march.[6]

The Elymi of Eryx, with their important port of Drepanum, promptly went over to Dionysius. There had evidently been some friction between them and their neighbour, Motya, arising probably from frontier disputes as a result of the growth of Motya and her spread to the mainland, and also no doubt from commercial rivalry. The Motyans, however, feeling

8 Motya (above) the docks; (below) the walls

secure on their island, and confidently expecting help from Carthage (which may have been their metropolis), prepared for a siege. They severed the causeway that ran in a northerly direction from their North Gate to the region of the necropolis on the mainland, a distance of about a mile and a quarter.[7] Motya (from mót, slime, or motua, a loom), probably one of the earliest Phoenician settlements in the West, occupied a low-lying, flat island, a little over one and a half miles in circumference, and was protected by a continuous line of wall with towers and bastions at frequent intervals. These fortifications had recently been modernized; Greek technique, if not Greek workmen, having been employed, especially in the most obviously vulnerable area of the great North Gate, where the walls stood some distance back from the water's edge. Motya island lay not quite in the middle of a shallow lagoon that measured about four miles in length (from north to south) and a little under two miles across at its widest point. Low, marshy ground enclosed the lagoon on three sides, those towards the open sea consisting of a peninsula (shaped rather like an inverted letter 'L') known as Aegithallus. The opening, almost a mile wide, faced south into the Bay of Lilybaeum, which was about half the length of the lagoon. Today these waters are in most parts only three or four feet deep; but in classical times there were, at any rate, channels which seagoing ships could use. Yet it seems likely that the lagoon was already becoming silted up, and that the Motyans (and the Carthaginians, when they used the area as an invasion point) were using the anchorage across the bay, at the site of the future Lilybaeum.[8]

The disposition of Dionysius' forces may be conjectured in the light of subsequent events. His main camp was probably at the northern end of the lagoon and his naval camp on the inner (the lagoon) side of Aegithallus, opposite the island. The transports were moored offshore, at the northern end of the Bay of Lilybaeum. He put in hand the construction of a mole to replace the damaged causeway (no doubt using its foundations), employing, I believe, the crews of the ships for this work; and then, leaving his brother Leptines in command before Motya, he took his infantry in a sweep across north-west Sicily, in order to give them some profitable employment while the mole was building. The native Sicans, to whom he would have presented himself as a liberator from Punic domination, went over to him; but the Phoenician cities, Segesta and the Campanian military colonies of Halicyae and Entella defied him. He ravaged the territories of Panormus, Solus and Halicyae, and made serious attempts to take Segesta and Entella, but, since his heavy siege equipment was at Motya, without success. Accordingly, he returned to Motya and threw thousands more of his men into the task of completing the mole.[9]

At Carthage, in the meantime, Himilco had been getting ships ready for sea. He sent 10 on a highly successful raid by night against the shipping in the harbour of Syracuse, which failed, however, to draw off the Greek fleet at Motya, as he had hoped it might. Late in the summer he sailed for Sicily with his best galleys, 100 in number, having received information that Dionysius' fleet was hauled ashore and in a state of unreadiness. He timed his passage, via Selinus, so as to arrive in the Bay of Lilybaeum at daybreak. He wasted (it would seem) some precious time attacking the transports that lay at anchor there, and sank a number of them; and then took his ships into the lagoon and threatened the beached galleys. However, the delay had enabled Dionysius to bring his infantry down to the camp, and Himilco drew back to the mouth of the lagoon and waited there, in battle formation, hoping to fight an action in the narrows, where Dionysius' superiority in numbers would be neutralized.

This, however, was the kind of situation – one presenting a challenge to his ingenuity – that brought out the best in Dionysius as a war-leader. He put his thousands of soldiers to hauling galleys, perhaps 80 of them, across the peninsula on rollers to the open sea, where they were launched. When Himilco saw what was happening, he turned his ships about and rowed to attack the Greek fleet as it took the water piecemeal, but Dionysius had lined the shore with catapults – his secret weapon – to cover the launching, and the decks of the galleys were thronged with archers and slingers. The hail of missiles – and especially the catapult bolts, the like of which had not been encountered before – so dismayed the Carthaginians that Himilco, who was never the most dashing of commanders and who, apart from the catapults, was now in danger of being attacked in front and rear by overwhelming numbers, broke off the action and sailed away to the south, leaving Motya to its fate. Polyaenus, giving a slightly more highly coloured account of this incident than Diodorus, confuses the matter by stating that the promontory was 20 *stades* – some 2½ miles – wide, instead of about 600 yards. This has led Whitaker to place the haulage of the ships at the *north* end of the lagoon and to suppose that they were dragged through shallows rather than over firm land. But it is better, I believe, to assume either that Polyaenus' source was guilty of gross exaggeration, or – more likely – that an error has crept into the text: after all, *gamma* (3) and *kappa* (20) might easily become confused.[10]

When his mole was completed, Dionysius moved up his siege train and his soldiers for the assault on the city. The main attack was probably directed against the northern sector of the wall, where the foreshore provided a flat, firm platform for his engines. Diodorus tells us how the rams beat in the bases of the towers and the catapults swept the battlements and how six-storeyed siege-towers (such as the Greeks had first encountered at the siege of Selinus) were moved up to the wall in

D ENVIRONS OF MOTYA AND LILYBAEUM

order to enable Dionysius' men to come to grips with defenders posted on the upper levels of the tall Phoenician houses adjacent to the wall.[11] Compared with the 'great sieges' of Plataea and Syracuse in the Peloponnesian War, this was Greek warfare on an altogether grander – on an Oriental – scale, and it presaged the siege of Tyre by Alexander, the exploits of Demetrius Poliorcetes and, even in many of its details, the siege of Carthage herself by Scipio Aemilianus.

The Motyans, who knew that they were in the fullest sense of the term fighting for their lives, resisted with a fury that surpassed that of the besiegers. They raised tall masts behind the wall, carrying yards to the ends of which protective containers were attached, from which men threw down fire on to the enemy's siege engines: fire which was quickly quenched. Then the wall was breached (near the west end of the old necropolis) and a fierce hand-to-hand struggle ensued, which developed into protracted and bitter street fighting, as the Greeks attempted to storm the hastily erected barricades and the tall houses from whose upper floors the defenders rained down missiles. Then the siege-towers were again brought into play, for they were dragged up to the nearest houses and the Greeks poured across gangways, on which many a desperate mid-air struggle took place, to fight their way into the buildings.[12]

After several days of this costly and inconclusive warfare (in which, because of the narrowness of the 'front', the defenders were able to maintain a local superiority of numbers), and after the Motyans had become accustomed to the routine of their enemy's attack, which always ceased at nightfall when the troops withdrew to the mainland, Dionysius mounted a night assault. A picked body of mercenaries under Archylus of Thurii scaled the ruined houses by means of ladders and seized a position – perhaps one of the stairs – by which Dionysius could lead a waiting force into the city. The Motyans rushed to repel the invaders, but Greek reinforcements continued to pour in, the bulk of Dionysius' army arrived by way of the mole and the defence was overwhelmed. The Greeks ran wild in the city and a massacre of the inhabitants ensued. Since every Motyan slain represented a loss to his treasury, and since he was, by the standards of those times, by no means an inhumane man, Dionysius attempted to halt the slaughter, although for the most part to no avail. Finally he posted heralds to advise the people to take refuge in those temples 'that were respected by the Greeks' – either, that is, those actually erected by the Greek residents to their gods, or (more likely, perhaps) those dedicated to Phoenician gods whom the Greeks popularly identified with their own, such as Melqart (Heracles), Reshef (Apollo) and Astarte (Aphrodite). The city and its contents were abandoned to the soldiery to plunder. Dionysius rewarded those who had distinguished themselves in the fighting, and crucified (or impaled) those Greeks – we are not told whether they were residents or mercenaries – who had fought under Deïmenes in the defence of the city: the specifically Hellenic character of Dionysius' crusade must not be lost sight of. The population of Motya he put up for sale as slaves, and it would seem that many – perhaps most – of them were, in fact, ransomed by their neighbours (perhaps by the Segestaeans), as was the common practice.[13]

It was now near the end of the campaigning season. The citizen soldiers were anxious to return to their homes, and if the Syracusans went home Dionysius would have to go with them. On the other hand, he wanted to begin the next year's campaign where he left off in 397. Accordingly he left a force largely composed of Sicels, under Biton of Syracuse, to garrison Motya, and deputed Leptines to keep watch, with 120 ships, on the waters of western Sicily and defeat any Carthaginian attempt to put an army into the island in the coming spring. Leptines was also to resume the siege of Segesta and Entella, presumably using for this the crews and marines of the fleet and perhaps some of Biton's men. Dionysius then marched his army back to Syracuse, the citizen soldiers dispersing to their various homes with instructions to be ready to march again the following summer.[14]

It would appear that the comparative ease with which he had captured the strong island city of Motya and the feebleness of Carthage's response to his aggression, together with the fact that he had already taken Himilco's measure as a cautious and unadventurous commander, combined to cause Dionysius to make – and not for the last time in his career – what is perhaps one of the most dangerous mistakes in a general's extensive repertory: that of despising his enemy. The key to Siceliot victory in the coming summer was held by Leptines, who, with his 120 ships (30 of them, perhaps, quinqueremes), was in a position to fall upon any Punic armada at the end of its 130-mile voyage over the open sea from Libya. What was required of him by the situation was unwinking vigilance and the energetic gathering of intelligence by means of agents and, with the return of spring, by regular patrolling. But the little that we know for certain of Leptines' history strongly suggests that although he was a man of exemplary courage as a soldier, a dashing leader and possessed of a jovial and attractive personality, he had very little power of judgement. Indeed, his conduct as commander of the fleet (a post so important that the dynast – perhaps on Spartan advice – did not venture to entrust it to anyone outside his immediate family) was so irresponsible, both now and later, that it encourages the suspicion that he resented having to play second fiddle to his brother and was obstinately determined, even at the risk of imperilling Dionysius' grand undertaking, to assert his own independence of thought and action. He failed to take either Segesta or Entella, and although Himilco's counter-intelligence measures may suggest that Syracusan agents were active at Carthage, they may equally be evidence merely of the old king's native caution. It certainly does not look as if Leptines' warships patrolled the waters south and west of Lilybaeum.

Carthage had not been idle during the summer and winter of 397/6. Her purpose now was to settle the troublesome Sicilian Question once and for all, by the capture of Syracuse and the subjugation of the whole island; and for this task she mobilized her Libyan resources, citizen, allied and subject, and hired mercenaries from Iberia. The figures given by Diodorus' sources for Himilco's armament (Ephorus, 300,000 infantry and 400 warships, Timaeus, 100,000 infantry) are really worthless. Ephorus says that Himilco had 600 transports, which looks reasonable; and if each transport, other than those carrying horses and chariots, carried 100 men, we arrive at a total of something over 50,000 men. To these should be added the levies of the Epicraty, giving a grand total substantially larger than that of Dionysius' army. Dionysius for his part collected his forces, probably about midsummer, and returned to the Epicraty. It seems quite clear, both from the subsequent course of events and from the fact that, on his return to Syracuse, Dionysius had only 180 ships *after* manning 60 with emancipated slaves, that Leptines' fleet was not reinforced for the campaign of 396. This was presumably on account of the difficulty and cost of providing rowers, and also because Dionysius did not believe that Carthage was capable of sending more than 100 or so ships to sea.

On his arrival in western Sicily, Dionysius began to lay waste the territories of Carthage's subjects. Halicyae went over to him, as a result, but Entella and Segesta held out, and the Segestans inflicted losses on their besiegers in a night sortie. Clearly the dynast did not have at his disposal for use against Segesta the sophisticated engines that had reduced Motya; and he could not commit himself completely to the siege of any Phoenician or allied city until he was satisfied that he would not have to face a Punic expeditionary force.[16]

In the late summer, when all his preparations were made, Himilco put to sea under cover of darkness and with screened lights (proof of the expertness of the Carthaginian seamen), having issued sealed orders to the captains of his transports to sail directly to Panormus: no doubt keeping outside the Aegates Islands. He himself with the battle fleet took a different course. Unfortunately at this point in his narrative either Diodorus' source let him down or Diodorus himself, in abridging his source, produced an account that does not make good sense. It runs as follows: 'the triremes sailed to Libya and proceeded along the coast. The wind continued favourable, and as soon as the van of the transport fleet was sighted from Sicily, Dionysius sent Leptines out with 30 triremes, with orders to ram and sink all the ships he could intercept'. Diodorus goes on to say that Leptines sank 50 transports, the rest of the convoy escaping under full sail to Panormus, where, in the next paragraph, we find Himilco and the warships. Clearly the reading '*Libuēn*' (Libya, 55.2) is corrupt. Post emends it to *'Libukēn'* sc. *thalattan*, 'to the Libyan Sea'; but this hardly helps matters (apart from the fact that elsewhere (13.54.2) Diodorus calls those waters *'to Libukon pelagos'*. It has been suggested that Himilco sailed eastwards along the south coast of Sicily in order to draw Leptines away from his station by the feint of an attack on Syracuse. But Himilco had over 250 ships – more than twice as many as Leptines – and had no reason to employ a diversionary strategy. Moreover, Leptines could not have been relied upon to fall for such a very improbable feint; and if he did not, the Carthaginian transport fleet would have been left at his mercy. And if Himilco really had employed this ruse – and employed it successfully – it is strange that it failed to find a place among Polyaenus' 'ruses of Himilco'![17]

Himilco was a cautious man, whose main concern was the shipment of his immense army to Panormus. Much the safest way of achieving this was to send his transports across the open sea – which is what he did – and to interpose his battle fleet between them and the much weaker Greek force at Motya. And so, for *'Libuen'* above we should read *'Lilubaion'* (Lilybaeum), with Dobraeus, although Eichstadt's *'Motuen'* (Motya), which seems to me a less happy emendation, would support the same conclusion. Once again Himilco had probably timed his sailing so as to arrive off Lilybaeum at daybreak, catching Leptines' ships still beached. The Greek admiral would, in the circumstances, have had no option but to remain where he was and prepare to defend his ships against attack. Himilco, then, apparently assuming that his transports were now out of Leptines' reach, proceeded on up the coast to Panormus, something like 80 miles distant. The leading ships of the convoy – which had no doubt straggled to some extent during the course of a voyage of 150 or more miles, much of it by night – were probably sighted from Mt. Eryx, from which the news would have been carried by a horseman to Motya. Leptines at once put to sea with 30 ships, – which, in spite of Diodorus' description of them as triremes, were, I believe, the quinqueremes: the crack squadron that we meet again, later in the year. He succeeded in catching and sinking 50 of the transports; something that cost the enemy no less than 5,000 men and 200 chariots, according to Diodorus. Were these, perhaps, the only chariots that Himilco had brought from Carthage? We hear nothing more, in the wars in Sicily during Dionysius' reign, of this weapon: one much favoured by the Carthaginians before the introduction of the war-elephant, in the first half of the 3rd century.[18]

Himilco added the levies of Panormus and Solus to his army (thus no doubt more than making good his losses at sea, although the total number of soldiers supplied by the Epicraty can hardly have amounted to the 30,000 mentioned by Timaeus); and then – such was the habitual cautiousness of the man – instead of marching directly on Segesta to confront Dionysius, he moved westwards, his right flank covered by the fleet, took Eryx, which – together no doubt with its port, Drepanum – was betrayed to him, and arrived before Motya. Leptines and the Greek fleet probably withdrew to Selinus when Eryx was lost, and Biton's resistance is unlikely to have been of any long duration. In fact, Himilco's strategy, although unheroic, was militarily sound. His army, huge as it was, was a motley, untried force consisting largely of light infantry, and in the last war the Greeks had handled such troops very roughly. It was sound policy to give his levies the chance to settle down and become a unitary force, by a spell of marching, siege work and camping, before committing them to battle against an experienced enemy. His strategy would also have served to stiffen the will to resist of his allies, bring deserters into his camp and undermine the confidence of his enemies.[19]

Dionysius now found himself in serious trouble. He had lost the command of the sea, Entella (about 19 miles south-east of Segesta) was still hostile, the loyalty of the Sicans was wavering, and now Halicyae (between Segesta and Motya) reverted to its loyalty to Carthage. Thus the roads over which supplies must reach him from the east, whether directly or by sea through Selinus, were either cut or threatened. He did not wish to be driven to attack Himilco's vastly larger army by the need to force a decision, since a defeat so far from home could be militarily and politically ruinous. But if he was not going to fight, the sooner he was back in his own part of the island the better. As has been said earlier, Dionysius was not by temperament a gambler; and, indeed, a readiness to retreat in good time before unacceptable odds is one of the marks of a good general: as the career of the Duke of Wellington would testify. Dionysius tried to persuade the Sicans to abandon their towns temporarily and migrate to eastern Sicily, where he would give them, either permanently or for the duration of the war, better lands than their own. Only a few communities, however, availed themselves, unwillingly and out of fear, of this offer; and Dionysius withdrew from the Epicraty, wasting the lands through which he passed in his march of at least fourteen days back to Syracuse, to which Leptines also withdrew with the fleet.[20]

No immediate pursuit followed, for Himilco was going about the business of subjugating Sicily in a characteristically methodical manner. It seems to me very likely that Himilco (as Stroheker has suggested), fully aware of the importance of the Bay of Lilybaeum as providing the most convenient bridgehead in western Sicily, took advantage of the partial destruction and depopulation of Motya to transfer the port and the town from the silted-up lagoon to the southern end of the bay, and to put in hand the building of a new city in the vicinity of the spring from which (according to Diodorus) it was to take its name: Lilybaeum. The former inhabitants of Motya were redeemed and settled on the site, to form the citizen body of the new city. Lilybaeum offered better commercial and naval facilities than land-locked Motya and, as history was to prove, could be made impregnable as long as Carthage was able to victual and reinforce its garrison by sea.[21]

Himilco knew very well that if Syracuse was to be taken or starved into surrender, he must gain decisive command not only of the waters around the city but also of the sea approaches from the direction of Italy and the Peloponnese, and that therefore his line of march must be along the north coast of the island to the Straits of Messana. The people of Himera, no doubt desperately anxious to atone for their having recently sent aid to Dionysius, offered their submission, and so did their eastern neighbour, Cephaloedium. Himilco despatched his fleet to the Lipari Islands, seized their chief city, Lipara, and exacted 30 talents from the islanders.[22]

In the autumn of 396 Himilco put his army in motion, probably proceeding by the coast road, with the fleet accompanying his march – although it would seem from the wording of a passage in Diodorus that the historian's sources were divided (or ambiguous) on the question of whether Himilco moved his army by land or sea. At the end of perhaps fourteen days he arrived in the territory of Messana and pitched camp at Peloris, some 11½ miles from the city. The Messanians' were isolated, their walls dilapidated and the fighting-men of their ruling class, the Knights, were at Syracuse with Dionysius: in effect, hostages for their countrymen's good behaviour. None the less, when they realized that Himilco was going to attack them, the Messanians sent their women and children and their treasure to places of safety and despatched a picked force to defend the approaches to their city; no doubt to where the coast road runs through a narrow pass between the mountains and the sea, where Himilco's superiority in numbers would be unavailing. Himilco countered this move by sending 200 ships loaded with troops directly to Messana, and although the citizens rushed back when they saw what was happening, they were too late to dispute the landing and were overwhelmed as the barabarians poured through the gaps in the city walls. Some of the population fell into Punic hands, but the greater part escaped; the majority to fortified hill villages, some to neighbouring towns. Fifty desperate men even managed to swim the Straits to Italy.[23]

Himilco wasted some time in fruitless efforts to take the hill forts, and then gave his army a period of rest in the city. The Sicels, apart from the people of Assorus, believing that the days of Syracusan over-rule were coming to an end, revolted to Carthage. Those to whom Dionysius had given the former territory of Naxos were induced by Himilco to unite to found a strong city just to the north of the site of Naxos, on the Hill of the Bull, to which they gave the name Tauromenium; and thither, when his men were rested, Himilco despatched the fleet under Mago, who was probably a kinsman of his. He razed the city of Messana in order to prevent its being reoccupied and rendered defensible in the rear of his advance, and then made a forced march to rejoin his fleet. South of Tauromenium, however, he found the coast road blocked by a recent flow of lava from mount Etna; and he therefore ordered Mago to take the fleet to Catane, while he with the army made a detour, by forced marches again, around the west side of the mountain, so as to come down into the coastal plain and rejoin the fleet at Catane. It would appear that he did not expect to be attacked either on land or sea before reuniting his forces, otherwise he would surely have delayed Mago's sailing until the army had made sure of Catane.[24]

At Syracuse, in the meantime, Dionysius, as might be expected, had risen to the challenge presented by Himilco's invasion and had been making vigorous preparations to resist it. He sent agents to Laconia to hire over 1,000 mercenaries, and he freed more than 10,000 slaves in order to provide rowers for 60 additional ships. This poses the question, Why was Dionysius obliged to emancipate slaves in order to commission these 60 ships, when only a few years earlier he had had at his disposal a work-force of over 60,000 able-bodied men, a large proportion of whom, at least, must be assumed to have been free men, and when he had sent back to Syracuse the previous winter some 80 ships, whose crews would have amounted to about 16,000 men (accepting Diodorus' estimate of 200 men to a ship)? I believe that we must assume that these 80 ships were wholly manned by mercenaries (which is what economic considerations would have dictated, anyway), and that these men had been paid off and had gone home. Even so, and accepting the fact that something like 20,000 citizens were now serving on Leptines' ships, we might expect that Dionysius could have found citizens with whom to man the additional 60 vessels. His inability to do so may be explained partly by the difficulty of collecting, at short notice, men who were not on the hoplite register, and who were scattered over a very wide area, partly by the natural unwillingness of farm workers, shepherds, charcoal-burners and the like to volunteer for sea duty, and partly – perhaps mainly – by his policy of provisioning and garrisoning numerous strong-points on Syracusan territory, with particular attention to the citadels of Leontini, into which was gathered the harvest of the rich plain. In this way he hoped to retain a hold upon the Interior and to maintain his communications with the rest of Sicily, should Syracuse be besieged. Moreover, the presence of scattered bodies of soldiers throughout the territory would expose Himilco's foraging parties to harassment and loss. The Campanian colonists of Catane were persuaded to move up to the more defensible Aetna, which had presumably been largely unpeopled since Dionysius expelled the exiles.

When he had taken all the precautions he could, Dionysius brought what was left of the Siceliot army north to Taurus, about 18½ miles south of Catane, near the site of ancient Megara (destroyed by Gelon), where there was also a sheltered anchorage. He had now only 30,000 infantry and 3,000 cavalry. Presumably the discrepancy between these numbers and those he had commanded earlier is to be explained by the secession of the Sicels and the Himeraeans and by desertions. Leptines brought the fleet up to Taurus; he had 180 ships, and of these (says our text of Diodorus) 'few were triremes'. I believe that this comment must be incorrect and that either Diodorus' source misled him or that the text has become corrupted and we should read 'few were *fivers*'.[25]

For once Dionysius seems to have had accurate information about Himilco's movements. He knew that the Carthaginian army was having to part company with the fleet, and he knew that the enemy fleet must appear in the vicinity of Catane long before the army. He knew also that the disparity between his own strength and Himilco's was rather less at sea than on land. He therefore decided to attack Mago as soon as he appeared off Catane, for he judged that the defeat of his ships would force Himilco to give up all thought of laying siege to Syracuse and (since he had himself destroyed Messana) retire for the winter to the Epicraty. Accordingly Dionysius moved his forces up to Catane and ordered Leptines to attack Mago's huge convoy, composed of some 500 vessels, more than half of them war galleys, as it ran before the wind towards the harbour. He gave his brother explicit instructions to keep his fleet in close order and not to break formation; a detail that must go back to Philistus.

When Mago, approaching Catane, saw the shore lined with Greek troops and the enemy battle fleet, cleared for action, bearing down upon him, he knew a moment of sheer panic. It should be remembered that (as far as we know) the Carthaginians had not fought a major sea battle since the sixth century, when they had clashed with the Phocaeans and with the Massaliots. In a fight with the Syracusans in 406, involving 80 ships, they had been defeated; and a large part of their present force had retired ignominiously before the Syracusan navy only the summer before. But Mago (who was a capable but not a great leader) pulled himself together; perhaps he realized that there were fewer ships in front of him than there had been off Motya, perhaps Leptines' dispositions (or rather, his lack of the same) gave him confidence. At all events, since flight in the teeth of the northerly wind was an impossibility for his transports, he resolved to fight the Greeks at sea rather than beach his ships and expose his men to attack by land and sea.

Leptines, however, who seems to have been temperamentally incap-

able of doing what his brother told him, instead of obeying Dionysius'
instructions and keeping his ships together, using his quinqueremes as
the spearhead of his attack and so reducing the advantage that Himilco's
superior numbers gave him, advanced with his 30 best ships (which I
believe to have been the quinqueremes), far ahead of the rest of the fleet.
This squadron inflicted serious losses on the enemy at their first onset,
but the Carthaginians, exploiting the odds of 8 to 1 in their favour,
crowded in on Leptines' ships, running their vessels alongside and
boarding, so that the battle developed into an infantry fight at sea, in
which superior numbers were bound to prevail. Leptines managed
somehow to extricate his squadron, but was driven off to the east; and
the rest of the Syracusan fleet, arriving in disorder, not merely leaderless
but already dismayed by the flight of their admiral, was heavily defeated.
Over 100 Greek ships were destroyed or captured, with the loss of more
than 20,000 men; for although the battle, especially in its last, bloody
stages, took place close to the shore, the crews of the stricken vessels
were butchered as they tried to swim to the safety of their own army by
men in light craft, positioned inshore of the main fleets.[26]

Dionysius at once fell back, probably towards Taurus; and Mago,
having occupied Catane, set about repairing and putting into service the
ships captured in the battle, so making good his own losses. Dionysius'
Greek allies, with their native predilection for an 'agōnal' decision, urged
the tyrant to fall on Himilco on his march, exploiting the element of
surprise; but his War Council was against a plan that would expose
Syracuse to attack by the victorious Punic navy – that would, indeed,
have provided Mago with the opportunity of repeating the success that
he had so recently achieved at Messana. Undoubtedly the decision not to
fight was the correct one in the circumstances; yet it marked another
retreat before the enemy without a fight, another admission of defeat. It
cost Dionysius the support of his allies who, having no desire to face the
rigours of a winter siege within the walls of Syracuse, made their way
back to their own cities or else took refuge in the strong-points that
Dionysius had recently provisioned.[27]

Himilco, after two days of forced marching, rejoined his fleet at
Catane. High winds compelled the Carthaginians to haul their ships out
of the water; but Himilco availed himself of the opportunity of resting
his troops and sailors. He also endeavoured, although without success, to
detach the Campanians at Aetna from Dionysius, to whom they had
earlier given hostages for their loyalty and with whom their best soldiers
were still serving. He then moved his whole force down to Syracuse. His
huge armada of warships and transports paraded in review order across
the Great Harbour, while the army marched round the western flank of
the city and occupied much the same ground, to the south of the river
Anapus, that Nicias had held in the late summer of 415. Himilco

9   Syracuse: temple of Olympain Zeus, with Ortygia in the background

established his headquarters in the precinct of Olympian Zeus, and set up his naval station at the mouth of the river. He drew up his army before the walls of the city and offered battle (which he must have known would be refused), while his fleet made a demonstration in front of the harbour; and then, having established his mastery of the open country, he spent what remained of the season scouring the territory and stocking his larder in preparation for a lengthy investment of the city. Supplies were also brought in by sea from Africa and Sardinia.[28]

With the approach of winter, Himilco concentrated his forces in his fortified camp in the Anapus plain, probably to the south of the river, demolishing the tombs that lined the Helorine road (including that of Gelon and Demaretē) in order to obtain cut stone. Someone at Himilco's headquarters was obviously familiar with the principal details of Nicias' campaign, and accordingly the precinct of Olympian Zeus, on its precipitous-fronted bluff (which the Syracusans had held against Nicias) was fortified, in order to protect the left-hand flank of his lines, a fort was built on elevated ground at Dascon, a promontory to the south of the Anapus, to cover the seaward flank and the anchorage and another fort was constructed at Plemmyrium, opposite the southern tip of Ortygia, for the purpose of securing the command of the entrance to the Great Harbour. Dionysius, too, did what he could to improve his position against the coming of spring, when serious military operations would be renewed. He sent his brother-in-law, Polyxenus, on an extended mission to Magna Graecia and Corinth and Sparta, to ask for assistance to preserve the Greeks of Sicily from destruction. He also sent recruiting officers to the Peloponnese to hire mercenaries, regardless of cost.[29]

With the coming of the spring of 395, Dionysius' embassies proved to have been productive. Syracuse's friends abroad, most notably no doubt the Corinthians, put together a force of 30 ships, with a Lacedaemonian – in fact, a Spartan full citizen – to command it. He is named Pharacidas by both Diodorus and Polyaenus, but many modern historians follow Beloch in identifying him with the Pharax who was Spartan *navarch* in the Aegean in the early summer of 397. Polyaenus states that this fleet, approaching Syracuse, fell in with a Carthaginian squadron and captured nine of its vessels, which the Spartan admiral manned with his own men and so slipped his force past the watchmen and patrols at Plemmyrium, who believed the new arrivals to be Phoenician ships.[30]

There was sporadic fighting in the spring and early summer of 395 which appears, on the whole, to have gone Syracuse's way. Himilco certainly assaulted the suburb of Achradina, attacking up the Helorine Road, and sacked the temple of Demeter and Korē. He also employed his ships to raid the coastal districts in the Camarina–Cape Pachynus–Syracuse triangle; and on at least one occasion his landing parties suffered heavy losses at the hands of the Syracusan cavalry commanded by Leptines. Diodorus reports an important victory gained in the Great Harbour by the Syracusan navy; but here, I believe, we encounter a product of the rhetorical tradition hostile to the tyrant. Diodorus' account of the incident and its political repercussions may be summarized as follows: Dionysius and Leptines sailed from Syracuse with warships, to escort a supply convoy. The Syracusans, left to themselves (*kath' hautous genomenoi*), engaged the Carthaginians in the Great Harbour: at first with 5 ships and then, when the enemy manned 40, with all their ships. They captured or destroyed 25 galleys and drove the rest back to their base, before which they offered battle, which was refused. Elated by their success, the Syracusans began to talk of ridding themselves of the tyranny. Dionysius returned at this juncture, summoned an Assembly and promised a swift end to the war. A Knight named Theodorus then delivered a vituperative oration (reported verbatim and occupying five chapters in the Loeb edition), calling for the deposition of the tyrant. Pharacidas thereupon mounted the rostrum, but instead of declaring for liberty he said that he had been sent to help the Syracusans and Dionysius against Carthage, not to overthrow Dionysius. Dionysius 'in great fear' dissolved the Assembly, but subsequently recovered his popularity through his amiability and generosity.

Now, this account simply will not do, as it stands. It fairly bristles with difficulties, some of such magnitude as to constitute virtual impossibilities, and its bitterly anti-tyrannical and highly rhetorical character stamps it as belonging in the realm of the historical declamation (the *meletē*), rather than in that of history. In the first place, is there any conceivable reason why Dionysius should have gone off with Leptines on convoy duty, running the risk of being taken or killed, or at least of being cut off from Syracuse? Even after his brother's bad showing at Catane, Dionysius continued to entrust the fleet to him; but if he *had* decided to go with Leptines, it would surely have been with every ship that could be made serviceable. Again, if he *had* departed from Syracuse, would he not have left someone whom he could trust (Pharacidas, or Philistus) in command there; and is it likely that the arsenals would have been left unguarded (by reliable mercenaries), so that the citizens were able to rush down to the shore and man the galleys, as the Athenians did in moments of crisis? Nor is it likely that the main Carthaginian fleet would have refused to put to sea and face the triumphant Syracusans, whom they must have heavily outnumbered even if (as may have been the case) they had sent some of their ships back to Carthage for the winter. Finally, the total number of Punic ships said to have been engaged (40) is the same as that attacked later in the year *without Dionysius' permission*.

In short, the whole account of the 'battle' looks very like an invention inspired by Pharacidas' capture of the Punic squadron described above and by the later Corinthian attack on the Carthaginians against Dionysius' orders – an invention designed to provide a historical background for the anti-tyrannical diatribe of 'Theodorus', and to display the Spartans in a bad light as the enemies of Greek freedom: the role in which Athenian opinion cast them in the years between the outbreak of the Corinthian War and the battle of Leuctra. The passage *may*, as Stroheker believes, be 'pure Timaeus', but I believe that it is much more likely to have come from a collection of rhetorical exercises (under the heading of 'Speeches against Tyrants') – unless, that is, it is a product of Diodorus' own pen. This is not, of course, to deny that Pharacidas may have spoken up at Syracuse in defence of Dionysius, and that the fact was reliably recorded. In Spartan eyes, the Strong Man and disciple of their friend Hermocrates was much to be preferred as master of Syracuse and controller of the corn supplies of Sicily to a disorderly democracy.[31]

The summer of 395 was an unusually hot one and the besiegers, lodged in cramped and crowded lines on low-lying and marshy ground, with doubtless wholly inadequate precautions taken against the dangers to health presented by impure water and primitive sanitation, were stricken by 'plague'. The symptoms of the disease are described by Diodorus in a passage that derives (directly, I believe) from Philistus, writing in imitation of the famous description of the plague at Athens; but it is not possible to identify it with any certainty. The doctors were powerless to check the spread of the disease, the dead were left unburied from fear of contagion (so making matters even worse), and the awful stench of corruption added to the horror of the disaster. Naturally the Greeks attributed the calamity to the wrath of the goddesses, over the spoliation of their temple.[32]

Dionysius was kept well informed by spies, deserters and prisoners of war of the state of things in the enemy's camp and of the incipient demoralization of the Carthaginian army; whereas the morale of his own men, stiffened by the arrival of the Peloponnesians, and by their success in numerous skirmishes, was high. He decided to strike Himilco by land and sea. This time, being in a position to choose the time and place of his attack, with substantial mercenary forces (including Campanians) at his disposal, and faced by a despondent enemy, he was able to produce and execute a more effective plan than that which had come to grief at Gela. Although the Carthaginians had suffered severely from the plague, they must still have greatly outnumbered Dionysius' army, shorn as it was of most of the allied contingents; so that a frontal attack upon the entrenched camp, whose ends were protected on its left by the bluffs on which stood the fortified precinct of Olympian Zeus (the *Polichnē*) and on the right by the marsh that stretched along the shore, would not be likely to succeed. Dionysius' plan shows how much he had matured as a tactician. It did, indeed, resemble his plan for the battle of Gela in that it called for a co-ordinated assault upon Himilco's position by three separate divisions; the strongest attacking the landward end, the weakest the centre and the third division, supported by the fleet, the seaward end. This time, however, the approach march was to be made under cover of darkness and the attacks were to go in at first light *against the flanks and rear* of the enemy's lines. And Dionysius was going to be there, to lead, direct and control the assault in person.[33]

On a moonless night Dionysius led his forces out of the city, across the Anapus and around the left flank of Himilco's position to the vicinity of the temple of Cyane (situated, no doubt, near the source of the little river of the same name). The cavalry and 1,000 mercenary infantry went ahead of the main body. South of Himilco's camp, the horsemen parted company and rode to the shore of the Great Harbour to attack the fort at Dascon, whose capture would make it difficult for the barbarians stationed at Plemmyrium to reinforce the main camp. Dascon was, moreover, the principal anchorage for the transports and, probably, Himilco's chief food depot. The mercenaries (described as expendable because of their mutinous character) assailed the rear of Himilco's camp, causing the attention of the defenders to be concentrated on this sector; they encountered a determined resistance and were cut to pieces. But they had served their purpose and kept the Carthaginians occupied while

Dionysius, with the main body, got into position to storm the *Polichnē*, attacking it from its unprecipitous side, and began the assault upon the camp. The ships, 80 of them under the command of Leptines and Pharacidas, arrived on cue. Some of them rowed to Dascon to assist the cavalry in the capture of the Punic depot, while the remainder attacked the main naval base. As the plan had intended, the barbarians were thrown into confusion, uncertain where the main attack was going to fall, and so prevented from making an effective use of their superiority in numbers to reinforce the areas threatened.

After the taking of the *Polichnē*, Dionysius rode across to Dascon and took command there. The Punic light warships drawn up on the beach were set on fire and a strong wind carried the flames to the anchored transports, so that soon the whole anchorage was in a blaze. Syracusans too old or too young for military service joined in the game, manning wherries and rowing across the harbour to plunder or tow home the crippled or abandoned supply ships. Imitating Thucydides again, Philistus describes the excitement of the population of the city, who thronged the walls, rejoicing at the tremendous spectacle of Himilco's fiery discomfiture. Nightfall brought the confused fighting to a close, with the main Carthaginian camp still intact, but with a large part – perhaps the greater part – of their triremes damaged or destroyed. Dionysius drew off his troops and bivouacked on the high ground near the Olympieum.[34]

Himilco had had enough. He opened negotiations with Dionysius, asking at first to be allowed to evacuate his army in return for 300 talents (his war chest) and finally accepting Dionysius' offer to grant him a four days' truce and the opportunity of evacuating, by night, the Carthaginian citizen element: abandoning the remainder to their fate. Accordingly, Dionysius pulled his forces back into the city. I see no good reason to doubt the authenticity of this compact, recorded by Diodorus, bearing though it does the imprint of the malice of the anti-tyrannical tradition.[35] Himilco was in fact in much the same desperate predicament that Nicias had been seventeen years earlier. It is true that he still held Plemmyrium (which Nicias had lost), but the Greeks commanded the Great Harbour and could assault his last strong-point whenever they wished. There was no likelihood of substantial reinforcements or supplies reaching him from Carthage, or from the Epicraty, and before long starvation and disease must compel him to capitulate. He did not, I believe, have sufficient ships left in a serviceable condition to evacuate his whole army by sea, even if he had been prepared to attempt to fight his way past the 80 Greek ships that would bar his passage. He must have been acquainted with the fate of Nicias' splendid army and known how when it attempted to retreat by land it had degenerated into a disorderly mob under the ceaseless harrying of a weaker force than that which now faced him. But Himilco possessed two advantages that Nicias had not

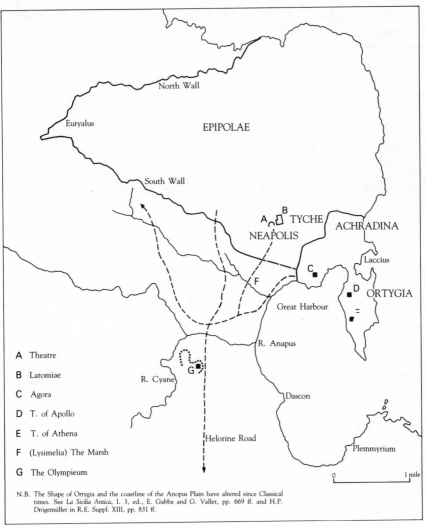

North Wall

Euryalus

EPIPOLAE

South Wall

A   B   TYCHE
NEAPOLIS   ACHRADINA

Laccius

C

D   ORTYGIA

Great Harbour

R. Anapus

R. Cyane   G

Dascon

Plemmyrium

Helorine Road

A   Theatre

B   Latomiae

C   Agora

D   T. of Apollo

E   T. of Athena

F   (Lysimelia) The Marsh

G   The Olympieum

0   1 mile

N.B. The Shape of Ortygia and the coastline of the Anopus Plain have altered since Classical
times. See *La Sicilia Antica*, I. 3, ed., E. Gabba and G. Vallet, pp. 669 ff. and H.P.
Drögemüller in R.E. Suppl. XIII, pp. 831 ff.

E   SYRACUSE

enjoyed. Nicias had been the commander of an army composed of citizens of a democracy and of its allies: his fate was inextricably bound up with theirs. Himilco, however, could feel no sense of obligation or loyalty towards the motley horde of 'barbarian' mercenaries that made up the greater part of his force. No tears would be shed at Carthage (which would otherwise have to pay them) if he returned home without them. His only duty was to his fellow citizens, and by preserving them he would save something out of the ruin of his great expedition. And he had those 300 talents.

For his part, Dionysius made his pact with the enemy for good political, economic and military reasons. After the disasters of the previous years and the overthrow of all the high hopes with which his people had embarked upon the great war of liberation, he urgently needed a spectacular success, and a breathing space, too, from warfare on the largest scale. By freeing his people at a stroke from the terrors, hardship and expense of the siege, and by destroying the disease-ridden camp of the enemy before the plague spread to the city, he would restore their trust in him as their leader. For we need not doubt that what the hostile tradition stigmatized as a betrayal was seen by the beleaguered Syracusans for what it was: a glorious victory. Dionysius knew – being a leader of mercenaries himself – that, deserted by its general and deprived of the stiffening influence of the Carthaginians, the army of Himilco would disintegrate. On the other hand, if he left Himiclo no alternative but to fight, the cost of crushing him, in terms of Greek lives, might be high, for the fiercest elements of his army could be expected to sell their lives dearly. And there was always the possibility that Himilco might succeed in fighting his way out: a defeat that could well cost Dionysius his tyranny. He must also have been familiar with the maxims that Thucydides puts into the mouths of his old chief, Hermocrates, and of the Spartan envoys after their set-back at Sphacteria: that 'in war the uncertainty of the future generally prevails', and that, for this reason, the prudent man is not greedy but is ready to make peace in the moment of success.

Dionysius was cautious by nature, and he badly needed those 300 talents of ready money; we hear of discontent among the mercenaries, and that usually indicates that their pay was in arrears. The cost of the war, which should have been more than covered by the plunder of the Epicraty, had brought the dynast into serious financial straits. Himilco might cheat him of the silver, either by slipping away with it by sea, or, if all else failed, by dumping it in the waters of the Great Harbour. The escape of perhaps 8,000 to 10,000 Carthaginians, although it would represent a serious loss to his treasury, would not affect the eventual outcome of the war; and Dionysius can hardly have failed to appreciate the damage that Himilco's desertion of his army would do to Carthage's prestige and to her good name as an employer of mercenaries, as well as to the reputation of the Magonid dynasty.[36]

So, by the terms of the agreement and under cover of darkness, Himilco conveyed his treasure into the keeping of the tyrant's officers in Ortygia, and, on the appointed day, put the Carthaginian citizens on to 40 ships and headed for the open sea. When his fleet reached the mouth of the harbour it was sighted by the Greeks, and as Dionysius delayed the pursuit, his Corinthian auxiliaries, who were no doubt the least well-disposed of his followers and the least amenable to his directions, manned their ships, gave chase and sank some of the vessels at the tail of Himilco's line. (It was this incident, I believe, that formed the basis of the anecdotal account of the 'spontaneous' attack on the Carthaginian fleet by the Syracusans, mentioned above.)

The report of Himilco's flight told Dionysius that he was now free to act against the Punic camp. He had already made his plan and called his soldiers to arms; and before the night was out he had blocked the roads leading into the interior and had his army ready to assault the camp at daybreak. The Sicels in Himilco's army – perhaps alerted to their peril by the general himself? – had already fled from the camp and escaped to their homes; but the rest of the barbarians, leaderless and demoralized, took to flight when the Greeks attacked. Some were captured at the road blocks, but the majority of them surrendered on the plain. A well-ordered body of Iberians, who offered a determined resistance, bargained successfully to be taken into the tyrant's service; but the rest of what had been an army was sold, the camp being given over to the Greeks to plunder.[37]

How acute Dionysius' financial embarrassment had become is shown by the fact that now (probably following the departure of Pharacidas and the Corinthians) he was faced by open disaffection on the part of his Greek mercenaries, who had (it will be remembered) been offered by his agents the most lavish inducements to enter his service. No doubt there were important Syracusan claims on his purse which he deemed it expedient to satisfy, including those of the gods, whose treasures he had 'borrowed' to defray the cost of the war, and which made serious inroads into his 300 talents and the proceeds of the sale of the prisoners. Moreover, he could not leave himself without some ready money for his forthcoming campaign. He attempted to silence the mercenaries by a display of firmness, and arrested their leader, a Lacedaemonian named either Aristotle (Diodorus) or Aristomenes (Polyaenus), an action which precipitated an open mutiny, in which (if there is truth in Polyaenus' anecdote) his life was threatened. However, he restored their good humour by offering them the town and territory of Leontini in lieu of cash. If (as I believe may have been the case) the former landowning citizens of Leontini (who may not have been very numerous) had been permitted to retain their fields and cultivate them *in absentia*, Dionysius must now have found other land for them, perhaps on confiscated Sicel territory. The mercenaries went off, 10,000 in number, to share out and colonize the town and its fertile lands; and their Lacedaemonian leader was sent back to Sparta to face trial – presumably for disobeying his government's instructions to support Dionysius loyally.[38]

Himilco's homecoming was a very different affair both from the triumphant return of Hannibal in 409 and from his own in 405, marred though the latter was by the plague which his army carried with it to Libya. The era of Magonid ascendancy at Carthage, which stretched back into the sixth century and which had added Sardinia, Libya and, for almost a decade, the greater part of Sicily to her empire, came to a close. Carthage's foreign policy was henceforth essentially unaggressive, concerned more to preserve what had been won – the commercial monopoly of most of the western Mediterranean and the overlordship of Libya and the North African seaboard, from the Syrtis to the Pillars of Hercules – than to extend her empire. It was probably in the wake of Himilco's inglorious return, perhaps after his death, that the Court of 104 Judges was instituted, to ensure the subordination of the individual to the state; had it existed in 395, Himilco would certainly have been arraigned before it. It was during the following half-century that the constitution (admired by Aristotle) with which we are (albeit very imperfectly) acquainted was established. The kingship disappeared and was replaced, as Head of State, by two annually elected *suffetes* (whom Greek writers, however, continued to call *basileis*, kings), and as head of the armed forces, by generals chosen by the Council and answerable for their actions to the Court of 104 Judges. The unfortunate Himilco mortified himself, in the Semitic manner, before gods and men, acknowledging his guilt in having desecrated the shrines of gods and in failing his ancestors (the Carthaginians maintained that Hamilcar had immolated himself to the Baals, before Himera) and his city. Eventually he starved himself to death.[39]

The disaster that had befallen Himilco's army – a disaster in which the Libyans (who were the first to succumb to the plague) had suffered particularly heavily – was quickly followed by the revolt of Carthage's Libyan subjects. Making common cause against the oppressor, they collected a large army which was swelled by runaway slaves and malcontents. They seized Tunis (this city regularly succumbed without much resistance to invaders and rebels) and drove the Carthaginians within the walls of their city, where the townspeople became a prey to superstitious fears. No doubt they offered the horrid sacrifice of their children to the Baals, and, attributing their misfortunes to Himilco's desecration of the shrine of Demeter and Korē, they introduced the cult of the goddesses into Carthage, appointing priests and attendants not only from their own aristocracy but also from among the leading Greek residents, whose position had, apparently, been unaffected by the events of the past three years: a significant indication of the different spirit in which Carthage and Syracuse had gone to war. There may, perhaps, be a connection between the establishment of this cult and the resemblance to Persephone borne by the head of the goddess Tanit on the coins struck at Carthage from about 340, when the mint there was reopened after an interval of some fifty years.

Having thus repaired their relationship with the gods, the Carthaginians set about making material preparations for restoring the military situation, building ships to replace those lost in Sicily and bringing in provisions from Sardinia. The Libyan rebels, for their part, lacked unity, effectual leadership and stores. Carthage was able to exploit their internal dissensions, and eventually the rebels dispersed to their villages and (probably by the end of 394) Carthage was able to reassert her shaken sovereignty over Libya.[40]

CHAPTER EIGHT

Dionysius' dealings with the Italiots and the Greeks of the Motherland

Dionysius had good reason to be grateful for the breathing space afforded him by the outbreak of the Libyan revolt. There was very little left of his *archē*; territorially, his power was reduced almost to what it had been in 405. But there were important differences between his position then and his position now. First, he had repaired his badly shaken prestige as a military leader; for, although he had failed to conquer the Epicraty, he had, with the help – as I am sure he reminded his countrymen – of the gods, inflicted on the Carthaginians a disaster almost of the magnitude of Himera. Secondly, the Sicilian Greeks owed the restoration of their freedom to him; Acragas, and therefore probably Gela and Camarina, were his allies, and the cities of the east coast and the Straits no longer presented a serious problem. Moreover, the Sicels (and Sicans) who had gone over to Carthage must have been disheartened by the completeness of Himilco's defeat. Thirdly, his regime, supported by a professional army and publicly approved by the leading military power in the Greek world, was securely established, and his leadership had restored his popularity with his countrymen.

His first task (after enlisting fresh mercenaries, to take the place of those discharged) was to begin the restoration of his empire in eastern Sicily. Himilco's destruction of Messana gave him the opportunity to achieve a long-standing ambition: to gain control of the Sicilian side of the Straits. He took the lead in restoring and fortifying Messana (and also perhaps enlarged its territory), bringing in 1,000 colonists from Locri, and 4,000 from Locri's colony Medma (if this latter figure is correct we must, I believe, assume either that a serious *stasis* had occurred in the city, or that Medma had been seized by Locri – presumably with Dionysius' approval – with the result, in either case that a large part of its citizenry had been driven into exile), He also brought in 600 Messenians, former allies of the Athenians, who had been serving in his army since their expulsion by the Spartans from Cephallenia and Naupactus, at the turn of the century. Dionysius spent what was left of the year 395 recovering control, by treaty (Agyrium, Centuripa, Herbita and Assorus) or by conquest (Menaenum and Morgantina), of the Sicel communities to the west and north-west of Syracuse. In the following year, 394, Herbessus (perhaps laid under siege the previous autumn) came to terms, and Henna was betrayed to him.

His settlement of Messenians, Sparta's inveterate enemies, at Messana, at a time when revolt against Sparta's hegemony in Greece was approaching boiling point, moved that city to protest; a protest which the dynast owed too much to Sparta and valued her friendship too highly to reject. He marched north, removed the Messenians from Messana where, perhaps now, he established a mercenary garrison in the citadel, seized a portion of the territory of Abacaenum to the west of Messana and planted the Messenians on the north coast. They named the new settlement Tyndaris (which was a name given to Helen, but which had also connections with the Dioscuri), and by admitting numerous immigrants rapidly increased their citizen body almost tenfold. Dionysius apparently received the submission of Cephaloedium and even of Solus, an ancient Phoenician colony on the borders of the Epicraty. It seems likely that he also renewed his former alliance with Thermae, and gained the friendship of Halaesa, which lay to the east of Solus. Perhaps it was about this time that the people of Solus took the first steps towards the removal of their city of a new site on the coast and towards increasing Hellenization.[1]

During these years, when Carthage was engaged in a struggle with her Libyan subjects, at first for survival and then for domination, and when Dionysius was re-establishing his empire in eastern Sicily, momentous events had been taking place in the East, which, because of his connection with Lacedaemon, were bound in the end to involve him, too. King Agesilaus of Sparta, sent out in 396 to take command in the war that had begun four years earlier to free the Greeks of Asia from Persian overlordship, had achieved some striking successes. But gold, discreetly administered to leading Greek statesmen, achieved for Persia what arms had failed to do; and an outbreak of hostilities between Thebes and the Phocians soon came to involve most of the chief cities of Central Greece in the so-called Corinthian War, whose purpose was to put an end to Sparta's high-handed domination; and which, by the summer of 394 had brought about the death of Lysander, the disgrace and exile of King Pausanias and the recall from Asia of Agesilaus.[2]

In 394, although the Lacedaemonians demonstrated in two major battles, near Corinth and at Coronea, that on land they were still unbeatable by the allied strengths of Argos, Thebes, Athens and Corinth (plus the allies of these), at sea their fleet was overwhelmed off Cnidus, in August, by the Persian navy under the satrap Pharnabazus and the Athenian Conon (the survivor of Aegospotami). The Spartan 'empire' in Asia collapsed, and her footing there was restricted to the

Hellespontine region. In the spring of 393, the victorious Persian navy crossed the Aegean, captured Cythera, and at Corinth its commanders discussed future policy with the synod of the Allies, and provided them with money. In the autumn, Conon visited Athens with 80 ships and supplied the money and labour for the rebuilding of the fortifications of Athens and the Piraeus. He resumed his citizenship and gave a vigorous lead to Athenian foreign policy; so that before long signs appeared that Athens' imperial aspirations were reawakening.[3]

Pharnabazus' subsidy enabled Corinth to man ships and gain control of the Corinthian Gulf; but it seems likely that after – or indeed even before – the disaster at Cnidus, Sparta had approached Dionysius with a request for naval assistance. Such a request would have put the tyrant in something of a quandary, for Sparta was embroiled with Corinth and Corinth was Syracuse's metropolis and had been generous in her assistance against both the Athenians and Carthage. We have no positive evidence that Sparta asked Dionysius for ships, but we do have the explicit statement of Lysias that, in the summer of 393, the dynast had got a squadron ready to assist the Lacedaemonians but then countermanded its despatch.[4]

The Lacedaemonians were not the only ones to approach Dionysius in 394. Conon, who had commanded Athenian fleets in the latter stages of the Peloponnesian War, appreciated the importance of Syracuse and the extent to which she could influence the course of the present struggle. Having spent the earlier part of his exile at the court of Evagoras, the phil-Athenian ruler of Salamis in Cyprus, he had no qualms about seeking the friendship of another military dynast; and there were others at Athens – where opinion was, in general, hostile towards Dionysius as a Syracusan, a friend of Sparta, and a subverter of democracy – who felt as Conon did. In the opening months of 393, the elderly dithyrambic poet Cinesias (abhorred by Aristophanes and Lysias, both of them staunch upholders of democratic liberty) proposed in the Council a laudatory decree in honour of Dionysius, his brothers and his brother-in-law Polyxenus. Cinesias' motion was in response to a report by one Androsthenes, who had, presumably, brought some conciliatory or flattering message from the tyrant. Perhaps the message had some connection with the festivals of Dionysus. Cinesias was a technical innovator in the dramatic field, and the stelē bearing the decree may have been set up near the theatre (where it was found).[5]

In the autumn of 393, Conon came to Athens, accompanied by Evagoras, who had assisted him and Pharnabazus to gain the command of the Aegean and who, consequently, was now accorded high honours by the Athenians. It was probably now that Conon sent two emissaries, Aristophanes, the son of a former colleague and fellow exile, and Eunomus, who was probably a Syracusan resident at Athens (metic) and

Dionysius' agent, at considerable expense to Syracuse, with the object of persuading the dynast to connect himself by marriage with Evagoras and to exchange his Lacedaemonian alliance for one with Athens. The emissaries failed to win over the tyrant, although they claimed the credit for his change of mind in the matter of the warships earmarked for Sparta. Quite apart, however, from Dionysius' unwillingness to engage in hostilities against Corinth, there were other and more cogent reasons why, in the late summer of 393, he would have wanted to keep all his available naval strength in Sicilian waters for the present.[6]

Dionysius' occupation of Messana in 395 had thoroughly alarmed the people of Rhegium. His enemies enjoyed considerable political influence there; and they had recently been joined by Heloris, to whom he had clearly given mortal affront. In 394, after Dionysius had withdrawn from the north-eastern corner of Sicily, the Rhegines established a colony, composed of the refugees from Naxos and Catane, at Mylae, almost midway between the new settlement of Tyndaris and Messana. Having thus, as they hoped, isolated Messana, they sent an army under Heloris (who enjoyed the reputation of a bold man of action) to attack the city. Heloris made a reckless assault upon the acropolis and was badly beaten. The victorious Messanians then marched on Mylae and expelled the new settlers, who were forced to disperse and find what homes they could.

Dionysius now decided to settle accounts with Rhegium, but first, in order to secure his communications with Syracuse, to make himself master of Tauromenium, which commanded the direct road from Syracuse to the Straits. He had probably made proposals earlier to the Tauromenians for an alliance which they had rejected. Late in the year he invested the hilltop city, and having a professional army at his disposal continued the siege past midwinter. But Tauromenium had for the Sicels something of the glamour of a legendary national centre; they may have received encouragement from the Carthaginians, and they held out grimly. On a moonless, stormy night, Dionysius led an assault up the snow-covered mountain against the naturally strongest and therefore most carelessly guarded sector of the acropolis. His attempt came close to success, but after fierce fighting he was repulsed with heavy loss, barely escaping with his life. Thereupon (although we are not told so by Diodorus), Dionysius probably raised the siege and returned to Syracuse. When the news of his discomfiture got about – no doubt exaggerated in the telling – the patriotic elements at Acragas and Messana (probably the 'old' citizens, in the latter case) got the upper hand, expelled his supporters and withdrew their cities from his alliance.[7]

Dionysius' timetable for the subjugation of Rhegium was further thrown out by the reappearance on the Sicilian scene of the Carthaginians – with whom, of course, a state of war still existed. Mago – presumably the admiral of 396 – was acting as military governor of the Epicraty and had been busy, with the forces at his disposal, consolidating his city's suzerainty over western Sicily; pursuing a policy of kindness towards the subject communities and forming alliances with other non-Greek peoples (including, probably, Tauromenium), to whom he would present himself as a protector against the threat of Syracusan domination. He may even have had something to do with the 'revolt' of Carthage's old best customer, Acragas. Dionysius' operations on the north coast and the defection of Solus must have alarmed Mago greatly; but the resistance offered to the dynast by Tauromenium, and the defeat of Dionysius and the subsequent 'revolts' of Acragas and Messana will have restored his confidence. Accordingly, in the summer of 393 he collected what forces he could and marched to the north-east corner of the island, where he could expect to find allies in Tauromenium and Abacaenum – the latter aggrieved by the seizure of part of her territory to accommodate the Messenian settlement. He ravaged the territory of Messana, no doubt hoping that, having offended Dionysius, the city might be coerced into joining Carthage. Messana, however, defied him, and so he withdrew westwards.[8]

Dionysius had been making his preparations for the attack on Rhegium (he may also have had to deal with unrest among his Sicel subjects, not recorded by Diodorus). Now he hurried north and confronted Mago in the neighbourhood of Abacaenum, where the Carthaginian had gone into camp. In the ensuing battle Mago was driven off the field with the loss of 800 men; and, as Dionysius did not follow up his victory, he retreated into the Epicraty.[9] If Dionysius had been contemplating a large-scale campaign against Rhegium, he would now have realized that the season was too far advanced to embark upon it this year. Moreover, he would not want to be tied down in Italy in 392, if Mago was likely to be back in eastern Sicily, perhaps with a larger army. On the other hand, his naval preparations were complete (had he, perhaps, in order to mislead the Rhegines, given out that the ships fitting out in the arsenal were intended for Sparta; and had he used the same story to improve the credit with their own people of his Athenian friends?). Anyhow, rather than waste the effort already made, he decided to try the effect of a surprise raid on Rhegium with a strong naval force.

Accordingly, only a few days after his return from Abacaenum, he headed for Rhegium with 100 warships, probably manned wholly or in part with fighting-men. Knowing that, with such a force, his only hope of success lay in exploiting to the full the element of surprise, he timed his arrival so as to attack the city under cover of darkness, setting fire to the gates and scaling the walls with ladders. Only the presence of mind of Heloris saved the city. Far from encouraging the handful of burghers who rushed piecemeal to the defence to fight the flames, Heloris bade them build fires in the path of their assailants and prevent them from advancing, until the bulk of their infantry could assemble and present an organized defence. Dionysius had not come with the intention of conducting a siege, and so, after ravaging the countryside, he concluded a year's truce (which would preclude the Rhegines from making a pact with Mago) and returned home.[10]

When Mago struck at Messana in 393, it is probable that his object was to secure an advanced base for the renewed offensive against Syracuse that his city was intending to launch in the following summer. During the winter and spring of 393/2, the Carthaginians collected a large army (80,000 strong according to Diodorus, who does not give his source), transported it to Sicily and put it under Mago's command. It was composed of Libyans, Sardinians and 'barbarians from Italy' – perhaps Ligurians – and was accompanied by only a few ships. This has rather the look of an 'economy' expedition, and reflects the shortage of silver at Carthage as a result of the Libyan revolt and the heavy losses of money and saleable goods in Sicily in 395. Mago marched through the interior of the island, winning over the native communities, as far as the upper Chrysas valley, to the west of Mount Etna; establishing his camp to the south of Agyrium, near the road that led to Morgantina. He was nervous of proceeding any further because Agyris, lord of Agyrium, the second most powerful dynast in Sicily, refused to desert his alliance with Dionysius, and Mago dared not push on either towards Syracuse or towards Messana, leaving so dangerous a potential foe in his rear. He therefore decided to wait for the Greeks (who, he was informed, were moving up from Syracuse to meet him) on ground of his own choosing, from which he could at the same time keep an eye on Agyris.[11]

As soon as Dionysius learnt that Mago was on the march, he called out the Syracusan levy-in-mass, and at the head of an army of some 20,000 men advanced to within a short distance of the enemy, going forward himself with a small body of men to Agyrium, to sound the ruler about his intentions; for although Agyris had rejected Mago's overtures, he had not as yet committed himself to assisting Dionysius. However, he now allowed himself to be persuaded by Dionysius' promise of a substantial augmentation of his dominion. He provisioned his ally, mobilized his own subjects and joined Dionysius in a campaign of ambush and harassment of the much larger Punic army that was calculated to force Mago to abandon his position because of a shortage of supplies, without resort to heavy fighting with its attendant risk of defeat.

Unfortunately, however, the Syracusan citizens wearied of a form of warfare to which the equipment, training and mentality of the hoplite were alike unsuited. Encouraged by their minor successes and by the passivity of the enemy to believe that they had the beating of him, they demanded that the issue be decided in the traditional Greek manner, by a pitched battle. Dionysius, with his habitual caution, refused to throw in what he regarded – probably rightly – as a winning hand: whereupon the Syracusans abandoned him and marched home. But it is significant that although they were marshalled under arms, and although the tyrant cannot have left very many soldiers behind to guard the cross-wall of Ortygia, the citizens made no attempt to shut him out of the city or to overthrow his rule, as they had done in 404. Their action was a practical protest against what they regarded as their leader's pusillanimity rather than against the regime itself. It is, however, most unlikely that they would have behaved in this independent manner if Syracuse had not been so heavily fortified or if the Carthaginian navy had been supporting Mago.

Deserted by perhaps half his army, Dionysius had no alternative but to fall back on his own city. Since the possibility of Mago's laying siege to Syracuse could not be ruled out, in which case the defenders would become dependent upon the fleet to ensure their food supply, Dionysius issued a proclamation freeing the slaves. Mago, however, had had the worst of the exchanges with Dionysius; the morale of his army – largely composed as it was of Libyan conscripts – was probably not high: and he had no fleet. It looks as if he too withdrew, into the Epicraty. An embassy from Carthage arrived at Syracuse, and when terms of peace had been agreed upon, the decree liberating the slaves was rescinded.[12]

Of the terms, Diodorus says simply that 'the articles were more or less the same (*paraplēsiai*) as those agreed upon earlier [i.e. in 405]; except that the Sicels should be subject to Dionysius and he should receive Tauromenium'. I believe that we must accept Diodorus' statement at its face value, and see in the treaty a recognition of the reality of the position. Carthage had demonstrated that Dionysius could not over-throw her rule in the west; and Dionysius had shown that, since Syracuse was impregnable, he could only be prevented from asserting, and reasserting, his power in the east by means which were economically unacceptable to Carthage: by the yearly despatch, or year-round mainte-nance, of vast military forces. So the treaty recognized Dionysius' *archē* (*his* epicraty!) – which the earlier treaty had not – but maintained the status quo in central Sicily; which, again, reflected the military situation, since Dionysius had been driven back into his own corner of the island. The Greek cities, therefore, while enjoying the autonomous manage-ment of their domestic affairs, remained tributary to Carthage, and of course Solus reverted to its old allegiance. So far from being confined to the Epicraty (comprising between a quarter and a fifth of Sicily), as Stroheker believes, Carthage still dominated well over half the island, and it was Dionysius' dominion that was restricted, to the eastern portion.[13]

Although from the Greek point of view the position in Sicily was very much less satisfactory than it had been in 409, there was one important compensation: Carthage had tried to conquer Sicily, *and failed*. The great days of her military expansionism under the Magonids were over; left to herself, it was unlikely that she would attack the Greeks again, and, from a purely book-keeping standpoint, the tribute was probably a small price to pay for peace, security and the resumption of a lucrative trade. There was not, after all, very much to choose between 'enslavement' by Carthage and its probable alternative, 'enslavement' by Dionysius. However, only Syracuse had escaped capture and sack, and none of the other cities ever fully recovered its former glory. Three had ceased to exist: Leontini, Catane and Naxos, although Adranum and Tyndaris had been founded and Tauromenium was, I believe, soon to become a Greek city. Moreover the Hellenization of the Sicels was greatly expedited by their close relationship, as allies or subjects, with one of the wealthiest and most advanced cities in the Greek world. All in all, it can probably be said that Hellenism in Sicily was in better shape than it had been for a decade, and the prospects were good for continuing stability and for full cultural and economic recovery.

If Diodorus' statement is true (and it probably is) that most of the Sicels – that is to say, the Sicels living in the region where Mago had been operating – had revolted, then Dionysius must have spent 391 and the earlier part of 390 restoring the overlordship that the treaty formally recognized. Abandoned by the Carthaginians, the Sicels of Tauromenium appear to have offered no further resistance and departed from their city, which the dynast re-peopled with 'the most reliable (*epitēdeiotatoi*) of his mercenaries; by which I take Diodorus to imply that they were Greeks. It seems clear, too, that Messana returned to her allegiance to Dionysius; perhaps as the result of a *stasis* fomented by his agents, which led to the ruling faction's opening the gates to the tyrant in order to preserve their own lives and property.[14]

By the end of the summer of 390, then, Dionysius had restored his *archē*; but for reasons historical, political, strategic and economic the logical frontier of his dominion in the north-east was not the western shore of the Straits but a line somewhat further north, drawn across the 'toe' of Italy, so as to give him a secure hold on both shores and thus effective command of this important waterway. Rhegium, indeed, like her neighbour Locri, whose territory comprised a narrow and not over-fertile plain confined between the mountains and the sea, should be regarded from the historical point of view as an extension of Sicily (the Straits at their narrowest are only about a mile and a half wide) rather than as a part of Italy. For a time, in the first half of the fifth century, Rhegium had been Messana's overlord; but her ruler's attempts to command the Straits had brought both cities into conflict with Syracuse, which therefore supported Locri against her. The mutual hostility of the two cities, separated by the river Hales, continued to be reflected in their respective relations with Syracuse. Locri remained a good friend to Syracuse and was well disposed towards Dionysius, whereas Rhegium, which had stayed neutral in the war between Syracuse and Athens, was consistently hostile to him, and had until recently been the asylum of the Syracusan and other exiles, before their removal to Croton, where they hoped to exert an influence upon a much larger body of Italiot opinion.[15]

For political reasons, therefore, Dionysius was eager to get control of Rhegium, so as to put an end to what was a standing threat to the security of his dominion; nor is he likely to have forgotten the many affronts offered him by the Rhegines. Possession of Rhegium would give him command of the Straits and make it that much the more difficult for Carthage to mount a major combined operation against him, and at the same time would make it easier for him to protect the movement of reinforcements from the Peloponnese. From the economic angle, as master of the Straits he would be the more able to prevent interference with Syracuse's trade with Italy and the Adriatic and with her import of essential raw materials. An excuse for settling, once and for all, his account with the Rhegines was supplied by the worsening relations – perhaps the actual outbreak of war – between Rhegium and Locri, which summoned its ally, Dionysius, to its aid. However, it was not only Rhegium that he now had to deal with, for an attack on Rhegium was likely to bring him into conflict with the formidable Italiot League.[16]

This confederacy, whose constitution was based on that of the early Achaean League and included a delegate council (*sunedrion*) to co-ordinate policy and strategy, probably had its beginnings in an alliance, formed in the late fifth century, between Croton, New Sybaris and Caulonia. This had subsequently been joined – perhaps (as Diodorus suggests) as recently as 392 – by other cities which felt their safety threatened, on the one hand by the inexorable advance of the Luca-nians, and on the other by the growth of Dionysius' power and his interest in south Italy, as manifested by his attack on Rhegium in 393. The Lucanians were Sabelli, whose ancestors had come from the high-lands of central Italy (Strabo calls them Samnites, and they were certainly of the same warlike stock). Since about 420 they had been overrunning the south-west of the peninsula and – bypassing Elea – had recently captured the old Sybarite colony of Laös, only about 30 miles west of Thurii. The cities of the confederacy had covenanted to support any member attacked by the Lucanians; and, probably in 392, the same obligation had been extended to cover equally a threat from the direction of Syracuse. Certainly the suspicion and hostility of the confederacy towards Dionysius was stimulated by the lobbying of the exiles now residing at Croton, the *hegemon* of the League.[17]

Very late in the season of 390, Dionysius transported to Locrian territory a formidable expeditionary force: 20,000 foot and 1,000 horse, accompanied by 120 warships. If we are to believe Diodorus, and if we are to take his words 'through the interior' (*dia tēs mesogeiou*) at their usual meaning, we have to assume that Dionysius marched his army from the borders of Locri by mountain paths across the peninsula and descended upon that part of the coastal plain of Rhegium that looks towards the Tyrrhenian Sea, ravaging and burning. The fleet sailed round the southern tip of the land and rejoined the army on the Straits, presumably to the north of the city, opposite Messana. It is astonishing that Dionysius should once again have mounted an expedition (a larger one than that with which the Athenians had assailed Syracuse in 415) so late in the year. He must have hoped that such an impressive show of force would frighten the Rhegines into submission before the other Italiots could collect their forces to oppose him. It is very likely that he was misled by over-sanguine reports of Rhegium's irresolution, emanating from Locri and from supporters of his cause in Rhegium itself.

The intrusion of the lord of Sicily into their world alarmed the Italiots for their liberty. Already predisposed against him by the hostile propaganda emanating from Rhegium and now from Croton (and perhaps also from Athens, the cultural capital of Hellas), the Italiots saw in Dionysius a threat to the freedom of Magna Graecia no less serious than that posed by the Lucanians. The terms of the alliance required them to come to the assistance of a member state; but with Locri in the enemy's camp they could not send an army by land, even had they been able to put one together so late in the year. However, a fleet of 60 ships was collected at Croton and despatched to Rhegium to reinforce her navy. As the Rhegines could man 20 ships of their own, this force would bring the strength of the combined fleet up to 80. Dionysius intercepted it, probably off Cape Leucopetra (south of Rhegium), with 50 ships, including his quinqueremes. The Italiots fled to the shore, not far from the city, and a brisk fight followed; the Syracusans endeavouring to secure and tow away the grounded vessels, the Italiots, aided by the levy-in-mass of Rhegium, resisting. Not for the last time, the weather came to the aid of Dionysius' enemies. A gale arose which forced the Sicilians to break off the engagement, enabled their opponents to haul ashore the threatened galleys and wrecked 7 of Dionysius' ships, many of the survivors falling into the hands of the Rhegines. It was midnight before Dionysius' flagship (the *Boubaris?*) struggled into the port of Messana. Dionysius was not the man to disregard so practical a warning; the gales marked the end of the sailing (and campaigning) season, and so he withdrew his forces from Italy.[18]

Before leaving Messana, he made an alliance with the Lucanians. He has been much criticized by historians for thus allying himself with the enemies of Western Hellenism; but it should be borne in mind that he was doing no more than many Greek states had done in the past and were to do in the future. Leaving aside the *medism* of many communities during the Persian Wars and the invitation to interfere in Sicilian affairs offered to Carthage by the tyrants of Himera and Rhegium in the early fifth century, we may instance the sending of a mission to enlist the support of Persia by the Peloponnesians, in the first year of the Great War; Sparta's employment of Epirotes against the Acarnanians in 429; the more recent attempt on the part of Athens to secure the support of Carthage against Syracuse; the pacts between Sparta and the Persians during the last decade of the Peloponnesian War; the co-operation between Athens and Persia after the battle of Cnidus and the proposal, carried by Antialcidas to the satrap of Sardes in 392, that a peace should be negotiated which would give the Great King a free hand in Asia – a wholesale betrayal of Hellenism by Sparta which was soon to become an accomplished fact. In Dionysius' eyes the Italiot League was the aggressor, in that it had intervened in his quarrel with Rhegium; and I doubt if any Greek State, in Dionysius' position, would have shrunk from utilizing barbarians against its enemies, on grounds of sentiment. There can be no doubt (in the light of what actually happened) that the dynast and his new allies agreed upon a joint campaign against the League, designed to inflict as much damage as possible upon its military strength and to involve it in a protracted struggle with the barbarians, at a (from Dionysius' point of view) satisfactory distance from the Straits.[19]

In the spring of 389, Dionysius sent Leptines with the fleet into northern waters (based himself, presumably, at Messana), with instructions to co-operate with the Lucanians against the powerful city of Thurii (founded by Pericles), an important member of the League. The Lucanians sent a marauding force into Thurian territory; and the Greeks reacted, first, by calling on their allies for assistance in accordance with the terms of the League, and, secondly, by mobilizing their own forces and marching against the invaders, who withdrew on their approach. The Thurians, over 14,000 infantry strong, with about 1,000 horse, followed up the retreat of the enemy (as, quite clearly, they had been expected to do), without waiting for their allies, and captured a well-stocked Lucanian border stronghold. Then, forgetting the advice given to their grandsires by the Spartan Cleandridas, that 'where the lion skin is no protection', they should 'stitch it onto a fox's', they advanced over-confidently, and without taking adequate precautions, across the mountains to attack the prosperous coastal city of Laös. This place, a former colony of Sybaris, had fallen into the hands of the Lucanians not long before.

When the Thurians descended into the coastal plain, at a place enclosed on three sides by hills, some of them precipitous, the whole might of the Lucanian tribal confederation, amounting to 30,000 foot and 4,000 horse, appeared in their rear. The ensuing battle ended in one of the worst massacres ever suffered by a Greek army, for the barbarians (who had an ancient grudge to settle with the Thurians) took no prisoners, and over 10,000 Greeks were slain. Some 4,000 escaped to a hilltop, and more then 1,000 plunged into the sea and swam out to Leptines' ships, which were heading towards the beach and which they took to be friendly Rhegine vessels. Leptines' fleet was obviously intended to close the fourth – the seaward – side of the trap; but (in the light both of his own conduct and that of his brother, later in the year) it seems to me reasonable to suppose that he had instructions to save as many Greek lives as he could, by offering the Thurians the opportunity of surrendering to him. He took the swimmers on board and negotiated their ransom with the Lucanians, standing surety, himself, for the one *mina* per head demanded. Nothing is said about the men who had taken refuge on the hill; presumably they were granted a truce.

Leptines now went far beyond his brother's instructions. He had already in his career displayed a propensity to insubordination, for displaying his independence and individuality, that, in a subordinate, amounted to irresponsibility. The truth of the matter probably is that he was not committed, heart and soul, to the cause of his brother's military glory. Shocked, perhaps, by the scene of carnage upon which he disembarked, and disgusted at the part his brother (and himself) had played in the slaughter of fellow Greeks by barbarians, and also, in all likelihood, influenced by personal vanity and the gratification of being hailed as their benefactor by the Italiots, he negotiated a peace settlement between the Lucanians and the Italiot League (which presumably had sent commissioners to the Laös region). This piece of diplomacy seriously embarrassed his brother's Italian policy, for it left the cities of the League at liberty to combine against him when he renewed his attack on Rhegium. Dionysius, not unnaturally, was furious. He relieved Leptines of his command and replaced him by a younger brother, Thearides. Subsequently Leptines was temporarily exiled from Syracuse, and his disgrace involved also the (future) historian, Philistus.[20]

It is better, I believe, to accept Diodorus' chronology of Dionysius' Italian campaign, and place his second invasion of the peninsula in the summer of 389, than to follow Stroheker and others and assign it to the next year. Although the cities of the League were not embroiled with the Lucanians (as Dionysius had hoped they would be), one of their strongest members had been knocked out, and policy would have suggested that such a serious blow should be followed up at once, not that the enemy should be given a whole year in which to recover. In the late summer, then, of 389, Dionysius sailed from Syracuse to Messana with a force of over 20,000 infantry, 3,000 cavalry, 40 warships and 300 transports. These 40 warships must have been a reinforcement for Leptines' former command, which consisted, I believe, of 30 ships (the fivers?) and was still lying at Messana under the command, now, of Thearides. Rhegium possessed no less than 80 ships, and Dionysius had no reason to assume that that many of the enemy could be contained by only 40 of his own ships. Indeed, to deal with only 10 Rhegine vessels stationed in the Lipari Islands (perhaps they had been intended to co-operate with the Thurians against Laös), he despatched 30 galleys (again, the fivers?) under Thearides, who captured them, crews and all, and brought them back to Messana. Dionysius' fleet, then, assembled at Messana, probably amounted to 70 galleys, and he was able to transport his army to Caulonia, some 25 miles north of Locri, without interference from the Rhegines. Siege operations were at once begun against Caulonia.[21]

Dionysius did not, as Diodorus (or rather, Diodorus' sources) would have us believe, aspire after the conquest of the whole of Magna Graecia. What he wanted was a defensible frontier to the north of Locri, which would secure his control of the Straits. North of Locri stood Caulonia, and beyond Caulonia was Scylletium, a dependency of Croton, the largest and most powerful city of the League. But between Scylletium and Croton lay some 40 miles of wooded, hilly country – a three to four days' march for an army of foot soldiers. It was here, on a line running across the peninsula from the northern border of Scylletium to the Tyrrhenian Sea, where the 'toe' is at its narrowest, that Dionysius determined to establish the northern frontier of his empire.

On receiving positive information that Dionysius was again invading Italy, the forces of the Italiot League mustered at Croton, to the number of 25,000 infantry and 2,000 cavalry. How many cities' contingents were represented in this total we do not know. It is unlikely to have included that of Taras; she was too remote to feel herself threatened by Dionysius, and jealousy of Croton, too, may have contributed to keep her neutral. Moreover (as Stroheker has pointed out) she would not have been likely to go to war against an ally of her metropolis, Sparta. Thurii may have sent a contingent, but Dionysius' statecraft had ensured that it was only a fraction of what it might have been. The command of this large army was entrusted to the Syracusan exile, Heloris. It was felt, says Diodorus, that his qualities of courage and enterprise, as well as his bitter hatred of the tyrant, would guarantee that the campaign would be fought to a decision.

When Heloris was ready, he set out for Caulonia to raise the siege, marching down the narrow coastal plain along the line of today's coast road and railway. His left flank was not protected by a fleet, perhaps, because the League had ceded the bulk of its ships to Rhegium. Heloris does indeed appear to have been the very model of a dashing cavalryman, for he rode not with the main body of his army but with the advance guard. This comprised the flower of his army and (on the basis of Diodorus' use of the word 'friends') was, I believe, wholly or in large part composed of the exiled Syracusan knights. At the close of perhaps the fifth day, he had reached the river Eleporus (today, the Galliparo), about 12½ miles north of Caulonia. In his dispositions for the night, Heloris revealed his ineptitude as a general. He remained with the advance guard, bivouacked in the vicinity of what is today the village of Marina di Badolato: a good mile ahead of the main body. Between himself and the main body lay a low but steep-sided hill which effectively cut him off from sight and sound of his army, his only means of communication with which was by runner. It is clear that he had concerted no plan of action for the following day with the leaders of the main body, although he could expect to encounter the enemy then. He sent forward no patrols to see where Dionysius was (obviously assuming that he would be awaiting the arrival of the Italiots in the vicinity of Caulonia), and he posted no pickets to give warning of the approach of an enemy.[22]

Dionysius had learnt a great deal about the trade of war since his fiasco at Gela. In particular, he had become aware of the importance of reconnaissance and intelligence. He was accurately informed about Heloris' movements, and as the Italiots approached the Eleporus he moved his army out from its lines. There is no mention of the fleet in our account of these events; but it seems to me a reasonable conjecture that he left it at Caulonia to maintain the siege, employing the crewmen as light infantry. He advanced about eight miles and then went into camp for the night, sending his scouts forward to reconnoitre Heloris' position. From them he learnt that the enemy's advance guard was camped a short distance south of the river, where the main body lay. Dionysius had his army on the move before daybreak, and at first light fell upon Heloris' camp. Although taken completely by surprise, Heloris and the men of the advance guard put up a gallant fight, hoping that the bulk of their army (which had been summoned to their aid by runners) would arrive in time to save them; but they were surrounded and nearly all of them, including Heloris himself, were slain. The main body of the Italiots arrived piecemeal; they had probably had no breakfast; their front was dispersed by the hill that lay across their path; no one seems to have been in overall command and they were blown by their run – much of it across rising ground. They encountered a well-led, disciplined, professional army drawn up for battle on the small plain just to the north of Marina di Badolato. The Italiots strove to form a coherent phalanx under the very spears of the enemy, but after a brave resistance and after suffering heavy losses, they broke and fled, over 10,000 taking refuge on the hill behind them.

This hill, although defensible, was waterless, and small enough too for the victors to be able to surround and beleaguer it. By the following morning, hungry and thirsty – with a river (largely dried up, no doubt,

THE BATTLE OF THE ELEPORUS

Based on Sheet 247 of British War Office map of South Italy, pub. 1943

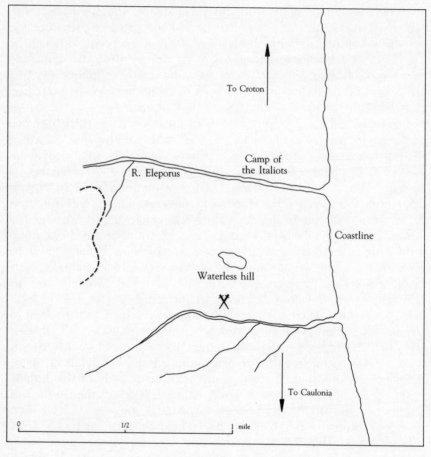

To Croton

Camp of
the Italiots

R. Eleporus

Coastline

Waterless hill

To Caulonia

0   1/2   1 mile

138

10   Caulonia: temple of Athena

but still carrying a trickle of water) only a few hundred yards away, and with the prospect of another waterless summer's day before them – the Italiots had lost heart and sent a herald to offer a ransom for their release. Dionysius' answer, not surprisingly, was, Surrender unconditionally. By the mid-afternoon the Italiots could hold out no longer and they gave themselves up, fearing the worst; for even in wars between cities, the enslavement of the rank and file and the summary execution of the leaders were not uncommonly the consequence of surrender at discretion. Dionysius, however, astonished his enemies by setting his prisoners free and concluding peace; not with the League but with those of its constitutent cities that he had not earmarked for incorporation in his empire. The Italiots, who may have lost some 15,000 men (and perhaps many more) in this one year, were in no condition to offer further resistance to Dionysius for the present. Indeed, their feelings at the moment were those of relief and gratitude, and they honoured the dynast publicly with golden crowns. But the prestige of Croton had been badly shaken and her hegemony of the League (which later passed to Taras) was correspondingly weakened. It was to be something like seven years before the League felt strong enough to give Dionysius any more trouble.[23]

Dionysius, who possessed that quality of 'celerity' that distinguishes the great commander, was determined to exploit to the full the psychological advantage conferred on him by the overthrow of the League, and moving

139

11 The Eleporus: site of the battle from the 'waterless hill'.

his forces south, he prepared to lay siege to Rhegium, which was now militarily and politically isolated and with its citizens' morale at a low ebb. The Rhegines were encouraged by Dionysius' generosity towards the Italiots to hope that his apparent implacability towards themselves might be appeased. Accordingly they sent an embassy to ask him to treat them with humanity. Dionysius agreed to leave them in peace, in return for a payment of 300 talents (he had sacrificed about 170 talents by setting the Italiots free without ransom), the surrender of their 70 remaining ships and the delivery into his hands of 100 hostages. When this demand had been complied with – no formal treaty appears to have been signed – Dionysius marched his army back to Caulonia. Although one Aristides of Elea had slipped through the Syracusan navy by a ruse and had brought 12 ships into the beleaguered city, the citizens could expect no further help from any quarter, and capitulated at once. Dionysius razed the city and ceded its territory to Locri; but in consideration of the Caulonians, having enabled him to complete this campaign before the onset of

140

winter, he spared the citizens and shipped them to Syracuse, where they were enfranchised and granted exemption (either from taxation or from military service) for five years, while they established themselves: a concession which suggests that the middle class, at least, was provided with lands. It seems to me very likely that they (along with the inhabitants of Hipponium) were enrolled among the colonists whom Dionysius established on the shores of the Adriatic in the following years.[24]

It looks as if Dionysius wintered in Italy, perhaps at Caulonia before destroying it, and it may have been at some time before the opening of the next summer's campaign that he incorporated the little city of Scylletium, some 25 miles north of Caulonia, in his empire: probably by agreement, since we do not hear of any military operations against her. Then, in the early summer of 388, Dionysius marched across the peninsula to Hipponium, which he treated as he had treated Caulonia. The territory of Locri, which was intended to serve as an autonomous

12 The Eleporus: waterless hill, from the river

(but subservient) buffer state between the Italiots and the Lucanians on
the one hand and Dionysius' possessions on the other, now stretched
right across the 'toe'. Medma, some 20 miles south of Hipponium, if it
still enjoyed an independent existence, was already an ally. Thus
Rhegium was completely cut off from the rest of Italy.

From Hipponium Dionysius marched down to the Straits and requested the Rhegines to supply him with provisions; promising to repay
the loans in kind when he returned to Syracuse. It is unlikely that the
account of these events given by Diodorus' principal source, Ephorus,
would have been anything other than sympathetic towards the people of
Rhegium. Dionysius' conduct is presented as wholly Machiavellian (was
he not, after all, the man who wrote the famous line, 'We cheat children
with knucklebones, men with oaths'?); indeed, it anticipated by almost
two and a half centuries the Romans' treatment of Carthage at the
commencement of the War of 149 to 146. Dionysius (we are told) had
been determined from the outset upon the destruction of Rhegium; he
had already stripped her of her ships and monetary resources, in order to
facilitate her defeat; and now he was only looking for a specious pretext
to go back on his hollow promises of the previous summer. He deliberately prolonged his stay in her territory, offering excuses (including
sickness) that were entirely insincere; intending to exhaust the Rhegines'
store of food and thus to drive them into a refusal to supply him further

13 Rhegium: silver tetradrachm, 400–390: (above) head of Apollo; (below) lion mask

which could be construed as an unfriendly act. As we do not have Philistus' account, we do not know Dionysius' side of the story; but it may well be that Diodorus' narrative is near enough to the truth. Dionysius would have been unlikely to hold himself bound by any consideration of fair play where the Rhegines were concerned; and Rhegium had not formally submitted to him the year before.[25]

143

Yet it seems to me probable that Dionysius, like the Roman Senate in its last, equally Machiavellian treatment of Carthage, believed that he had discovered a *humane*, because un-bloody, solution of the problem of reducing to submission a strong city whose reduction by force would entail great cost in lives and money and could end only in the death or enslavement of the whole population. Dionysius probably congratulated himself that he had spared the Rhegines the horrors of siege, sack and servitude by rendering it impossible for them to contemplate resistance. He himself knew when to cut his losses and he would have credited the Rhegines with an equally realistic attitude. What he would have done with them if they had capitulated without fighting is hard to say. They were probably too numerous and had been for too long his enemies to be incorporated (like other Italiot communities) in the Syracusan citizen body. Perhaps he would have been satisfied with the surrender of their arms, the destruction of their walls and their acceptance of a strong garrison; perhaps he would simply have expelled them, to find whatever homes they could. It seems to me reasonable to suppose that, with the Olympic Festival, to which he intended to send a splendid embassy, imminent, he would have been anxious to appear in as good a light as possible in the eyes of the Greek world.

However, the Rhegines allowed themselves to be persuaded by Phyton, one of their leading men, to reject whatever final demand Dionysius made upon them, and the dynast, after very correctly handing back the hostages that he had taken, laid siege to the city; constructing huge war machines and, at the outset, in the hope of taking the place by storm, launching daily assaults upon the walls. Knowing that they could now expect no mercy, the Rhegines, under Phyton's leadership, mobilized their resources and resisted heroically. They made several sallies to burn the siege engines, caused the besiegers heavy casualties (and suffered heavy casualties themselves), and even succeeded in inflicting a dangerous wound on Dionysius himself.[26] In the summer of 388, the 98th Olympic Festival was celebrated, and Thearides (Leptines was still in disgrace) was entrusted with the conduct to Olympia of a magnificent *theoria*, sent in Dionysius' name. Patronage of Delphi and Olympia had always been a feature of Greek tyranny, and Hieron had won great renown for his Olympic victories, in the previous century. Dionysius' four-horse chariots and pavilions with purple hangings and cloth-of-gold displayed the wealth (and therefore hinted at the power) of the lord of Sicily; the sacred envoys (*theoroi*), deputed to offer sacrifice in his name, advertised his piety towards the gods; and the rhapsodes had the task of displaying the tyrant in the light of a cultured, erudite, essentially civilized man. The whole display (making allowance both for a little natural vanity on the dynast's part and even, perhaps, for a little piety) was a lavish exercise in propaganda.

Diodorus, drawing as ever on the tradition hostile to the dynast, fairly revels in the details of the total failure of Dionysius' pretentious mission. The tyrant's bad verses were derided by the public, his pavilion was attacked, his chariots collided and ran off the course and the offended critical sensibility of the very gods requited itself upon the hapless *theoroi* on their return voyage by wrecking them in the Gulf of Tarentum. The orator Lysias, the son of a Syracusan merchant who had settled at Athens and a passionate champion of democracy, inveighed against the tyrant in his Olympic oration; coupling him with the Great King as an enemy of Greek liberty, calling upon his listeners to ban the tyrant's *theoria* and even to tear down his pavilion, and urging the Greeks to depose him and liberate Sicily. What the whole truth of the matter is, we shall never know. No doubt Dionysius' chariots were unsuccessful, no doubt the rhetoric of Lysias fomented the ill will of a public to which the very word 'tyrant' was anathema; and no doubt the story of Dionysius' discomfiture lost nothing in the telling. But there is no escaping the fact that Dionysius displayed that complete insensitivity to the feelings of others which was a feature of his character, in trying to capture the imagination and favour of the Greek world by making a lavish display of his wealth at a Panhellenic festival, thronged with visitors from Magna Graecia and Athens, only a year after he had allied himself with barbarians in order to overthrow the Italiot League, and had followed this up by destroying two Greek cities and besieging a third, for the purpose of destroying that also. And this, too, at a moment when the King of Persia was preparing to subjugate the cities of Asia and crush Evagoras, the friend and ally of the Athenians.[27]

As the campaigning season in southern Italy drew to a close, Dionysius, finding that he could not force his way into Rhegium, fell back on blockade and waited for starvation to do his work. The siege was maintained through the winter and well into the following summer; by which time the inhabitants, having eaten their oxen and horses, and being denied by the enemy access even to the grazing that had sustained their beasts, were dying like flies, and the survivors were too weak to offer further resistance. And so, after a siege lasting almost eleven months, they surrendered unconditionally. The survivors, according to Diodorus, numbered something over 6,000, a figure which seems very small, even allowing for losses in battle and the more serious loss of life as a result of famine, for a large and populous city which, only twelve years earlier, had been able to send out an expeditionary force of 6,600 men and 50 ships. It may well be that women, children and slaves were not included in the total; and I would expect that a considerable number of the inhabitants made their escape during the winter, when the vigilance of the besiegers would have been likely to relax.

Phyton was unwise enough to allow himself and his family to fall into the victor's hands. Dionysius regarded him as the man responsible for everything that the siege had cost him, in his own blood and that of his men, in the execration of his name by the Greeks and in treasure, and he punished him accordingly. Phyton passed into legend as a patriot and a victim of the cruelty that is found in tyrants; and his torments, the constancy with which he bore them, and the horror and revulsion with which they were beheld, even by the tyrant's soldiers, are described with gusto by Diodorus, following no doubt the Italiot, Ephorus. Of course the execution by the victors of a general (indeed, of a whole army or a whole population) who had caused them a great deal of trouble and expense was by no means un-Greek. The Syracusan Demos had killed the Athenian commanders after the Great Siege; Lysander executed the Athenian generals and other prisoners that he took after Aegospotami; and the Spartans and the Athenians put to death, respectively, the populations of Plataea and Melos. But, according to Diodorus, the victor himself recognized that his treatment of Phyton was exceptional (*parēllagmenōs*). The unfortunate man was displayed before the walls, lashed to one of the tallest siege-towers and then flogged through the city while a herald proclaimed that he was being punished for having persuaded the city to choose the war; the plea put into his mouth by the historian, that he was being punished for refusing to betray the city to Dionysius being, after all, an admission of the same offence from a different standpoint. Phyton was finally drowned, as was his whole family. The survivors of the siege were shipped to Syracuse, and there those who could find someone to pay a *mina* for their ransom were set free, the remainder being sold as slaves.[28]

Dionysius razed the empty city (sparing, presumably, its temples, and probably other buildings as well. He did not turn its territory over to the Locrians; but kept it in his own hands, subsequently building a palace there and laying out extensive gardens. The whole of what had originally been known as Italia, the land of calves (*Fitulos, italos vitulus*), that is to say, the 'toe' of Italy south of a line from Scylletium to Lametus, comprising an area of some 2,000 square miles, was now directly or indirectly subject to Dionysius. The greater part of this area consisted of the enlarged territory of his loyal – and dependent – ally, Locri. A useful bonus accruing to the dynast from this extension of his empire was the access it offered him to the timber of the Sila mountains. To mark the northern limit of his empire and to render it defensible against the marauding Lucanians – no longer convenient allies – as well as against the Italiots, he began the construction of a wall across the isthmus at its narrowest point. This wall was intended to serve a similar purpose to that served by other Greek 'long walls': in conjunction with Dionysius' command of the sea, it attached 'Italy' to Sicily.[29]

With Rhegium under blockade and its fall merely a matter of time, Dionysius in 387 had been at liberty to give a part of his attention to the

Corinthian War, in which both sides had sought to enlist his support. After their initial successes, the Spartans were by then finding the struggle – which had reached a stalemate – a greater burden than they could easily sustain. Athens, emboldened by the restoration of her defences, and inspirited by the leadership of able and aggressive men like Thrasybulus (killed in 390), Chabrias and Iphicrates, had begun reasserting herself in the Aegean. Sparta badly needed reinforcement at sea, and she naturally turned to the ally who owed her a favour. It is not fanciful to suppose that Spartan agents sounded Thearides about his brother's ability to help their country when he was at Olympia in 388; and in the spring or early summer of 387 an ex-navarch, Pollis, was sent to Sicily, presumably to ask the dynast to despatch ships to the eastern Aegean, where the Athenian fleet outnumbered the Lacedaemonian. Dionysius agreed and Pollis was able to sail to the Aegean to give the navarch, Antialcidas, the good news that 20 galleys under Polyxenus would be coming to assist him. Perhaps the fact that Corinth had temporarily become merged in Argos may have influenced Dionysius' decision; for now many of the 'best' Corinthians were fighting alongside the Lacedaemonians. Pollis had agreed to give a passage home to Plato, who had been touring Italy and Sicily; and he dropped him off at Aegina, where the unfortunate philosopher was promptly arrested as an enemy alien and had to be ransomed by his friends. Needless to say, the story as told later in the Academy attributed the Founder's mishap to the treachery of Dionysius (one version even had him sell Plato as a slave at Syracuse!).[30]

However, the Athenians had already taken a step which virtually ensured the downfall of their hopes of rebuilding an Aegean confederation. In 389, 'with greater chivalry than discretion', they had sent a naval squadron to assist Evagoras in his revolt against Artaxerxes and thus alienated the already wavering good will of the Great King. In addition to this, Conon's old ally, Pharnabazus, a prince on the whole favourably disposed towards the Athenians, had been replaced as satrap of Dascalon by Ariobarzanes, whose guest-friend was the Spartan diplomat Antialcidas. Thus, by the summer of 388, Sparta was ready to renew the attempt to secure the active support of Persia that had come to nothing in 392. Antialcidas was appointed navarch, and in the autumn proceeded to Asia. He journeyed up-country to Susa, where he renewed his former friendly contact with the pro-Spartan Tiribazus (now probably a high official at Court). Together they got Artaxerxes' approval for the notorious document embodying the 'King's Peace'. In accordance with the terms of this, a general peace was to be accepted, the cities and islands of Greece were to be autonomous (apart from Clazomenae and Cyprus, which were to belong to the King, and Lemnos, Imbros and Scyros, traditionally the property of Athens), and the cities of Asia were to recognized as the King's.[31]

Antialcidas returned to the coast in the spring of 387, and found the

Lacedaemonian fleet of 25 ships being blockaded by 32 Athenian galleys at Abydos, on the Hellespont. Antialcidas resumed command of his fleet and out-generaled his adversaries into sailing past him into the Propontis, leaving him in control of the Narrows and free to rendezvous with Polyxenus, whose squadron he knew to be approaching the Hellespont. He succeeded in capturing 8 Athenian triremes coming from Thrace to reinforce their main body, and when Polyxenus arrived with his 20 ships, their combined force outnumbered the Athenians. Xenophon describes Polyxenus' squadron as coming 'from Syracuse and Italy', which suggests that Locri had been persuaded to contribute one or two vessels – unless, of course, it means merely that the squadron was despatched from Rhegium, perhaps on the fall of that city. Further reinforcements arrived from Tiribazus (newly appointed Satrap of Lydia) and from Ariobarzanes, bringing Antialcidas' total strength up to 80 vessels and giving him complete command of the Hellespont and the ability to cut off Athens' vital imports of grain from the Black Sea. Athens' position was now almost as hopeless as it had been after Aegospotami; but because it was not completely hopeless (her fleet was still undefeated and she herself was not blockaded by land), she leapt at the chance of making peace on reasonable terms; and her allies had their own sufficient reasons for desiring peace.[32]

Delegates of the warring cities were invited to Sardes and Tiribazus read them his master's rescript. The Thebans protested against terms of peace that would dissolve the Boeotian confederacy of which they were *hegemon*; but under threat of invasion by Sparta and her allies (backed by Persia) they gave way. By this treaty, too, Syracuse's metropolis, Corinth, recovered her separate identity. The common peace was signed by all, probably in the summer of 386, and the cities of Asia and Evagoras were given up to the Great King. Sparta, whose confederacy was an alliance of free peoples, not a *sympolity* like the Boeotian League, was left with her power intact and with the prestige of champion (*prostatēs*) and keeper of the common peace. Because of the help that he had sent to Sparta at a critical moment, Dionysius was associated in men's minds – above all at Athens – not with a love of peace but with membership of the unholy triad of Sparta, the Great King and himself, whose power was arrayed against the liberty of the Hellenes: as, indeed, Lysias had gone some way towards proclaiming already, in his Olympic oration.[33]

A dynast who indulged not in personal luxury and extravagance but in the most costly public luxuries – fleets, mercenary armies, grandiose building programmes and wars of conquest – was bound to concern himself with the commercial prosperity of his dominions and especially of his capital city; since a vigorous foreign trade served the importation of essential raw materials and the harbour dues and (probably) metic tax brought money into the city's treasury, which the dynast could tap at need. Besides, a flourishing overseas trade disseminated a varying measure of prosperity throughout all classes, and the improved standard of living increased the tyrant's popularity and so helped to disarm dissatisfaction with the regime. Nor are we entitled to discount the probability that Dionysius genuinely desired the welfare of his people and took a very ordinary human pleasure – which was also a reputable pleasure in Greek eyes – in being honoured as his countrymen's benefactor. Certain it is that the cities of Sicily prospered at this time. Plato, visiting the island in 388/7, comments with austere disapproval on the wealth and luxury that he found prevailing.

A commercial policy, particularly one that was oriented towards the import of raw materials rather than export, would – like that of Carthage – be likely to favour trade with backward peoples, through the medium of barter, rather than with advanced, sophisticated competitors. Trade with native Africa and Spain was prohibited by Carthage; and so Dionysius, with the Straits of Messana under his control, naturally turned his eyes northwards. The Adriatic, which, since the collapse of the Athenian Empire, had not seen very much Greek commercial activity, offered a ready field for exploitation. It had been opened up in the seventh century, when Phocaean merchant adventurers had entered its waters. Epidamnus and later Apollonia had been founded in the course of Corinth's great 'imperial' expansion beyond the entrance of the Corinthian Gulf; Parians had colonized Anchiale, and Cnidians and Rhodians had settled as far north as Corcyra Nigra, as well as on the coast of Apulia. At the mouth of the Po, at the end of trade routes stretching back into central Europe, Etruscans had founded the city of Spina. But with the diminution and then the failure of Athenian trade in the second half of the fifth century, and with the overthrow of the Etruscans of the Po Valley by the Celts, Greek interest in the northern Adriatic had fallen away, and Spina had declined.

That Dionysius entered the Adriatic in order (as Diodorus suggests) to secure military bases from which to make a descent upon Epirus and sack the great international religious centre of Delphi, we need not believe for a moment: the charge derives from the fourth-century stereotyped portrait of The Tyrant as one who cared nothing for the rights of men or gods. It seems to me probable that the earliest version of this story credited Dionysius with predatory designs upon the important oracular shrine of Zeus at Dodona, in Epirus, and that Delphi was a later 'improvement'. Nor do I consider it likely, considering the remoteness of the regions in which he took an interest, that his purpose was to establish bases in the Ionian Sea in order to secure his communications with the Corinthian Gulf and Central Greece: which is the view of Stroheker. Dionysius must have been fully aware that Carthage owed her strength and her resilience to her empire. His purpose, I believe, was to build up a maritime empire in the Adriatic to counterbalance that of Carthage in the western Mediterranean – an empire that would provide him with silver, tin, timber, horses and mercenaries: Celts imported from the country of the Senones, to match Carthage's Iberians and Ligurians.[34]

By 385 Dionysius had already taken the first steps towards the establishment of his power in the Adriatic. 'Not many years earlier [i.e. than 385] he had sent colonists into the Adriatic and founded the city called Lissus'. 'Not many years' could mean, either, that Diodorus knew the date but could not be bothered to give it, or else that he was following an authority equally imprecise. The most likely time to which to assign this venture seems to me to be the period immediately following the destruction of Caulonia and Hipponium, when Dionysius may have been embarrassed to find land for all his new citizens. Lissus stood at the mouth of the river Drilo, in northern Illyria, north of the venerable Corinthian-Corcyraean colony of Epidamnus. The hinterland was rich in mineral ores (including silver), and an important trade route ran up the Drilo to the lower Danube basin. Lissus was used as the base for further expansion into the central Adriatic region; and Stroheker has argued convincingly that the unfortunate lacuna in the text of Diodorus at this point covered the account of the planting of a colony on the island of Issa, off the Illyrian coast, where Dionysius established a naval station under an *eparch*. From Issa, settlements spread to Corcyra Nigra and the mainland.[35] Presumably the foundation of Lissus was connected with the treaty concluded by Dionysius with the Illyrians, which (Diodorus informs us) was negotiated through the good offices of an exiled Molossian prince, one Alcetas, at that time residing at the dynast's court. The Illyrians, involved in hostilities with the neighbouring Molossians, would have been extremely glad of the assistance of the most powerful State in the Greek world, and prepared to be correspondingly grateful to Alcetas.

The Molossi of Epirus, a tribal state (*koinon*) whose ruling family claimed descent from Achilles, had formerly been allies of the Lacedaemonians (through their common hostility towards the Acarnanians, although the latter were in 385 the unwilling allies of Lacedaemon). However, Alcetas' father, Tharyps (or Tharypas), had been educated at Athens, having probably been sent there when he was still a minor, shortly after the defeat of the Peloponnesians and their allies (including the Molossians) before Stratus in 429. Tharyps was credited with the Hellenization of his people: that is, with the introduction of written laws and certain Greek-style political institutions. We know from an inscription that he was granted Athenian citizenship, and we may conjecture that this was in grateful recognition of his having brought his people into friendship or alliance with Athens. Alcetas, Tharyps' son, had

150

inherited not only his father's Attic citizenship but also (as events were to show) his partiality for Athens. At this time, however, Alcetas had been excluded from the succession, presumably by a claimant in the Spartan interest; for Sparta had taken steps in 401 to reassert her influence in western Greece, and appears to have enrolled the Molossi among her allies.[36]

Dionysius will have hoped, by making Alcetas king of the Molossians, to secure for himself a powerful friend and ally, whose kingdom would comprise the eastern shores of the Straits of Otranto, the gateway to the Adriatic. Accordingly, he sent 2,000 soldiers and 500 stands of arms to assist an Illyrian invasion of Epirus, for the purpose of establishing Alcetas as ruler. At the same time he agreed to assist a colonizing venture into the Adriatic on the part of the islanders of Paros, to the island of Pharos, to an island which either was already called Pharos or which derived its classical name from the new settlers. Pharos lies some dozen miles to the east of Issa, and the Parians built and fortified a city there, apparently without coming to an arrangement beforehand with the natives of those parts.

The Illyrians overran Epirus and inflicted a crushing defeat on the Molossians, killing some 15,000 of them. But Sparta was not prepared to see the whole north-western flank of her 'empire' fall into the hands of the Illyrians, or to see the regime which she may have been instrumental in installing overthrown. She sent an expeditionary force to assist the Molossians and as a result the Illyrians withdrew from the country. Diodorus does not tell us what became of Alcetas; but we know that in 375 he was ruler of the Molossians, so it is possible that Dionysius (or Leptines) negotiated an understanding between him and the Lacedaemonians, which resulted in his being accepted by the latter as king. However, in 375 he joined the new Athenian confederacy, which had been established in 377. A mysterious reminder of Alcetas' sojourn on Ortygia seems to be traceable in an inscription, set up at Athens in 373, in honour of one Alcetas, son of Leptines, a Syracusan. From King Alcetas both Alexander the Great, through Olympias, his mother, and Pyrrhus were descended.[37]

The island of Issa lies about 150 miles distant from the country of the Senones (the later Ager Gallicus), and it is probable that Dionysius' agents made contact with the tribe. These were the Celts who descended on central Italy in 391 and sacked Rome in the following year. It seems to me more likely that they entered into treaty relations with Dionysius than through a contact made with the raiding party itself, some of whose members penetrated as far south as Iapygia. In 384 the new Parian colony on Pharos was attacked by over 10,000 Illyrians from the mainland, summoned by the natives of the island. The Illyrians (belonging to the

Ardiaei and Pleraei, different tribes from those with which Dionysius had made his alliance) came across the narrow straits in small boats, and inflicted serious losses and damage on the Greeks. However, Dionysius' military commander (*eparch*) at Issa, coming to the assistance of the Parians with a strong force of warships, caught the barbarians, presumably on their return journey to the mainland, and overwhelmed them, killing over 5,000 of the raiders and capturing some 2,000. These I assume, were sold or ransomed.

From the parts about Illyria, Dionysius extended his 'colonial empire' across the Adriatic to northern Italy. In Picenum, just south of the borders of the Senones' country, on the only good natural harbour in this part of Italy, Ancona was founded – *dorica Ancona*, Juvenal calls her – by Syracusan exiles, according to Strabo. However, this story may merely represent a desire on the part of the inhabitants, at a later date, to dissociate their ancestors from a tyrannical regime; for, as Stroheker points out, Dionysius would have been unlikely to allow his enemies to occupy so important a site, which would pose a threat to Issa and give them a measure of dominance over this commercially important region. Of course, if the colonists (or a significant portion of them) were drawn from the peoples expelled from southern Italy by Dionysius who were granted Syracusan citizenship, Strabo's statement would conform to inherent probability. At Numana, a few miles to the south, there was a trading post.

Between the mouths of the Po and the Adige, Dionysius probably recolonized the old Venetian – later, perhaps, Etruscan – city of Adria (then a port, but today, with the extension eastwards of the coastline, over 13 miles inland). Theopompus attributed the foundation of Adria to Ionios, who hailed from Issa. Some ancient drainage channels, falling into the river Tartarus, on which Adria stands, were known in Pliny's day as the *Fossae* (dykes) *Filistinae*; and the name is usually connected with the historian Philistus, who as an exile resided at Adria. It has been suggested that Philistus (who never wavered in his loyalty to the regime) was relegated (to use the Roman term) rather than exiled, and perhaps served as Dionysius' governor at Adria. Perhaps, too, there is some connection, now lost, between Philistus' presence in the northern Adriatic and the tradition (mentioned above) that Ancona was founded by Syracusan exiles.

Control of Adria not only allowed Syracusan merchants to tap the produce of central and northern Europe, such as amber and tin, but also facilitated trade with the Veneti, great breeders of horses and mules, on whose territory Dionysius established a stud farm. He entered into treaty relations with the Senones, thus at one and the same time averting friction with Ancona's neighbours and providing himself with a valuable source of (expendable) mercenary light infantry. It seems likely that the pretty fancy, that the Gauls – Galatae – and the Illyrians sprang from the union of Polyphemus and Galatea, belongs to the court poetry of contemporary Syracuse and perhaps to the pen of Philoxenus himself.[38]

CHAPTER NINE

The nature of Dionysius' empire

It is time to consider the nature of Dionysius' empire, and to begin by asking, What was the relation, first, between Dionysius and the Syracusans (for he is regularly referred to as 'the tyrant of the Syracusans'), and secondly, between him and the other Greek cities and the Sicel communities? One cannot, of course, talk about the 'constitutional position' of a tyrant: tyranny is, by its nature, antithetical to the concept of constitution, for a constitution (the laws – *hoi nomoi*) was founded in justice and tyranny was the product of violence (*bia*). The *polis* – the word *polis* has, in Greek, to do duty for 'city', 'Community' and 'State' – was considered to be a commonwealth (*koinōnia*): a political community that possessed in common a material city and its territory. With the erection of a tyranny, ownership of the city passed into the hands of an individual, the citizens no longer had a city and 'commonwealth' lost its meaning. Sophocles spoke for Greece when he said, 'That which is subject to one man is no *polis*'. In a *polis*, power (*kratos*) belonged to the citizen body, whose instruments the magistrates were, responsible (*hypeuthynoi*) to it. But a tyrant was responsible to no one, power had passed to him together with the ownership of the city, and his power was absolute. The Chorus in Aeschylus' *Suppliants* say to King Pelasgus,

> Mark well, thou art the Polis, thou art the People,
> a Prince not answerable to judgement.

'He [Dionysius] is master of the city' (*kratei tēs poleōs*), says 'Theodorus'. The rule of a tyrant, however mild, however beneficial, however much it respected the laws, was an act of violence, because the tyrant was not answerable to the Law. Only Law could rule as king (*basileus*) in a Greek city; a tyrant could only be a master of slaves (*despotēs*), and his subjects, no matter how free he left them to manage their private, and even their civic, affairs, were none the less his slaves.[1]

Dionysius belonged in the tradition of the Sicilian tyrannies, not of the metropolitan and Ionian; he was the political heir of Phalaris, Hippocrates and Gelon, not of Cypselus, Peisistratus and Thrasybulus. Compared with the Dorian States of the Isthmus region and the cities of Asia, the Sicilian colonies were of recent origin. They were the product

154

not of large-scale movements of tribes and peoples of the Dark Ages but of small settlements organized by rulers or noblemen of established cities of the early archaic period, and their members formed a privileged class in the developed colony, having no sense of identity with the rest of the inhabitants, who consisted of the descendants of later settlers. This made for political instability in the late archaic age; but the tyrants who emerged, being members of the aristocracy – even if, like Phalaris, they exploited social grievances – had nothing in common with the 'Demos'. This was the age of economic expansion and of wealth-getting and the Sicilian tyrants were tempted into militarism by the fact that the hinterland was occupied by less advanced peoples who could be reduced to subjection; and so they devoted themselves to empire-building and to war – war waged, at any rate in part, with mercenary armies. They were war-lords rather than city-rulers.

There was, however, an important difference between the earlier Sicilian dynasts and Dionysius. They belonged to an age when the national *polis*, as distinct from the aristocratic, had not yet emerged in Sicily. The memory of hereditary or elective monarchy was still green in the sixth century, and the tyrants were themselves members of the traditional ruling class. Dionysius was a middle-class citizen and he belonged to a world in which the national *polis* was regarded as the only really acceptable organization of civilized society by all but the most backward Greeks. The regime that he subverted was a republican regime that had endured for two generations and that had, within the last decade, been more or less assimilated to the most advanced in the Hellenic world. However, in his conception of monarchy and in his ambition he showed himself a tyrant of the native Sicilian pattern; he was first and foremost a soldier, and although in his rise to power he borrowed from Peisistratus' notorious repertory of ruses (so that Aristotle, rather carelessly, classes him among those who had seized power by demagogy), it was by taking advantage of a military, not a social, crisis, by exploiting his own military reputation and by acquiring control of the armed forces of his city that he established, extended and consolidated his rule.[2]

Dionysius' career shows clearly that he desired power not for its own sake but as the means of achieving military glory: the *kleos* so important to the heroes of Homer. One of the very few sayings attributed to Dionysius (which may, of course, have had its origin in one of his plays) is, that the greatest benefit that ruling confers on a man is the ability to carry out his plans quickly (Demosthenes said something rather similar, when speaking of Philip of Macedon). The possession of absolute power enabled Dionysius to put into execution his grand design for the expulsion of the Carthaginians from Sicily at what he conceived to be the most propitious moment. He stood poles apart from, for instance,

Peisistratus, who devoted his life to the task of restoring and cementing the social harmony (*eunomia*) that Solon had proclaimed at the panacea for social evils. Peisistratus had been essentially a man of peace (although he had distinguished himself in the war with Megara and showed himself a skilful general at Pallene), and he managed to maintain friendly relations with all Athens' neighbours (even with Sparta and Argos at the same time); and certainly by the fourth century, and probably even by the end of the fifth, his reign was looked back upon as a Golden Age.[3]

We know that Peisistratus was able to exercise indirect rule over the Athenians without doing violence to the constitution by ensuring, presumably by the implied but never open threat of force, that the Archonship (the Presidency) was always held by someone whom he could trust, but we know nothing about Dionysius' *modus operandi* in the field of politics. We do know that in 405 he was elected General Plenipotentiary, an office that was annually re-elective. Some modern historians believe that, after the suppression of the Great Revolt, he assumed this title in perpetuity (having, of course, been deposed by the Demos in the early summer of 404). In favour of this suggestion it may be argued that he would have needed to hold the office in order to be able to convene the Assembly, deal with foreign embassies and command the armed forces. Moreover, because he would have been anxious to legitimize his rule as far as possible (Dionysius being a pupil of the sophists and tyranny enjoying an evil name in intellectual circles), he would have wanted a show of constitutionalism in order to disarm criticism. It is true that none of our sources gives any support to the suggestion; but this silence may be explained by the hostility of the tradition which would have suppressed the fact, in order to emphasize the despotic character of the regime. There are, however, cogent grounds for supposing that Dionysius did not, in fact, hold any office: in particular, the silence of the inscriptions and especially of that containing the text of a treaty (concluded at the very end of his reign) between Athens and himself. Dionysius must have been most anxious to propitiate the notoriously touchy Demos – which at that juncture, was itself no less anxious to reciprocate any propitiation offered. To have been able to describe himself as *Strategos Autokrator* (a title that the Athenians themselves employed) would have supplied just that touch of legitimacy which diplomacy would approve of (and which Stroheker believes him to have been looking for), and so rendered less unpalatable his assumption of the title, Lord of Sicily.[4]

There is, however, no good reason to suppose that, after 404, Dionysius felt that he *needed* to hold any office. Peisistratus, who had been concerned to preserve the Athenian constitution, did not feel the need, and nothing that we know about Dionysius suggests that he felt any concern for the constitution of Syracuse or any desire to preserve its institutions or its spirit. Dionysius was concerned only with power, and the Greeks (except perhaps in a very special way at Sparta) did not regard power as something vested by the people (who were the source of power) in a magistrate, in order that he might govern them: as the Romans did. In a *polis*, power resided in the citizen body, and the magistrates were the instruments – Aristophanes could present the magistrates of a radical democracy as the slaves – of the sovereign people: they possessed the *authority* to act (*exousia*), not the power (*kratos*). Once, however, a tyrant had taken possession of a city, so that the power passed from the keeping of the citizens into that of the dynast, the holding or not holding of office by the latter was, politically, an irrelevance. Of course Dionysius, had he wished, could have assumed the title of General, or he could have had himself annually re-elected, but such actions would have been meaningless: the title would have enhanced neither his power nor his political respectability.

Nor do I believe that Dionysius, pupil of the sophistic movement though he no doubt was, was particularly anxious to legitimize in the eyes of the Hellenes a regime that all the world knew to have been established by violence – the capture of the city by force of arms – and to be maintained by what was in effect a mercenary garrison. Unlike his contemporary, Evagoras of Cyprus, he could not claim to be the descendant of Homeric kings of Salamis, nor did he (like Evagoras) have Athenian statesmen and sophists for his friends and apologists. His only friend in Greece was Sparta, and she had never scrupled to support tyranny when she thought that it was in her interest to do so, however much she might boast of her hatred of tyrants. I believe that Dionysius was too much of a realist (at least in political matters) to waste time on 'cosmetic' treatment of what was patently a military dictatorship, merely to mitigate the criticism of Athenian or Corinthian intellectuals. Like Solon (although in a very different connection) he looked for the justification of his efforts at the bar of Time, in the conquest of the Epicraty and the creation of a Greek realm in Sicily and southern Italy whose extent and power would far surpass those of all the great kingdoms that had gone before. Everyone associated with him would have some share in his glory; and this, together with the immense accession of prosperity that must follow upon the final pacification of the island, would (at all events, in *his* eyes) outweigh such trifles as the loss of political freedom.[5]

The relation between Dionysius and the citizens of Syracuse was defined and established in 403 at the end of the Great Revolt. Some 7,000 men – and, although we are not told so in as many words, the narrative of Diodorus implies that they were men of substance, hoplites – had joined the Knights at Aetna. That is to say, the greater part of Syracuse's field army was now congregated, under leaders of its own choosing, in a stronghold beyond the borders of the State. Such a body, if it decided to do so, could have proclaimed itself an effective political society; it could have made Aetna one of the strongest *poleis* in Sicily and one well able to enlarge its territory to support an increased population at the expense of its Sicel or even Greek neighbours. As the centre of Greek opposition to Dionysius, it could have posed an enduring and probably fatal threat to his regime. For this reason, and also because he did not wish to see his own city, Syracuse, depopulated – and of its best elements, at that – Dionysius was anxious to bring about the return of the exiles. For their part, the Syracusans wanted to come *home*, to recover their farms and their town houses, to be reunited with their wives and children, to worship again at the familiar altars, to greet the tombs of their ancestors, to meet at the hallowed centres of phratry and cult, to resume their membership of the *polis* that was the source of their rights, that gave them their identity. When Dionysius sent his emissaries to Aetna to invite the Syracusans to be reconciled with him, the middle-class citizens, the hoplites, were in the mood to come to terms; but the Knights, whose property had already been sequestrated and who were not prepared to serve a tyrant, remained irreconcilable.

In view of the strong bargaining position that they enjoyed, it seems to me unthinkable that the hoplites would have been induced to return by no more than the promise of an amnesty. In fact, a formal treaty must have been sworn by the dynast and the representatives of the citizens, as between two hostile parties. This fact is, indeed, implied in the word 'reconcile' (*dialuesthai*), a word regularly used of the settling of international disputes; and the failure of Diodorus to enlarge upon the treaty and to specify its terms may be readily explained by the reluctance of his sources to mention something that might seem to modify the impression that they wished to convey of Dionysius' regime as one of unrelieved despotism. I believe that by this treaty Dionysius formally recognized the autonomy of the city; that is to say, he guaranteed the right of the citizens to live their lives and to administer the domestic affairs of the city in accordance with the laws. But he went further than that; it is clear both from the History of Diodorus and from the anecdotal material that under Dionysius the Syracusans enjoyed a fundamental right of free citizens: that of deciding on questions relating to war, peace and taxation. It is therefore probable (to put it no higher) that they also enjoyed the right of administering justice freely and according to the laws of the city. On their side, the citizens undertook not to molest Dionysius in his castle of Ortygia and to entrust to him, as *Hegemon* of the Syracusans (Duce, Führer), the conduct of their military affairs (*ta pros tous polemous*). This would mean that in anything bearing directly upon war – including the defence of the city – once the Assembly had given its approval, Dionysius would assume, in effect, all the powers of a General Plenipotentiary, but without assuming the title.[6]

Since we have no information about the methods by which tyrants directed the affairs of their cities (how, for instance, did the 'liberal' Peisistratus, about whom we know more than we do about any other tyrant, ensure a compliant Presidency at Athens?), because tyrants, being (again with the exception of Peisistratus) anti-political, were of little interest to political thinkers, and since we know next to nothing about the constitution of fourth-century Syracuse, it is best not to speculate too much on the relation between Dionysius and the machinery of State. As a citizen, of course, Dionysius had the right to address the Assembly, and it seems to me reasonable to suppose that, as *Hegemon*, he was given the right either of convening it himself or of requiring it to be convened. I consider it most unlikely that he interfered with the selection by lot of the civil magistrates, whose role was wholly administrative and who were powerless to thwart him; but the generalship (*strategia*), the most important executive office in a *polis*, was quite another matter. All the functions that constituted the province of the *strategia* and gave it its authority (and its attractiveness) – the leading role in foreign affairs, defence, military policy and finance, as well as the command of the armies and fleets of the State – were (with a qualification in the matter of finance) now performed by the dynast or his appointees. I believe that the *strategia* may be assumed to have been suspended during Dionysius' reign, and that Dionysius continued to appoint the officers of the citizen levies (after the rearming of the People) – the counterparts of the Athenian hipparchs and taxiarchs – as he had done when *Strategos Autokrator*. The organization and officering of the mercenaries was, of course, entirely his affair. The command of the fleet, whose ships and arsenals were, in effect, his property, was entrusted to one or the other of his brothers, and after their deaths to admirals undoubtedly appointed by him. What organization he employed to officer and man the ships we do not know, except that, for the great 'national crusade' of 398, the complements of half the fleet were drawn from the citizens of Syracuse.

A question that cannot be answered with any certainty is whether or not the Syracusan military levies were employed by Dionysius in any of his later wars. Polyaenus tells us that, after disarming the people (presumably with reference to the events of 403), Dionysius rearmed them temporarily in order to meet a sudden military threat (*kindynou kairos*). 'After the battle', he disarmed them again before readmitting them to the city. This story has, I believe, a basis of fact: that, on some occasion between 403 and 398, Dionysius did restore their shields to the hoplites for a specific military operation. Although the most likely occasion, from the stand-point of the historian, is (as I have suggested in an earlier chapter) that of Dionysius' expedition against the Chalcidian cities, it looks as if either Polyaenus or his immediate source, itself anecdotal, has introduced the element of crisis from the abortive attempt of the Straits cities to liberate Syracuse in 399, and invented the battle in order to heighten the drama. However, by 400 the Syracusans had come to terms with their situation, and their good behaviour on this occasion must have helped to embolden Dionysius to put in hand his preparations for the war with Carthage, which included the rearming of the citizens, who were to play an important part in the fighting and to whose steadfastness much of the credit for the final victory must go. It is, however, most unlikely that Syracuse was asked to declare war against the Italiots; and after the fiasco of 392 – when, at the height of a campaign against a formidable Punic army operating only some 60 miles from the city, the Syracusans, disagreeing with the strategy of their *Hegemon*, simply marched home from the front – it would have been entirely reasonable for Dionysius to conclude that the citizen levies were not to be relied on in the field. Once he had established his empire and perhaps acquired a regular source of silver as a result of his contact with Illyria, he had the money to hire as many professional soldiers as he needed. No doubt a great many Siceliots, including Syracusans, took service with him; but if, as I believe to have been the case, the Syracusan phalanx was not involved in the war against Carthage in the '70s, and therefore not in the disaster of Cronium, it would help to explain both the rapidity of Dionysius' military recovery and the absence of any tradition of a great national calamity's having afflicted Syracuse during his reign. If the farmers of Syracuse were not called away to fight in the dynast's wars after 392, his forbearance can hardly have failed to lull, if *not* dispel, the resentment of the Demos towards the regime.[7]

Most of the anecdotal material connected with Dionysius is calculated to illustrate his petty cruelty and paranoia. The least vituperative parts are those which deal with his methods of raising money; and although these protray him as deceitful and rapacious, they do in fact make two very important points in his favour: first, that when he wanted money from the Syracusans he had to ask for it, and, secondly, that the methods which he employed to raise it were very much the same as those employed by the governments and generals of city-states in time of emergency. We are told that the basic difference between monarchies and republics in the matter of raising revenue was that the former habitually levied a direct tax in the form of tithes (*dekatē*) on their subjects, either as an impost on agricultural produce or as one on livestock, whereas the latter did not. Now, it is nowhere stated explicitly that Dionysius imposed tithes on the Syracusans (as Peisistratus certainly did on the Athenians); but there is, in the *Politics* of Aristotle, the remarkable assertion that, *in order to impoverish his subjects*, Dionysius exacted the whole of men's properties over periods of five years: that is, that he imposed an annual levy of 20 per cent on property. The alleged purpose of the levy betrays the origin of the story: the stock-pot of 'characteristics of tyrants', familiar to fourth-century writers. Some historians assume that this was an emergency measure, lasting only five years, but any such assumption comes up against the *fact* that Dionysius had to ask the Syracusans for funds, and that they would hardly have been likely to vote for their own impoverishment. The best explanation, I believe, of this notice is that it is a careless – or, more probably, a malicious – adaptation for attribution to Dionysius of a rather naïve anecdote relating to the proto-tyrant, Cypselus of Corinth. Cypselus, it is said, in pursuance of a vow to Zeus, took a tenth of each Corinthian's property every year for ten years. However, by virtue of the income earned by the Corinthians from the remaining nine-tenths, at the end of the ten-years' period every man's property was intact, although Cypselus had taken the whole of it! It would, I believe, be very unsafe to use this passage in the *Politics* as evidence for the levying of a regular tithe (or worse) by Dionysius.[8]

On the other hand, there are plenty of indications that the Syracusans, like other Greek peoples, were subjected to special imposts and levies of various kinds. Thus the pseudo-Aristotelian *Economics* depicts the tyrant calling a meeting of the Assembly and asking for a levy of 2 staters (the equivalent of 4 drachmas) per head, which he at once refunds; and then, having established his good faith in matters financial, he asks for it again and this time spends the money on ships. The inference is that this demand was, first, exceptional, and, secondly, in the power of the Assembly to refuse. Another passage, dealing with a tax on livestock, could be taken to show either that this tax was a regular annual impost although its exaction was sometimes remitted, or that it was not. Yet another anecdote (recounted by Polyaenus) tells us that Dionysius, 'being short of money', asked the People for taxes and was refused, on the grounds that they had no more to give him.

The most that these passages can be said to prove (apart from the one referring to the livestock tax, which, besides being ambiguous, has the odour of 'a good story about tyrants' about it) is that when Dionysius found himself short of funds he asked the Syracusans for extraordinary contributions. But it must be remembered that, when faced by an emergency, free cities too had recourse both to levies on property (*esphorai*) and to 'emergency' taxes. For instance the Athenians voted numerous levies when they were under serious financial pressure as a result of the Peloponnesian War, beginning in 428 when the *esphora* amounted to no less than 6½ times the highest annual tribute paid by an allied (i.e. subject) State. Nor should we forget the Athenian system of

14 Syracusan tin-bronze drachma, period of Dionysius, 'war emergency coinage': (above) Head of Athena (the Guardian of Cities); (below) dolphins and starfish

liturgies, which kept the fleet in commission and financed, in large part, the cultural side of the city's festivals. On the other hand, there are two pieces of indirect evidence for the existence of an annual tax at Syracuse; first, the statement of Diodorus that the Caulonians transported to Syracuse were granted exemption (*ateleia*) for five years (*ateleia*, however, can signify merely exemption from military service); and secondly, that of Justin, that Dionysius' successor remitted three years' taxes (unfortunately, the tone of the whole passage is not such as to inspire much confidence in its historical accuracy: it may, however, reflect a reliable tradition).

I believe that there is good reason to assume that in 403, as part of their compact with Dionysius, the Syracusans undertook to pay him a regular subsidy, perhaps on the understanding that it would be remitted when his own coffers were full; for even Dionysius' enemies agree that he did not covet money to pay for his own pleasures or personal display (although he had a proper appreciation of display for *state* purposes). The cost of achieving Syracuse's long-standing ambition, to subjugate the Sicels and Chalcidic cities of eastern Sicily, was something that the Syracusan people could legitimately be asked to contribute towards: particularly as they were not being required to risk their lives, unless in the last campaign. Yet the city must have been relatively poor although the citizens were prosperous and their standard of living such as to offend visiting intellectuals. There was, in 403, no revenue coming in from the Sicels (after this date, as they were brought into subjection, their tribute went into the coffers of the dynast); and Dionysius controlled much of the port area (Plato mentions the customs officers and merchants who would do the tyrant's bidding), and consequently a large proportion of the harbour dues and (probably) *metic* tax would have accrued to him. If Syracuse was going to pay her *Hegemon* a substantial subsidy, it could only be raised by direct taxation, which her citizens could well afford. Of course, the tithes of Syracuse would not have sufficed to support the large mercenary army and the ships that Dionysius maintained. To pay for these, he relied on the tribute of his tributary allies, subjects and dependencies, on the harbour dues, perhaps a *metic* tax, plunder and the sale of slaves and booty. Dion (who, towards the end of the tyrant's life, seems to have enjoyed his confidence in both diplomatic and financial matters) is quoted as saying that Dionysius, like a good housekeeper, had his whole empire organized under his personal supervision. He certainly paid close attention to finance, and anecdotes indicate his appreciation of business acumen. He did not like to see money lie idle, and he was, for a military dictator, singularly generous to a merchant who made a corner in iron. So far, indeed, from desiring to impoverish his fellow citizens, he appears to have presided over an era of outstanding prosperity.[9]

Considering the essentially hand-to-mouth nature of all ancient public financing, ultimately dependent as it was upon a narrowly finite supply of silver, one need hardly be surprised to find that all governments, free no less than despotic, were obliged occasionally to resort to expedients that were nicely compounded of the confidence trick and plain extortion. Quite respectable was the practice of borrowing the treasures of the gods – who were, after all, really the highest class of citizen and could therefore legitimately be required to make loans to the city. At the outbreak of the Peloponnesian War, both sides openly planned to make use of temple treasures to defray the cost, and, indeed, the adornments of Phidias' celebrated statue of Athena were made removable, with something of this sort in mind. Thus the citizens of Antissa appropriated funds collected specifically for the festival of Dionysus, and the Byzantines sold lands belonging to religious guilds and ancestral cult associations.

Tyrants, however, were regarded as men without respect for religion or custom, and so it was a matter of course that when Dionysius borrowed from the gods of the city he should be described as 'plundering the treasures of all the Syracusan temples'. Specifically, he sheared the golden locks of Apollo, seized the robes of Zeus and 'ordered the archons' to sell the treasures of the temple of Asclepius; and the pseudo-Aristotelian treatise on economics accuses him of the wholesale plundering of all the temples of their valuable furniture and vessels and of the adornments of the statues of the gods. That such appropriations as he did make were borrowings and not thefts we need have no doubt; for we have no good reason to suppose that Dionysius was really irreligious – nor is it likely that the man who, in the days of his prosperity, sent rich offerings to Delphi and Olympia would have left the shrines of Apollo and Zeus in his own city in a desecrated condition. If the robes referred to above were those of Olympian Zeus, then their removal may merely have been for safe keeping, at the time when his great temple was about to fall into Carthaginian hands. The temple of Apollo was on Ortygia and was therefore under the dynast's protection; the temple of Asclepius was evidently on the mainland, and so the sale of its treasures was conducted by the city magistrates, either in response to a vote of the Assembly, proposed by Dionysius, or in obedience to an edict issued by him as war leader. At all events, since all these borrowings were undoubtedly occasioned by serious military (and hence, financial) crises, the action of the dynast in no way contravened accepted Greek practice. Slightly different is the charge – probably false – that he stole a valuable offering from the temple of Lacinian Hera, in the territory of Croton; and it is significant that the goddess whose temple he plundered in his raid on Etruria – elsewhere, the country of pirates – is always referred to by the name of her Greek equivalent, Eileithyia (or, incorrectly, Leucothea), and not as Uni (or even Juno), in order to emphasize Dionysius' impiety. This was also the purpose of the story, referred to in Chapter 8, that

Dionysius intended to plunder the shrine of Dodona, and of the absurd tale, repeated without qualification by Cicero (who certainly knew better), that the tyrant actually despoiled the statues of Persephone at Locri and of Zeus at Olympia and Asclepius at Epidaurus: the two last charges being 'improvements' on the anecdotes related above.[10]

A monetary system based on silver, such as the Greek, clearly was going to get into serious trouble whenever the supply of the precious metal ran short. This happened more than once at Syracuse, which depended on imported silver, and it may be assumed to have happened in the wake of each serious military set-back. Mercenaries had to be paid in silver, and were apt to become troublesome if their pay was too much in arrears: a very large part of the silver that Dionysius could lay his hands on was earmarked for this purpose. And at the close of the disastrous third Punic War, he had to find no less than 1,000 talents in order to pay off the war indemnity. In these monetary crises he did what governments before and since have done and devalued the domestic coinage. On one occasion he persuaded the People to sanction the temporary replacement of the silver coinage in private hands by a token issue in iron. As conditions improved, the owners of the silver were reimbursed with interest and the iron coinage was withdrawn. On another occasion Dionysius (again, by means of a vote of the Assembly? We are not told) had all the silver called in and reminted, the weight of the stater (the didrachm) being reduced by half. With these 'new' didrachms he repaid outstanding public debts and reimbursed – at face value – those who had handed in their silver. It was probably during the Great Siege, following the sack of the temple of Demeter and Korē, that Dionysius convened the Assembly and told it that the goddess herself had informed him that she wished all the women of Syracuse to deposit their ornaments in her temple: Dionysius subsequently removed the ornaments 'as a loan.' Later, he caused a temple tax on all female gold jewellery to be instituted.[11]

All these expedients, however, as well as others, such as (apparently) a mock sale of his palace furniture and the use of trust funds, during the minority of orphans, to supply his needs, can be paralleled by the actions of free cities and their officers. Clazomenae, for instance, also struck a temporary iron coinage in an emergency, and the Athenian admiral Timotheus was, on one occasion, compelled to pay his men in a token copper currency. The Ephesians obliged their women to remove their gold ornaments and lend them to the State and the Lampsacenes imposed what was in effect a 50-per-cent impost on essential foodstuffs. Nor should one forget the trick played by the Segestans upon the guileless Athenians in 416, in order to convince them that their city possessed abundant treasure with which to finance a war. In short, it is probably fair to say that, under Dionysius' rule, the property of a citizen of Syracuse was as secure as that of a citizen of any free city; and it seems quite clear, even from the uniformly hostile tradition, that extraordinary levies and compulsory loans were resorted to only in times of national emergency, that to obtain these the tyrant was obliged to get the approval of the Assembly and that this approval might be withheld. There is no evidence that the administration of the mint was taken away from the city authorities, and the coins struck during the 'reign' continued to bear the traditional types.[12]

However, the most damning, if only because in various forms the most often repeated, charge against Dionysius is that of cruelty arising out of a morbid suspiciousness of all about him. The objects of his suspicion would fall into two categories: the first, those whom we may call his Syracusan enemies, those suspected of plotting to abolish the tyranny and liberate the city; and the second, his Ortygian or domestic enemies, members of his circle of friends and adherents who might be plotting to remove *him* without overthrowing the tyranny. As regards the persecution of the first of these categories, the charge of cruelty rests wholly on assertion, anecdote and generalization. Thus, Nepos declares that Dionysius 'spared the life of no one whom he thought to be a conspirator against his power'. Plutarch states that Dionysius destroyed more than 10,000 citizens. Now if this figure is intended to represent the total number of Syracusans who fell in Dionysius' various wars it might be regarded as rather conservative; for it would include those slain at Gela, in the Great Revolt, in the siege of Motya, in the naval disaster off Catane (where 20,000 men are said to have perished, most of whom could have been Syracusans), in the land fighting against Himilco and later against Mago, on the Eleporus and also at Cabala and Cronium (for even if the citizen levies were not involved there must have been many Syracusans serving as mercenaries). However, the tone of the passage and the use of the verb *anairein* suggest that Plutarch wants us to believe that 10,000 people were *put to death* by the tyrant – especially as he goes on to say that Dionysius also strangled his mother and betrayed his brother to the enemy. His 'myriad or more' may therefore be taken simply as the 'countless' of polemical exaggeration.

Polyaenus tells us that from 'information received' from female entertainers, instructed to report to him on the loyalty or the reverse of their clients, Dionysius was able to execute or exile many disaffected persons. There ladies are, presumably, the same persons as the 'tale-bearers' (*potagogides*) mentioned by Aristotle as being connected with Syracuse (but not specifically with Dionysius), and by Plutarch (who, however, makes them masculine) as being creatures of the Dionysii (in one place) and of the *Younger* Dionysius (in another). If Polyaenus' story is not sheer invention – based, perhaps, on instances of tale-bearing by individual ladies – and if it does not, in fact, properly belong to the latterly chaotic reign of the Younger Dionysius, it may refer to the activities of the *demi-monde* of Ortygia. In any event, it is scarcely good evidence for a pogrom.

Polyaenus also says that Dionysius massacred the mutinous ex-servicemen whom he had settled at Leontini; but as Diodorus does not mention any such action and as the massacre of something like 10,000 tough fighting-men would have required the exertions of a large army to accomplish it, and as Dionysius could hardly have been insensible to the effect that such a deed – totally unnecessary anyway – must have on potential recruits, it is best to dismiss the tale as pure invention. Diodorus, indeed, representing the historical as distinct from the anec-dotal tradition, says nothing about a persecution of the 'republican opposition' at Syracuse after 398. Indeed, he brings the 'Theodorus' episode to an end – the occasion on which a bitter harangue is supposed to have been delivered in the Assembly against the tyrant, to the applause of the People – with the restoration of cordial relations between Dionysius and the citizenry and without any suggestion that the despot bore any ill will against his political opponents. The assertions of Plutarch and Polyaenus appear to have no foundation in *fact* but only in the sophistic-Platonic picture of The Tyrant as one who systematically destroys all the Best Men, putting suspects to death without trial.[13]

The most sustained and – because of its author's intellectual and literary eminence as well as the known fact of his personal acquaintance with Dionysius' Syracuse – the most damaging criticism of the regime comes from Plato. Plato cannot name Dionysius as the tyrant at whom the famous passage in the *Republic* is aimed, since the 'dramatic' date of the *Republic* is 410. It is presented as a generalization, an elaboration of the well-known passage in Herodotus; and, indeed, the account of the origin and rise of tyranny has more to do with Peisistratus than with Dionysius, who exploited a military rather than a social crisis. But thereafter the references to Syracuse are unmistakable, particularly to any reader acquainted with the story of Plato's journey to Sicily. Thus, at the outset, the tyrant fulfils his promises to the Demos that has put him in power. He cancels debts and reapportions the land and he comes to terms with or crushes the city's external enemies. But he cannot give her peace; he must be for ever stirring up war, and this for three reasons. First, in order to make himself indispensable to the people as their leader; secondly, to impoverish them by taxation and so compel them to devote all their energies to the earning of a livelihood; and thirdly, to rid himself of the most independent – and therefore the boldest – spirits by exposing them to the enemy.

However, the tyrant's militarism is bound to render him bitterly unpopular, and for this reason his most manly partisans will criticize his policy and he will be obliged to get rid of them, until at last he has neither friend nor enemy remaining who is worth anything. Indeed, he must identify the brave, the noble, the intelligent, the well-to-do, and purge the city of them, ridding the body politic of its best elements and leaving behind the worst. Becoming ever more unpopular, he is increasingly dependent on his guards, who become ever more numerous and are at last recruited from emancipated slaves. Only his partisans and the 'New' citizens admire and consort with him. He welcomes playwrights to his court because, like him, they are 'clever' chaps (*sophoi*) and sing the praises of tyranny (it is perhaps significant, in the light of the story about Antiphon, that Plato does not accuse the tyrant of putting them to death when they fail to pander to his vanity). In order to support his armed camp, the tyrant plunders the property of the gods and of the citizens whom he has destroyed, so as to lighten the burden on the Demos, but in the long run it is the Demos that will be compelled to pay for his excesses. It will attempt to expel him and his followers but will not be strong enough to do so, and he will take away its arms. The tyrant will triumph, but his position will be one of awful isolation; virtually a prisoner in his citadel, he will be unable to travel abroad or to frequent the great festivals.[14]

When Plato came to Sicily via southern Italy as an enquiring tourist, probably between the late summer of 388 and the early spring of 387, he did not come with an open mind. Indeed, it would have been very remarkable if any Athenian of his generation had been able to do so. The great Syracusan disaster, in which almost every citizen of Athens must have lost a kinsman or a friend, was only twenty-five years distant. Athens was still technically at war with Syracuse, Dionysius was the ally of Athen's enemy, Lacedaemon, he had destroyed the Chalcidic cities of Sicily, Athens' old allies, and he was at that very time engaged in subjugating the cities of southern Italy. Like the Great King, like Sparta, he was the enemy of Hellenic liberty. If Plato visited Croton, still smarting from its defeat at the Eleporus, he must have met the (probably very few) survivors of the Syracusan aristocracy exiled since 403. Certainly, in his travels, he must have encountered and equally certainly must have accepted the Italiot view of Dionysius and his regime. The Locrians (among whom he stayed, according to Cicero) may have painted a rather more favourable picture of the tyrant, but they are unlikely to have portrayed him as a philosopher king.

That Plato was not invited to Syracuse by Dionysius (as some versions of the 'legend' maintained) is clearly attested by the Seventh Letter, which is followed by Plutarch; and the silence of the Letter and the language of Plutarch (*Dion*, 4.3) imply that he did not lodge in the palace. Dion, the son of Hipparinus (whom the Academic tradition placed on an equal footing, initially, with Dionysius himself), was then twenty years old: at his most vulnerable, intellectually. He became a disciple of Plato, who captivated the young man, filled as he was with the intellectual arrogance of gifted youth and flattered by the attentions of his brilliant instructor, a man twice his age. From Dion, therefore, Plato probably got a picture of the regime that chimed with his own preconceptions. The Academy retailed stories of Plato's entertainment by Dionysius himself and of his dispute with the despot and its painful sequel; but it appears to me to be very significant that the Seventh Letter (whether that letter be regarded as emanating from Plato himself or from his School, shortly after his death) does not give the slightest hint that Plato ever met the dynast, and there is very little doubt in my mind that he did *not*. Dionysius may very well have been in camp before Rhegium; Pollis' ship, on which Plato was to be given passage home, may have been berthed at Syracuse, or Plato may have travelled by road to join it on the Straits.

There is, however, no good reason to suppose that if Plato had met the tyrant his opinion of him would have been affected. Quite apart from the reasons that he had as an aristocrat and an Athenian to abhor the Sicilian tyrant, there was another and more compelling one, arising out of his conviction of the nature and purpose of society. When Plato arrived at Syracuse he had already reached the conclusion that the duty of the Statesman was not to make his citizens richer or more feared than their neighbours but to make them more virtuous: thus and only thus opening to them the possibility of attaining true happiness. He had, in short, arrived at the conception of the Philosopher King. To this conception Dionysius, whether his ruling passion was the lust for military glory or (as Plato chose to present it) the lust for power for its own sake, who had made his city prosperous, luxurious even, and – reflecting his own power – formidable in the eyes of Greeks and barbarians, was the very antithesis. Indeed, he would have appeared the more deplorable in Plato's eyes because he was a highly gifted and well-educated man, and therefore should have known how to make a better – that is, a truly philosophical – use of his position and his power.[15]

But when Plato arrived at Syracuse, a domestic crisis was already brewing on Ortygia, which within a few months of his departure was, I believe, to produce the only really serious conspiracy of the reign; one directed not against the regime but against Dionysius himself. It centred around his brother Leptines and provided posterity with the material that enabled it to portray Dionysius as one possessed by a morbid suspiciousness which caused him to destroy his closest friends and associates. It is true that there is no specific mention of this conspiracy in our sources, but this omission can be satisfactorily explained; and the circumstantial evidence for a conspiracy appears to me compelling. That Dionysius must have *believed* that his life, or at least his position as monarch, was threatened by Leptines is surely incontrovertible; for Leptines *was* banished from

Sicily, and the length of the interval – perhaps as much as three years – between his public offence and his exile must dispose of the idea that the latter was punishment for the former. What needs to be examined is the question, were there or were there not good grounds for Leptines' banishment, or did Dionysius indeed suffer something like a brainstorm which produced acute delusions of conspiracy, but apparently without its having any lasting effect upon his intellectual powers or his power of leadership?

At this point it may be useful to recapitulate in tabular form (for ease of reference) the events leading up to the presumed conspiracy. Thus:

390 (winter)	Dionysius forms an alliance with the Lucanians, directed against Thurii.
389 (spring)	Rout of the Thurians. Leptines removed from his command for negotiating peace between the Thurians and the Lucanians. Leptines honoured by Thurii.
389 (summer)	Battle of the Eleporus. Deaths of Heloris and his friends.
388	Siege of Rhegium. Thearides' mission to Olympia. Thearides falls out of favour as a result (?).
388/7	Plato visits Syracuse. The 'conversion' of Dion.
387	Plato expelled from Syracuse. Fall of Rhegium, return of Dionysius to Syracuse, disbandment of the greater part of his army. Polyxenus sent with a fleet to the Aegean. The King's Peace.
386 (Diodorus' date)	Dionysius seized by a condition akin to madness (*maniōdes diathesis*), suspects all his friends of plotting against him, executes many and exiles not a few, including Leptines and Philistus who go to Thurii.

Now there is one passage in Plato's description in the *Republic* of tyranny that seems to me to throw light upon this question of a conspiracy, which, following Diodorus, may be dated to 386. It is the passage that describes the alienation of many of The Tyrant's closest and apparently most loyal adherents because of their open rejection of his extreme militarism: an insight that Plato no doubt owed to his sojourn at Syracuse and his friendship with Dion. The first important defector had been Heloris, probably Dionysius' adoptive father and one of the faithful in the darkest days of the Great Revolt, who is to be found, not very many years later, among the Syracusan exiles in Italy, Dionysius' most inveterate enemy. It makes good sense to suppose that Heloris broke with the dynast over the latter's proposal to dissolve the Peace of Himilco (which Carthage appears to have been anxious to preserve).

Leptines, a man very unlike his brother as well as we can tell; extrovert, debonair, high-spirited (and therefore, it is said, popular at Syracuse); was almost certainly jealous of Dionysius' pre-eminence and felt that he should be allowed to share his power (as his actions in the spring of 389 show; perhaps he was influenced by the Spartan view, that the navarchy was virtually a second kingship). Leptines was – or became – closely associated with Philistus, who believed passionately in monarchy but may well have disapproved of militarism. Did he, perhaps, consider that Syracuse should accept the partition of Sicily and turn her eyes northwards and eastwards, towards Italy, the Adriatic and Greece; allying herself with, and assuming the hegemony of, the Italiot confederation, becoming the bastion of Hellenism in Magna Graecia and acquiring honour and respectability in the eyes of Greece? Such a policy could scarcely fail to please Sparta. Certainly Leptines seems to have had reservations about his brother's Italian policy, and to have disapproved of his methods.

Impulsive, lacking in judgement, yet with a very good opinion of himself which his popularity will have encouraged, Leptines must have been deeply mortified, perhaps to the point of utter recklessness, by his dismissal and disgrace; it would hardly be surprising if he allowed himself to become the centre of a palace conspiracy whose object was to transfer the monarchy from his brother's hands into his own. Philistus would have been in the plot, and also, perhaps, Polyxenus. Plutarch attributes Philistus' disgrace to the discovery of his secret marriage to an illegitimate daughter of Leptines – a story which, if true, is quite consistent with the supposition of a conspiracy. Polyxenus (who is not heard of again after his voyage to the Aegean) apparently fled the land without Dionysius' knowledge, 'having become his enemy', and this, too, would fit in with the notion of an abortive palace conspiracy.[16]

The conspirators would have had to wait until Dionysius' return after the end of the fighting in Italy before attempting any move against him, since there would be no hope of overthrowing him whilst he was in the field, surrounded by his soldiers. On his return, however, the greater part of his mercenaries would have been paid off from motives of economy, and Philistus, as Captain of the Citadel, would perhaps be in a good position to take the necessary action. Dionysius, secretive as he no doubt was, is unlikely to have made a secret of his intention to renew the war against Carthage as soon as he had absorbed his recent gains and strengthened his financial position. Is it fanciful to suppose that when Polyxenus (who was, of course, a connection by marriage of Leptines as well as of Dionysius) had talks with Spartan statesmen at the Hellespont – including the subtle Antialcidas – it was conveyed to him that Sparta would view with approval a change in the orientation of Syracuse's foreign policy, that Syracuse should concern herself more with the nipping in the bud of nascent Athenian imperialism than with a fruitless struggle with Carthage? Polyxenus must have returned home in the late summer or autumn of 387, and without doubt brought a message *of some kind* from the Spartans to his lord. That Dionysius would have rejected out of hand any suggestion that he should turn his attention from Carthage to the affairs of metropolitan Greece we need not doubt, although it is certainly true that from now on he took a greater interest in the Adriatic. This he did, however, merely in pursuance of his grand design against Carthage. But if Polyxenus brought to Court any such message as I have conjectured above, he may have stirred up his already disaffected kinsmen to take certain fatal steps – or perhaps to do no more than talk incautiously.

For it could well be that the matter had never gone beyond talk, and that this talk was reported, perhaps with exaggeration and misrepresentation, by enemies at Court: one thinks of Dion and Hipparinus. Now it is certainly true that Dionysius had been under very considerable strain for many years. He had campaigned almost without respite since 390 and during that time had received a serious wound. His pride and self-esteem as an artist (which, even without the testimony of our sources, we might assume to have been both large and vulnerable) had suffered a wound no less severe from the fiasco of his Olympic *theoria*. It may be that his brutal treatment of Phyton is referable to his mental condition. Yet the evidence of conspiracy – at any rate, as it was presented to him – must surely have been very strong, to cause him to banish from his dominions the brother whose negligence, disobedience and, lastly, whose flat disloyalty he had condoned over the course of a decade. His anger and resentment would, of course, have been the greater because of the trust that he had always placed in these men (Polyxenus does not seem to have fallen under suspicion), who were among the closest to him; but however much the true balance of his mind may have become temporarily disturbed, it is to be noted that he did not have the culprits (real or supposed) put to death, and that he later forgave Leptines and reinstated him in high command. He never wholly forgave Philistus or allowed him back to Sicily, although it seems likely that he employed him as his agent or even as his viceroy in the Adriatic. Perhaps he believed that Philistus, the cleverer and more sober character and the older man, had seduced Leptines from his loyalty. It is a measure of the carelessness of Diodorus' writing that he states that Philistus, too, was pardoned and returned to Syracuse, although Timaeus certainly, and Ephorus probably, knew that this was not the case. However, the chapters that deal with these matters (6 and 7 of Book XV, in the Loeb edition) are of a parenthetical character and probably derive from the anecdotal (note-book) material rather than from the historical.[17]

If the treachery (or the evidence presented to him of the treachery) of his most trusted associates did induce in Dionysius a period of intense – perhaps even paranoid – suspiciousness, it would hardly be surprising. Even in a democracy the discovery of a serious conspiracy may result in a 'witch hunt'; and without looking for modern parallels we may recall the fever of suspicion that attacked the Athenians as a result of the mutilation of the Hermae. Diodorus says that 'many' of Dionysius' friends were executed; but in fact if all the individually identified instances of Dionysius' 'cruelty' are reckoned up, they amount to only eleven persons, of whom three at least appear to be totally unconnected with the (presumed) conspiracy – and, indeed, not one of the eleven cases is above suspicion of being the product of malicious invention. There is, first of all, the Guard commander, Marsyas, said to have been executed for having told Dionysius that he had dreamed of killing him. No doubt the reason given for his execution belongs to the Academic tradition that ascribed all the tyrant's crimes to the moral degeneration inseparable from the possession of irresponsible power; but the survival of a *name* (one of only three), and the fact that the conspiracy (real or imagined) involved the Captain of the Citadel, gives a certain credibility to the story of the execution of an officer of the Guards. Similarly, truth may underlie the anecdote of the sentry put to death for handing Leptines his spear in Dionysius' presence. The story of the barber, killed because he made a joke in bad taste, is probably no more than a version of the 'Dionysius-was-so-paranoid-that-he-did-not-dare-to-allow-a-razor-near-his-throat' myth; but there just might be something more behind it. In the same way it would be unwise to assert that the stories of the two young men slain for taking a sword into the tyrant's ball court, and of the death of the other young man who talked treason in his cups, did not derive from real events. There is also the today otherwise almost unknown playwright, Antiphon, said by Aristotle to have been put to death, apparently by some form of crucifixion, by Dionysius. Something more will be said about Antiphon in Chapter 12, but for now let it suffice that Philostratus (second century AD) knew a tradition that he had been executed for plotting against the tyrant. And there is also one Leon, of whom nothing is known beyond the statement that he was put to death after having been twice reprieved; but we cannot say for certain which of the Dionysii was concerned.[18]

In summing up, then, it appears to me that there is strong circumstantial evidence for the historicity either of a positive conspiracy designed to replace Dionysius by his brother Leptines, or at least of a falling-out between the dynast and his brother (the latter supported certainly by Philistus and probably by Polyxenus) of such seriousness that the dynast became convinced of his brother's disloyalty. Towards this conviction he *may* have been influenced by the prompting of Dion, who certainly had a double motive, dynastic and now philosophical, for wanting to secure for

himself the favour and trust of the tyrant: an object which, in the course
of the next few years, he undoubtedly achieved. An additional motive
would have been that of revenge, if, as I believe may have been the case,
it was Philistus, as Captain of the Citadel, who was responsible for
packing Plato off from Syracuse. Certainly the enmity that Philistus
displayed towards Plato and Dion in the next, unhappy, reign is presented as having been extremely bitter. However, whether there was a
conspiracy to depose Dionysius, or whether the latter was merely led to
believe that there was, Dion's non-participation in it left him, morally
speaking, in a somewhat anomalous position; for, as a Good Man, he
ought to have supported a movement to overthrow a tyrant – a movement which must inevitably have weakened the tyranny. When he was
at Athens, therefore, engaged in enlisting the support of the Academy
for his proposed overthrow of Dionysius the Younger, he would have
been likely to keep quiet about the earlier conspiracy and encourage the
idea that the banishment or execution of Leptines and others was to be
ascribed to the mixture of calculated cruelty and paranoia that was
accepted in intellectual circles (and, indeed, by then, popularly) as
inseparable from the tyrannical condition. Philistus, hoping always for
pardon and recall (and following, perhaps, the example of his literary
model, Thucydides) would naturally have been reticent about the reason
for his own, and therefore for Leptines', disgrace. As a result, the conspiracy, like so many other things that might seem to contradict the
accepted picture of the despot Dionysius – things like the votes of the
Athenian Council and of the Assembly in his honour, the gold crowns
bestowed upon him together with the gift of Athenian citizenship, and
the solemn treaty – was allowed to disappear from the record of those
times.[19]

If the reason why some of Dionysius' closest supporters went or were
driven into exile is that they conspired to put an end to, or that they
merely criticized, his militarism too incautiously, it is impossible not to
sympathize with them. Victory over Carthage and Dionysius' glory, in
whose reflected light they were to bask, must have seemed very prob-
lematical in 387; and it was for the good of Syracuse, not for the
realization of Dionysius' dream, that the best of his friends had helped
him to the monarchy. Once suzerainty over the Sicels and the Greek
cities of the east coast had been firmly established (and Carthage had
made no attempt to interfere with this), it was peace – or rather, since
Greeks normally took a Clausewitzian view of war, it was the absence of
large-scale, unproductive and essentially unnecessary wars – that would
provide Syracuse and its people with prosperity and the regime with
popular support, so dispelling the atmosphere of suspicion and veiled
oppression that is inseparable from despotism. Peisistratus of Athens, the
beau ideal of the 'liberal' and popular tyrant, had been conspicuously a

man of peace. Yet if we have to sympathize with those who had become disillusioned with the crusade against Carthage, we must recognize the fact that Dionysius saw himself as a Man of Destiny and one therefore entitled to the loyalty of his friends; nor can his treatment of Leptines and Philistus be regarded as either despotic or cruel. How long, we may ask, would Leptines have lasted in wartime Athens? His carelessness as a commander and his pigheaded recklessness contributed perhaps more than any other single factor to the ill success of Dionysius' wars with Carthage. Had he been an Athenian general, we need have little doubt that he would have been punished severely for allowing Himilco to land his army in Sicily in 396 without having to fight a major battle at sea, and I cannot believe that death would not have been his portion, once for throwing away his fleet at the battle of Catane, and again for taking it upon himself to make peace between the Lucanians and Thurii. Indeed, it may well have been the same recklessness that cost his brother what would have been a decisive victory at Cronium – and cost him his own life.

Envy being (as Herodotus pointed out) a universal human failing, it would be absurd to pretend that Dionysius' regime was untainted by envy, suspicion, corruption and perhaps serious injustice. Not only Ortygia but the city of Syracuse, too, was a State in which advancement, power and wealth depended on the favour – or at least on the absence of disfavour – of the dynast: a typical breeding ground for intrigue. In addition to the political stresses and strains that gave rise to the conspiracy (or suspicion of a conspiracy) discussed above, Dionysius had two 'queens', two households, under his roof, and although we are told that he did his best to keep both his wives happy, there is anecdotal evidence of a struggle for primacy between them. Dionysius is said to have had his Locrian mother-in-law put to death for administering contraceptive drugs to Aristomache; and although this may be no more than a version of the hoary wicked-mother-in-law myth, spiced by the malice of Dion, Aristomache's brother (whom Doris' prior fecundity robbed of the advantage of being uncle to Dionysius' successor), there must have been intense rivalry between the two 'queens' to produce the first son, and the 'Syracusan' camp, in their disappointment, may well have accused their rivals, either with or without good grounds, of underhand practices. If Doris' mother did in fact administer drugs (the word *pharmaka* also connotes poison) to her daughter's rival – or if she failed to clear herself of the suspicion of having done so – her execution would not have offended contemporary ideas of justice.

But Plato's most serious charge against Dionysius is that his absolute power bred in him a suspiciousness that led him to get rid of *all* men of excellence – of all men who could be his friends – leaving only a residue of creatures and sycophants. Dionysius, if he had really been asked to debate the matter with Plato, had plenty of material from which to fashion his reply. He could have pointed out that Dion, his brother-in-law, a paragon of virtue and the brightest of Plato's disciples, remained at his side to the end, enjoying his (almost) complete confidence even though (we are told) he openly disapproved of tyranny on principle and dissociated himself from the dissolute Court. And there were others. Secondly, he could have remarked that Plato was merely serving up, in expanded form, the strictures on tyranny made familiar by Herodotus. And thirdly, that the free *polis*, inbred and exclusive in its membership, intensely jealous of its rights and privileges, divided by latent class resentment which tended to become active in time of stress, could show a far more impressive history of envy, suspicion and judicial murder than his tyranny. He could have pointed out the fundamental injustice of the Athenian institution of ostracism (adopted for a time by free Syracuse); he could have reminded his Athenian critics of the Terrors of 411 and 404, when political assassination and judicial murder were frequent, and of the notorious trial and condemnation of the generals, in 406; he could have instanced the numerous occasions on which loyal citizens had been exiled or executed simply for failing to satisfy the Demos; and he could have suggested that his *potagōgides* (if they *were* his and not his son's) were hardly more obnoxious than Athens' sycophants.[20]

Yet when all this had been taken into account, the fact remained that Dionysius found it exceedingly difficult to discover loyal and efficient servants, whereas Athens did not; and for this misfortune the banishment from Syracuse of so many of the governing class – something that was not the result of Dionysius' deliberate policy (as Plato would have us believe) but was inseparable from tyranny itself – was to blame. Plato accuses the tyrant of identifying the individual members of this class, (which he styles the Best Element (*to beltiston*)) and making away with them: in fact, of putting into practice the legendary advice given by Thrasybulus to Periander. But the expulsion of the Knights from Syracuse was not the outcome of Dionysius' suspiciousness but of their own abortive coup against him. For it is in the nature of aristocracy that it cannot serve a master: it can only lead. The noblemen of pre-Dioclesian Syracuse (like those of pre-Periclean Athens) saw themselves as the leaders, the patrons (*prostatai*) of the people. But democracy – radical democracy – demands service, and so does tyranny. So Greek aristocracy was unhappy under rampant democracy and there was no lack of mutual envy and suspicion between the Quality and the Demos at Syracuse, from the '50s of the fifth century onwards; which helps to explain the ease with which Dionysius secured for himself, first, the generalship and then the acquiescence of the Demos in his assumption of supra-constitutional power immediately afterwards. Nor should it be forgotten that, towards the end of the Great Revolt, the Demos rejected the co-operation of the Knights and compelled them to return to Aetna.

However, the Syracusan nobles had found it possible to play an active part in public life under the democracy, because the Demos, aware of their superior education and their tradition of leadership, permitted them to continue to hold the elective military commands (although subjecting them to constant interference and to the threat of dismissal or worse from demagogues and Assembly), and to play a not insignificant role as counsellors and advisers of the Assembly. They could still think of themselves as the rightful governing class, could still distinguish themselves; and, being both numerous and wealthy, could hope for the return of better times following a re-revision of the laws. Dionysius, however, had taken upon himself the direction of military affairs and the protection of the city, and also the patronship of the People. In fact, the city no longer had a foreign policy, except in so far as the Assembly was permitted to accept or reject wars and treaties decided upon by the dynast in consultation with his Privy Council of relations and friends. It was the tyrant who appointed, at his own discretion, the force commanders and the corps commanders and admirals, he that planned the campaigns and reaped the glory. Any noble who wished to play a significant part in the public and military life of Syracuse could do so only as Dionysius' appointee and subordinate: in effect, as his servant. This situation would have seemed to most of them intolerable and their resentment, being no secret to the dynast, would have made it difficult for him to employ them, even if they were willing to be employed, in positions of trust. Yet he had made an effort to effect a reconciliation with the exiles, for he desperately needed able, experienced and (in *his* interpretation of the word) patriotic men to assist him in the carrying out of his grand schemes; and the career of Dion shows that really loyal subordinates could be both rewarded and trusted. But the resentment of the old governing class towards the 'upstart' tyrant effectually deprived the regime of the services of Syracuse's natural leaders, and left the ruler dependent upon anyone whom he could find willing to work for him: relatives, foreign *condottieri* and such natives, old or new upper-class, competent or incompetent, as were prepared to take orders from a tyrant. Small wonder, then, that a critic as strongly influenced both by the prejudices of his caste and the circumstances of his upbringing and by his philosophical convictions as Plato should summarily describe the tyrant's entourage as sycophantic and worthless. That Dionysius was not always well served by the men whom he appointed to command his troops and, particularly, his ships is very true. But then efficient leaders had not been numerous in free, republican Syracuse either. Athens, it has to be admitted, had been, and, indeed, in the first half of the fourth century remained, singularly fortunate in that respect.[21]

One of Dionysius' greatest disappointments must have been the unwar-like nature of his eldest son. He was accused of keeping his son out of public life, so that when he succeeded to his father's power he was wholly inexperienced in statecraft and unable to keep what his father had so laboriously won. But, as has been said already, Dionysius was essentially a war-lord, not a civil statesman; and if the the young man had neither the physique (he is said to have had bad eyesight) nor the aptitude nor the stomach for fighting, he could not have been either of much real interest or of any real use to such a man as Dionysius. I have suggested that the dynast played no formal role in the affairs of Syracuse and we are told that he kept the management of his empire under his own close supervision. If the young man could not be employed as a soldier – and therefore could not be appointed to the governorship of a city – it is difficult to see what part he could play in a world where only the military man counted.

The Younger Dionysius (who has, if anything, been worse treated by the writers of antiquity than his father) is said to have been devoted to debauchery and bad company; which may well be true, and if true, is hardly surprising. He showed himself, on his accession, opposed to war with Carthage, with which he concluded what could have been a lasting peace. But unhappily for him, one of the things that he inherited from his father was the latter's right-hand man, Dion, son of Hipparinus, an enigmatic figure, who may well have been planning to transfer the control of the empire from the Locrian branch of the family to his own, the Syracusan, under the form of a Platonic monarchy. It is useless to indulge in 'might have beens' with regard to the fate of Syracuse and Sicily if Dion and Plato had left the young man alone to pursue his mild debaucheries; but it is at least possible that they would have been spared a great deal of devastation and misery.

Much of the malice displayed by the Greek literary tradition towards Dionysius and his son stems, without any doubt, from the eagerness of the Academy to justify their Founder's conduct and to shift as much of the blame as possible for what befell Sicily in the '50s and early '40s from Plato's friends to the tyrants. Like the intellectuals who visited Russia in the Twenties and Thirties of the present century, Plato came to Syracuse in order to see what his preconceptions had led him to believe that he would see, and his convictions will have been hardened by what he was told in southern Italy (although Pythagorean Taras was not actively hos-tile towards Dionysius and Locri was friendly). Plato came to contemplate the vices that his philosophy assured him he would find in a tyranny: the reign of envy and suspicion, the repudiation of the rule of law, the exile of the 'Best Element', the emancipation of slaves, the waging of ceaseless war and the prevalence of a gross materialism wholly at variance with his own ideal of society. His preconceptions, I believe, received confirmation as a result of his intercourse with the young Dion, who was mortified by the prospect of having in the future to play second fiddle to the despised son of his sister's foreign rival, and ready to be converted to a Platonic view of present conditions and future possibilities. Plato's critique of the regime is largely unoriginal and tendentious; but because of the high esteem in which he was held in antiquity, it set the tone for all subsequent comment. Even the fact that he does not accuse the tyrant of sensuality and personal display and extravagance may have served to spare Dionysius one unmerited reproach, at least![22]

In Plato's (or the Platonic) Seventh Letter we encounter the same theme, that of the tyrant's failure, because of his suspiciousness, to find loyal and able associates, applied this time to the governance of the empire – and applied with no less disingenuousness. Dionysius (it is said) could not establish lasting regimes loyal to himself in the Greek cities that he had restored, although he employed both creatures of his own and his brothers. He made one *polis* of all Sicily, but almost came to ruin through lack of reliable friends. Comparisons are drawn, to Dionysius' disadvantage, with the satrapal organization of the Persian Empire by the 'good king' Darius, who trusted his associates, and with the Athenian Empire, which endured for 70 years because it found 'friends' in the (subject) cities. Now there are not a few considerations which lead one to question the validity of a comparison between a quasi-feudal sixth-century Oriental monarchy and a fourth-century Hellenic tyranny; nor is there any mention of the numerous revolts against Persian rule. Moreover, it cannot be said that the Persian kings, including Darius, were very happy in their relations with their Greek subjects – and it is with Dionysius' failure to win over the Greeks that Plato is concerned. The comparison with the Athenian Empire is even more dishonest. The writer of the Letter can hardly have been unaware of the admittedly tyrannical nature of that Empire and of the numerous revolts that occurred over almost the whole period of its existence; of the severity with which these were put down and punished; of the part played by the Athenian navy in the horrible civil war that devastated Corcyra, or of the means by which the Melians were incorporated into the Empire; of the garrisons, cleruchies and constant naval activity which policed the Empire and ensured its 'loyalty'. Above all, perhaps, he forgets that Athens' 'friends' in the cities belonged to the very class, the demagogues and friends of radical democracy, that Plato himself most disapproved of. Finally, the statement that Dionysius made one *polis* of the whole of Sicily is simply a rhetorical flourish, made for its emotive effect. What the writer has in mind is that Dionysius had made the whole of Sicily into one *State*; but the Greek language has no word for 'State' as distinct from 'community'. To say that Dionysius had made the whole of Sicily into one *empire* would be pointless; and so the writer uses a term which would convey to the Greek mind the impression that Dionysius was not just a man who could not preserve an empire but was one who, by reason of the flaw in his character, could not prevent the dissolution of that homogeneous community (*polis*) upon membership of which depended the possibility of enjoying the good life.

The Athenian Empire came into existence as a voluntary federation of free peoples with a common purpose; and during the period between the two Peloponnesian Wars, at all events, it performed a most useful function by excluding the Persians from the shores and waters of the Aegean, by preserving the freedom of the seas and by extending to the member States the benefits of the best legal system and the best currency of the day. Moreover, it exercised a civilizing and educative influence that was recognized by the more enlightened of the Athenians. Dionysius' empire, on the other hand, was founded and maintained solely in order to supply the dynast with the sinews of war. Yet it cannot be denied that the Athenian Empire degenerated into something not so very different, in many respects, from that of Dionysius, when it could be written of it: 'For by now you [Athenians] hold your empire as a tyranny, which it may have been unjust to take but which it is perilous to give up'. Dionysius' empire had, from the standpoint of the Sicels, never been anything but a tyranny. For a brief time prior to the third Punic war, the Siceliots regarded it as a free association of cities; but after the signing of the peace treaty with Carthage it became a tyranny. Of Dionysius' Italiot subjects, only the Locrians were wholly free – and even they may have fallen under the yoke, in the '80s.[23]

Modern historians have accused Dionysius of destroying the *polis* and so of betraying Greek freedom and Hellenism itself. Dionysius, being a tyrant, was the enemy of political liberty (and therefore of the *polis*, the very embodiment of liberty), and as ruler of an empire he could not tolerate the existence of strong *poleis* within it. Therefore, because his empire was not a voluntary league of free peoples (as Plato would have been happy for it to be), its only principle of cohesion was supplied by the person of the dynast, and as soon as that was withdrawn the empire fell apart, leaving Hellenism defenceless.

This criticism, which the actual course of events would appear to render a just one, does not take into account several important factors. First, the Greek cities of Sicily were, from the outset, confronted by a Super-power in Carthage, with which they could not hope to cope individually. Secondly, they never even discussed (as far as we know) the creation of a formal league such as the Italiots established, which might, by repressing old mutual antagonisms and setting up an effective machinery for the raising and handling of joint armies, have enabled the Siceliots to meet their adversary on a more equal footing. Thirdly, when

Dionysius emerged as the accepted lord of Syracuse, in the summer of 404, all the Greek cities west of a line drawn roughly from the western borders of Messana to those of Syracuse were either isolated or subject to Carthage; and to this may be added the consideration that, had the cautious Dionysius not been in overall command at Gela in 405, the Greeks might very well have suffered a disastrous defeat in an old-fashioned agōnal battle, which could have left Carthage the mistress of Sicily. Lastly, it was not until the last decade of his reign (and not, as Berve and Stroheker maintain, since 392) that Dionysius' archē included, on a permanent basis, the Greek cities of the north and south coasts of the island.

Now it is clear that Dionysius, tyrant though he was, respected the autonomy of the Syracusans; and, since we are told that Carthage's subjects joined him voluntarily and that he 'treated them fairly', and since Carthage had respected *their* autonomy, we may conclude that Dionysius did likewise. That he supported regimes friendly towards himself we need not doubt: these will have been the regimes that brought their cities over to him in the first place. Certainly his subjects were required to surrender, in effect, their foreign policies to him, and to contribute to his war chest. In some cases he appointed governors (if Plato is to be believed, which is by no means axiomatic), perhaps as garrison commanders. But although all this certainly constituted 'enslavement', as the Greeks understood the term, it did not amount to the destruction of the *polis* or the abolition of more than certain aspects of political liberty. Athens did all these things to the cities of *her* empire, and in addition she took their land for cleruchies and punished revolt by wholesale executions. Sparta, in her role of liberator, did far worse, with her system of decarchies and harmosts. By the strictest of standards, the cities of Boeotia were enslaved by Thebes.

The fact is that the *polis* had never been very healthy in Sicily, where the sixth and fifth centuries had witnessed more tyranny and *stasis* than political stability. Besides this, the cities had almost all suffered siege, capture and sack, from which none ever fully recovered, and they were subjects of Carthage, apart from a brief interlude in the '90s, for some twenty years. It is true that Dionysius' empire was by its nature ephemeral and dissolved with the downfall of his son, but so too was the Athenian Empire, which fell to pieces on the destruction of the Athenian navy (which was, at bottom, what held the Empire together). Yet a further twelve years passed before the Carthaginians reappeared on the scene: plenty of time, one might think, for the cities to recover from less than thirty years of over-rule by the Dionysii and to put their houses in order. It hardly seems fair to blame Dionysius, who freed the Siceliots from Punic domination (Plato gives him the credit for 'restoring', *katoikizas*, the plundered cities), for their inability to preserve their freedom after the dissolution of his empire. Timoleon acquired great credit in antiquity for having 'restored' Sicily; yet Timoleon's Sicily, which enjoyed almost a quarter of a century of independence, did not create a league for mutual defence, did not renounce internecine strife, and was unable to preserve itself from subjugation by Agathocles.

Dionysius' relations with the Italiots is a somewhat different matter. He did, briefly, ally himself with the Lucanians and thus contributed to the heavy defeat of a major Greek city. Yet that city did not fall into the hands of the barbarians until more than a generation later. He overthrew the League which had been established for the purpose of resisting the encroachment of the tribes (demonstrating that the League was, perhaps, unequal to the task of containing the Lucanians); but the quarrel with the Italiots was not of his seeking. He had tried to gain Rhegium's friendship and had been unceremoniously rebuffed; and the hostility of that city, the old enmity between her and Syracuse's 'ancient ally', Locri, plus the intrigues of Heloris and his friends, drew him into open war with her and so into war with the League. Yet just as the Dionysii kept the barbarian at bay in Sicily, so did they in Italy. In fact, it was only a Super-power that could hope in the long run to overcome the wealth of Carthage and the relentless pressure of the Italian tribes; although some of the Greeks of Magna Graecia, with the periodic assistance of military adventurers, did manage to preserve their independence until the '80s of the next century. Indeed, in the Motherland itself, within twenty years of the 'liberation' of Syracuse, it was demonstrated that no city – that not even a combination of the strongest cities – could withstand a Super-power: in this case, the 'worse than barbarian' kingdom of Macedon.

Dionysius passed his adult life in continuous warfare in pursuit of *his* vision of Hellenism and Hellenic liberty: the liberty of a Sicily united under his rule from barbarian domination. It was a fact recognized by his very detractors in antiquity that he saved hellenism in Sicily; and, indeed, the hellenization of the Sicels under his sway actually strengthened it in central and eastern Sicily. Had Tychē and the gods been as kind to him as they were to Timoleon, he would have made Sicily Greek from sea to sea. But what he actually achieved, and what he might have achieved, were something that no *polis* (and, indeed, in the light of history, no combination or league of cities) could have achieved. The age of the truly independent *polis* was coming to an end; an end foreshadowed, indeed, by the forced alliances, leagues and empires of Sparta, Thebes and Athens, which were able to coerce, and if need be destroy, the independent *polis*, more than a century before the rise of Macedon.[24]

At its greatest extent (in the year of Dionysius' death) the empire comprised all the Greek cities of Sicily, probably all the Sicel and many of the Sican communities, certain non-Greek towns of the Epicraty, the whole of the 'toe' of Italy from the northern borders of Croton down to the Straits, and certain possessions in the Adriatic. In most cases, but certainly not in all, the peoples of the empire paid tribute. The Siceliots who had put themselves under Dionysius' protection in the '80s in order to escape from the domination of Carthage must have undertaken to assist the lord (*archōn*) of Sicily in his wars; but if what has been said above about his non-employment of the Syracusan militia after the 90s is true, it would probably apply to them; and in that case their assistance will have been in cash and perhaps in cavalry. Some if not all of the more important cities probably had military governors appointed by Dionysius, the civil administration being put into the hands of men whom he felt he could trust. Some of the cities were military colonies, some were free allies, like Agyrium and, in Italy, Locri. But whatever the means he employed to keep control of an empire whose sole purpose was to serve the military ambition of the dynast, he would appear to have been more successful in holding it together then Plato would have us believe – although the member cities (like the great majority of those that composed the Athenian Empire) were always on the lookout for a favourable opportunity to revolt. It would, for instance, be surprising if unrest had not followed the disastrous termination of the third Punic War; and if it did, it would perhaps explain Plato's (if it is Plato's) 'he barely survived' (*mogis esōthē*). But Carthage's domestic troubles and her unwillingness to keep large standing armies in Sicily in peacetime discouraged revolt during the last years of the 'reign'.[25]

The tyranny of Dionysius, then, belonged firmly in the native Sicilian tradition of the military monarchy, established in the first half of the sixth century by Phalaris of Acragas. He had not seized power for the purpose (and the satisfaction) of rectifying social abuses, or for the distinction that power confers on its possessor, or for the inner gratification arising from the sheer possession of power, but as the means of supplying his thirst for military glory with the resources for waging war. The Syracusans, as the price of their being permitted to conduct the affairs of the city in accordance with their laws, had given him the control of military matters. However, as war-leader, he would have had to be consulted – as the board of generals used to be consulted – on all matters even remotely connected with the defences of the city, its armed forces, its finances and its relations with other peoples. But Dionysius was a man of hyperactive temperament. He was quick to act and impatient of delay. Highly intelligent, he could identify problems and quickly devise solutions for them, and he hated inefficiency, waste and lawlessness. When not campaigning – that is to say, for something like half the year – he would be quite unable to sit in idleness and not interfere in what was going on, on the other side of the cross-wall that marked the agreed boundary of his civic authority. The construction and repair of public buildings, the proper worship of the gods, the maintenance of law and order, the provision of employment for the landless – in general, the well-being and prosperity of the city – were all matters that Dionysius would have regarded as being very much his business, both as a Syracusan and as the War-lord of the city, upon whose reputation any shortcoming of that city would reflect.

When he made his compact with the Syracusans, I have little doubt that Dionysius fully intended to honour it in the spirit as well as in the letter; but however little interest he professed in the 'parish-pump' politics of the city, his own nature and the nature of politicians at all times and in all places would have ensured that he became involved in them. As Augustus was to discover when he sought to detach himself somewhat from civil government, the very existence of a war-lord with powerful armed forces devoted wholly to himself casts its shadow over the whole political life of the State; and at Syracuse, this private army was largely composed of foreign mercenaries and was camped upon the very doorstep of the city. Inevitably the war-lord dominated Syracusan public life and his presence restricted the free play of democracy. Dionysius would have been bound to put the weight of his influence behind those citizens whom he regarded as well disposed towards himself. Politicians on the make would have seen the advantage to be gained by attaching themselves to him and claiming to consult and represent his interests; more honest men would have been driven to consult him and to elicit his approval of their views by the conviction that failure to do so would be interpreted as hostility towards him. No doubt his support was canvassed by candidates for elective office, and although there was probably more than one 'Theodorus' in the city who was prepared to speak out against him (for it is worth noting that, at the close of the Theodorus episode in Diodorus, there is no suggestion that either Theodorus or the Syracusans who approved of his speech were punished), if supporting the leader's policies and doing his work in the Assembly was the way to advancement, there would be no lack of men to follow this course. Probably, like Pericles in the latter part of his career, Dionysius addressed the Assembly in person only when the most important matters were coming under discussion, leaving it to his 'friends' to take care of ordinary matters.[26]

Even the administration of justice, the corner-stone of liberty, can hardly have escaped. From the very first, Dionysius must have been appealed to, to advise, to arbitrate, to rectify real or supposed injustices. It is likely that, once his overlordship was consolidated and generally accepted as something that was there to stay, he came to constitute a kind of non-statutory high court and court of appeal. Of course, on Ortygia – for it was Ortygia, not Syracuse, that was the capital of his empire – he ruled absolutely, dispensing justice and directing the lives of kinsmen, friends, toadies, followers, mercenaries, merchants and servants, with the help of a privy council of friends. Indeed, the truth is that the cross-wall with its fortifications that divided the Island from the mainland was as much a symbol and a safeguard of the liberties of the Syracusans as it was of the overlordship of the dynast. On the Island Dionysius' word was law, but in Syracuse he had to get his way by respecting the forms, employing the methods and (at any rate, up to a point) accepting the restraints and curbs of democratic government. If Dionysius had crossed the wall with force, to coerce or chastise the Syracusans, the covenant between them would have been broken and their working relationship destroyed.

Indeed, not only is there no instance in the tradition of despotic (in the looser sense of the word) behaviour on the part of Dionysius towards his fellow citizens, there is more than one passage – quite apart from the openly laudatory chapters of Diodorus that derive directly from Philistus – that attests the mildness and generosity of his rule. His son spoke to the first meeting of the Assembly that he convened after his accession to power of the loyalty (*eunoia*) that the Syracusans had shown his father. Had Dionysius lived in the last decades of the century, when the Macedonian notion of the military kingdom became familiar to the eastern Mediterranean world, he would undoubtedly have proclaimed himself king (*basileus*), and so have given his regime a kind of legitimacy. But monarchy, in the days before the rise of Macedon, was inseparable from tyranny. Philosophers could accept the idea that a monarch, by sedulous avoidance of all the traditional vices of the tyrant, might rule his people virtuously, or, by his own selfless cultivation of philosophy, govern in accordance with the dictates of True Knowledge. None the less, monarchy remained a universally unacceptable form of government, although a monarch who did not oppress his subjects might be tolerated and even popular. But the man in the street was happiest with some form of democracy, and the intellectual preferred, as a practical alternative to ideal aristocracy, the *politeia* approved by Aristotle and the 'oligarchs' of fifth-and fourth-century Athens.[27]

CHAPTER TEN

The third Punic War

In the fifteenth book of his World History, Diodorus' account of the events of the fifth and fourth centuries in Sicily and Magna Graecia, comparable up to this point in substance and detail to that of events in metropolitan Greece and the Aegean, falters. In chapter 13 of the Loeb edition, which deals with the dynast's operations in the Adriatic, the narrative breaks down after the founding of Lissus; it recovers in chapter 14; and then, in chapters 15, 16 and 17, under the single year 383/2, and in two sections of chapter 24, under the year 379/8, it takes in the *whole* of the third Carthaginian War, its causes and its outcome. Yet this was a war which Dionysius was compelled to fight on two fronts, in Sicily and in Italy; it saw the submission to him of the leading Greek city in southern Italy, it included probably the two largest land battles of his career; and it lasted, in all probability, *at least* six years: nevertheless the text that we possess gives to it less than half the pages that it devotes, for instance, to the largely, or wholly, fictitious meeting of the Assembly at which 'Theodorus' delivers his tirade against tyranny!

Clearly something disastrous has befallen the transmission of Diodorus' text. Stroheker's explanation, that Philistus, upon whom Diodorus' immediate source or sources relied for *facts*, being then in exile, was not in a position to provide material of the same quality as heretofore, seems to me to be wholly unsatisfactory. In the first place, Philistus is said to have written *the greater part* of his history in exile. He must have had his correspondents at Syracuse, and if (as seems possible) he in fact enjoyed a position of trust at Adria, he is hardly likely to have been completely out of touch with such momentous contemporary events. After all, exile had not prevented his model, Thucydides, from collecting his material; and he had time to revise his work, after his eventual recall to Syracuse. Moreover, Philistus was not the only contemporary historian of Sicilian affairs: there were also Hermeias of Methymna and Polycritus of Mende. Finally, there are notices of events belonging to this period in later writers other than Diodorus – in Justin, Dionysius of Halicarnassus, Aelian and Polyaenus – which we do not find in Diodorus. But if there was ample contemporary material available, it is hardly credible that

15 Croton: silver didrachm, ca. 400: (above) eagle; (below) tripod

both Ephorus and Timaeus (who were personally interested in the history of Magna Graecia and Sicily) would have dealt so very cursorily with a period of such great historical interest; especially as the outcome of the war could be adduced as an object-lesson on the doom that Nemesis keeps in waiting for the hubristic.[1]

However, if we may reasonably assume that both Ephorus and Timaeus gave full accounts of the events between 383 and 375, the conclusion is inescapable that Diodorus, himself a Sicilian who had, up to this point, given Sicilian and Italian affairs their fair share of his attention, would have told us at least as much about this war as he had about the two preceding wars. The only satisfactory explanation is that at some remote point in the stemma of the sadly corrupt (*degener* – Vogel) archetype from which our extant manuscripts derive, the passages dealing with the third Punic War were (with one minor omission) *collected together* in order to provide a single connected narrative of this war, whose dramatic effect – fought as it was in two widely separated theatres and culminating in a truly tragic peripeteia – would have been enormously heightened if it were excerpted from the framework of an annalistic universal history and presented to the reader as a coherent unity. Perhaps the publisher (or his patron) had been influenced by the strictures passed by Dionysius of Halicarnassus upon Thucydides' arrangement of his material by summers and winters: an arrangement which breaks up the continuity of the narratives of the various campaigns. The section of Diodorus' book containing this connected account of the war was subsequently lost, and the resultant gap in the history of the decade was filled by a clumsy epitome, which was inserted under the year 383/2 because the section dealing with the events of 384/3 ends with the statement that Dionysius was obviously going to make war on the Carthaginians. I think that it is significant that our chapter 24, sections 1 to 4, whose account of a Carthaginian naval expedition to south Italy and of the outbreak of plague at Carthage belongs to the general narrative of the third Punic War, but does not mention *Sicily*, has been left in. Certainly as regards their whole manner and style, chapters 15 to 17 read like an epitome, rather than a continuation of Diodorus' own narrative.[2]

Let us, then, examine what information we have been given about this momentous period, taking the text of Diodorus first. By the end of 384/3, it was clear that Dionysius was going to fight the Carthaginians. In 383/2, he made alliances with Carthage's disaffected allies and rejected Carthaginian demands for their return to her control. Carthage made an alliance with the Italiots and in consort with them embarked upon war. She raised large citizen and mercenary forces, appointed Mago general and moved 'many tens of thousands' of troops (the uncharacteristic vagueness of this figure is surely significant) into Sicily and Italy. Dionysius, too, fought on both fronts. There were numerous engagements by land and sea in both theatres, and two important battles. Dionysius was victorious at Cabala and Mago was slain. Carthage then offered to make peace, but Dionysius demanded that she evacuate Sicily. All the above events are contained in a single chapter (15). The

Carthaginians in Sicily tricked Dionysius, and 'in the course of a few days' Mago's son restored the morale of the beaten army, and subsequently fought a battle at Cronium in which Dionysius' army was routed. Carthage again offered to make peace and peace was in fact concluded. These events are treated in our chapters 16 and 17. *Later*, in our chapter 24, under the year 379/8, we are told that the Carthaginians sent an expedition to Italy and restored the city of Hipponium to its exiles. Then plague struck Carthage, and Libya and Sardinia revolted.[3]

Justin (who, however, runs together Dionysius' first major Italian campaign, the third Punic War and the fourth) tells us that the dynast fought a long and at first unsuccessful war against Croton. Then he made a pact with the Senones and with the aid of Gallic auxiliaries renewed the struggle. Dionysius was still in Italy when the arrival of the Carthaginians, after the ending of the plague, summoned him back to Sicily. Polyaenus gives us a slightly *different* account of what took place after the battle of Cabala from that of Diodorus and also an account (in all probability) of events preceding the battle of Cronium. Aelian says that 'Dionysius led 300 ships full of hoplites against Thurii, but his fleet was destroyed by the North Wind'. From Dionysius of Halicarnassus we learn that the dynast captured Rhegium and Croton and held them for twelve years. This 'twelve years' can, of course apply only to Croton (Dionysius, at the time of his death, had held Rhegium for almost twenty years), and the carelessness of the notice suggests to me that the twelve years may, in fact, refer to the length of time that Croton was subject, that she may have broken away from the empire during the earliest years of the reign of Dionysius II, and may, therefore, have been taken shortly *after* the 379 that Dionysius' words would seem to imply. And in Strabo we read that in Italy those outside (i.e. to the north of) the Wall prevented its completion. There are two other passages in Diodorus which may help to throw some more light on the problem of the chronology of the war. In 374, the Spartans sent a naval squadron to Corcyra; giving out, however, that its destination was Sicily. Beloch has suggested that the ostensible purpose of the expedition was to strengthen Dionysius' hand in the peace negotiations with Carthage. It seems to me more likely that Dionysius had asked for (and later, perhaps, countermanded) a show of force by Sparta to bolster up his position as overlord of eastern Sicily, shaken by his conclusion of an unfavourable peace. The other passage tells us that the historian Hermeias of Methymna ended his Sicilian History with the year 376/5. Of course Hermeias may have died or become incapacitated in that year; but it is tempting to surmise that he chose as the terminus of his work the conclusion of a peace in Sicily that must have given the appearance of finality.[4]

As regards the chronology of the war, then, all that Diodorus really gives us is a *terminus post quem* for its outbreak (383/2), possibly a *terminus ante quem* for its conclusion (375), and one other date. We can, however, deduce a little more from what I take to be his epitomizer's account of the war. Both the narrative and inherent probability support the assumption that peace followed closely upon the Carthaginian victory at Cronium. In addition, the narrative suggests that in Diodorus' full account of events, the two battles of Cabala and Cronium were not separated by any very long period of time. Thus from Diodorus we may conclude that the serious fighting in Sicily was confined to the last few years of the war. This supposition bears out Justin's statement, that Dionysius was recalled from his Italian campaign by the arrival of the Carthaginian expeditionary force in Sicily, whose despatch had been delayed by the plague that had attacked Carthage – a plague that is also reported by Diodorus – together with the revolt of Libya and Sardinia. But this plague, recorded in the non-epitomized chapter 24 of Diodorus, broke out in the late summer of 379, and Carthage can hardly have recovered from the effects of this, *and* recovered her revolted dependencies, before the late summer of 378. It is most unlikely, therefore, that Carthage was in a position to send a large expeditionary force to Sicily before the summer of 377. The two major battles, then, may be assigned to the years 377 to 375, and the peace to the latter year.

By the summer of 384 Dionysius had established his power in the Adriatic, and was ready to turn his attention once again to the achievement of his greatest ambition, the expulsion of the Carthaginians from Sicily. For this he needed a large army, composed wholly or at least in great part of professional soldiers, and to obtain these, he needed ready money. So he conceived the idea of making Carthage's oldest non-Phoenician allies pay for his war, and of making at the same time a demonstration of his power that would rekindle the Hellenic sentiments of those Siceliots who, as tributaries of Carthage, must feel themselves to be enslaved. The Etruscans had been allies of Carthage against Greek expansion in the western Mediterranean since the sixth century. They had commercial treaties with her, probably more favourable than that with which the not commercially-minded Romans were content. The Greeks considered them pirates, which probably means that their warships were active in preventing 'unauthorized' Greek traders from sailing north of Campania. Hieron of Syracuse had taken a powerful force into the Tyrrhenian Sea in 474 and had crushed 'the Etruscans' off Cyme, and republican Syracuse had raided the coasts of Etruria and Elba in 454. Perhaps it is not surprising then that Etruscans had aided the Athenians in their attack upon Syracuse in the Great War. Now, in 384, Dionysius, giving as his motive the wish to suppress piracy, launched what was in fact a massive piratical foray into Etruscan waters.[5]

His primary objective was the principal port, called by the Greeks Pyrgoi (Towers), of Agylla, one of the most important States of Etruria, later and more familiarly known as Caere. The people of Agylla had close treaty and cultural ties with Rome, and despite their commercial relations with the Greek world had aided the Carthaginians, a century and a half earlier, to drive the Greeks out of the upper Tyrrhenian Sea. Perhaps it was from Pyrgi that the Etruscan ships that served under Nicias had come: if so, the fact might have contributed to Dionysius' choice of target for his raid. All our sources (anxious to convict the tyrant of sacrilege) agree that the richest booty was provided by the sack of the famous temple of a goddess whom Strabo calls Eileithyia, who may be equated with the Roman Juno Lucina, and she in her turn with the Etruscan great goddess Uni. From a bilingual inscription found on the site of Pyrgi we know that the people of Agylla had dedicated a shrine to Astartē in their precinct of Uni (with whom Astartē may also be identified). This, together with the name – in Latin, Punicum – given to one of the ports of Agylla, provides evidence of a Phoenician 'colony' and of a strong commercial connection with Carthage, the principal representative of the Phoenician race in the West. The sack of Pyrgi and its temple (whose riches were probably a legend in Sicily), apart from filling his coffers, was intended by Dionysius to convey a signal warning both to the Etruscans and to Carthage that the Tyrrhenian Sea was the preserve of neither people, and that Syracuse could strike heavily wherever she wished. At the same time it would offer encouragement to any of Carthage's subjects who were meditating revolt.[6]

Diodorus, in the last 'original' – i.e. not epitomized – chapter dealing with this period, gives the size of the Sicilian armada as 60 triremes; pseudo-Aristotle, as 100 ships; and Polyaenus as 100 triremes as well as horse transports. It has been suggested that these discrepancies may be reconciled by supposing that they all represent a true figure of 60 triremes and 40 horse transports. We know from Thucydides that a horse transport could carry 30 horses; and it appears unlikely (to say the least) that Dionysius took 1,200 cavalry with him. But Thucydides also tells us that a fleet of 100 ships, 'including horse transports', could convey a force of 4,000 hoplites and 300 cavalry; and probability, and the account of the raid, suggest that Dionysius must have commanded a force of this sort of strength.[7]

Once again Dionysius displayed his appreciation of the military value of surprise, landing his army under cover of darkness and overrunning the weak defences of the port at first light. The citizens of Agylla came down from their hill town to repel the invaders; but Dionysius had plenty of time to draw up his men and the Etruscans were routed. He plundered their territory, no doubt ransomed the many prisoners he had taken, and withdrew to his ships: according to Strabo, he also raided Corsica. In terms of loot, the expedition was worth some 1,500 talents to the dynast.[8]

Under the year 383/2, Diodorus – that is to say, his epitomizer – says that Dionysius, looking for a reasonable excuse for the war against Carthage upon which he was already resolved, 'saw that the cities subject to Carthage were favourably disposed towards revolt, offered his friendship to those that wished to revolt, made an alliance with them and treated them fairly'. The wording of this passage suggests that the cities concerned were Hellenic and Hellenized communities rather than native Sican towns. If, as I believe to be the case, the Greek cities of the north and south coasts were still obliged to pay tribute to Carthage, the list of the disaffected would have included Selinus, Acragas, Gela, Camarina and Himera.

There are several references in the anecdotal material to Dionysius' interest in Himera. Polyaenus (seemingly with some confusion with the capture of Rhegium) describes his seizure of Himera by force, the oft-quoted story of the Dream of the Woman of Himera mentions his coming to the city, and there is the account of Leptines' being sent thither, to take over garrison duty; so it looks very much as if Dionysius gained control of this city, either by force or by agreement, and the most likely time for this to have come about is during the period between the second and the third Punic Wars.[9]

The words 'treated them fairly' in the passage from Diodorus quoted above probably mean that Dionysius guaranteed the autonomy of the cities and offered them a reduction of their tribute. Perhaps, like the Athenians a few years later, he substituted some more palatable word (such as 'contribution', *syntaxis*) for the odious word 'tribute' (*phoros*). Diodorus' epitomizer continues: 'At first the Carthaginians sent ambassadors to the dynast and asked for the return of the cities; but he took no notice, and this turned out to be the origin of the war'. I believe that we must assume that these events – the secession from Carthaginian control of numerous communities, the mounting indignation and alarm of Carthage, the drift towards war – in fact occupied several years. If Dionysius was campaigning in Italy when the Carthaginians landed an army in Sicily (as would appear from Justin's – admittedly very confused – account to be the case), we may infer that he did not feel that he had anything to fear from Carthage before 378; and that therefore her treaty with the Italiots and her commencement of hostilities against Dionysius do not precede by very much the naval expedition in support of the Italiots, dated by Diodorus to 379.[10]

What seems to have happened is that Dionysius' plans for the conquest of the Epicraty were thrown out of gear by the outbreak of hostilities in

Italy. Although the Italiots had voted golden crowns to Dionysius for his generosity after the Eleporus battle, they must have been deeply offended by his subsequent treatment of Caulonia, Hipponium, Scylletium and, above all, Rhegium; nor can their anxiety have been anything but increased by the extension of his power into the Adriatic. But the last straw must have been the disclosure of Dionysius' plan to build a wall across the peninsula, ostensibly to protect his empire from the inroads of the Lucanians, but regarded by the Italiots as a move to sever permanently from Greek Italy the region that was first called Italia.

It was, I believe, the decision of the Italiots (who were still under the hegemony of Croton) to destroy this wall before its completion that led to the outbreak of war, sometime between 383 and 381. Justin tells us that Dionysius landed large forces in Italy and, 'having conquered Locri', attacked Croton. Of course, Justin – who is apt to run one war into another – may simply have confused Rhegium with Locri; but Plato speaks of Locri as having been 'conquered and enslaved by Syracuse': and this expression hardly seems appropriate to the Younger Dionysius' assumption of *legitimate* authority there, following his flight, in 356, from Syracuse, or even for his subsequent seizure of the citadel and establishment of a despotism (we are unfortunately dependent once again upon Justin for this information). Indeed, Justin's account, as well as the notices in our other sources, rather suggest that Dionysius the Younger went to a city which was already subject to him. If that is so, we must assume either that the Italiot League had overrun the northern parts of Dionysius' Italian realm and compelled the Locrians to join the League, or that a popular revolt against the stable oligarchic regime had carried the city into the camp of the League. In either case, Dionysius' first task would have been to recover Locri (now, perhaps, putting it under the rule of an appointee of his own), and his next, to teach the Crotoniates and their allies another lesson. The latter, however, offered so vigorous a resistance that (if Justin is to be believed) the citizens of Croton became hopeful of victory. A reason for their optimism was, I believe, provided by the disaster, noted by Aelian, that overtook a sea-borne attack upon Thurii, whose capture (or submission) would have virtually isolated Croton from the rest of Magna Graecia.[11]

Dionysius' ships were wrecked by a northerly gale, in gratitude for which the Thurians accorded Boreas the honours of a citizen and benefactor (he was also worshipped by the Athenians, the founders of Thurii, for having given them similar assistance against the Persians). Aelian says that the expedition consisted of 300 ships 'laden with hoplites'. This figure, if reliable, would suggest an expeditionary force of warships and transports, carrying perhaps over 20,000 soldiers: a credible enough number, if the object of the expedition was to crush Thurii, which must by now have partially recovered from the disaster of 389.

Aelian says only that the fleet was wrecked, not that the crews and soldiers were killed, and we may perhaps assume that the loss of life (mercenary life, of course) was not of catastrophic proportions. It is tempting to conjecture that the dynast's brother, Thearides, commanding the galleys, met his death in this disaster. Aelian preserves an anecdote to the effect that Dionysius allowed his brother to be killed in a sea fight. Unfortunately Aelian calls the brother Leptines, and we know that Leptines was killed in the land fighting in Sicily. Plutarch, naming no names, says that Dionysius betrayed 'his brother' to the enemy. Thearides is not heard of after 388; but if he did perish in or about 380, the recall and reinstatement to favour of Leptines may have followed. Like absolute rulers everywhere and at all times, Dionysius suffered from a chronic shortage of trustworthy lieutenants, and Leptines must have promised to behave himself. Thearides' widow (who was also his niece, being Dionysius' 'Syracusan' daughter, Arete) was remarried to her maternal uncle, Dion, the son of Hipparinus. When Leptines was recalled, he married his brother's 'Locrian' daughter, Dicaeosyne.[12]

It may have been Dionysius' display of sea power in the Tyrrhenian Sea that encouraged the defection, over two or three years, of Carthage's Greek subjects and their enrolment in Dionysius' alliance. We should expect that the earliest defectors would be the cities furthest from Carthage; and it was, perhaps, the revolt of Selinus (which clearly *did* revolt) that decided the Carthaginians to take action. Loath, nowadays, to embark on large-scale military adventures, they found themselves obliged, when their representations to the dynast went unheeded, to put a stop to further encroachment upon their Epicraty. Even in the heyday of her Magonid-inspired imperialism, Carthage had never been able to respond quickly to a threat to her Sicilian possessions; she had always required time to collect the large mercenary armies on which she relied. Now, having decided on war (the fact that Dionysius was fully occupied in Italy must have been an important factor in influencing her decision to fight), she employed diplomacy in order to gain time and approached the Italiots with the offer of an alliance which the Italiots were very ready to accept. This treaty should, I believe, be assigned to late in the year 380 (after the loss of Dionysius' fleet off Thurii), and the Carthaginian expedition to Italy to the summer of 379. Diodorus tells us, under the year 380/379, that Dionysius sought an alliance with the Spartans, then at the zenith of their power after having dissolved the Olynthian League. This action may reasonably be connected with the difficulties that the dynast was experiencing in Italy, the loss of a fleet and the entrance of Carthage into the war.[13]

Dionysius was committed to the defeat of Croton and so the Carthaginians, who needed until the summer of 378 to get together the large army that would be required in order to restore their position in Sicily, sent a naval task force to Hipponium, on the north side of the peninsula. Dionysius, it will be remembered, had removed the inhabitants to Syracuse, and the verb employed (*metoikizein*) implies that they were incorporated into the citizen body there. Many, however, including the richer elements, probably escaped before the capture of the town and went into exile at Croton or Thurii; and if so, it would be to these (no doubt augmented by other exiles) that the Carthaginians now restored the city.[14] If this expedition was intended to relieve the pressure on Croton, it failed to achieve its object. Dionysius had by now established friendly relations with the Senones and had strengthened his army with Gauls, the effect of whose participation in the war may be gauged by the impact that a quite small body of them had upon the Greeks of the homeland a few years later.

Carthage was prevented either from sending further aid to the Italiots or from launching a major offensive in Sicily by an outbreak of the plague, probably in the high summer of 379. The effects of this were sufficiently serious to encourage not only the Libyans but also the natives of Sardinia, Carthage's principal granary, to revolt and make common cause against their overlord. The situation was made the more alarming by an attack of national hysteria in the city itself. However, the Carthaginians propitiated the baals, no doubt feeding the fires of moloch with their children; and having restored their morale and rid themselves of the plague (with the coming of cooler weather?), they addressed themselves to the task of crushing the rebellion. This, says Diodorus, they completed quickly; but they can hardly have done so before the end of 378.[15] They had then to collect mercenaries for the war in Sicily (the plague must have inhibited the recruitment of Iberians and Ligurians, and the Libyans had to be crushed before they could be conscripted); and so it seems impossible that Mago could have been able to land an army in Sicily before the summer of 377. (Mago is styled 'the king' by Diodorus, but the Greeks had no word other than *basileus* to translate the Phoenician *shofet* – Latin, *sufes*; and it seems probable that, following the disgrace of Himilco, the kingship had been replaced by an annually elective dual suffeteship.)

Carthage, before this, had probably sent some troops to reinforce the citizen militias of her Phoenician subjects in Sicily and Dionysius had responded in kind. We learn from Aeneas Tacticus that Leptines was sent at some unspecified date to Himera, to relieve part of its garrison and to stay there until recalled. Stroheker believes that this may have been during the years 388 and 386, between Leptines' diplomatic *bêtise* in 389 and his exile. I believe, however, that it fits better into the period immediately after Leptines' return from exile.[16]

Let us suppose, then, that in the early summer of 377 Mago transported an army to Sicily; undoubtedly a large army, but probably, as a result of the plague and the revolt of Libya, not as large as that which Himilco had brought over in 397, and including a larger proportion of Carthaginian citizens. I would put the fall of Croton some time between the summer of 378 and the summer of 377. Undoubtedly the city did fall to the dynast's arms, for apart from the notice in Dionysius of Halicarnassus, Livy states that the citadel was taken 'per dolum', which probably means that it was betrayed to Dionysius. It may be that, on the capture of the citadel (taken from the seaward side), the Crotoniates asked for terms, which Dionysius, rendered anxious to extricate himself from Italian affairs by the militancy of Carthage, granted them.

He also concluded peace with what was left of the Italiot League; which seems to be implied by the comment of Dionysius of Halicarnassus, that the Italiot cities had to choose between submission to Dionysius or to the barbarians – clearly an exaggeration, for cities like Taras certainly preserved their independence of both. On the other hand, we have an anecdote of Polyaenus that deals with the dynast's efforts, seemingly successful, to win the friendship of Metapontum and other Italiot communities, and Taras was on good terms with Ortygia in the reign of Dionysius' son. Perhaps it was at this time that the dynast sent the father of Echetrates of Phlius (a Pythagorean visited by Plato at Locri) on a mission to the Italiots, as reported by Diogenes Laertius. Taking into consideration the loss of a fleet and his failure to take Thurii, Dionysius had none the less strengthened his position in Italy. Locri probably, and Croton certainly, were now subject to him; any Syracusan exiles who still survived must have had to move on; and the hegemony of the League, whose hostility was no longer directed towards him, passed to distant Taras (the colony of his ally, Sparta), and its centre was later established at Heraclea, a colony of Taras. I consider it likely that re-founded Hipponium also came to an understanding with the dynast.[17]

Arrived back in Sicily, probably in the late summer, Dionysius set out with all the strength he could muster to halt Mago's advance, which the narrative of Polyaenus (for what it is worth) suggests lay through the centre of the island. He encountered the Carthaginians at a place, still unidentified, called Cabala (ta kabala) and there won a spectacular victory. The enemy were routed and left their suffete, Mago, together with more than 10,000 of their soldiers dead on the field, and another 5,000 men in the hands of the victors. The survivors of the rout took refuge on a defensible but waterless hill, and sent a herald to ask for terms of peace. Dionysius demanded the withdrawal of the Carthaginians from Sicily and the payment of the cost of the war. The Carthaginians pretended to accept Dionysius' conditions, but said that they did not have the authority to hand over the cities (Diodorus), to give a definitive answer (Polyaenus).[18]

At this point, unfortunately, the narratives of Diodorus' epitomizer and of Polyaenus, hitherto in remarkable harmony, part company over certain important details. 'Diodorus' says that the Carthaginians 'out-generaled Dionysius with their customary knavery' (a phrase that might be Diodorus' own: *punica fides* was a commonplace in his day). They asked for a truce *of a few days*, to enable them to consult their government; that is to say, a truce of sufficient length to enable them to send messengers to Carthage to obtain the consent of the Council and for the messengers to return. Dionysius agreed, delighted at the prospect of taking over the whole of Sicily. The Carthaginians then buried their general with great magnificence and replaced him in the command by his son, who spent the whole period of the truce drilling his army and restoring its morale. After the expiration of the truce, both sides lined up for 'the battle', which took place at Cronium. Polyaenus, however, says that the Carthaginians asked to be allowed to withdraw to the coast, so that they could consult the *navarch*. Dionysius disregarded Leptines' protest and permitted them to move camp. Once reunited with their fleet, the Carthaginians 'sent Dionysius' embassy back empty-handed'.[19]

It is perfectly clear that neither of these accounts is acceptable as it stands. The matter of the waterless hill is highly suspicious, for a start; and not just because it appears to be a 'doublet' of the Eleporus incident. Defensible waterless hills abound in the Mediterranean area and, in fact, a Carthaginian army was trapped in precisely this manner by Masinissa in 150. What I do not find credible is that Dionysius, with his triumph at the Eleporus fairly fresh in his memory, would have granted the enemy a truce – which could hardly have been one of less than ten days (to enable a messenger to get to Carthage, receive an answer and return), during which time he would have had to supply his beaten foes with food and water, when he had it in his power to reduce them to unconditional surrender in a couple of days. These enemies were barbarians, whom it was his purpose to drive out of Sicily, and whose good will, consequently, he had no need to cultivate. If he had some thousands of Carthaginian citizens, including members of the aristocracy, in his hands, can anyone doubt that Carthage would have accepted his conditions, however harsh? Diodorus' epitomizer does not mention a withdrawal of the Carthaginian army, only a truce; and, as it stands, his narrative would imply, first, that Mago's son was appointed general by the Carthaginians trapped on the hill; secondly, that he regenerated his army, still on the waterless hill and in full view of the Greeks who were provisioning him, within a few days; and thirdly, that he then faced them – and defeated them – with at least 15,000 fewer men than his father had had. Polyaenus' account, although expecting us to believe that Dionysius gave the beaten enemy permission to march out of the trap in order to consult their admiral, does appear to preserve an important fact: that the

Carthaginian army was allowed to retire to the coast and join up with its fleet. The manifest absurdity of 'Diodorus'' narrative is due to the ineptitude of the epitomizer, whom the dramatic element of peripeteia has deceived into telescoping the events of two campaigns into the space of 'a few days', whereas Polyaenus is concerned only with the tricking of Dionysius by the Carthaginians. Both stories go back, I believe, ultimately to an 'official' account which appeared in Philistus' history, and which sought to excuse Dionysius' failure to follow up his victory by introducing the element of Carthaginian knavery.[20]

Once again (as so often happens when one is attempting to write the story of Dionysius' reign) we are forced to fall back on a conjectural reconstruction, from unsatisfactory source material, of the true course of events. What actually happened must, I believe, have been something like this. The Carthaginians were driven in rout from the field; they retired on to higher ground and asked for the customary truce in order to bury their dead – including their suffete. Dionysius' own army may have suffered serious casualties and it will, anyway, have been engrossed in the profitable tasks of securing prisoners and stripping the fallen, and so Dionysius granted the truce (which is reported by 'Diodorus' and implied by Polyaenus). The Carthaginians, taking a leaf out of their enemy's own book, took advantage of the truce to slip away (probably by night) to the coast, to link up with the fleet; and they then went into winter quarters: I would suggest, at Panormus. Negotiations were then opened for a peace treaty (Dionysius had some 5,000 prisoners in his hands, and these may have included many Carthaginian citizens), and the dynast sent an embassy to Carthage, where his terms were rejected. Mago's son, whose name was probably Himilco, was appointed general of the army in Sicily and in the following summer was substantially reinforced. Perhaps the passage in Polyaenus which describes how a Punic convoy escaped from Dionysius' warships refers to this despatch of reinforcements.[21]

After the battle of Cabala and the failure of his embassy, Dionysius (I believe) retired to Syracuse for the winter, leaving a part of his forces (under Leptines?) to prosecute the siege of native – probably Sican – towns, including Cronium. Polyaenus recounts how a Himilco employed a smoke-screen in order to gain entry to the town of Cronium, outside which 'Dionysius' generals' were encamped. Since this incident (which seems to me to bear the stamp of authenticity) does not fit into the story of Himilco, son of Hanno (who disposed of an overwhelming superiority of numbers in both the wars that he fought against the Greeks), it must belong to the prelude to the final battle of this war. Himilco raised the siege – or rather, forestalled the siege – of Cronium; his reinforcements eluded the attempt of Dionysius' ships to intercept them and reached him at, or in the vicinity of, Cronium; Dionysius, with the troops that he brought from Syracuse, arrived in the neighbourhood and assumed overall command of his forces; and the two armies faced one another for what was bound to be the decisive battle of the war.[22]

The Greek army was drawn up with Leptines commanding one wing and Dionysius the centre, with the pick of his mercenaries. The Greeks had another glorious victory almost within their grasp when Leptines, performing prodigies of valour, was slain, and, as so often happened in the pitched battle when a leader fell, his wing was dismayed and routed. The other wing was also driven in and, the panic spreading to the centre, the whole army was put to flight. The barbarians gave no quarter – Himilco had a father to avenge – and 14,000 of Dionysius' men were killed. The defeated army found refuge in its camp and nightfall put an end to the fighting. The Carthaginians, like Dionysius the year before, made no attempt to follow up their victory, and retired into Panormus; which suggests, first, that Cronium lay somewhere in the western half of the island and, secondly, that (as in 377) the battle was fought at the very end of the campaigning season.[23]

As has been said above, the Carthaginian aristocracy had by now at last asserted its corporate authority over the Magonids and had turned its back on the aggressive policies associated with that family. They had come to terms with the idea that Syracuse was impregnable and that, as long as Dionysius was alive, no war of conquest in Sicily was finally winnable, except perhaps at a cost that was far higher than they were prepared to pay. Moreover, Carthage had suffered heavy casualties, the effects of the plague had probably not fully worn off, there may still have been pockets of unrest in Libya and Sardinia and the economic cost of the revolt and of the campaigns in Italy and Sicily must have been enormous. And lastly, Dionysius still had 5,000 prisoners in his hands. So Carthage was very ready now to make peace on the basis of what she regarded as an equitable partition of Sicily.

Dionysius, for his part, was in no condition to continue a struggle which the least superstitious person might be excused for regarding as ill-fated. He did not enjoy Carthage's – by ancient standards, almost inexhaustible – wealth; which, as the Romans, something over a century later, were to discover to their cost, enabled her to replace lost armies by drawing on the backward but warlike peoples of Africa, Spain and Italy. It is most unlikely that Dionysius had sufficient reserves of silver in his treasury to be able to hire soldiers to replace the fallen; but if he could not raise a fresh field army by the spring of 375, and if he did not make peace, the Carthaginians would be bound to advance into eastern Sicily; and experience had taught him that in that case the Siceliots and the Sicels would fall away from him, the Italiots would probably take up arms again and his hard-won empire would, in a twinkling, dissolve into nothing. In Dionysius' heart relief must have contended for mastery with astonishment, when the victors of Cronium sent ambassadors bearing overtures for peace.[24]

The treaty was concluded, I believe, sometime between the end of the campaigning season of 376 and the spring of 375. The terms reported by Diodorus' epitomizer were as follows: both parties to keep those possessions of which they were previously masters (*kyrioi*), but the Carthaginians to receive in addition (*exaireton* – a word which could signify 'as a special reward of valour') the city and territory of the Selinuntians and the territory of Acragas up to (i.e. to the west of) the river called Halycus. This passage indicates that the little town of Heraclea Minoa at the mouth of the Halycus (which certainly passed into Punic hands) was at that time a dependency of Acragas. Now one would, I believe, expect 'previously' (*proteron*) above to signify, 'under the terms of the previous treaty' (i.e. that of 392); and if that were so, we should have to accept that not only was Acragas recognized by that treaty as a part of Dionysius' empire but so too was Selinus. However, I have given reasons in Chapter 8 for supposing that in fact Dionysius, who had at that time been driven back into his own corner of the island, was suffering considerable political and financial embarrassment and had seen Acragas throw off her allegiance to him, was prepared to accept Carthaginian overlordship of the Greek cities, or, at the very least, the neutrality – the non-alignment – of those cities. I believe that we have here another example of the carelessness of the epitomizer, and that 'previously' must be taken to mean something like 'prior to the outbreak of hostilities'. Nor does the writer tell us anything about the northern end of the new frontier: specifically, was Himera to be in the Epicraty or in Dionysius' *archē*? Stroheker says that it may have reverted to Carthage, and I think that this is probably correct, so that the boundary line now ran roughly from the new western borders of Acragas northwards to the eastern borders of Himera.

From this treaty it followed that Dionysius' suzerainty over the Greek cities to the east of the Halycus line (as well as over the Sicels) was explicitly recognized: and, I believe, explicitly recognized for *the first time*. Carthage wanted peace in Sicily, and to secure it she was prepared to accept Dionysius as the ruler of the greater part of the island – as the overlord of his own people and of the Sicels (who, like the population of Himera, were becoming Hellenized), just as Selinus, now included in the Epicraty, was becoming assimilated to her Phoenician neighbours. Dionysius was obliged also to pay a war indemnity of 1,000 talents. Plato (or the writer of Plato's Seventh Letter) says that Dionysius 'agreed to pay tribute (*phoros*) to the barbarians'; and, since it seems unlikely that he would have been able to find, or to raise quickly, a sum as large as 1,000 talents, he may have undertaken to pay it in instalments: which would, in effect, constitute a payment of *phoros*. Dionysius was, no doubt, also required to hand back the prisoners taken at the battle of Cabala.

It must have seemed to the Carthaginians, counting, like good businessmen, the costs of imperialism – Dionysius' as well as their own – that now a permanent, because reasonable, *modus vivendi* could be said to have been established between themselves and the Greeks. For Dionysius, however, who never ceased to dream of a Sicily wholly united under his sway, the cessation of hostilities meant no more than the provision of a breathing space in which to recuperate his strength, until a favourable opportunity should offer itself of renewing the struggle with Carthage with a good prospect of decisive success.[25]

CHAPTER ELEVEN

Affairs in Greece, the fourth Punic War, the death of Dionysius

First Italian and then Sicilian affairs had occupied Dionysius' attention between 384 and 375, to the exclusion of events in metropolitan Greece. Diodorus states that the dynast had been anxious to strengthen his ties with Sparta in 379, when the Lacedaemonians were at the zenith of their power – and when a war on two fronts threatened Syracuse. But, in the grand tragic manner in which the vicissitudes of Greek history so often come about, the first moves in the overthrow of Sparta's long hegemony were being made at the close of the same year. The liberation of the Cadmea, the citadel of Thebes, occupied since 382 by a Spartan garrison, and an ill-conceived attempt by a Spartan officer to seize the Piraeus, led to open war between the Lacedaemonians and Thebes, the latter actively supported by Athens. Dionysius was deprived of the possibility of Peloponnesian aid and must also have viewed with misgiving the emergence in 377 of the second Athenian Confederacy and Athens' recovery of the command of the Aegean by the battle of Naxos in the autumn of 376. Even more alarming, at this critical juncture of his affairs, must have been the foray into the Ionian Sea of Conon's son, Timotheus, in 375, and the establishment of a hostile cordon of Athenian allies (including his old associate, Alcetas, now king of the Molossians) across his route to the Corinthian Gulf and the Peloponnese. [1]

Resentment of the growth of Theban power, allied to war weariness and shortage of funds, led Athens to make peace with Sparta, during the winter of 375/4. However, Timotheus' action in establishing a body of exiles hostile to Sparta on Zacynthian soil, and Athen's in enrolling them in her Confederacy (as the Zacynthian Demos), led to Sparta's sending 25 ships to aid the Zacynthian oligarchic regime, and, probably in the late summer or autumn of 374, a further 22 to support the insurgent oligarchs of Corcyra. In order to mislead the democrats of Corcyra into admitting these ships into their harbour, it was given out that they were on passage to Sicily. It seems to me probable that Dionysius, following his defeat at Cronium, being desperately short of money, men and ships, had asked Sparta for assistance in anticipation of a serious revolt of his subjects – a revolt which did not, in fact, occur. The Spartans, however, having decided to send the aid, were able to utilize the ships and their ostensible mission for their own ends.

The control of the eastern Ionian Sea continued to be a bone of contention between Athens and Sparta, and the year 373 saw both parties preparing to send strong forces into the area; in connection with which, the Spartans wrote to Dionysius, reminding him of his interest in this theatre. The dynast had by then apparently recovered, both financially and militarily, from the late war, and he agreed to send a squadron of 10 ships (Polyaenus says 11) under Crinippus and Cissidas, to join the Lacedaemonian fleet before Corcyra.[2]

Timotheus, the Athenian commander, was detained in the Aegean by the need to collect funds to pay his rowers and as a result Mnasippus, the *navarch* of 373/2, was able to drive the Corcyraean democrats into the city and lay them under siege. However, the Corcyraeans, reinforced by some 500 Athenians under an able officer, Ctesicles, gained the upper hand, and by the time Iphicrates (Timotheus' successor) arrived the Lacedaemonians had withdrawn. By a combination of good reconnaissance and planning on his part and culpable carelessness on that of the Syracusans, Iphicrates succeeded in capturing 9 out of the 10 ships of Dionysius' squadron. The crews of the ships were permitted to find Corcyraeans prepared to stand surety for their ransom, but their admiral was less fortunate. Iphicrates kept him under guard, hoping to get a large price for him, either from Syracuse or in the open market. But Crinippus had lost more than just his military reputation and most of his ships. He had also been conveying some chryselephantine statues that Dionysius intended to dedicate at Delphi and Olympia (deprecatory, in the light of his recent misadventure? as thank offerings, for the establishment of peace within his empire?); these the Athenians seized. Iphicrates received instructions from Athens to sell the treasures, and from the proceeds of the whole operation he raised no less than 60 talents – a godsend for a commander with clamorous mercenaries and rowers to pay. Apart from the shame of failure, Crinippus probably felt that he had little to look forward to in either a lifetime of slavery or a return home to face the anger of his master, and took his own life. Dionysius sent a strong protest to the Athenians, accusing them of sacrilege, but we do not hear that it produced any result.[3]

Athens' relations with Thebes were by now the reverse of cordial, and Callistratus, the architect of her second maritime Confederacy and the most influential statesman at this time, was anxious for a return to the common peace that had once been a matter of shame to the Athenians and of reproach to Sparta (as being dictated by the Great King), but which was now the corner-stone of Athens' foreign policy. Sparta, too, deterred from undertaking any military operations beyond her borders by earthquakes (she will hardly have forgotten the great earthquake and the revolt of the helots, almost a century earlier), wanted peace; and so the common peace was renewed in the summer of 371. Thebes, however, refused this time to accept the dissolution of the Boeotian League, of which she was the *hegemon*, and she was excluded from the treaty by King Agesilaus. Twenty days later, King Cleombrotus, advancing by the coast road into Boeotia in order to chastise the Thebans and 'liberate' the cities, was killed and his army driven off the field at Leuctra, and the century-and-three-quarters-old myth of Spartan invincibility in an agōn-al conflict was destroyed. The Athenians received the news with any-thing but enthusiasm, and called a peace conference at Athens to confirm the settlement already signed – from which the Eleans, and, of course, the Boeotians, dissociated themselves.[4]

With the defeat of Sparta, a 'wind of change' began to blow through the Peloponnese. A movement to form a single Arcadian State that could defy the claim to hegemony of the Lacedaemonians was supported by Elis and Argos, and gathered impetus with the arrival of a powerful allied army under the Theban Epaminondas, in the winter of 370. Not venturing to attack the unwalled city of the Spartans, Epaminondas ravaged Laconia and then struck his heaviest blow by re-founding the city of Messene and reconstituting the Messenian nation, so long enslaved. In this crisis – the worst in their history up to that time – the Spartans appealed for assistance to Athens, in accordance with the terms of the second treaty of 371; and it is clear that they also approached Dionysius. Sparta had stood by Dionysius loyally in more than one serious crisis, and he undertook to repay his debt the following summer. The Athenians, however, were able to respond at once, and they sent Iphicrates with troops to her aid.

After a winter campaign of eighty-five days, Epaminondas returned home, having reduced Sparta from the level of a 'super-power', destroyed the *pax peloponnesia* and totally upset the balance of power in Greece. In the spring of 369, Sparta concluded a full alliance with Athens, and so at last the way was opened for a *rapprochement* between the Athenians and Sparta's lifelong ally, Dionysius. The Athenians sent Chabrias with an army to the Isthmus, where an allied force of 20,000 men was assembled and a line of fortifications built, to bar the passage of the Boeotians into the Peloponnese. Epaminondas, however, attacked the southern end of the line, broke through the allied defences, devastated the territories of Sparta's allies and gained control of Sicyon. He then withdrew to the Isthmus and made a determined attempt to seize Corinth.[5]

Immediately after this, about midsummer, Dionysius' auxiliaries ar-rived on the scene. They proved to be a formidable reinforcement, comprising over 20 warships and 2,000 Celtic and Iberian mercenaries; the latter presumably being men paid off by Carthage after the late war –

unless, of course, they were men taken at the battle of Cabala who had agreed to transfer their services to their captor. An anecdote of Plutarch's suggests that it was now (although it may have been in the year following) that the Greeks of the homeland encountered the catapult for the first time. The comment of the Spartan king's son, Archidamus, is characteristic; 'Heracles! That's the end of manly courage!' The newcomers, and especially their 50 horsemen, gave so much trouble to the enemy, who were scattered over the plain of Corinth, pillaging and burning with impunity since the allied horse did not venture to attack them, that after a few days the Boeotians retired to their homeland. In order to give the Lacedaemonians their master's money's worth, Dionysius' men, before returning to Sicily, invaded Sicyon, defeated the Sicyonians and captured a stronghold. The Spartans rewarded them for their services and they departed, leaving behind them a deep impression on the minds of the Greeks. It was probably during the winter, or in the spring of 368, that Athens voted a gold crown to Dionysius, presumably in recognition of the assistance that he had sent the allies in the preceding summer.[6]

Probably early in 368, the satrap of Hellespontine Phrygia, the philo-Laconian Ariobarzanes, sent an emissary, Philiscus of Abydus, to Greece, to try above all to bring about a renewal of the King's Peace. A conference was held at Delphi, but the talks broke down over the question of the independence of Messenia. Philiscus then devoted his master's money to the recruitment of 2,000 mercenaries to assist the Lacedaemonians. It seems likely that Dionysius associated himself with this attempt to restore the common peace. An inscription found at Athens proves that, towards midsummer, he wrote directly to the Athenians: first, about the rebuilding of the temple of Apollo at Delphi (destroyed in the winter of 373/2), for which an international subscription had been opened the previous year; and secondly, about 'the peace', which line 25 specifically identifies as the King's Peace. The decree praises Dionysius, the Lord (*archon*) of Sicily and his sons Dionysius and Hermocritus, inasmuch as they were good friends of Athens and her allies and support the King's Peace. The decree goes on to confer citizenship, with *deme* and *phratry* of their choice, upon Dionysius, his sons and his descendants. Athens' diplomatic *volte-face* was now complete.[7]

Although Dionysius had matters of the very greatest urgency engaging his attention in Sicily itself in the early summer of 368, he sent a force under Cissidas to the Isthmus to assist the defenders of the King's Peace. The language of Xenophon and the achievements of the corps in battle suggest that this force was of at least the same strength as that sent the previous year: it certainly included both Celts and horsemen. The Spartans persuaded their allies to allot these troops to them, and

Archidamus attached them to the army that he led into Arcadia. It would appear, in the light of what occurred, that Archidamus was under the impression that he had the use of these soldiers for the same length of time – five months (less, presumably, travelling time) – as in the year before. In fact, Cissidas had either been instructed to bring them home well before the end of the summer, or else (which I consider to be less likely) received an urgent summons, which he did not communicate to Archidamus, recalling him to Syracuse. Be that as it may, at the moment when Archidamus' withdrawal from Arcadia was being threatened by an allied Arcadian and Argive army, Cissidas announced that it was time for him to go home. The outcome of the enemy's attempt, with the support of the Messenians, to cut off, first, Cissidas, and then Archidamus, when he marched to Cissidas' aid, was the famous Tearless Battle, in which a large number (Diodorus says over 10,000, but that must be too many) of the allies fell, without the loss of a single Lacedaemonian.[8]

At Syracuse – or, rather, on Ortygia – Carthage's anxiety for peace in Sicily, manifested by her reluctance to follow up, militarily, her crushing victory at Cronium and her readiness to accept Dionysius as overlord of the greater part of the island, must have encouraged the idea that, with the ending of the Magonid domination, she had ceased to have the will to resist another determined assault upon the Epicraty. News of the recurrent attacks of the plague and of the disaffected state of Libya and Sardinia will have reinforced this opinion; and there was other, more specific, evidence to support it. Carthage had not yet really entered that era of political stability praised by Aristotle; and a certain Suniatus, described as the most powerful man at Carthage, who belonged to the hellenizing faction among the nobility, was prepared to betray the interests of his city, no doubt with the object of making himself tyrant. Dionysius quite clearly had made good the losses of the previous war both in men and treasure. He was now over sixty years old, and it is a reasonable assumption that he was feeling his age. Hyperactive, he had never spared himself, physically or mentally, and he had been seriously wounded at least twice. He had come close to achieving his life's ambition a few years earlier, and he may have felt in his heart that if he did not succeed now, when all the omens seemed to be so favourable, he never would. He must have determined on war in the summer or autumn of 369, and made his preparations, building and repairing ships and war engines and hiring mercenaries, so as to be ready to launch his offensive in the summer of 368.[9]

Seeking, like aggressors in every age, to establish a specious *casus belli*, he proclaimed (what may, after all, have been the truth) that the inhabitants of the Epicraty had violated the territory of his empire. Carthage, it is clear, was not taken wholly by surprise; but as a result of what was already becoming an habitual unwillingness to take up arms, in conjunction with serious disunity within the ruling class, she failed to make preparations to match those of Dionysius. However, passages in Diodorus, Justin and Polyaenus indicate that she did send troops to Sicily, under the command of Hanno, and that these, although too few to face the dynast's army in the field, provided an adequate garrison for Lilybaeum; for it would have been a reasonable assumption that Dionysius would follow the route of his advance in 397, in order first to liberate Selinus, and that from Selinus he would proceed to Lilybaeum. Clearly, these troops were meant to reach the Epicraty before the arrival of the Greeks, but were delayed – perhaps by the difficulty encountered in enlisting mercenaries at very short notice. Suniatus kept Dionysius informed of events at Carthage and of the delay, with the result that Dionysius' fleet was in position to intercept Hanno's ships: probably at Selinus. The Carthaginians, however, inferior in number and with their ships laden with troops, none the less managed to out-general Dionysius' inexperienced commanders by making a feint of offering battle and then taking to their heels while the Greeks were confusedly trying to get their galleys into battle order. Yet once again – and not for the last time – Dionysius had been let down by his navy. Having successfully completed his mission, Hanno either took or sent his ships back to Carthage.[10]

Dionysius' expeditionary force was one of the most formidable ever put into the field by a single Greek Power. 30,000 infantry and 3,000 cavalry were accompanied by no less than 300 warships (if Diodorus' figures are to be credited): Dionysius clearly expected Carthage to make a major effort at sea. Including camp-followers and servants, he must have moved something like 100,000 men into western Sicily. Selinus – still Greek enough to welcome him as a liberator – and Entella went over to him immediately. He ravaged the Epicraty and forced Eryx to capitulate: a success which put the good harbour of Drepanum at his disposal. He then moved his army to Lilybaeum and laid siege to the city; but the Carthaginians had made it too strong a place (as the Romans were to discover) and had garrisoned it too well for it to be takable by ancient siege technique. It seems clear that Dionysius did not open his campaign until mid- or even late summer (until after the return from Greece of Cissidas and his battle-hardened men?), and that he planned much the same disposition of his forces for the winter as he had made in 397. He sent more than the half of his ships back to Syracuse and left the rest – 130 in number – at Drepanum, to be ready for service in the spring to prevent the Carthaginians from transporting reinforcements to Sicily. Diodorus says that he did this because he believed a report that the arsenal at Carthage, and with it the entire Punic fleet, had been destroyed by fire. I confess to finding attractive the idea that the wily Carthaginians utilized the traitor Suniatus' couriers to convey this piece of disinformation to the enemy, in order to confirm him in a decision which financial considerations would anyway have enjoined upon him. For Suniatus had by now been detected in his treason, and the authorities had not only silenced him but had also taken steps to stamp out the dangerous spread of the Hellenic language – and with it, of course, Hellenic culture and even sympathies – and had prohibited the teaching and study of Greek. Henceforth, all dealings with Greeks were to be conducted through interpreters.[11]

Diodorus' narrative of this war is much less detailed than that of the earlier campaigns, and he does not tell us the names either of Dionysius' admiral (may it have been Cissidas?) or of the commander-in-chief of the Carthaginians: Justin, however, says that it was Hanno. So it was probably Hanno who led 200 galleys in a surprise attack upon the harbour of Drepanum. The Greeks were taken completely by surprise, and the Carthaginians captured and towed away most of their ships. It was the end of the campaigning season, an armistice was agreed upon, the Carthaginian fleet returned to its base and Dionysius marched his army back to Syracuse. Dionysius' empire had now attained its greatest extent. Panormus, Solus, Lilybaeum and Elymian Segesta were now the only major cities remaining under Punic control; Dionysius' army was undefeated, he still had 170 ships in his ship houses at Syracuse and he would be able to find the rowers to man them. Diodorus makes no mention of any large-scale recruitment of mercenaries by Carthage, during the winter, and it is clear that she did not put an army into Sicily in the spring of 367. We need have no doubt that the dynast intended to reopen the campaign in the summer of that year; and it can hardly be denied that the fate of the Epicraty hung in balance.[12]

It was probably during 368 that Isocrates, the mentor of Timotheus and one of the strongest proponents at Athens of the idea of Panhellenism, who formerly had seen Dionysius as one of the principal threats to Greek liberty, wrote an open letter to the dynast, of which, unfortunately, only a small portion has survived. Addressing Dionysius as the foremost man of the Hellenic race and the most powerful, Isocrates appeals to him to help to save Greece. Athens, he says would gladly join him in a common effort. Precisely what it was that Isocrates was inviting Dionysius to undertake must remain (like so much else concerning him) a matter for conjecture; but it is unlikely that it was the leadership of a Panhellenic crusade against Persia. Dionysius, he says, can now assume responsibility for the affairs 'of our region' (*ton topon ton hēmeteron*); so it is more likely (as Stroheker believes) that he saw the dynast as the guarantor of the Common Peace, in place of the weakened Sparta and the always unsatisfactory, because barbarian, King of Persia.[13]

It is clear that diplomatic contact was maintained between Ortygia and Athens during the winter of 368/7. Dionysius, since the end of the preceding *archōn*-year, had been an Athenian citizen, and as such had been granted a chorus at the Lenaean festival, to be held about the end of January. The tragedy that he sent to the competition was *The Ransom of Hector*; chosen, no doubt, because its theme was that of reconciliation. There is no real reason to suppose either that any expense was spared in the production or that the play itself was markedly worse than the general run of contemporary drama: the consensus of hostile criticism of the poetry of a tyrant can scarcely be regarded as unprejudiced. At all events, the play was awarded the first prize, which in the circumstances is hardly surprising. Anything less would have been tantamount to a calculated insult offered to a potentate with whom it was now Athens' policy to establish the friendliest possible relations.[14]

Probably less than two months later, in March 367 (although a date just *before* the Lenaea has been proposed), the Athenians passed a decree which, after praising Dionysius, 'the Lord (*archōn*) of Sicily', for his support of Athens and her allies, goes on to enumerate the terms of a formal alliance for mutual defence to be concluded with him and his descendants in perpetuity. The proposer was the same Pandios who had introduced the honorific decree of 368. The wording of the decree parallels fairly closely that of other treaties drawn up by the Athenian *Boulē*; but the presence at Athens of an embassy from Syracuse suggests that the initiative and probably a draft of the treaty came from Dionysius; and it rather looks as if the *Boulē*, in its anxiety to propitiate the dynast, had not thoroughly considered all the implications of its provisions.[15]

Unlike, for instance, the treaty of alliance concluded by Athens a few years earlier with Corcyra, this treaty did not bring Dionysius into the Athenian Confederacy: after the preamble, there is no mention of the Allies. It simply requires Dionysius to come to the assistance of Athens by land and sea, when requested, with all his available might, if her territory should be attacked, and himself to refrain from any such attack. This is the usual formula. Athens, for her part, undertakes to send all the aid she can, by land and sea, 'if Dionysius or his descendants or any part of his realm (*hosōn archei*) should be attacked', and herself to refrain from any such attack. Thus this treaty recognized by implication the legitimacy of Dionysius' regime and of his empire; and if it were interpreted according to the letter, it would leave the dynast at liberty to attack an ally of Athens, and at the same time would entitle him (and his descendants) to ask for Athenian aid either to defeat any attempt to liberate one of his subject cities or to suppress a revolt of the Syracusan people against his rule. So strong had been the impression made upon the minds of the Greeks by Dionysius' barbarian skirmishers that Athens was prepared to go to these lengths in propitiating a tyrant whom, until less than half a dozen years before, she had regarded with abhorrence.

Dionysius' envoys presented their copy of the treaty to the Council, the generals, the hipparchs and (presumably) the taxiarchs to be sworn to; and Athenian envoys carried the city's copy to Sicily, for ratification both by Dionysius (on his own and his sons' behalf) and by representatives of the Syracusans. The mutilation of this latter portion of the inscription is particularly tantalizing, since if it were complete it would throw some light upon the nature of Syracuse's institutions, about which we know so little that no certain restoration of the missing words can be made. All that we can suggest is that the chief civil magistrates (*archontes?*), the Council (which must have existed, but for which there is no epigraphical or even literary evidence), and some catagories of military officers were designated. At first sight it might seem strange that the city of Syracuse, which is not referred to in the body of the treaty and which must, therefore, have been regarded as a part of Dionysius' empire, should have been included among the signatories. Part of the explanation, no doubt, is that the signing of this treaty was seen as terminating a state of war that had existed, because never formally ended, between Athens and Syracuse for almost half a century. Indeed, there was still in existence – although probably forgotten by both parties – a treaty of alliance between Athens and Carthage! But it is also clear that the citizens of Syracuse were understood to enjoy still the fundamental right of a free people to decide for themselves on questions of peace and war, and solemn treaties; and the Lord of Sicily was sufficiently astute to appreciate the fact that the participation of Syracuse in this treaty would render it more digestible for Athenian democratic stomachs.[16]

The treaty, reflecting as it did the altered climate of international politics since Leuctra, represented a considerable propaganda triumph for the dynast. Dionysius the warmonger and scourge of Hellenism had been accepted as a respectable ornament of the Hellenic family by the city which was universally regarded as the cultural leader of Greece. From the standpoint of the Athenians, Dionysius might well prove a more reliable friend than the Great King, who had never really trusted them. Athens' second maritime Confederacy was beginning to assume some of the aspects of her former empire; and she, like Sparta, now, and Thebes, was looking for a formula for a common peace tailored to her particular interests; interests which now seemed much less likely to conflict with those of Sparta and Sparta's friend than with those of the Great King. In the words of Leon, Athenian ambassador to the Persian court in the following autumn, 'It was time for them to look for some other friend instead of the King'. And they were right, for on that occasion Artaxerxes sided with Thebes against Athens and Sparta.[17]

The treaty was sworn to at Athens; but it may very well be that it was never ratified at Syracuse, that the ambassadors arrived home only to find their master dying or lately dead. Diodorus gives us, rather as a parenthesis, an account of Dionysius' end that seems to derive from an anecdotal rather than a historical source: one, like the source or sources of Diodorus' other anecdotes, that was more interested in the tyrant's *literary* pretensions than in his political or moral depravity. According to this story, Dionysius' death was brought on by the excesses in which he indulged in celebration of his Lenaean victory. Although the account has been tailored to fit the moral – that hubris in a poetaster brings fitting retribution, do what he will to avoid it – there may be a basis of truth to the story; in which case we must suppose either that the celebrations and Dionysius' resulting illness occupied a period of a month or more, or that the treaty should indeed be dated to a prytany prior to the Lenaea. It is better, I believe, to accept the first alternative and to assume that, whether ratified or not, the treaty was from the beginning a dead letter. Dionysius' son had no ambition to play the role of patron of metropolitan Greece, and within very little more than a decade his empire was in dissolution. By 343 the Athenian public and its orators had forgotten all about the treaty and Dionysius had become, once again, the despot who formerly threatened their freedom.[18]

There appears to exist a veritable conspiracy of silence among our sources in respect of this treaty. Even if the treaty was not ratified, Philistus must surely have heard of it; but if he mentioned it, the mention either did not reach or did not interest the writers of the Roman era; and yet, as a striking example of the political *volte-face*, it might, one feels, have attracted attention. It is, of course, a fact that Diodorus tells us very little about Sicilian affairs in the last fifteen or so years of Dionysius' life. He does not, for instance, mention the *rapprochement* between Athens and Dionysius after Leuctra, or the votes of the Athenian Assembly in his honour, or the participation of his troops in the Tearless Battle: matters that one would expect Philistus to have mentioned, although of course Ephorus (and Timaeus) may well have omitted them.

Plutarch tells us that Dion conducted the most important of Dionysius' embassies, and the embassy sent to secure this treaty surely comes into that category. Dion, indeed, may have played a prominent role in all the major diplomatic moves of these latter years; and it is a fact that, not many years later, the Spartans were to accord him the rare distinction of admitting him to their citizenship: presumably for 'services rendered'. But if Dionysius was deathly sick in the early spring of 367, it is likely that it was Dion who drafted the treaty and despatched the embassy; remaining, however, at Ortygia himself, in order to be at the centre of affairs. Plutarch passes on to us Timaeus' account (which is likely to have originated with Dion himself) of how Dion wished to visit the bedside of the dying man, in order to try to secure a share of the political inheritance for his own nephews, something that would have given him a more authoritative voice in the government. He was, however, refused admission by the doctors in attendance, who then poisoned their patient in order to prevent any further discussion of the matter. If, then, this treaty, still-born though it was, could be regarded as a diplomatic 'score' for Dion, it is quite likely that Dion's bitter enemy, Philistus, would not have mentioned it; and Dion himself, during his sojourn at Athens, when he was busy making friends and winning support from people who had forgotten their short-lived ties with Dionysius, would not be over-anxious to remind them what a good servant he had been to the despot. Thus neither in the historical nor in the Academic – the anecdotal – tradition would the memory of Athens' adoption of the tyrant and of her treaty with him survive.[19]

CHAPTER TWELVE

Events following the death of Dionysius

Before we consider the questions, what kind of man was Dionysius, and what place in history are we to assign to him, it will be as well to give a brief account of the events that followed his death, and of the overthrow of his empire. The Younger Dionysius, although admitted by Antiquity to belong to 'not the worst class of tyrant' (unlike his father), has been treated by it, if anything, even more spitefully. The father's political and military achievements were on the whole recognized: he held the tyranny for thirty-eight years and left behind him an empire 'secured with bonds of adamant'; he saved Sicily from being enslaved by the Carthaginians. The son, however, was seen to be not a patch on his father. He was pusillanimous (*anandros*), he relaxed the adamantine bonds, not out of decency (which would have been commendable) but from slothfulness, and he permitted a handful of men to wrest from him the greatest military power in Greece. Admittedly his character had been 'maimed and crushed' in youth by lack of (higher) education; he had been deliberately cut off from communication with men of learning (that is to say, with Pythagoreans and Platonists) by his father, and encouraged to live a life of debauchery (*potous kai gynaikas* – wine and women), enlightened only by a little amateur carpentry, for fear that he should become a threat to the regime. But however large a portion of the blame for his poverty of character was to be laid at his father's door, it was remembered against him that he had been twice offered, and had rejected, the golden opportunity of founding a Philosopher's Kingdom which would have brought justice and contentment to the peoples of Sicily and proved a stronger bastion against the barbarian than the realm of his father, and would also have redounded for all future time to the credit of Plato and his School. Dionysius had sinned against the Light, and (what was worse) had made Plato look foolish. He had to be portrayed as a person wholly contemptible.[1]

He himself is said to have complained that he had inherited everything from his father except his Luck (*tyche*); and although there was an element of truth in this, there does seem to be very little doubt that it was his own inadequacy – as a war-lord, that is; not necessarily as a man – that was his undoing. The mainspring of his father's life, of his empire, had been the prosecution to a triumphant close of the struggle with Carthage; deprived of that motivation, for Dionysius II was not by inclination or choice a man of war, what purpose could the role of war-lord have for him except to provide him with the sinews of leisure and dissipation? Indeed, he appears to have attempted to dissociate himself from his father, to the extent of claiming to be the son of Apollo (who had cuckolded his father). It is small wonder that, in abandoning his father's militarism, he allowed the adamantine bonds to become loosened and created an atmosphere at Syracuse which encouraged disaffection on the part alike of the citizens and of the subject cities.[2] Yet it is clear that Dionysius II was not a wholly feeble ruler. He maintained his power intact for ten years, and although he made peace with Carthage (thus displaying a capacity for sound judgement), he fought a successful war against the Lucanians, gave assistance to his father's old ally, Sparta, and took energetic steps to counter piracy in the Adriatic. He also partly restored Rhegium and renamed it Phoibia (in honour of his true – that is, his Olympian – father). But the survival of a *personal* empire like that of Dionysius demanded that the Archon devote all his energy and ability to it, and this the Younger Dionysius had neither the temperament nor the inclination to do. And, indeed, since it was clear that Carthage was not going to wage aggressive war against him, it must have seemed to him and his friends that there was no good reason why he should not be content merely to enjoy the opportunity for self-instruction and pleasure with which his power and wealth furnished him. What he seems, however, to have failed to appreciate was that although the citizens of Syracuse and of the cities were prepared to tolerate the domination of a war-lord as long as Carthage could plausibly be represented as posing a threat to their peace and safety (and to Hellenism), they would become less ready to do so once it was clear that war with Carthage was a thing of the past. A pacific war-lord was an expensive luxury that Syracusans and Sicilians found they could do without.[3]

However, since the career of the Younger Dionysius is not part of the subject matter of this book, only a very brief account of the events that followed the death of the great dynast must suffice. For our knowledge of these we are dependent on Diodorus, who seems in the main to have followed Ephorus, but who unfortunately telescopes the happenings of the first decade after 367 into a single chapter, under one year; on Plutarch (Life of Dion), and on the Letters of 'Plato' (especially the Seventh). There is also some anecdotal material. Plutarch drew upon Timaeus, Theopompus and Timonides (who was one of the 'liberators'), as well as upon Ephorus. Partly as a result of this diversity of sources, but

214

probably in greater measure owing to Diodorus' careless over-compression, there are quite serious divergences between him and Plutarch: whose account is, however, the more trustworthy.

The accession of Dionysius the Younger (who had already established the nature of his character as unwarlike, impressionable and pleasure-loving) produced a struggle for influence between the friends of Dion, the brother of Aristomache and, after Dionysius himself, the richest and most influential man in Syracuse, and those who were jealous of his position of (virtually) chief minister. Dion's enemies were also alarmed both by his ambition and by his Platonic aspiration to transform the *archē* into a Philosopher's Kingdom, which they saw as a threat no less to the security of the regime than to their own luxurious existence. Dion appears to have been genuinely committed to the idea of converting the young dynast (who must have been about twenty-nine at this time) to Platonism; a plan which if it succeeded would have compensated him, in terms of influence, for the failure of his sister to produce the heir to the throne; and in order to achieve his end he moved heaven and earth to bring Plato himself to Syracuse, to teach the dynast the way to the philosophical life. Alarmed by the prospect of being so seriously disadvantaged in the intellectual field, Dion's enemies (who are identified as the tyrant's boon companions, and who included Socrates' old friend Aristippus of Cyrene and Damocles) prevailed on Dionysius to recall Philistus from exile, in order to reinforce the monarchical and anti-Platonic party.[4]

The order of the events of the ten years of Dionysius II's reign seems to be fairly well established, but (with one exception) it is impossible to assign any event to a specific year with any certainty, until towards the end of the period, when Plato's meeting with Dion at Olympia in the late summer of 360 provides us with a *terminus ante quem*. Plutarch describes the first meeting of the new ruler's *synedrion*, at which the most important matter on the agenda was that of peace or war with Carthage. Neither Dionysius nor Carthage desired a renewal of hostilities, but the finding of a peace formula satisfactory to both parties was not easy, since Heraclea Minoa and Selinus had been 'liberated' and (together with Drepanum) were probably garrisoned, and Carthage would hardly have been likely to agree to a treaty that gave the Greeks such an important foothold in the Epicraty. She would, however, have been aware of the unwarlike character of Syracuse's new leader and would have hoped to improve her position by patient negotiation rather than by war. Dion (we are told) offered to conduct the peace talks on behalf of Dionysius, and subsequently, being anxious to acquire kudos as a peacemaker, wrote a most imprudent letter to the Punic government, advising them to negotiate only through himself (as having their interests at heart). Plutarch does not credit him with the actual conduct of the peace negotiations, and his language certainly suggests that these had not taken place before Dion's fall.[5]

Philistus must have returned in 367 or 366, and Plato arrived, an honoured guest of the dynast, some little time afterwards. Dionysius at once altered his ways, and the study of letters and of philosophy replaced the former licentiousness of the Court. The smouldering hostility between the two 'parties' at Court was fanned into a blaze, and Dion's enemies united their voices in an outcry to the effect that he was planning either to engineer the transference of the monarchy from Dionysius' hands to those of his own nephews or to abolish it altogether. The letter mentioned above fell into Dionysius' hands and gave Philistus' friends just the handle that they needed to get rid of Dion. The dynast, perhaps fearing to take more violent measures against the most powerful of his Syracusan subjects, packed Dion off into what he promised would be only temporary exile (this happened three months after Plato's arrival), and rather unwisely allowed Dion's relatives to send his movable wealth after him to Athens, where (and elsewhere as well) he cut a brilliant figure. Dionysius kept Plato a virtual prisoner in the citadel, at first in order to separate him from Dion and later because (according to Plutarch) he conceived a 'despot's passion' for the old gentleman. However, a war breaking out – which I take to be the war against the Lucanians, mentioned by Diodorus: a war presumably brought on by Lucanian attacks upon Dionysius' Italian dominions – the dynast sent Plato home, promising to recall Dion and requesting that the exile take no steps against him in the meantime. It was, no doubt, with a view to improving his reputation among his father's friends in mainland Greece that, apparently in 365, Dionysius sent a trusted officer, Timocrates, with 12 ships to assist the Lacedaemonians, and the soldiers of this force took part in the recapture of the strategically important frontier town of Sellasia, 'liberated' (and perhaps burnt) by the Thebans after Leuctra.[6]

Dion was living in considerable style at Athens, his host being one Callippus, and attending the Academy, where Plato's nephew (and successor as head of the Academy) Speusippus became his closest friend. Dion visited other cities, and at Sparta was even accorded the rare honour of being presented with the citizenship; partly, perhaps, as a reward for diplomatic services rendered under the old tyrant, partly with a view to enlarging him in the eyes of Dionysius – a gesture that he would of course repay after his expected reinstatement in favour. Meanwhile Dionysius, having prosecuted the war against the Lucanians (his detractors said, in a dilatory manner, but there is no need to believe them) and having won battles, made peace, presumably on terms that guaranteed the security of his northern frontier (I believe that it may have been about this time that Croton regained its independence). He returned to Syracuse, probably sometime during 364/3, and there surrounded himself with a collection of learned men; devoting himself enthusiastically to the study of philosophy (with numerous 'publications'), but without comprehension of the true Platonic method. He also discontinued the remittances that he had hitherto been sending to Dion (who had, perhaps, been behaving with less discretion than the generally friendly tradition would have us believe). Plato now came under intensive pressure from several directions to return to Syracuse and effect a reconciliation; and finally he agreed and went back there, probably in the spring or summer of 361.[7]

He found that the dynast had made great advances in his studies – indeed, he regarded himself as a finished philosopher – but was quite incapable of assimilating the true Platonic doctrines. Dionysius not only persisted in refusing to recall Dion but now sequestered his property and, using his authority as her brother, gave Arete, Dion's wife, in marriage to Timocrates: he refused, moreover, to allow Plato to depart from Ortygia as he wished. There being now no wars on his frontiers (for peace had by this time been concluded with Carthage, a peace by which the Halycus frontier was restored: was this, perhaps, the occasion on which Damocles was said to have bungled a diplomatic mission?), Dionysius most imprudently attempted to cut the pay of the mercenaries. This naturally provoked a mutiny, the dynast was obliged to revoke the measure, and Heracleides, the commander of the troops, accused of inciting his men to revolt, went into hiding. His uncle, Theodotes, tried, with Plato's assistance, to bring about a reconciliation with Dionysius, but failed; and after the flight of Heracleides and his friends, first to the Epicraty and thence to Greece, Plato came under the tyrant's suspicion and was imprisoned under frightening circumstances. Eventually, through the good offices of Archytas, the distinguished Pythagorean of Taras, Plato was released and allowed to go home, in the summer of 360. He travelled by way of Olympia (it was an Olympiadic year) and there conferred with Dion.[8]

Dion was now determined to recover his rights, his property and his wife by force. Plato pleaded the obligations of his guest-friendship with Dionysius and refused to give his support or countenance to violence; but Speusippus (who had accompanied his uncle to Syracuse) encouraged Dion with assurances that Syracuse was ready to revolt, and accordingly he began to make his preparations. No city, of course, would give him official support, and the fame of Dionysius' strength must have deterred individuals or captains of bands from enlisting in his service. However, three years later (in midsummer of 357), Dion set off with a small force of mercenaries (something like 800 men), and having been blown off his course landed at Heraclea Minoa, on the borders of the Epicraty. The military governor, Synalus, was a guest-friend of Dion and gave him some assistance, and he marched on Syracuse by the southern coast road, collecting contingents from Acragas (Plutarch describes these as 200 horsemen from among 'Acragantines living at Ecnomus'; presumably they were aristocratic exiles, expelled from their city by the partisans of Dionysius), from Gela and Camarina and from some Sican and Sicel towns. He was also joined by volunteers from Italy and, apparently (for Diodorus' language is unclear at this point), from Messana – perhaps exiles. The adamantine bands having been loosened, the break-up of Dionysius' empire had begun.

When Dionysius, an exile at Corinth, told King Philip that he had failed to inherit his father's luck, he must have been thinking bitterly of the fact that when Dion reached Syracuse, at the head of a force amounting to 5,000 men (according to Plutarch), or 20,000 (according to Diodorus) – the truth (as so often in such matters) lies, perhaps, somewhere between the two – he himself was away from home: the awareness of which fact was probably the decisive factor in determining so many of his subjects to throw in their lot with Dion. The tyrant's absence was connected with the new towns which he had founded in order to counter piracy in the Adriatic, and he himself was staying at Caulonia, while Philistus, his *navarch*, was operating in the Adriatic with a powerful fleet. Timocrates, left by Dionysius in charge of Syracuse, allowed himself to be cut off on Epipolae by the desertion of his followers and fled; and Dion and his brother Megacles made a triumphal entrance into the city and proclaimed the liberation of Syracuse and of Sicily. They were elected Generals Plenipotentiary; this was (to borrow a hackneyed phrase) Dion's finest hour.[9]

The rest of the story – a story of almost twenty years of violence, treachery, destruction and finally heroism and restoration – must be told very briefly. Dionysius returned to the citadel (still held by his guards) a week after the liberation and a stalemate ensued between him and Dion, whose initial popularity, undermined by his apparent willingness to reach a compromise with his kinsman, began to decline. His position was further weakened by the arrival from Greece, the following year, of Heracleides with reinforcements; Heracleides found allies among the more radical of the citizens and was elected *navarch*. He gained a signal success by defeating Philistus in a sea battle (in which the old historian perished), and as a result of this Dionysius, after failing in an attempt to secure fairly generous terms from the Syracusans, abandoned Ortygia, leaving his young son Apollocrates in charge, and withdrew to Locri. *Stasis* at Syracuse followed his escape, and Dion and his mercenaries (whose pay had been stopped by the radical faction, supported by Heracleides) withdrew to Leontini, which had revolted from Syracuse. Dion was, however, recalled (probably in the spring of 355), to recover the city which had been overrun and sacked by Dionysius' general, Nypsius, and he was reinstated in his plenipotentiary generalship –

although Heracleides (with whom he was formally reconciled) was given the *navarchy*, and continued to intrigue against him. It was becoming impossible for Apollocrates to hold out on Ortygia, and he finally abandoned the citadel and, with his family and the troops of the garrison, sailed away to rejoin his father at Locri.[10]

Dion was now the (elected) ruler of all Syracuse, but he presented an imperious and haughty front to the citizens and summoned counsellors from Corinth to assist him in drawing up a new constitution which would lean strongly towards aristocracy rather than towards the democracy that had proved so unstable (and which, as a Platonist, he of course abhorred). Heracleides, however, maintained so vigorous an opposition that Dion at last acquiesced in his murder. He did not live long to enjoy his virtually monarchical position. Callippus, his Athenian friend (but who was not, as the Academy was careful to point out, a member of Plato's School) fomented a plot against him and at last, in 353, procured his murder by a group of Zacynthian mercenaries. Dion's followers were expelled, taking refuge in Leontini, and Callippus seized power and ruled Syracuse for thirteen months, until he was himself killed (at Rhegium) in 352, being succeeded as tyrant by Hipparinus, the son of Dionysius I and Aristomache. After two years Hipparinus was succeeded by his younger brother, Nysaeus, who in 346 was expelled by the Younger Dionysius, embittered by the revolt of Locri and the massacre of his family.

The *pax dionysiaca* had been destroyed by Dion; Sicily was laid waste and its cities were de-civilized; some were deserted, others occupied by ex-mercenaries and barbarians. In southern Italy, with Dionysius' power overthrown, a warlike confederation of peoples arose, styled the Brutii, and many Greek cities (including Thurii) fell into their hands. At Leontini, a Syracusan adventurer, one Hicetas, established himself and was accepted as the champion of liberty by the republican elements at Syracuse; but he was in communication with the Carthaginians, who, having composed their domestic problems, were once again contemplating the extension of their suzerainty over the whole chaotic island, and whose assistance Hicetas intended to use in order to make himself master (as their puppet ruler) of all Syracuse.[11]

The Syracusans appealed to their metropolis for help, and in 345 Corinth sent them Timoleon, son of Timaenetus, who was living under a cloud as the result of his having slain his brother for aspiring to the tyranny. Timoleon arrived in Sicily with 10 ships, having eluded a Punic squadron based at Rhegium (the Carthaginians had sent a powerful force to Syracuse, to co-operate with Hicetas who had seized the city), and by a combination of diplomacy and good generalship liberated Syracuse, put down tyranny in Sicily and in 343 won a spectacular victory over greatly superior Carthaginian forces on the river Crimisus, in western Sicily. Dionysius retired to Corinth, where he eked out a frugal existence,

The Family of Dionysius[12]

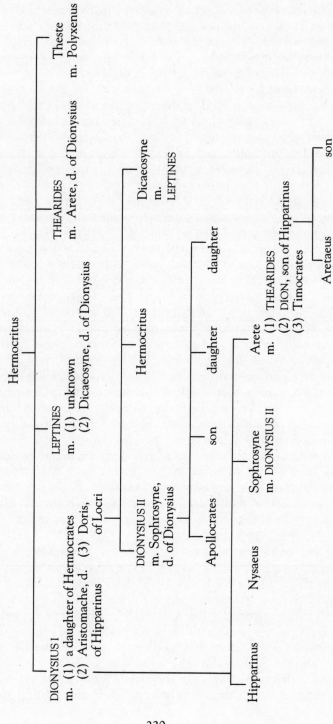

perhaps as a schoolmaster; the butt of visiting intellectuals (like Diogenes) and potentates (such as Philip of Macedon) and providing Academic moralists with a striking example of the punishment that Universal Justice has in store for the hubristic and for the enemies of Platonism.

The Greek cities of Sicily were united in an alliance under the hegemony of Syracuse (the Crimisus victory had been followed by a peace treaty that defined the line of the Halycus as the eastern frontier of the Epicraty), tens of thousands of colonists were brought into the island from Greece to re-people the depopulated cities, Syracuse received a new constitution of *politeia* form and the laws of Diocles were again revised. Timoleon retired from public life and ended his days, old, blind, but honoured as an adopted son of Syracuse, in 334; having afforded Sicily the opportunity to recover from the devastation and anarchy of the post-Dionysius period and given Syracuse a respite from tyranny and *stasis* that endured for over twenty years, until the rise of Agathocles put her once more under the sway of a lesser, but more brutal, tyrant than Dionysius I.[13]

CHAPTER THIRTEEN

Dionysius – the man and the soldier

Let us now try to arrive at some kind of picture of the man who is the subject of this book; and first let us consider that which was created, disseminated and accepted by Antiquity and which is almost (but not quite) unrelievedly defamatory. Stroheker sees Athens as the provenance of most of the stories about Dionysius, for she was already the chief literary and philosophical centre of Greece, she had a long tradition of hostility towards tyranny, and for all but the last few years of Dionysius' reign he had been either the ally of her enemy, Sparta, or, as in 387, actively hostile towards herself. The period of reconciliation was a short one, and with the death of Dionysius and the withdrawal of Ortygia from the affairs of metropolitan Greece the favourable view of him faded quickly from the minds of the Athenians. The Middle Comedy, which in the fourth century replaced the Old Comedy that we associate principally with the name of Aristophanes, has been credited with the invention of much of the derisive material that came to be accepted by the Academy as providing the authentic picture of the tyrant, after the disastrous failure of Plato and his associates, first to reform and, subsequently, to liberate Syracuse. In Stroheker's view it was Timaeus, working at Athens from perhaps 317 for the greater part of his life, who transmitted this picture to the age of Diodorus and Cicero.[1]

It seems to me that the only one of these assumptions which can be accepted without serious reservations is that relating to the role of the Academy. Undoubtedly during Dionysius' lifetime, although there were a few men at Athens favourably disposed towards him, the great majority of the citizens must have felt about him much as Lysias did – when they thought about him at all. For Dionysius was a *remote* enemy, engrossed in the conquest of Sicily and in his wars with Carthage, and it was only in the '80s that he began to appear as a threat to Athens. Evidence (as distinct from assertion) of the hostility towards him of the writers of Attic Comedy is scarcely impressive. In 388 (the year of Lysias' Olympic oration), when Dionysius' stock at Athens was falling towards its lowest point, Aristophanes, the old master of invective, remarks, simply, that it is disgraceful to compare Thrasybulus (the Liberator) with Dionysius.

Ephippus makes a disparaging reference to Dionysius' poetry. (The obscure coined word, *Dionysokouropyrōnen*, which appears in Strattis – who wrote a comedy about Dionysius' sympathizer, Cinesias – does not refer to the dynast at all.) The only other comic passage that has been recorded, from a play by Eubulus entitled *Dionysius*, may be assumed to date from the last years of the tyrant's life, and is complimentary. In fact, the anecdotes upon which rests the dynast's reputation for paranoia are not the kind of thing that we should expect to find in Middle Comedy, with its abandonment of the parabasis and reduction of the role of the chorus.[2]

A man who did, apparently, pillory Dionysius on the stage, and that at about the time when the Court, and perhaps the mental balance of the dynast himself, were disturbed by the conspiracy (or suspected conspiracy) of Leptines, was Dionysius' former boon companion, Philoxenus of Cythera. There are three versions of his falling out with the tyrant. According to one, he seduced the tyrant's mistress, Galatea, was incarcerated in the Quarries, and there had his revenge on the despot by composing his dithyramb of the *Cyclops*, which he later produced at Athens and in which Polyphemus (the Cyclops), made up to resemble Dionysius, pressed his uncouth affections upon the reluctant numph, Galatea. The two other versions turn on the sensitiveness of the tyrant to criticism of his poetry, displaying the enviousness inseparable from the possession of absolute power. The first of these (whose author, Diodorus, is our earliest authority for the story) has it that Dionysius threw the dithyrambist into the Quarries for one night, for speaking his mind about the dynast's poetry; releasing him, however, the next day and apparently becoming at least temporarily reconciled with him. The second of these versions, which might be described as a blend of the other two, throws Philoxenus into the Quarries for criticizing the tyrant's bad verses and has the poet write the best part of his *Cyclops* while immured there.[3]

The only important detail that all three versions have in common is that Philoxenus was thrown into the Quarries, and this item is itself open to grave suspicion. The alleged offence was given in the palace (or at least, on Ortygia), and one is entitled to ask why the tyrant should have gone to the trouble of carting the poet across half Syracuse to the Quarries, in order (according to one version) to lock him up for the night. The Quarries had been used in the late summer of 413 as a POW camp because the Syracusans had then needed somewhere in which to confine something like 7,000 Athenian prisoners. If they were still used as a prison – for debtors, perhaps – they would have been in the charge of the city, not of the dynast, who must have had plenty of places in which to incarcerate a too-outspoken poet until, presumably, he recanted his ill-considered criticism. The truth of the matter probably is that in the innovatory production of the *Cyclops*, put on at Athens (perhaps in

389), the cave in which Cyclops-Dionysius lived was *called* the Latomiae, a name calculated to awaken sinister memories in Philoxenus' Athenian audience, many – if not most – of whom had a kinsman who had suffered in them. This piece of stagecraft, then, gave rise to the story of the poet's incarceration in the Quarries; and it may be that it is to Philoxenus that Dionysius owed the beginning of his reputation for homicidal sensitivity to literary criticism.[4]

The anecdotes upon which rests the tyrant's reputation for intense suspiciousness, morbid fear of assassination and readiness to put even his closest associates to death smack of palace gossip, of the political pamphlet, of the lampoon and of the philosophical essay rather than of the comic stage. They were, I believe, the products of the stoas, the lounges (*leschai*), the *palaestrae* and the symposia; the equivalent in the fourth century of the exchanges, clubs and common-rooms of today, where 'good stories' about prominent, and particularly about unpopular, public figures are coined and passed on: and as such are unlikely to have been confined to Athens. Syracuse itself, the cities of Sicily, Croton, Thurii, Taras, even Locri, probably contributed to the corpus of anti-Dionysiac material. There were also the writers of formal history, men to whom the authenticity of a story was of less moment than its effectiveness. Philistus, whose account of Dionysius' reign was said to have suppressed everything of an unflattering nature, was not the only man writing about Sicilian affairs in the fourth century. There were Hermeias of Methymna, Athanas of Syracuse, Timonides of Leucas (an Academician) and Polycritus of Mende. The last three wrote about the reign of the Younger Dionysius and the civil war, but they are unlikely not to have made references to the older tyrant; and, indeed, we know that Athanas mentioned Dionysius' use of strange words in his dramas, and this may have been in connection with the tyrant's literary touchiness. Moreover, Theopompus of Chios devoted three books of his *Philippica* to the history of Sicily under the two Dionysii.[5]

The anecdotes fall into two main categories, which we may call the 'historical' and the 'moralizing', and it is with the second category that we are concerned here. These are the stories designed not so much to tell us something about the historical Dionysius as to delineate the very type of The Tyrant and therefore the most contemptible and the most unhappy of beings. For a tyrant was, by the very fact of his being a monarch, a bad thing: 'Nothing is more inimical to a city', says Euripides. He represented the triumph of Force (*bia*) over Justice. It is true that if he respected the laws, and truly exerted himself for the benefit of his citizens and not merely to satisfy his own greed or ambition, he might be allowed *some* virtue. So Peisistratus enjoyed a good and improving reputation in the later fifth and the fourth centuries, and was placed by Athenian national pride in the list of the Seven Sages. None the less, monarchy was identical with tyranny, as Herodotus makes clear in the 'debate of the satraps'. So, in the *Supplices* of Aeschylus, the 'good' king Pelasgus has to insist upon the sovereignty of the People; and in the play of the same name by Euripides the Theban herald's, 'Who is the *tyrant* of the land?' provokes from King Theseus (by now the mythical ancestor of Athenian democracy) the sharp rejoinder, 'The Demos is king (*anassei*)'; and in his righteous indignation Theseus goes on to use both 'tyrant' and *basileus* to express the idea of despotism. Similarly, in Euripides' *Ion*, the hero (who of course became a good king of Attica) rejects the idea of monarchy outright. However, in the fourth century, partly perhaps as a result of Athens' friendly relations with Evagoras of Cyprus, a distinction began to be made in thoughtful circles between king (*basileus*) and tyrant; the former ruling over 'willing subjects and in accordance with the laws', the latter over 'unwilling, and not in accordance with the laws'.[6]

Although I cannot agree with Stroheker that Dionysius regarded himself as a king rather than a tyrant (in that the Syracusans had agreed to accept him and displayed loyalty towards him), I do believe that he would have indignantly rejected the imputation of tyranny, on the grounds that he was not the *ruler* of Syracuse but its war-leader. However, the ordinarily intelligent Greek of, say, the 380s, would have found no difficulty in assigning Dionysius to his proper category. He would have appeared to him as a tyrant who by demagogy and with the aid of a bodyguard had overthrown an established democracy, expelled the 'best men', reapportioned the land, freed slaves, defeated a popular revolt by the use of mercenaries (including barbarians), disarmed the People, and shut himself away from them in a fortified citadel, maintaining himself in power with the aid of a large mercenary army which the People were required to pay for, and waging endless wars in order to impoverish his subjects and justify his position as war-leader. Worse than all that in the eyes of an Athenian, he consistently sided with Sparta and therefore indirectly with Sparta's friend, the Great King, the foe of Greek liberty. He had destroyed Athens' ancient allies, the Ionian cities of Sicily and he had taken as his own allies the barbarians who were threatening the existence of the cities of Magna Graecia. Could any man fit more completely the accepted pattern of The Tyrant?[7]

That pattern, established by the sophists before the last quarter of the fifth century, has been mentioned already. We encounter it first in Herodotus and later in Euripides. The fundamental objections to tyranny, that it represents the rule of force and the denial of liberty, had been established by Solon, but it is Herodotus who gives us the first fully drawn portrait of The Tyrant. Being answerable to no one (*aneuthynos*) he becomes totally corrupted, hubris being added to man's natural condition of envy. Consequently he envies the best elements and rejoices in the worst. He listens to calumny and is offended equally by those who flatter him and by those who do not. He changes (for the worse) the established laws, he carries off women, he puts men to death without trial, for he heeds the injunction laid on Periander by Thrasybulus, to cut down all outstanding men in the city. Euripides reminds us of this precept in his brief delineation of The Tyrant, adding that tyrants extort from their subjects the profits of their labour. He also introduces us to the idea that was to dominate the thinking of the philosophical schools about tyranny from the fourth century onwards, the idea of the *misery* of the tyrant. Nothing could you find more wretched than tyranny. Ion declares that tyranny is grievous (*lupēra*), for no ruler can be happy or fortunate who is for ever looking askance in fear for his life, has only the vile (*ponēroi*) for friends and puts good men to death. Nor is his wealth any remedy.[8]

It was the malignity (*kakoetheia*) of Plato, and after his death of the Academy that he founded and of the Peripatetics, that fitted Dionysius definitively to the established pattern; laying particular emphasis, as might be expected, upon the moral degeneration of the man whose ruling passion was the lust for power. Plato had visited Dionysius' Syracuse, but (as has been said already) the silence of the Seventh Letter makes it, I believe, unlikely that he met and disputed with the dynast, as the legend pretends – a legend invented, first, to illustrate the intellectual and moral superiority to the tyrant of the Founder of the Academy, and secondly, to provide a reason (the resentment of the baffled despot) for the sale of Plato as a slave (whether by Dionysius himself at Syracuse or by Pollis at Aegina). The legend had several ramifications: one tells how Plato was offered 'Persian' robes by Dionysius (and of course refused them), another, that he visited Mount Etna in company with the tyrant, and a third, how Pollis was punished for his wickedness by being defeated in battle and drowned by the tidal wave that overwhelmed Helice in 372. Plato does not name Dionysius in the *Republic* – he could not, for 'dramatic' reasons – and Stroheker believes that the passage was not aimed specifically at our tyrant. However, it seems to me absurd to suppose that any educated Greek reading this section of the *Republic* and knowing of Plato's sojourn in Syracuse (and, presumably, of its embarrassing sequel) would not immediately have connected it with Dionysius; and indeed it appears to me to be a fair assumption that, from the day of the foundation of the Academy, the empire of Dionysius was held up as the very type of the 'perverted' form of monarchy. As I have suggested above, I think it likely that the young Dion did nothing to disabuse his tutor of his prejudices. Dion was an ambitious young man, filled with youth's unrealistic passion for liberty; he was also an aloof, haughty and autocratic person, and no doubt very conscious of the humiliation of being compelled, a member of the old governing class, to serve an upstart tyrant and his low-caste associates. Although he schooled himself for the next twenty years to play the part of a loyal and trustworthy minister (and was regarded as such by Dionysius), he was not committed to the struggle against Carthage, and there are indications, first, that he would have liked to secure at least a share of the succession for the sons of his sister (which would have put him in the position of a regent), and secondly that – perhaps from the highest motives – he would not have been averse to acquiring the monarchy for himself.[9]

As has been suggested in an earlier chapter, when Plato visited Syracuse it was at a time when the dynast's household was under considerable, and probably increasing, tension, and when Dionysius himself was absent, in camp before Rhegium. Leptines was in disgrace and may have been meditating revolt, and Philistus – who either already was, or was soon to become, Leptines' unacknowledged son-in-law – was, as Captain of the Citadel, in charge of the defence and security of the city. I think that it was Philistus who packed Plato off home, having been rendered anxious by what he would have regarded as his intrigue with Dion. That Plato *was* packed off certainly appears to have been the case from the 'legend', and is inherently probable (always provided, of course, that the whole story is not pure invention); for would an Athenian citizen have chosen, if he were a wholly free agent, to set off for home in an enemy warship commanded by a leading Spartan who had come to Sicily to ask for naval assistance against Athens? In the Academic tradition Philistus appears as antipathetic to Plato; and if the story of the philosopher's seizure by the Aeginetans is true (as I believe it to be), Plato would be likely to hold Ortygia to blame for his embarrassment, which would provide an additional reason for the hostility of his School.

But far worse was to come. Plato allowed himself to be drawn into the struggle, first, for the control of the Younger Dionysius, between the Old Guard reinforced by Philistus, recalled from exile, and Dion, whose true motives are difficult to assess; and later, between Dionysius and Dion, following the retirement of the latter from Syracuse; and Plato can hardly be said to have emerged from this imbroglio with either his dignity or his credit unimpaired. Civil war, three- and at times four-cornered, resulted, Dionysius' empire collapsed, tyrants came and went in Syracuse and in the cities, Dion was murdered (the Academy was at pains to dissociate itself from that crime) and the island was ravaged and depopulated. Plato's involvement with Dion and the equivocal part played in the confusion by the Academy and certain of its members, meant that the Academy was very much on the defensive where Sicily was concerned and very ready to blacken the reputation of the Dionysii.[10]

However, even had no untoward event marred his visit to Sicily, Plato could not have felt anything but repugnance towards a regime which was in every way the antithesis of his own Ideal State. Certainly it would not have been possible for him to endow the tyrant with two qualities – uncomfortable and indeed rather suspect in a democracy, but beginning to catch the imagination of the fourth century, with its rising tide of individualism – namely, lordliness (*megalopsychia*) and love of honour (*philotimia*). These were the qualities of a man who zealously sought glory and preferred a glorious death to mere living; a man prepared to confront any danger, if so be he could establish his fame for all time. By Aristotle's time, *megalopsychia* had been adopted by philosophy and given a high moral connotation, becoming 'an ornament of the virtues'. Dion is presented by the Academic tradition, as one who would have been the very embodiment of this quality, had it not been for a fatal tendency towards the haughtiness and insolence that are, as it were, the perversion of true 'greatness of soul'. Dionysius, however, was a tyrant – he was *the* tyrant – and so could not possibly be 'lordly', 'great-souled', or 'honour-loving'; he had to conform to the pattern established by the fifth century and it had to be shown that he was ambitious only for *power*.

Herodotus had been concerned mainly about the effect that a tyrant had on society; but to Euripides, and to the fourth century with its interest in the condition of the individual's soul, the unhappy state of the despot himself was a matter of importance. Men must be most earnestly dissuaded from envying, and so perhaps being tempted to emulate, the life of the tyrant. It had, indeed, always been assumed that the tyrant who managed to live his life to its full span (as many tyrants did) must be the happiest of men. Equality was not for him and he could do whatever he wished; tyranny was 'fair of face', it was 'the ultimate cynosure of mortal eyes'. Even a brief reign was something to be desired: 'If I could have ruled, possessed wealth in abundance and been tyrant of Athens for only one day, I should have been willing thereafter to be flayed for a wineskin and to have my line obliterated'. Dionysius, therefore, must not only be shown to be despotic – cruel, suspicious, an apt disciple of Thrasybulus of Miletus – but he must be portrayed as the *unhappiest* of men: self-immured in his citadel, cut off from intercourse with free Greek spirits, tortured by perpetual fear and suspicion, utterly friendless.[11]

Their Founder having shown how Dionysius corresponded to the accepted pattern of The Tyrant in all respects save one (did he, perhaps, owe his freedom from the charge of violating women to the fastidiousness of his brother-in-law, Dion?), the Academy collected the corroborative details and transmitted them to posterity. There was, I suggest, already plenty of such material available in one form or another in mid-fourth-century Athens, and some may well have been brought by Dion when he came to Athens and set himself to obtain the active support of the

Academy for the proposed liberation of Syracuse. At that time the Academy was very much concerned to justify its interference in Syracusan affairs, an interference that contributed, in the event, to the ruin of Sicily; later, however, its purpose was rather to belittle Dionysius, regarded as the *type* of The Tyrant, to reduce his stature from that of the most powerful man of his age, and therefore, it might be supposed, the happiest, to that of a creature so contemptible, so consumed by envy, suspicion and *fear* that he could be denied even the attributes of a soldier. There was not a hint that Dionysius might, in the '80s, have had good reason to suspect Leptines and others: his actions were ascribed to paranoia. It may be that *at that time* Dionysius was nervous of assassination, and I have suggested in another chapter that if he was it may not have been without cause. So, under the insidious promptings of Sejanus, was the fine soldier, Tiberius. It is not everyone who possesses the fatalism of a Julius.

But Dionysius had to be shown to be ridiculous, and so the stories current at Athens were incorporated (with variations, as time went on) as moral parables in the lectures delivered and in the essays and pamphlets penned by members of the Academy and later of the Peripatos. Their purpose was to portray Dionysius as a monster of cowardice – of the very antithesis of *aretē* – and he had to be shown as one living in a continual agony of fear. Some of the stories may seem to us to be too silly to be worthy of the notice of great philosophical schools; but there is nothing so silly that it will not be believed by those who want to believe it, and the purpose of the stories was to emphasize not the awfulness of the tyrant but his ridiculousness, his contemptibility. That they were not too silly for the Academy is shown by the fact that they were not too silly for Cicero. Thus all who approached the tyrant were forced to change their clothes in case they might be carrying a hidden weapon. The man who cut his hair might cut his throat, and therefore the despot slew his barber for reminding him of the fact, or else he taught his daughters to do his barbering for him or had his hair singed instead of cut. When he approached the wife of the night – she was, of course, obliged to receive him stark naked – he did so by way of a drawbridge that spanned a moat dug around the marriage bed.

A careless remark could indeed cost lives at Syracuse, and I have mentioned in an earlier chapter the various young men whom an indiscreet remark destroyed. Timaeus tells us that the tyrant made away secretly with the Woman of Himera. This was the lady who dreamt that she was taken up to heaven and there beheld, before the throne of Zeus, a large 'red' man, loaded with chains. She was informed that he was the Evil Spirit – the bane – of Sicily and Italy, who, if he got free, would destroy the lands. When, at a later date, she encountered Dionysius she cried out that he was the bane who had been revealed to her. Three months later, she 'disappeared'. Dionysius was also said to have murdered his mother, although this story was probably no more than a variant of the story that he had put his mother-in-law to death.

Since he dared not enter the agora, Dionysius addressed the people from a lofty tower (there may, of course, be a basis of fact to this story; for it would not have been unreasonable for him to summon an Assembly in front of the cross-wall and to speak to it from one of the towers, especially during the last few years of his life). One of the oldest-established traits of The Tyrant was his enviousness (a sign of his unbalanced condition, for did he not possess everything he could want?); and in the case of Dionysius this manifested itself in the form of a bitter resentment of any hostile criticism of his poetry. I have already considered the case of the dithyrambist, Philoxenus – with whom, of course, this charge may have originated, for it might have occurred to him that it would put him on good terms with his new Athenian patrons. Another victim of the tyrant's sensitiveness, according to one version of the story, was the playwright Antiphon; but he may very well have been put to death (if, of course, he *was* put to death) for conspiracy or suspected conspiracy.[12]

There was, of course, no possibility of the tyrant's enjoying true friendship: apart from anything else, his penchant for ridiculing those whom he injured was hardly calculated to endear him to persons of sensitivity. Since he had destroyed all the Best Men and so been compelled to rely wholly upon the support of enfranchised slaves and mercenaries, it followed that his Court must consist only of such people, whom a Roman aristocrat (and snob) like Cicero would naturally describe as fugitives, criminals and barbarians. The Academic tradition always ignored the discrepancy between its picture of Dionysius' Court and the high favour in which the Platonist, Dion, continued to be held, despite his displaying an independence of spirit and incurring an unpopularity with the courtiers which should surely have led to his speedy downfall. The lasting friendship with the tyrant of Socrates' former companion, Aristippus of Cyrene, was explained by reference to Aristippus' parasitical and hedonistic character and philosophy. Care was not always taken to distinguish between father and son when ridiculing 'Dionysius'. Cicero tells the well-known story of the Sword of Damocles (itself patently an absurd invention) in connection with the father, which was presumably the form in which he received it, although we know from Timaeus that Damocles was an associate of the son. Even the half-way favourable anecdote of Dionysius' clemency towards Damon and Phintias (a clemency preceded by an unexplained death sentence), is probably no more than an invention designed to illustrate the steadfastness of Pythagoreans.

If all these anecdotes were accepted as valid evidence they would, of course, add up to a formidable indictment of paranoia. However, as Stroheker has pointed out, once the hostile nature of their sources and the intrinsic worthlessness of most of them have been appreciated, their mere number adds nothing to the credibility of the effect that they are intended to produce. As a Lord Chief Justice, referring to the value of evidence, once remarked, 'Nought added to nought still equals nought. And it remains nought if you add a third or a fourth nought to it, or, indeed, any number of noughts'.[13]

Stroheker sees the malice of Timaeus as the principal channel by which the defamatory anecdotes were passed on to the Ciceronian and later ages, but I believe that this is only partially true. Timaeus lived for much of his life at Athens, where he had connections with the Peripatetics. Diodorus regarded him as a truthful historian who showed unacceptable bias only in the case of his old persecutor, Agathocles; Plutarch, however, strongly deprecated Timaeus' vilification (*blasphēmia*) of Philistus, whom he disapproved of as a staunch upholder of tyranny. But neither Diodorus nor Polybius (in his bitter attack on Timaeus, in Book XII) accuses Timaeus of prejudice against Dionysius; however, we must remember that in the eyes of both these writers Dionysius was the very model of the despotic tyrant, with all but one of the vices attributed by philosophy to tyrants, and that therefore only statements that were self-contradictory or inconsistent with what had gone before, that were at variance with the accepted tradition or that consisted merely of unseemly abuse, would be regarded as evidence of prejudice. Certainly we can attribute at least one derogatory story to Timaeus: that of the dream of the Woman of Himera, a story already familiar, in its essentials at least, to the Athenians of Demosthenes' day and probably introduced by Timaeus into his History as a corrective of Philistus' story of the pre-natal dream of the dynast's mother. Diodorus and Josephus tell us that Timaeus 'corrected' Philistus' errors (Philistus was said to have suppressed Dionysius' most unholy deeds – *ta anosiōtata*), and it seems to me very probable that he also regularly 'corrected' Philistus' judgements and the motives that he assigned to his hero, in accordance with his own very different sentiments.[14]

However, I believe that Timaeus was not the only, or even perhaps the most important transmitter of material damaging to Dionysius' reputation. Timaeus, whatever may have been his shortcomings – and in fact we possess too little of his work to be able to make a worthwhile assessment of his historiographical integrity – regarded himself as, and may be said to have been, a 'serious' historian; and although he no doubt accepted as true and therefore incorporated in his work numerous historical anecdotes, and also accepted (because he had been brought up to do so) the verdict of the Athens of his day on the character and motives of the tyrant, I see no good reason to suppose that we should hold him responsible for the onward transmission of what I have called the corpus of 'moralizing' material. There can be no doubt that Diodorus was familiar with Timaeus' history and (to put it no higher) took it into account when writing his own; and if Timaeus had dealt extensively in moralizing anecdote, we might perhaps expect to find more of it in Diodorus.

In fact, Diodorus give us only four examples, of which three deal with the tyrant's literary pretensions and his inability to accept adverse criticism. Two of these appear in what is really a parenthetical passage concerned with Dionysius' attachment to the arts, following the fall of Rhegium, and the third is to do with his death. The first two comprise the least defamatory of the Philoxenus stories, and the version of Plato's sale as a slave that makes no mention of either Pollis or Aegina; something that would, I believe, be remarkable if it came from Timaeus, whom one would expect to have known all about Pollis, particularly as his voyage to and from Sicily was connected with the momentous events then taking place in the eastern Aegean. In his account of Dionysius' death, Diodorus again does not appear to have been following Timaeus, who gives the event an added touch of drama. Stroheker has described the 'Theodorus episode' as 'pure Timaeus', but I find this hard to accept; first, because we do not possess enough of Timaues' writing to be able to say what is or is not 'pure Timaeus', and secondly because (as I have suggested above) the improbabilities of the historical narrative that forms its introduction put the whole passage into the realm of the political pamphlet or the rhetorical exercise rather than into that of history.[15]

We may be sure that the earlier biographies and *memorabilia* of Plato emanating from both the Academy and the Peripatos included material highly critical of both the Dionysii; and if we possessed the *Tyrannies in Sicily* and the *Retributive Destruction of Tyrants* produced by Aristotle's pupil, Phaenias of Eresus, we should probably find there many, if not all, of the stories that became the common currency of ancient moral philosophy. Dionysius represented Tyranny and the well-known anecdotes were introduced, in order to point a moral, into the philosophical literature which was, I believe, their principal channel. Cicero, who had studied at Athens and was – like Brutus, to whom the *Tusculan Disputations* were addressed – sympathetically inclined towards the Academy, is our earliest source for most of the 'moralizing' stuff, and he regurgitates it (in the Tusculans) in order to illustrate the text, that he could conceive of nothing 'more disgusting, more lamentable, more detestable' than the life of the wicked and unjust man, beset by fear and suspicion. I am sure that Cicero found these stories not in the historical writings of the Greeks but in the philosophical; and we know that he took the view that orators are allowed to depart from the truth when dealing with history in order to make their point more effectively.

Cicero, composing philosophical works at a time when the spectre of tyranny haunted the faltering Roman republic, cared very little whether the tales about Dionysius that he was passing on were true or false; they were recounted solely in order to make a moral point (after all, Cicero had read and appreciated Philistus, and knew that there was another side to the story). All men who wrote for publication must have done what Pliny expressly says he did, and made notes of everything that they read; so that a Cicero or a Diodorus or a Plutarch had plenty of anecdotal material at his disposal, to which he could readily refer without having to consult the author whenever he needed a reference. Philistus was still read in Cicero's and Diodorus' time, but he was considered, no doubt correctly, the inferior of Thucydides as a stylist, and therefore in many respects as a model. Moreover he was unashamedly biased in favour of monarchy and of Dionysius, so that he omitted from his work all mention of the tyrant's by now well-established shortcomings and atrocities. His authority, therefore, would have had little weight against that of the more morally acceptable anecdotists.[16]

The other side of the classical picture is extremely meagre. Timaeus and Valerius Maximus tell us a little about Dionysius' physical appearance: he was a big man (by ancient Greek standards), freckled and fair-haired – or, if we take the freckles into account, perhaps red-haired. He was strong and capable of great feats of endurance (his fondness for playing ball must have contributed to his fitness). Cicero describes him as an ardent man of action, and Scipio Aemilianus reckoned him to be one who combined in the highest degree activity and daring with intelligence. Cicero also mentions his moderation (*temperentia* = *sōphrosynē*), a rare virtue in a tyrant, and Nepos says the same: 'he was not at all sensual, he was not a voluptuary, he was not rapacious. In short, he was greedy only for perpetual personal power'. Aelian tells us that the reason why Dionysius did not write comedies was that he was not a lover of laughter; but against this must be set the statement of Suidas, that he *did* write comedies, the story of Athenaeus that turns on the hearty laughter of Dionysius and his friends, the description of Philoxenus as one of his drinking companions (before their falling out), and the fact that his Court was attractive enough to encourage Socrates' hedonistic friend, Aristippus, to sojourn there. Moreover his favourite method of winning people over was to feast them – scarcely the conduct of a misanthrope. The Athenian comic poet Eubulus, in a play most probably produced after 370 entitled *Dionysius*, says that he was stern towards flatterers but good-humoured with those who jested at his expense – a description that reflected the radically changed attitude of the Athenians towards the dynast, but which is interestingly at variance both with the accepted pattern of The Tyrant and with what Antiquity in general had to say about Dionysius. We are told, too, that he was interested in history and in medicine, as well, of course, as in music and poetry. [17]

In fact Dionysius' whole career, and such of his few recorded sayings as seem to be genuine, convey the impression that he was the very embodiment of *megalopsychia*: the characteristic of the man who devotes his life to the pursuit of glory and is prepared to face any danger in it, the man to whom fame is dearer than life itself. When we first encounter him, we find him risking (and very nearly losing) his life and liberty in a reckless attempt to establish the high-minded and 'charismatic' Hermocrates as tyrant; an attempt which, if it had succeeded, must have proved a short-cut to fame for the young and socially undistinguished Dionysius. When, four years later, besieged on Ortygia, he believed that his own cause was irretrievably lost, he thought not of how he might negotiate his safety with the Syracusans but of 'what sort of death he should embrace, so as to make the dissolution of his regime not wholly inglorious'. Once he was well established as tyrant, he might have ruled securely over a large part (perhaps even the greater part) of Sicily, maintaining peace with Carthage, had power alone been the object of his ambition.

Let us consider again the picture of Dionysius in action, that Philistus gives us.

> He personally attended to the work [the building of the north wall of Epipolae] along with his friends, during the whole period; he visited every section and lent a hand to anyone who had run into difficulty. He laid aside completely the dignity of his position as ruler and put himself on a level with the commonalty; he faced up to the heaviest tasks and endured the same toil and hardship as the rest, so that a great competitiveness was aroused and some men even added part of the night to the labours of the day, so great an enthusiasm had taken possession of the masses.

This display of 'togetherness' with the People (like his display of magnanimity after his victory on the Eleporus) had, of course, a calculated purpose; here, to encourage a feeling of common effort in a common cause, of the unity of Hegemon (for it is as *leader*, not ruler, that he presents himself) and people. But the picture is not just that of a born leader of men and one who knows how to get things done, it is also that of a man who cares about the impression that he is creating; like Sarpedon, taking his stand among the foremost Lycians because to do so was the duty of a king, upon whom all men gazed as upon a god. When engaged in one of the toughest military operations of his career, the siege of Rhegium, Dionysius went to great trouble and expense to send a *theoria* to Olympia in order to display to the Greek world not just his power and wealth – the rewards of his *aretē* as a soldier – but also the treasures of his mind – of his *aretē* as a poet. In the last year of his life, when he could contemplate an empire that comprehended the greater part of Sicily, 'secured by chains of adamant', he was still planning the conquest of the Epicraty and the winning of the glory that yet eluded him. Even the story of his death, as told by Diodorus (which may be true in its essentials) – his submission of a play at the Attic Lenaea and his joy at winning the prize, which led to his overindulgence at the celebratory banquet – illustrates his thirst for fame: the fame that is the acknowledgement of victory, which is itself the highest realization of *aretē*. [18]

Stroheker sees Dionysius as a disciple of sophistic rationalism and a cynic in matters pertaining to the gods. In fact, we cannot say for certain how he viewed the supernatural, but it seems to me probable that he would have subscribed to the widely held view that Chance (*tychē*) ruled the world – particularly when things were going wrong. Dionysius, however, was essentially a man of action, not a sophist, and he spent his whole life pitting himself against external perils, including those of the winds and waves, in the pursuit of a definite goal. Such a man, I believe, would not be likely to turn his back upon the ancient and familiar rulers of the Universe, whom one could approach as a suppliant (or, indeed, as a businessman, with concrete proposals) and whose relationship to Tychē was so ill-defined that they were regarded both as validating the decrees of Tychē and also as bestowing upon a man his individual *tychē*, or 'luck'. A man of war like Dionysius would probably have played safe and, without being deeply religious, would have paid all due honour to the gods whilst making a mental reservation in respect of Tychē. For this reason I am inclined to disagree with Stroheker's assumption that the story of the dynast's mother's dream was an ingenious invention, published after the establishment of the regime in order to bring Dionysius into the company of men like Cypselus, Phalaris, Peisistratus and Pericles, whose future greatness was presaged in this way. To my mind the essential detail of the story – that Dionysius' mother gave birth to a satyr – gives it the ring of truth. It is something quite different, because so apparently inconsequential, from the dream of the Woman of Himera: a tale concocted, I believe, specifically to countervail Philistus' story. It would not be so very remarkable for a pregnant woman to have a dream connected with a god of fertility whose worship was especially associated with women and who enjoyed, as we know, an important public cult at Syracuse; nor that the Galeotae should give a flattering interpretation of it: many a mother-to-be must have been promised high distinction for a son who, in the event, never came to anything. Again, it is possible (we have no information on the matter) that Dionysius was the name of the future dynast's grandfather, and if this was the case it would not be so strange for his mother to dream that she had borne a member of Dionysus' entourage. If the story is true, or if – what amounts to the same thing – Dionysius *believed* it to be true, its significance would be very great; for the words of the Galeotae would have endorsed the feeling of dissimilarity to his fellow men that besets the introvert and would have encouraged him to regard himself from an early age as a person set apart and marked out for greatness by Destiny. In any case, we may safely assume that someone as astute as Dionysius would have anticipated in his conduct Aristotle's advice to tyrants, to appear conspicuously zealous in what pertains to the gods.[19]

Cicero's account of Dionysius' upbringing (based as it probably is on Philistus) makes it probable that he enjoyed the Higher Education of a well-to-do young man of his day, attending the lectures of Sophists, whose boast was that they inculcated aretē, excellence, in their pupils. No doubt he heard the popular definition of Justice discussed – a definition to which his actions throughout his life suggest that he subscribed – *to do good to one's friends and harm to one's enemies*. Nor could he have avoided being steeped in Homer. Homer was the basis of a gentleman's education, and the sophists (in Jaeger's words) 'regarded Homer as an encyclopaedia of all human knowledge . . . and as a mine of wisdom for the conduct of life'. Certainly they agreed with the Homeric conception of the purpose of education: to train a man to be 'a doer of deeds and a speaker of words' – the speaking of words, of course, being the field in which they particularly excelled, although there were those who were prepared to lecture on the principles underlying even military activity. But it was not in the world of Homer but in that of the *polis* that they claimed to train young men, teaching them political *aretē*. Since higher education was not directed towards banausic ends, the rewards of *aretē* were fame and honour; for (as Jaeger says) *aretē* and glory are inseparable: they had been so in epic, and they remained so in the *polis*. A hero (in our sense of the word – an *anēr agathos*) put forth his *aretē* in order to achieve victory and win glory. He did not strive for *interior* satisfaction, any more than he abstained from offending against the code of his society in order to win the plaudits of his conscience. The Greek conscience was entirely public.[20]

When the heroic age was replaced by the age of the *polis*, *aretē*, victory and good and ill fame acquired a new significance. In time of war, indeed, the civic hero stood, like his epic counterpart, in the forefront of the battle; but he was under discipline, he put forth his *aretē* in concert with his peers in the phalanx, neither hanging back nor pressing forward, and the victory that he strove for was the common victory of his city. So far was his glory from being diminished by an enemy's private victory over his body (as an epic hero's was), that if he fell in battle his city accorded him special honour and conferred upon him what was probably the most substantial form of immortality that the old Greek world had to offer, the immortality of his name: 'Beneath the soil though he be, he becomes immortal'. But even when he was not 'standing firm in his place [sc. in the phalanx], both feet well planted on the ground, biting his lip', a man could still display his *aretē* by his conduct as a citizen; for in the *polis* all the aspects of virtue – Aeschylus mentions self-restraint (*sōphrosynē*), justice (*dikē*), courage (*aretē*), and respect for religion (*eusebeia*) – are subsumed in respect for Justice (*dikaiosynē*), the corner-stone of the *polis*. [21]

However, as civic life became more complex – particularly after the development of popular regimes of various kinds, ranging from the warrior society of Sparta to the radical democracy of Athens – and the competition for civic distinction became concerned with more than just the pronouncement of the most acceptable judgement in a lawsuit, men began to look for instruction in political technique (*politikē technē*): they wanted to be taught the art of success in the *polis*, the art which Aristophanes described as that of making the worse cause appear the better. Not everyone, however, among the educated upper classes was satisfied with the *polis* as it had developed by the close of the fifth century. Just as there were well-to-do, clever, educated men who found the political atmosphere of a democracy distasteful and the rewards that democracy accorded to political *aretē* ignominious and who therefore withdrew from public life, so there were others who sought to replace democracy by a regime more in keeping with their own ideas of what constituted a society of equals, and so to create the opportunity of winning more conspicuous distinction in a more discriminating circle.

As a very young man, Dionysius was, I believe, such a one, and attached himself to Hermocrates' band of young men; indeed, I consider it most likely that Thucydides had Dionysius in mind when he introduced what appears to be a rather inconsequential attack on the 'young men in a hurry' into the 'debate' between Hermocrates and Athenagoras, in Book Six. Of course, by the time Dionysius was old enough to begin to play an active role in Syracusan politics, Hermocrates was in exile; and once it became apparent that the Demos (or at any rate its leaders) was too nervous of his individualism to accede to his friends' plea for his reinstatement, if ceased to be a matter of supporting a reactionary statesman who aspired to constitutional leadership (*prostasia*), but of planning an armed coup that could hardly have had any other purpose than that of establishing him as sole ruler (if only, perhaps, temporarily). Dionysius' egoism was too powerful to be satisfied with the uncertain rewards of civic virtue offered by a fickle Demos, under which public acclaim could change overnight into public odium. Patriotism, anyway, is only possible if a person is able to 'identify' himself with his country, whether rationally by a deliberate act of will or irrationally, from sentiment or mere unthinking habit; but after the failure of Hermocrates' coup, whatever sense of loyalty Dionysius may have felt towards the Syracuse that had killed his leader and come close to killing himself must have been at a very low ebb.[22]

Filled as Dionysius was, by inclination reinforced by teaching, with the Homeric ambition always to excel in valour (*aristeuein*) and be distinguished above others, the fate of Hermocrates had shown him that there was no likelihood of his achieving his aim within the framework of a democracy, or, indeed, of any form of free political society; and since he could no longer subscribe to the political – the Tyrtaean – ideal of *aretē*, and would have been equally unattracted by the philosophical conception of *aretē* as moral virtue, he was left with the simple heroic. No hero's reputation stood as high in Sicily as that of Gelon, who had expelled the Carthaginians from the island in 480 but had not sought to extend his empire to include the western (the Phoenician and Elymian) corner. Hermocrates, however, by his foray into the Epicraty, had shown Dionysius how, by again driving the Carthaginians from Sicily and by incorporating the Epicraty in his own pan-Sicilian empire, he could achieve fame surpassing Gelon's. The defeat of contemporary Carthage (much more powerful now than she had been almost a century earlier) would be an achievement comparable to the overthrow of Xerxes and would reward the *aretē* of the man who accomplished it with the greatest glory in Greek history; and to win such glory there was nothing – neither his own life nor the lives of any number of his countrymen – that Dionysius was not prepared to sacrifice; for he was, like Alexander the Great and like Hannibal, that most perilous kind of romantic: the man morally as well as intellectually and physically capable of turning colossal fantasy into reality. That he in fact failed where Alexander succeeded is, I believe, due less to his inferiority as a man to the Macedonian than to the inferiority of the resources with which he had to work. And at least, unlike the great Barcid, he died with both his power and the possibility of yet accomplishing his dream intact.

Aristotle was expressing a sentiment whose origin can be detected even in Homer when he declared that the man who could not live in a political society must be either defective (*phaulos*) or more than human. (He noted, too, that such a man was 'a lover of war'. Did he have in mind both Dionysius, whom he would certainly have classed among the 'defectives', and his old pupil, Alexander, who demanded to be worshipped as a god?) Certainly Dionysius rejected the *polis*; the cross-wall between Ortygia and the mainland was, for all its gates, the barrier between himself and the life of a citizen. But although he had cut himself off from daily contact with public opinion in the city, and indeed from contact with the sentiments of the Hellenic world at large (so that he could commit such a gaffe as to send, at that particular juncture, his grandiose *theoria* to Olympia), he seems never to have lost sight of his humanity or to have likened himself to the gods (although he is said to have claimed to be in their confidence – for fiscal purposes). Nor, I believe, did he see himself as a tyrant, not because (as Stroheker suggests) he regarded himself as a king, but because he would not have seen how the accepted pattern of The Tyrant could apply to himself, who was the *leader* of the Syracusans, not their ruler. Tyranny, as he remarked (most probably in one of his plays), is 'the mother of all injustice', and he named his three daughters after three of the chief virtues, Aretē, Sōphrosynē and Dicaiosynē (had he had a fourth, he would assuredly have called her Eusebeia), in order to advertise to gods and men their father's love of virtue, evidenced by his valour, his avoidance of hubris and his policy of aiding his friends and smiting his enemies.[23]

If Dionysius' whole career is proof of his passion for glory, three of the very few sayings attributed to him (the first of which may be a quotation from a play) are equally revealing. One was that the chief advantage of power (*archē*, which Cicero would have translated by *imperium*) is that it enables a man to do what he wants without delay (*tacheōs*), another, that he prayed that he might never be without employment (*scholazein*), and the third, that he advised his son not to jeopardize his power by hubris. To these sayings may be added the story (perhaps apocryphal, but none the less significant), that he was encouraged to despise death by the sight of an ox being killed as a sacrifice. These are the indications of a man contemptuous of death, hyperactive (in the common, not the clinical, usage of the word) and impatient of delay, introspective and yet well enough versed in the character of his race to know that Greeks would tolerate injustice longer than they would insult (something that he forgot, however, in 388). That he was impatient, also, of criticism (especially if he regarded it as ill-informed) is likely enough; and Dion's comment, that he undertook the personal supervision of everything himself, suggests that he was not good at delegation. During the early part of his reign he is recorded as consulting his Privy Council about important matters; but with the defection of Heloris and, later, with the exile of Leptines, Philistus and Polyxenus and the deaths of Thearides and Hipparinus, he was perhaps thrown largely upon his own intellectual resources (although he is said to have consulted Leptines, after his reinstatement, upon a question of military policy). Towards the end of his life he appears to have given Dion a considerable amount of administrative liberty, and no doubt a *synedrion* of some sort continued to function and supplied a measure of continuity to the succeeding reign. As the ruler of an empire Dionysius appears to have been very much more efficient and successful than his enemies gave him credit for being; and at the end of his life, in spite of the serious losses in both men and ships that he had incurred in his last major wars, he ruled an empire that was secured 'by bands of adamant' and which, militarily speaking, was the strongest of the Hellenic Powers.[24]

Between the fall of Rhegium and the outbreak of the second Italiot war, Dionysius enjoyed a brief respite from military activity; but, as he himself admitted, inaction was hateful to him, and it is to this interlude in his wars that Diodorus, no doubt correctly, dates his most intensive literary activity, although he had always (we are told) had a passion for poetry and had already produced the verses which received such a rough reception at Olympia. On the subject of Dionysius' poetry the judgement of antiquity is unanimous: it was altogether bad and laughable. It was said that, in an effort to gain inspiration, he had acquired the note-books of Aeschylus, but without avail (had he, perhaps, saved these relics from the sack of Gela, where Aeschylus had ended his life?). Only a few lines from Dionysius' tragedies have survived and they are quite undistinguished both in form and matter. Certainly Dionysius believed himself to be a poet, for he was a man with a vision, and poetry is the language of the visionary; and because that vision was a grandiose one, it called for writing on a commensurate scale. Tragedy was 'the representation of the noblest life, of weighty matters' (*spoudaiōn*), and the writing of tragedies would enable him to display his *aretē* as a poet and to win the applause (the Homeric reward for 'speaking words') of thousands of persons at a time, for he had, of course, a 'captive' audience at Syracuse. (The statement of Tzetzes, that he had competed several times at Athens without success before his victory in 367, must be rejected, since it is quite inconceivable that he would have been granted a chorus before the date of his belated reconciliation with the Athenians and his admission to Athenian citizenship.)[25]

Dionysius wrote tragedies (and perhaps comedies too) because he believed in his talent, not (as Stroheker suggests) in order to provide literary justification for his regime. But, as Aristotle points out, the writing of poetry demands a composer either with a natural gift or with a touch of madness; and it seems only too clear that Dionysius no more had the divine spark of poesy in him than Sophocles – who served as a general – possessed the gift of generalship. Yet in Dionysius' defence, and in the defence of his very many contemporaries whose works have survived no better than his, it may be said that by the time he had leisure to devote to dramatic composition, the vein of classical tragedy had been pretty well worked out, and what was being written then must have seemed either derivative, hackneyed and boring, or else, as the result of the poet's attempting to avoid these failings, fantastic, stilted and mannered. Aristotle complains that the *dramatis personae* were characterless and talked like rhetoricians. Dionysius' plays, described as dull and sprinkled with unfamiliar words and neologisms, displayed the faults of their age. However, although no doubt a good deal worse than the best of his day, they need not have been as bad as the worst; and they would have had to be very good indeed to have won the approbation either of contemporary dramatic critics, or of those later writers who had been brought up to regard the literary pretensions of the arch-tyrant as anything but wholly ridiculous.[26]

The patronage of poets and men of letters had, from earliest times, been a feature of kingly and dynastic courts, and Dionysius, being himself a poet (if only in his own estimation), had an added reason for wishing to give lustre to his court by playing host to distinguished writers. Diodorus says that 'many men of letters stayed at his court'; but unfortunately, when we come to names, it is often difficult to tell whether a particular individual sojourned at the court of the Older or of the Younger Dionysius. Some, of course, may have spent time at both. I have already given my reason for assuming that Plato did not, in fact, enjoy Dionysius' hospitality, but several poets and sophists are known to have resided on Ortygia. Philoxenus, the dithyrambist, has been mentioned already, as has Antiphon, known only for having been executed (apparently) by Dionysius, and for the saying, so apposite to the dynast's approach to the problems of warfare, that 'we defeat by technique (*technē*) those who surpass us in strength'. The Sicilian writer of mimes, Xenarchus, is known to have been patronized by Dionysius, but we cannot be sure whether the tragic poet Carcinus was a guest of the father or of the son. The sophist Aristippus of Cyrene (a close friend of Socrates), who was criticized in antiquity for his luxurious life-style, was apparently well established at Dionysius' table (he accepted the 'Persian dress' that Plato refused, of course), and it is possible that another former associate of Socrates, Aeschines Socraticus, was a 'parasite' of the father before becoming one of the son. It is clear, therefore, that the dynast's court was not composed wholly of the dregs of society.[27]

As I have suggested above, it may have been due to Dion's aristocratic disinclination to spread scandal about his family connections, that Antiquity had comparatively little to report on the subject of Dionysius' domestic life. It was agreed that he was not rapacious (that is to say, that he respected the laws of property) and that he was not a voluptuary: he displayed *temperentia*, which is the equivalent of *sōphrosynē*, one of the most highly prized social virtues. It was indeed said, and it is inherently most likely, that his brothers and his close associates became extremely wealthy. Hipparinus, for instance, was (according to Aristotle) impoverished at the time of Dionysius' accession to power, yet in 367 his son was apparently in a position to equip 50 galleys out of his private means. No doubt the basis of these fortunes was laid when the sequestrated properties of the Knights were redistributed, and they were augmented by gifts of booty in the best Homeric tradition. Dionysius' conduct towards his wives was wholly in keeping with Greek ideas: it was even said that they took turns in accompanying him on his campaigns. Neither the perfunctory suggestion of homosexuality (he was, after all, a Greek) in one of Cicero's anecdotes, nor the story that he had a mistress named Galatea is good evidence of his depravity.[28]

In a monarchical household in which there were two equal 'queens', both from aristocratic families, one the daughter of a citizen, the other a foreigner, it would hardly be possible for there *not* to have been constant rivalry, and at times considerable strain; yet apart from the 'conspiracy' of Leptines (which was really a public rather than a domestic matter), the only major scandal to emerge was the reputed execution of the dynast's Locrian mother-in-law, a matter which I have touched on already. Doris, his Locrian wife, bore Dionysius two sons, Dionysius and Hermocritus, both of them older than the two sons of Aristomache, Hipparinus and Nysaeus: Hermocritus was of an age to be granted Athenian citizenship, together with his father and his elder brother, in 368. It was said that Dionysius deliberately stunted his eldest son's intellectual growth and kept him out of public life in order to prevent his becoming a threat to his own power; an unlikely enough story, in view both of the perennial shortage of helpers that he suffered and of the fact that he always employed his kinsmen in positions of authority even after they had, like Leptines, proved to be unreliable. If it is true that the young Dionysius was not actively employed by his father in affairs of State (although his inclusion in the Athenian honorific decree suggests that he may have been) the most probable reason, as I have noted in Chapter 9, is that he was physically as well as temperamentally unsuited for military service; and indeed after he acceded to power he does appear to have left to others any fighting that had to be done. We must also consider the possibility that he disapproved of his father's foreign policy and made no secret of the fact. We know that he disowned his paternity (in favour of an Apolline origin) and largely abandoned Dionysius' militarism.[29]

Hermocritus makes no mark on the page of history other than that supplied by the Athenian Demos, and we may reasonably conjecture that he died in the early years of his brother's reign. Justin followed a tradition that saw the new reign begin with a blood-bath, in which first the Younger Dionysius' uncles and then his brothers were put to death, but there is no hint of anything of the sort in Diodorus, Plutarch or Plato, and we know that Hipparinus was alive in 352 and Nysaeus in 346. Whether or not the fact that the Elder Dionysius associated his two eldest sons with himself in communications to foreign Powers should be taken to indicate that they actually enjoyed some share in the governance of the empire – perhaps as members of his *Synedrion* – we cannot say; but his doing so would have had the effect of accustoming Syracusans and foreigners alike to the dynastic character of the monarchy and so facilitating the succession of the Younger Dionysius, who, by marrying his half-sister, had united the two inner branches of the family. No doubt Dionysius, student of history that he was, hoped that his younger sons would co-operate loyally with the eldest, as the Peisistratids had done, and so strengthen the monarchy. However, we hear no mention of any of the sons except Dionysius, until after the overthrow of the regime. [30]

Dionysius the Elder made use of the marriage of his daughters (as he did of his own and his sister's) for dynastic purposes: behaving in the public sphere as any well-to-do Greek father or brother would have behaved in the private. He gave Theste, his sister, in marriage to the well-born Polyxenus, the maternal uncle of his first wife, thus connecting himself by a double link with the old aristocracy of Syracuse. So respected was Theste by the citizens as well as by her brother that she retained their affection and regard not only after the treason and flight abroad of her husband but even after the dissolution of the tyranny. Of Aristomache's two daughters, Arete (probably the elder) was married first to Thearides and, after his death, to Dion; and Sophrosyne was joined with her half-brother, the younger Dionysius. Doris' daughter, Dicaeosyne, married Leptines after his return from exile. [31] Dionysius' policy of intra-familial marriage (which does not appear to have offended Greek susceptibilities, accustomed as they were to the marriage of near relations in order to keep property in the family) was forced upon him by the dearth of trustworthy Syracusan adherents of good enough family to make them suitable to be members of a monarchical house, as well as by a disinclination to elevate outsiders to a position where they might become contenders with the family for the 'throne'. It might be interesting to speculate whether Dionysius' marital policy, studied in the pages of Philistus, played any part in influencing that of Ptolemy Philadelphus and his sister and their successors.

It remains to try to arrive at some estimate of Dionysius as a soldier, the calling that dominated his life, and to do so under two headings, first, that of intelligence and skill, and second, that of leadership. At once let it be said that he is surely one of the most underrated generals in history. At the very outset of his career, when (as far as we know) he had never before held an independent command, he brought to the military problems posed by the situation before Gela a wholly fresh and sophisticated approach; and even if it cannot be claimed, in all fairness, that his plan of battle deserved to succeed, yet it certainly represented the first radical – the first intellectual – handling of a tactical problem for some two and a half centuries. It was he who saw the military value of the Punic siege-towers and introduced them into Greek warfare, he who pioneered the use of artillery and quinqueremes and employed the former, at least, to good effect. He gave his irresponsible brother Leptines the *correct orders* for the battle of Catane, and had Leptines carried them out the story of the second Punic War would have been different (although, of course, not necessarily more successful in its outcome). The planning of the operations that resulted in the defeat and expulsion from Sicily of Himilco and in the dissolution of his army was of the highest order, and (in spite of the misconstruction put upon his motives by Antiquity) we should admire the good sense which Dionysius displayed in permitting Himilco to save himself, a policy which put Himilco's barbarian mercenaries at his mercy. His generalship in the campaign against Mago and his conduct of the Eleporus campaign merit the highest praise and the same may be said of the planning and handling of the expedition against Pyrgi. Far more than Demetrius, the son of Antigonus, he deserves the sobriquet 'Poliorkētes' (the Besieger), for it was he who introduced the Greeks to 'modern' siege technique – technique that was copied by Alexander the Great's engineers. Before Dionysius' day, starvation and treason were regarded as the most effective means of overcoming a city's resistance – not that he disdained to use these methods when assault proved ineffectual. All in all, his record of successfully prosecuted sieges must be one of the most impressive in ancient history.

The loss of that section of Diodorus' Histories that dealt with the second Italiot and the third Punic wars, in which Dionysius won his greatest and most spectacular victory and also suffered his worst defeat, is particularly grievous, for it places the historian rather in the position of one who has to evaluate the generalship of (say) Hannibal without knowing any of the details of Cannae and Zama. All that we can say is that the battle of Cabala was clearly an outstanding achievement (although it seems equally clear that Dionysius' judgement failed him disastrously in the days immediately following), and that, whatever happened at Cronium, the language of the epitome suggests that the battle was not lost through any failure of Dionysius' generalship.

One of the (many) areas in which we are lamentably ignorant is that of the composition and equipment of Dionysius' field armies. That he appreciated the value of light infantry and made considerable use of it is well attested. His guards, whom at the outset of his career he equipped with costly gear and presumably organized in sub-units and trained, thus partly anticipating the achievement of Iphicrates, were clearly light infantryment (as is proved by their mobility). It was with them (and some horsemen) that he overthrew the Knights; it was presumably light infantrymen that he led up the precipitous slope of Tauromenium; it was with the assistance of Celtic light troops that he defeated the Crotoniates; and it was Celts that he sent to the aid of the Lacedaemonians. The

Iberians whom he took into his service were light troops and many of his Greek mercenaries were probably trained as peltasts. Peltasts, Greek (as distinct from 'native') light infantry, were developed as a regular, disciplined arm by Iphicrates during the Corinthian War and were employed alongside (and, in peculiarly favourable circumstances, even against) the phalanx: skirmishers had previously been provided either by hireling tribesmen or by the poor-citizen element, the latter being of little military value except, perhaps, against a defeated enemy. Peltasts are specifically mentioned by the author of Plato's Seventh Letter as forming part of the garrison of Ortygia – probably the Guard – in the Younger Dionysius' reign. However, although Dionysius, having first-rate 'native' and probably also Greek light-infantry material at his disposal, made intelligent use of it, it was the heavy infantryman, the hoplite, who remained the backbone of his army; for the effectiveness of the phalanx against Carthage's light troops – the Libyans and Iberians – was well established and light troops would have been ineffective against the Carthaginian citizen troops and the Campanians, who had no doubt adopted the phalanx formation. Indeed, the phalanx continued to dominate the set-piece battle until the Romans appeared on the Greek military scene. Dionysius did not possess the cavalry resources available to the kings of Macedon or to Hannibal and Scipio, and there is nothing to suggest that he made any novel use of this arm.[32]

It is not uncommon for men possessed of a talent for planning and organization as impressive as that of Dionysius to be found wanting when a sudden crisis – the occurrence of the unexpected – calls for improvisation: Dionysius' ability in this direction may fairly be said to have amounted to genius. Yet he seldom displayed rashness: he was not a gambler. Gela, his first battle, was a planner's battle – only that the plan contained fatal flaws. But the overthrow of Himilco's forces in front of Syracuse was excellently planned and the Eleporus battle was planned, in that Dionysius had taken care to acquire intelligence of his enemy's movements and dispositions. His successful sieges were thoroughly planned. When he was not in the field his restless energy found an escape in planning. The great war machine that he directed, comprising an impregnable citadel and arsenal within an impregnable circuit of city walls, ship-houses, barracks, 300 ships with reserves of stores, artillery, thousands of stands of arms, a permanent force of mercenary soldiers and the organization and resources to expand it into the most formidable land army that a Greek could muster – all this was entirely Dionysius' creation, built up from his first reorganization of the Syracusan army when he became General Plenipotentiary. He planned and organized the partial reshaping of Syracusan society during the winter of 405/4, when he established his 'inner kingdom' on Ortygia. He planned and supervised the walling of Epipolae and the massive re-arming of Syracuse for the Carthaginian war in a manner characteristically spectacular and even extravagant, which won the admiration of posterity. The expansion of his power into Italy and the Adriatic was part of a comprehensive plan to safeguard the northern flank of his future operations against the Epicraty and to provide the financial and material resources for sustained campaigning. We can only guess at the influence that his indefatigable pursuit of efficiency must have had upon the lives of the Syracusans; in his own household it extended at least to his sleeping arrangements with his wives.

Of course Dionysius did not plan and organize in splendid isolation. Philistus' purpose, where it shows through Diodorus, was to exalt and magnify the dynast; but he makes it clear that Dionysius, at all events in the earlier part of his reign, had the assistance of a group of able and devoted friends (of which Philistus himself was one), his *synedrion*. But whatever part their advice and collaboration may have played in the creation and direction of the State, it is clear that the mainspring of the whole enterprise was Dionysius himself.[33]

Since the love of military glory was the inspiration of his life and since, in the small, very personal world of classical antiquity, it was to the leader in any great enterprise that the greatest glory accrued, it was as a leader of men that Dionysius would have wished to be immortalized by History. I have quoted above the passages in which Philistus (through Diodorus) has given us a picture of Dionysius as the leader of his people, and the account of the overthrow of Himilco's forces in front of Syracuse gives us a glimpse of him as a leader in battle. He also led the perilous (and almost fatal) night assault on Tauromenium. Indeed, there can be no doubt that as a leader he was quite outstanding and, taught by the fiasco of Gela, he seems thenceforth always to have led from the front, as a commander of pikemen must if he is to be successful. Beyond question he was one of the greatest leaders of *mercenary* armies, in this category inferior perhaps only to Hannibal – and Hannibal enjoyed important advantages denied to Dionysius: a formidable army created by his father and his brother-in-law, and the warlike tribes of Numidia and Iberia to draw upon for his soldiery. Had Dionysius had that kind of material, or the splendid tribal and citizen fighting material available to the kings of Macedon and to the greatest Roman proconsuls, he would, I believe, have left behind a reputation to rank with theirs. As a war-lord and as a soldier I would account him the superior of Pyrrhus.

Antiquity noted with distaste the apparent contradiction between Dionysius' unflagging aggressiveness on the one hand and, on the other, his readiness to retreat before an enemy, to make peace without risking the decisive battle that the strategy of ancient city warfare hinged upon, and even to grant terms to an enemy who appeared to be at his mercy. Naturally it put the worst interpretation upon his conduct, attributing it to an unwillingness to free Syracuse finally from danger and so deprive his regime of its only justification for continuing to exist. The true reason, however, although equally egoistical, is to be found in the nature of his ruling passion, the pursuit of fame. Dionysius' whole life was inspired by a vision of destined greatness – of glory – and this, of course, implied that he was one who would not flinch in the face of danger. And so, where a careful consideration of the pros and cons of accepting battle showed that victory was achievable, he would expose himself to mortal peril in order to achieve it. But the introvert whose conception of glory was Homeric, not Tyrtaean, could not be satisfied with the prospect of a glorious death as the reward of his valour (unless as a counsel of despair), for nothing could compensate such a man for the loss of his life: a world from which he would have passed away could have no interest for him. Such a man would not lead a forlorn hope, would not be found dead in a last ditch. And so Dionysius was always ready to accept defeat, to accept the necessity of retreat when confronted by forces which his military sense told him he could not fight with a good prospect of success.

However much he believed in his *tychē* he was not at heart a gambler, as Hannibal, as Caesar, was. He was always acutely aware (he could hardly have been otherwise) that all his policies and strategies were governed, ultimately, by the supply (or at least, by the prospect) of silver. Dependent as he was upon mercenary forces both for the security of his regime and for the successful prosecution of his grand design, he could neither allow himself to be isolated with his army in western Sicily nor cooped up indefinitely in the south-east corner of the island, cut off in either case from his major source of revenue, the tribute of the Sicels. Unpaid mercenaries (as he knew to his cost) were notoriously unreliable, and Dionysius could not afford to 'sit out' a long war. If, therefore, victory – or at least a profitable interim success – did not come quickly, he was likely to be obliged to make peace (or a truce) in order to give himself time of recuperate his finances. Since his spirit was always buoyed up by the conviction of the ultimate triumph of his arms, he could find the moral courage to yield to necessity, to conquer the false pride that cannot accept a set-back or loss of 'face', and, putting his discomfiture behind him, to begin the rebuilding of his resources for another attempt.[34]

Ours is an age that has suffered more, perhaps, from the evils of imperialism and military dictatorship than any preceding age; and therefore, when we attempt to assess the merit and the proper place in History of one who was (in modern terms) a military dictator and a tireless imperialist, it is all the more important that we avoid 'the moral anachronism of judging a man of one age by the standards of another'. How we regard Dionysius must to a large extent depend upon our attitude to war (for Dionysius was, above all, a man of war) and military glory. The perverse ingenuity of modern science has made war so mutually destructive that there is a tendency today among the more advanced peoples to reject the idea that it may *ever* be indulged in, even in the last resort (unless, perhaps, on a very small and rigorously localized scale). Again, the experience and recollections of two World Wars, coupled with the vast scale and consequent anonymity of war today, as well as the technological advances which, in reducing the possibility of human error, reduce at the same time the elements of humanity and human virtue, have combined to produce a rather cynical attitude towards glory. The notion, therefore, of a national leader's waging mighty wars for the enlargement of his personal glory will appear wholly repugnant to the present age. But the Greeks of the Classical age, although agreeing that war was an evil – 'sweet only to him that hath not experienced it' – none the less looked upon it in general as a practical means of achieving a logical end; and since both politics and war were very intimate and personal matters and since the individuals who composed the body politic of a city had been taught from childhood that their personal honour was identical with the honour of their city, they could easily be persuaded that the preservation of national honour and the winning of national glory constituted such an end. War, therefore, regarded as a 'basic human trade' – something to be avoided as much as possible, but in the long run probably inescapable – could break out for reasons that were not entirely connected with the gaining of some material advantage. And so the Greeks, as well as fighting over disputed borders or to gain control of cultivable land or harbours, sometimes fought – or at least believed that they fought (which comes to much the same thing) – for national honour; and indeed national honour was an important, and probably the most loudly proclaimed, ingredient in the explosive mixture of motives that produced the disastrous Peloponnesian War.[35]

It was not primarily as a warmonger that antiquity criticized Dionysius, for the rightness of his struggle against Carthage was recognized by Greeks and Romans alike. The Punic invasion of 410 revived memories of that of 480 and reawakened long dormant fears, which were sharpened by the second invasion, that of 406. By sacking Selinus, Himera, Acragas, Gela and Camarina, the Carthaginians established themselves in the minds of the Greeks as the inveterate enemies of Hellenism: that is, of civilization. It was recognized that Dionysius had preserved Sicily from subjugation by Carthage, and as long as Selinus alone remained under her heel, his wars were seen as wars of liberation.[36] It was not for his warlike policy towards Carthage that Plato condemned him, but for his despotism towards the Greek cities and for the nature of his empire, whose cohesive principal was force, not justice and friendship, with the result that he could never bring his wars to a satisfactory conclusion. His destruction of the Chalcidic cities was, of course, another matter, especially in the eyes of the Athenians, although in this he was doing no more than carrying out the policy initiated by Gelon and pursued by republican Syracuse; nor was it to be expected that the sound military reasons for his conquest of southern Italy would be appreciated by his critics. Dionysius of Halicarnassus says that the tyranny of Dionysius was 'the last and greatest disaster' that befell the cities of Italy, which had to choose between the two evils of enslavement by Dionysius or by the barbarians. Schooled to regard Dionysius only as the model of The Tyrant, antiquity saw his love of war merely as an expression of his love of despotic power. He fought the Chalcidians and the Sicels and the Italiots and he deliberately prolonged the war with Carthage in order to justify his position of war-leader and to keep his subjects occupied, to impoverish them and to cream off their best (and therefore most dangerous) elements. Had he been an elected *prostatēs* of the people (like Pericles), or a legitimate king – even a barbarian (or worse than barbarian) king – the ancients might have been prepared to admit that what motivated him was the love of glory. Demosthenes, no mealy-mouthed critic of the ruler of Macedon, could none the less concede that Philip's sole aim was glory (*doxē*), that his subjugation of great cities was something glorious, wonderful, enviable, and that his desire to rule Hellas was the product of his *megalopsychia.* For Philip was a *king,* whereas Dionysius was a tyrant only, and therefore only an insensate greed for *power* could be attributed to him.[37]

Although Dionysius' empire might appear superficially to anticipate the Great Kingdoms of the Hellenistic age, it belonged essentially to the past. He was the political heir (if one may use the term 'political' of a potentate whose regime implied the rejection of almost everything that the *polis* stood for) of Gelon, Hippocrates and Phalaris: his empire was not the forerunner of the kingdoms of Ptolemy, Seleucus and Eumenes. Yet in one sense he may be seen as the precursor of those who laid the foundations of the Hellenistic age; for it is surely not merely fanciful to suppose that restless and ambitious princes, living (like Dionysius himself) on the fringes of the restrictive world of the *polis* – men particularly susceptible because of their royal (or semi-royal) status and heroic ancestry to the appeal of the Homeric ideal of *aretē* – perceived the Homeric, the romantic, quality of Dionysius' vision and were inspired to emulation. His career is known to have provided an inspiration to more than one minor potentate and to have been of interest, at least, to those two kings of Macedon, father and son, who in the second half of the century bestrode, the one Greece, the other the known world, like Colossi.[38]

For Dionysius had reintroduced into Greece, after an interval of two generations, the idea of a personal empire as the prize of victory, as the reward of *aretē*. In the 370s, a Thessalian nobleman, Jason, the lord of Pherae, appeared upon the Greek international stage and for a brief but hectic space of time bade fair to dominate it. The picture which Xenophon gives us of him has many points of similarity with what we know about Dionysius. He describes Jason's tireless activity, his self-control and sobriety, his appreciation of the value of the mercenary soldier in wars of conquest, his qualities as a leader of men and as a 'soldiers' general', his astuteness (not devoid of a certain nobility) as a statesman and negotiator, his appreciation of the importance of the economic factor as the basis of power and, most strikingly, the grandeur of his design. This was nothing less than to make himself the greatest man in Greece by first of all securing Thessaly (becoming, by election, its *tagos* or military leader) and then Macedon, with its immense resources and potentialities, by building up an irresistible alliance of cities and peoples, by wresting from Athens the command of the sea and from Sparta the hegemony of Greece by land, and (if he so decided) by crowning his career by the overthrow of the Great King himself. The picture is that of a man avid for fame rather than for power for its own sake. Xenophon, who had no interest in the affairs of the Western Greeks, describes him as the greatest man of his time, and Diodorus, commenting on his ambition to become the *hegemon* of the Greeks (so anticipating Philip of Macedon) describes the hegemony as 'the prize of valour' (*epathlon aretēs*). May we not suppose that Jason saw in Dionysius (then, in the late '70s, at the height of his power) at once a model and a challenge?[39]

It is said that the example of Jason inspired his neighbour, Philip, to emulation, and that his method – the creation of a powerful alliance around the nucleus of a first-rate national army stiffened by devoted professionals – showed him the way, and this can hardly be otherwise than true. Yet Jason's grand design was still-born, and it was Dionysius, not Jason, who was in fact the greatest man in Greece in the 70s, as Isocrates perceived. Philip had studied Dionysius' career for himself: by the time he came to the throne, the works of Philistus were available. He is said, when he visited Corinth, to have asked Dionysius' son, when did his father find the leisure (*scholazein*) to write poetry: a question that seems to echo the old dynast's prayer, that he might never be without employment.[40]

When Alexander, from Upper Asia, asked Harpalus to send him some books (Homer of course he always had with him), his boyhood friend, who must have been familiar with his taste (and may of course have received a specific list), sent him, in addition to the Attic classics, the histories of Philistus. Ehrenberg has described for us the impetuous desire, the longing for the unattained (*pothos*) that gave direction to the 'obscure faith and conscious will-power' that would have carried Alexander to the end of the earth – if his followers' *pothos* for their homes and families had not frustrated him. Yet what was it that filled Dionysius' heart if not 'an impetuous desire, a longing for the unattained'? In Dionysius' case the object of his desire remained defined and limited by his repeated failure to achieve it, whereas Alexander's 'longing' was set free of all limitation by the overthrow of Darius, whose kingdom was bounded by the unknown and, to Greeks, by the infinite. May not the young Alexander, steeped as he was in Homer and caring only for valour and fame, have recognized in Dionysius' pursuit of fame something akin to his own longing, and seen in his achievements (as he did in those of his own father) something to be emulated and surpassed?[41]

It was not, then, to the satraps-become-kings, rulers of huge, heterogeneous barbarian (or part barbarian) kingdoms which required to be pacified, organized, administered, defended and ruled, that Dionysius could serve as a model and an inspiration, but rather to the seeker after fame, the nympholept, to whom his career demonstrated how an individual – even a relatively obscure individual – could, if he possessed the highest *aretē* and gave free rein to it, create an empire out of nothing and win the highest renown in Greece. Certainly he provided an example to Agathocles (whom Scipio coupled with him, as outstanding examples of the intelligent man of action), the last of the great 'classical' tyrants; for Hieron II, although he came to power in much the same way as Dionysius, developed, under Rome's protection, into a king in the Hellenistic tradition. Dionysius' reputation stood higher, we may be sure, among soldiers and statesmen in the fourth century than it did among philosophers; and I think it probable that, in time, the Syracusans became proud of their *Hegemon*, in the reflection of whose greatness they could themselves bask, and felt a genuine loyalty towards him. For he had made their city impregnable and he had shown that Carthage could be defeated: as long as he lived, the people of Syracuse at least must have felt secure. To the objection that after 405 the Punic menace was of his own contriving and that Carthage, left to herself, would not have threatened Greek freedom, it may be replied that the Peace of Himilco left the Greek cities defenceless and tributary 'allies' of Carthage; that in the course of time Carthaginian influences would have permeated their societies (as they seem to have done in the case of Selinus, and, in the third century, in that of Acragas); that, if the spirit of the cities had revived, they would inevitably have resumed their age-old quarrels among themselves, into which Carthage would almost certainly have been drawn; and finally, that after the collapse of Dionysius' empire, Carthage renewed her attempt to conquer all Sicily.[42]

Yet for all his undoubted greatness, Dionysius' career and his generation-long feud with Carthage belonged in the dwindling world of Western Hellenism, out of the mainstream of Greek history, whose orientation, since the close of the archaic period, had been mainly towards the East. With his death, and with the rise, only six years later, of Philip of Macedon, the affairs of the Western Greeks ceased to be of very much interest to the people of the Motherland, apart from a few Corinthians and some persons at Athens. The failure of the Younger Dionysius to hold on to his power and the dramatic success of Timoleon in achieving (albeit without benefit of Platonism) the Platonic ideal of a Sicily united against the barbarian by bonds of friendship rather than of adamant, served to dim the memory of Dionsius' military achievements and of the fact that he had halted, for half a century, the tide of 'barbarism', Semitic and Italic, which had threatened to swamp Western Hellenism, and that, at the end of his reign, Carthage had been penned in the western corner of the island. His fame was finally obscured by the deeds of Philip and his extraordinary son. Alexander captured the imagination of the civilized peoples of the Mediterranean and later of western Europe – 'so doth the greater glory dim the less' – and the malice of the Academy completed Dionysius' obscuration. The Archon of Sicily, the bulwark of Hellenism in the West, the greatest man in Greece, the honorary citizen of Athens, crowned by her with golden crowns for his services to peace, was largely forgotten, and only the despot, the paranoiac and the poetaster was remembered and handed down to posterity.[43]

An introvert and wholly egoistic, an unfaltering believer in his own genius and (apart from a few moments at the height of the crisis of 404/3) in his destiny by right of the omens attending his birth, Dionysius directed all his restless energy and ambition into the pursuit of the unsubstantial: of unrivalled fame, the prize of victory, the recognition by the world of peerless *aretē*. Yet for all that, it is probable that in the winter 406/5 he needed the encouragement and stimulation of his friends to bring him (like Macbeth) to the sticking-point: that he required their assurances that he, uniquely, was the man to rescue Syracuse from democratic fumbling and save Sicily from enslavement by Carthage. Yet once in power he would permit no obstacle to stand in the path of the achievement of his purpose, would shrink from no sacrifice of self or friends or servants or subjects to attain it. He would regard his friends, Syracuse and Sicily as being merely accessory to his own purpose, and their interests and rights as things to be respected and championed only so long as they did not appear to conflict with those of his grand design. Seeing great issues in black and white terms, himself, he would be intolerant of those who did not; and in the case of those friends who had helped him to power, not in order to realize his Homeric dream of personal glory but for the preservation of Syracuse, whose welfare the best of them (men like Philistus) placed above private interest, he would be insensitive to their intellectual and emotional reactions to what they regarded (I believe) as his change of purpose, in the '90s, and unable to see in their mounting opposition to his militarism anything other than disloyalty. In much the same way he mistook the obedience of the Syracusans to his orders as general, in the summer of 404, for a passive acceptance of his assumption of monarchical power.

Yet he was loyal to those who did not fail in their loyalty to him, generous to his servants, jovial with his courtiers, his soldiers and the citizens of Syracuse. He possessed in the highest degree courage, determination and the gift of leadership, exposing himself to the same dangers and sharing the same hardships as his followers, and as a general he must be accounted the inferior of only very few of the famous soldiers of antiquity. He was a master of organization and diplomacy. Moderate and self-restrained in his private life, he loved learning and poetry, and I find it pleasant to reflect that, as a result of his victory at the Lenaea, he died confirmed in the belief that he possessed the lyric and dramatic gifts that nature would in fact appear to have denied him.

Nevertheless, it is difficult to avoid the conclusion that this truly extraordinary and multifariously talented man, who raised himself from obscurity to the position of the most powerful individual in Greece, was one of those of whom, at the end, it is said, He never grew up. Dionysius never settled into 'a green and smiling age'. Had death not taken him in the spring of 367, he would have been on horseback and at the head of his army in the Epicraty by midsummer, for his destiny was still unachieved and the goal towards which he had striven all his life lay before him still. Desire, in *his* old age, remained intact indeed, but hope was far from extinct. His victory at the Lenaea must have seemed to him an omen of the supreme victory, with its reward of glory, that still eluded him. Repose, now, and the memory of past triumphs – old age's consolation – could not have satisfied him. Emotionally he remained to the very end the same ardent and sanguine youth who, more than forty years before, had so nearly thrown away his life in a quixotic attempt to make his boyhood's hero the master of Syracuse and, perhaps, the Lord of Sicily.

NOTES

Principal works consulted in the preparation of this book:

Andrewes, A., *The Greek Tyrants* (London, 1956)

Bengtson, H., *Griechische Geschichte* (Munich, 1950)

Berve, H., *Die Tyrannis bei den Griechen*, 2 vols. (Munich, 1967)

The Cambridge Ancient History (*CAH*), esp. vol. VI (Cambridge, 1953)

Caven, B., *The Punic Wars* (London, 1980)

Dunbabin, T. J., *The Western Greeks* (Oxford, 1948)

Finley, M. I., *Ancient Sicily*, rev. edn. (London, 1979)

Gabba, A., and Vallet, G., eds., *La Sicilia Antica*, 5 vols. (Naples, 1980)

Harden, D. B., *The Phoenicians* (London, 1962)

Jacoby, F., *Die Fragmente der Griechischen Historiker*, 3 vols. (Leiden, 1950)

Maurin, L., 'Himilcon le Magonide', *Semitica* (Paris) XII (1962)

Mossé, C., *La Tyrannie dans la Grèce antique* (Paris, 1969)

The Oxford Classical Dictionary (*OCD*), 2nd edn. (Oxford, 1970)

Pauly/Wissowa/Kroll, *Realencyclopädie* (*RE*), 68 vols. (repr. Munich, 1958–80)

Stroheker, K. F., *Dionysios I* (Wiesbaden, 1958)

Tod, M. N., *A Selection of Greek Historical Inscriptions*, 2 vols. (Oxford, 1944–48)

Warmington, B. H., *Carthage* (Harmondsworth, 1964)

Woodhead, A. G., *The Greeks in the West* (London, 1962)

The above works are cited in the notes by author's surname only (e.g., Stroheker), or by the abbreviation indicated; all other sources are cited in full at their first occurrence.

Texts: For convenience of reference (especially for the general reader), all classical sources are cited in the Loeb Library editions, where these are available. In the cases of Polyaenus and Justin, the editions used are the Teubner (1970) and that of Ruehl (1886), respectively.

B. C.

INTRODUCTION

1 Photius, cod. 131.
2 Jacoby III B. 551–68. On Philistus: Nepos *Dion*, 3. 1; Cic. *Ad Q F* 2. 11. 4, *De Or*. 2. 57, *Brut*. 66, *De Div*. 1. 39. Theopompus also devoted three books to the reigns of the Dionysii: Diod. 16. 71. 3.
3 *OCD* (A. H. McDonald).
4 For a very full discussion of Diodorus' sources, see Stroheker, ch. 1.
5 Jacoby III B. 581–91.
6 On Timaeus' reputation: Suidas, s.v. Timaios; Diod. 5. 1. 3, 13. 90. 6 f., 21. 17. 1 ff.; Athen. 6. 103, 272 b; Polyb. 12 *passim*.
7 Polyb. 12. 15, 23 ff.
8 Diod. 14. 65–69; Polyb. 12. 25a, b. Diod. 20. 1–2
9 Diod. 12. 54. 7; Polyb. 12. 25k. 2; Thuc. 4. 58; Diod. 13. 33. 1; Thuc. 7. 86. 2; Plut. *Nic*. 28. 5. Diod. 15. 7. 1, 4, 15. 74. 1–4; Plut. *Dion*, 6. 3.
10 On the other hand, we are told that Ephorus was sympathetic towards Philistus himself: Plut. *Dion*, 36. 2. Diodorus' purpose: Diod. 1. 1–4. 5.
11 Polyb. 12. 25–28 *passim*.
12 Polyb. 12. 15, 23. Diodorus goes so far as to reject Timaeus' account of Agathocles' career, because of its prejudice against the despot: Diod. 21. 17. 3.
13 Diod. 5. 1. 3. *RE* V. A. 2. 1847, no. 39 (Stegemann).

254

14 Polyb. 12. 15. 9. See also n. 12 above.

15 The Constitution of the Syracusans: Athen. 10. 435e; Suidas, s.v. Kallikurioi.

CHAPTER 1

1 The eclipse: *RE* VI. 2. 2355 (Boll). For the final stages of the Athenian expedition: Thuc. 7. 50. 3–87. 6; Diod. 13. 12. 6–19. 4; Plut. *Nic.* 23 ff.

2 Thuc. 6. 35 ff., 103, 7. 2. 2, for Syracusan disunity.

3 Thuc. 4. 65. 3 f.

4 Thuc. 6. 53, 60, 61. The debates on strategy: Thuc, 6. 47–50. 1, 7. 47–49, Plut. *Nic.* 15. 3.

5 Gelon: Hdt. 7. 155–6; Diod. 10. 29–11. 38. 7; Berve I. 140–6.

6 Diod. 11. 68, 72. Ar. *Pol.* 1304a 6.

7 Thuc. 6. 49. 3; Diod. 13. 56.2; also Plut. *Dion* 27. 1.

8 Diod. 14. 18. 4. There were 5,000 Athenian hoplites (Thuc. 6. 43. 1), and the Syracusans faced them with a phalanx 'twice as deep': Thuc. 6. 67. 1–2.

9 Some historians, e.g., Berve I. 226. Polyaen. 1. 43. 1. The terms *penestai* (lit. toilers, and therefore, very poor) and *penesteia* (Ar. *Pol.* 1264a. 35, 1269a. 37) were used of the serfs of Thessaly.

10 A pointer to the number of the tribes may be given by the number of the generals: 15 (3 × 5) under the *politeia*, 3 (3 × 1) in an emergency, 20 (5 × 4) and 25 (5 × 5), in the 'reformed' constitution: Thuc. 6. 72. 4, 73. 1; Plut. *Dion* 29. 1, 28. 2. For the Boeotian 'council': I. A. F. Bruce, *An Historical Commentary on the 'Hellenica Oxyrhynchia'* (London, 1967), App. 2.

11 Thuc. 6. 38. 5.

12 For Diocles: see below, ch. 3.

13 Diod. 11. 72–76, Ar. *Pol.* 1303a 11.

14 Diod. 11. 86. 4, 87. 1–4. Presumably Heraclea. Minoa capitulated.

15 Ar. *Ath. Pol.* 22. 3–6, 25. 1–4; Plut. *Cim.* 15–17. Diod. 11. 87. 6. For Corax: Cic. *Brut.* 46.

16 Diod. 11. 88. 6–92. 4, 12. 8, 29. 1. R. Meiggs and D. M. Lewis, *Greek Historical Inscriptions* (Oxford, 1969), nos. 63, 64. There is little agreement among scholars about the date of these early treaties.

17 Diod. 12. 30.

18 Thuc. 1. 24–45. Treaties; see n. 16 above. Thuc. 2. 62. 2, 1. 44. 3. Thuc. 3. 86. 2.

19 Thuc. 1. 88, 139. 3. The antagonism of Dorians and Ionians: e.g. Thuc. 1. 124. 1, 5. 91, 8. 25. 5; in Sicily: Thuc. 3. 86. 2,

6. 77. 1, 6. 82. 2, 7. 5. 4, 7. 57.

20 K. J. Beloch, *Gr. Gesch.*, III² 2. 102; Tod II. 133. 21. Isoc. *Ep. Phil.* 65. Cic. *Tusc.* 5. 20. 58. Stroheker, p. 37.

21 Cic. *De Div.* 1. 39; Stroheker, p. 38; *vaticinium ex eventu*: Ael. *VH* 12. 46. Cic. loc. cit.

22 Thuc. 3. 86. 4; Diod. 12. 53. 1–2.

23 Diod. 12. 54; Thuc. 3. 86, 88, 90, 4. 1, 2, 48. 6, 58–65; Diod. 12. 54. 7; Polyb. 12. 25k. 2.

24 Hermocrates: Thuc. 6. 36–40 (speech of Athenagoras), 6. 72. 2, 99. 2, 7. 21.3–5, 7. 73; Diod. 13. 11. 4, 18. 3–4, 19. 5; Xen. *Hell.* 1. 1. 30 f., Plut. *Nic.* 28. 2, 4.

25 Thuc. 4. 59–64, esp. 59. 2–4, 60. 1, 61. 1–3, 64. 4–5. Thuc. 6. 34. 2.

26 Thuc. 5. 4. 2–4, 5–6.

27 Thuc. 6. 6. 2–6. 26. 2; Diod. 12. 82. 3–84. Thuc. 5. 115. 2, 6. 93. 1.

28 Thuc. 6. 32–35.

29 Thuc. 6. 41, 45. Diod. 13. 4. 1; Thuc. 6. 72–73, 96. 3, 75–80.

30 Thuc. 6. 99. 2. Polyaen. 1. 43. 1. Thuc. 6. 103. 3–4; Diod. 13. 7. 4. Thuc. 7.2; Diod. 13. 7. 6. Plut. *Nic.* 19. 4, 5.

31 Thuc. 7. 21. 3 f., 7. 73, Diod. 13. 18. 3–4. Diod. 13. 19. 5; Thuc. 7. 86.2; Plut. *Nic.* 26. 1–2, 28.

32 Thuc. 8. 26. 1, Diod. 13. 34. 4. Athenian refugees at Catane: Thuc. 7. 85. 4, Lys. 20. 24. The barbarian mercenaries: Diod. 13. 44. 2.

33 Thuc. 8. 9–10, 26. 1, 17. 4–18. Diod. (13. 34. 4) says that the Syracusans sent 35 ships, but this is clearly a mistake: see ch. 3.

34 Diocles: Diod. 13. 19. 4, 13. 35; Ar. *Pol.* 1274a. See Beloch II. 1. 403 (n. 4).

35 Diod. 13. 34. 6; Ar. *Pol.* 1304a 27.

36 For these hostilities: Diod. 13. 56. 2. The Syracusans in the Aegean: Thuc. 8. 84. 2, 4. Hermocrates and Tissaphernes: Thuc. 8. 85. 2–3. The sea battle: Thuc. 8. 104–6; Diod. 13. 39. 3–40. 4. For the oligarchic revolution at Athens: C. Hignett, *A History of the Athenian Constitution* (Oxford, 1952), pp. 268–80, App. 12.

CHAPTER 2

1 Diod. 13. 43. 1–4. It must be remembered that, whatever their origin (they claimed to have fled from Troy), the Elymi were not Greeks: Thuc. 6. 2. 3; Cic. *Verr.* 2. 4. 72.

2 Athens' relations with Carthage: Thuc. 6. 88. 6. The mercenaries: Diod. 13. 44. 2.

3 Justin 19. 1. 1–8, 2. 1–6. Maurin. Diod. 13. 43. 5.

4 Diod. 13. 43. 4–6 (Hdt. 7. 167; Diod.

13. 59. 5).

5 Hannibal's diplomacy: Diod. 13. 43. 6–7.

6 Diod. 13. 44. 3–4, 5–6.

7 Acragas' ñeutrality: Thuc. 7. 33. 2, 58. 1; and *stasis*; Thuc. 7. 46, 50. 1. Diod. 13. 81. 4.

8 Diod. 13. 49. 3–51; Xen. *Hell.* 1. 1. 14–18. Hermocrates: Xen. *Hell.* 1. 1. 27–31; Diod. 13. 63. 1; Thuc. 8. 85. 3.

9 Xen. *Hell.* 1. 1. 31, 1. 3. 13.

10 Diod. 13. 44. 5–6, 54. 1–5.

11 Diod. 16. 67. 2; Plut. *Tim.* 17. 2; Diod. 16. 77. 4; Plut. *Tim.* 25; Diod. 23. 8. 1. For Selinus' walls: Diod. 13. 55. 7.

12 Diod. 13. 54. 3–6.

13 Diod. 13. 59. 3, 54. 3.

14 Diod. 13. 54. 6–7, 55. 5–8, 56. 1–2. Harden, p. 129.

15 Xen. *Hell.* 1. 2. 8; Diod. 13. 64. 5.

16 Diod. 13. 56. 2, 59. 1. This advance force is much too large to be a *corps d'élite*, and Parke's explanation of the *epilektoi* at Athens clearly applies here: H. W. Parke, *Athens and Euboea* (London, 1929), p. 247.

17 Diod. 13. 56. 3–58, 59. 1–3.

18 Diod. 13. 59. 4–9, 61. 3.

19 Diod. 13. 60. The arrival of the ships: Diod. 13. 61. 1; provided by Pharnabazus: Xen. *Hell.* 1. 1. 25. 25 ships at Ephesus: Xen. *Hell.* 1. 2. 12; the Selinuntian ships: Xen. *Hell.* 1. 2. 10.

20 Diod. 13. 61.2; Thuc. 6. 64–66. Diod. 13. 61. 3–6.

21 Diod. 13. 62. Maurin, p. 23.

22 Diod. 13. 79. 8. Himera: Inst. di Arch., *Palermo*, Intro. 1. p. 7.

23 Thuc. 3. 68. 2–4, 5. 116. 3–4.

CHAPTER 3

1 Diod. 13. 63. 1–3; Xen. *Hell.* 1. 131; Beloch II. 1. 407.

2 Diod. 13. 63. 3–4; Stroheker, pp. 33–4.

3 Diod. 13. 63. 6.

4 Hom. *Il.* 2. 204; Hdt. 3. 80–82, esp. 82. 8–9.

5 Suidas, s.v. Philistus. Thuc. 6. 38. 1–3, 5, 39. 2, 40. 2.

6 Ar. *Pol.* 1306a 1. Hdt. 7. 154. 2.

7 Diod. 13. 75. 2–5.

8 Diod. 13. 75. 6–8.

9 Diod. 13. 75. 9: Heloris: Diod. 14. 8. 5.

10 Diod. 13. 79. 8, 80. 1–2.

11 Cyrus: Diod. 13. 69. 3; Xen. *Hell.* 1. 4. 3; Alcibiades: Diod. 13. 73. 6–74; Xen. *Hell.* 1. 5. 16–17. The rejection of peace: Diod. 13. 53; Aeschin. *De fals. leg.* 76. Athenian

embassy to Hannibal: *SEG* 10. 136; Stroheker, p. 36 and n.

12 Diod. 13. 80. 2–5, cf. 11. 20. 2.

13 Diod. 13. 79. 8, 13. 80. 6. For an indication of Hannibal's time of arrival: Diod. 13. 91. 1. Ships left at Panormus and Motya: Diod. 13. 88. 4.

14 Diod. 13. 81. 2–3, 84. 3, 85. 2–3.

15 For the luxury of the Acragantines: Diod. 13. 81. 4–84. 6, esp. 84. 5–6. Diod. 13. 86. 1–3.

16 Diod. 13. 86. 4–5. For Dionysius: Diod. 13. 96. 4, 14. 66. 5; Dem. *Lept.* 161; Polyaen. 5. 2. 2.

17 Diod. 13. 87. 1–3; Polyaen. 5. 7.

18 Diod. 13. 87. 3–5.

19 Diod. 13. 88. 1–5.

20 Diod. 13. 88. 5–8.

21 Diod. 13. 89, 90, 96. 5; Polyb. 12.25. 1–5. Warmington, pp. 99–100.

22 Diod. 13. 91. 1, 89. 4, 93.1.

CHAPTER 4

1 Diod. 13. 92. 1.

2 For Polycrates: Polyaen. 1. 23. 2; Hdt. 3. 120. 4; Berve I. 107 ff. For Peisistratus: Hdt. 1. 59. 5; Ar. *Ath. Pol.* 14. 1. For Gelon; Hdt. 7. 155. 2; Ar. *Pol.* 1302b 32.

3 Polyb. 15. 35. 6; Nepos, *De Reg.* 2. 2.

4 Youthfulness suspect: e.g., Thuc. 6. 12. 2, 13. 1, 38. 5, 39. 2; Dem. *in Mid.* 18; cf. verb, *neanieuomai* ('behave like a young idiot'), e.g. Isoc. 20. 17.

5 Criticism of Daphnaeus: Diod. 13. 87. 5, 91. 2–3.

6 Diod. 13. 91. 3; Plut. *Mor.* 175d; Xen. *Hell.* 1. 7. 8.

7 Diod. 13. 91. 4–92. 1; Ar. *Pol.* 1305a 26 (Thuc. 7. 73. 3).

8 Diod. 13. 92; Thuc. 6. 103. 3, 7. 49. 1.

9 Diod. 13. 93. 1–4, 94. 2.

10 Diod. 13. 93. 4–5, 94. 1–3.

11 Diod. 13. 94. 4–5; Ar. *Pol.* 1306a 1. Gelon as General Plenipotentiary: Diod. 11. 26. 5–6.

12 Diod. 13. 94. 5–95. 1; Plut. *Dion* 3. 2., Pl. *Ep.* 8. 353b, 354d, 356c.

13 Diod. 13. 95. 3.

14 Diod. 13. 95. 4–96. 2; Cic. *De Div.* 1. 73. At Diod. 13. 113. 1, Dionysius' foot guards number 600.

15 Diod. 13. 96. 2 (Peisistratus' proclamation, Ar. *Ath. Pol.* 15. 5).

16 Diod. 13. 96. 3. Demarchus: Thuc. 8. 85. 3; Xen. *Hell.* 1. 1. 29. Polyaen. 5. 2. 2.

CHAPTER 5

1 Diod. 13. 108. 2. For Gela: A. S. von Stauffenberg, *Trinakria* (Munich, 1963), pp. 129 ff. Ov. *Fasti* 470, cmp. Verg. *Ae.* 3. 702. Life of Aeschylus (OCT, ed. Page), p. 332, 11. 20 ff.

2 Diod. 13. 108. 2–3.

3 See Stroheker, p. 199, n. 64, for a discussion of the problem. Diod. 13. 108. 2–5. Polyb. 12. 25f, g.

4 Diod. 13. 108. 6–9.

5 Diod. 13. 109. 1–2. Stroheker, p. 44. Polyb. 12. 4a.

6 Diod. 13. 109. 3.

7 Diod. 13. 109. 4–110. 7 (author's translation).

8 Stroheker, p. 45.

9 Diod. 13. 111. 1.

10 Polyaen. 5. 7. 4.

11 Hom. *Il.* 2. 362.

12 Diod. 13. 111. 1. If (as suggested above) light-armed troops were not included in the totals reported by Diodorus, Dionysius may have had many more than 30,000 men.

13 Diod. 13. 111. 1–5.

14 Diod. 13. 112.

15 Diod. 13. 113.

16 Diod. 13. 114. Maurin, p. 36.

17 Diod. 13. 105–6; Xen. *Hell*, 2. 1. 22–28, 2. 2. 7–9; Plut. *Lys.* 10–11.

18 The revolt of the Sicels: Diod. 14. 7. 5.

19 Diod. 13. 114. 1–2.

20 For Halaesa: Diod. 14. 16. 4. Finley, p. 72, and Warmington, p. 85, for decline of Hellenism.

21 Diod. 13. 114. 2, 14. 8. 5.

22 For the Greek notion of enslavement, Thuc. 1. 141. 1. For Gelon: Hdt. 7. 153. 2–5; note that in 161. 1, he is addressed as 'King' (*basileus*). Diod. 14. 66. 1–3.

23 Diod. 14. 7. 1–3.

24 Diod. 14. 7. 4–5.

CHAPTER 6

1 Diod. 14. 7. 5–7.

2 Diod. 14. 8. 1–2.

3 Athens' surrender: Diod. 13. 107. 4; Xen. *Hell*. 2. 2. 23; Plut. *Lys.* 15. Diod. 14. 8. 3–6, 20. 78. 3; Plut. *Mor.* 783d, *Dion* 35.5; Ael. *VH* 4. 8. The 'winding-sheet' aphorism was remembered by the last ruler of Carthage, Hasdrubal: Caven, p. 290. Polyaen. 5. 8. 2.

4 Lysander: Plut. *Lys.* 13–21, *passim*. The harmosts: Thuc. 8. 5. 2; Diod. 14. 10, 1, 13; Xen. *Hell.* 2. 4. 28, 3. 5. 12–13; Plut. *Lys.* 14. Spartan refusal to destroy Athens:

Xen. *Hell.* 2. 2. 19; Andoc. *De Pace*, 26. 21. Aretas/Aristos: Diod. 14. 10. 2, 70. 3.

5 Diod. 14. 9. 1–4.

6 Diod. 14. 10. 2–3; Athen. 10. 51. 438c. Diod. 14. 9. 4–8.

7 For the 'constitutional' question: see below, ch. 9. For Peisistratus: Thuc. 6. 54. 6; Ar. *Ath. Pol.* 16. 7–9.

8 Diod. 14. 10. 4; Polyaen. 5. 2. 14.

9 Diod. 14. 9. 8–9, Polyb. 7. 2.

10 Diod. 14. 10. 4. The Campanians: Diod. 15. 3. No doubt many poor or adventurous Syracusans also took service with Dionysius. Lysander's visit (undated by our sources): Plut. *Mor.* 229e. Lysander's troubles: Diod. 14. 13. 7–8; Plut *Lys.* 18 f.; Xen *Hell.* 2. 4. 29, 36.

11 Diod. 14. 14, 15. 1, 16. 1–4. Plut. *Mor.* 855c.

12 Diod. 11. 49. 1, 14. 15. 1–3; Polyaen. 5. 2. 5, 14.

13 Diod. 15. 15. 4, 37. 5.

14 Diod. 14. 40. 1–2.

15 Diod. 14. 40. 3–7.

16 Diod. 14. 18, Stroheker, pp. 62–4.

17 See Introduction. Diod, 14. 18. 2–8. (author's translation).

18 The Athenian wall: Thuc. 1. 90. 3. *Archē* is the equivalent of the Latin *imperium*, power, and Diodorus, writing in Rome, may have had this word in mind. The ability to inspire one's subjects was regarded as kingly (*basilikos*): Xen. *Oec.* 21. 10–12.

19 Diod. 14. 41. 1. Maurin, p. 36.

20 Caven, esp. pp. 291 f.

21 Diod. 14. 41. 3–43. 4 (author's translation).

22 For the catapults: see E. W. Marsden, *Greek and Roman Artillery* (Oxford, 1969), esp. pp. 5–12, 54–6, 58–9.

23 Harden, p. 130. Diod. 14. 41. 3, 42. 2–5.

24 Diodorus (16. 70. 3) credits Dionysius with the possession in 367 of '400 triremes', and Aelian (*VH* 6. 12) improves upon this, making the ships out to be sixers and fivers. Probably by 'triremes' Diodorus there meant simply battleships. For what it is worth, Aristotle (ap. Pliny *NH* 7. 207) credits the Carthaginians with the invention of the quadrireme.

25 The 30 crack ships: Diod. 14. 55. 2, 60. 2; also 14. 103. 2. The first fiver was sent to Locri in the early summer of 397: Diod. 14. 44. 7.

26 Diod. 14. 47. 1–2. Berve I. 230; Storheker, pp. 70 and 207 (n. 62).

27 Diod. 14. 43. 4, 44. 1–2. For Lysander's

comeback: Xen. *Hell.* 3. 1–4; Plut. *Lys.* 22. Cinadon: Xen. *Hell.* 3. 4–11; Ar. *Pol.* 1306b 35.

28 Diod. 14. 41. 2. Reports of the plague: Diod. 14. 45. 3, 47. 2. For Himilco's security-mindedness: Polyaen. 5. 10. 2.

CHAPTER 7

1 Diod. 14. 44. 3–6, 107. 3. The Academy made the Rhegine rejection of Dionysius' proposal the basis of a highly defamatory story about him and the *Locrians*: Plut. *Tim.* 6. 3 f.

2 For Locri: Schol. Pind. *Pyth.* 1. 36; Diod. 11. 68. 4; Thuc. 3. 86. 2, 4. 24. 2. Diod. 14. 44. 6. King Anaxandridas: Hdt. 5. 39–40.

3 Diod. 14. 44. 7. The *Boubaris*: Phil. fr. 69 (Jacoby III B. 567). Ael. *VH* 13. 10.

4 Diod. 14. 45. 2–47. 2.

5 Diod. 14. 47. 2–3.

6 Diod. 14. 47. 4–7.

7 Diod. 14. 48. 1–2.

8 For Motya: see J. I. S. Whitaker, *Motya* (London, 1921). Cf. Diod. 13. 54. 2, 4.

9 Diod. 14. 48. 3–5, 49. 3. For the siege of Motya: Whitaker, ch. 6, pp. 75–91.

10 Diod. 14. 49. 1–2, 50. 1–4; Polyaen. 5. 2. 6; Whitaker, pp. 81–3.

11 Diod. 14. 51. 1. For the point of attack: Whitaker, p. 154.

12 Diod. 14. 51. 2–52. 4.

13 Diod. 14. 52. 5–53. 4, 22. 10. 4.

14 Diod. 14. 53. 5.

15 Leptines' character, and his probable relations with his brother, are discussed in ch. 8, 9, 12 and 13 below.

16 Diod. 14. 54.

17 Diod. 14. 55. 1–3; Polyaen. 5. 10. 2. C. H. Oldfather, in Loeb edn. of Diodorus, VI. p. 165.

18 Diod. (Loeb), VI. p. 165n. Diod. 16. 67. 2, Harden, p. 128, Caven, p. 4.

19 Diod. 14. 55. 4.

20 Diod. 14. 55. 5–7.

21 Stroheker, p. 74; Diod. 13. 54. 4, 22. 10. 4; Polyb. 1. 42. Whitaker, p. 94.

22 Diod. 14. 56. 2.

23 Diod. 14. 56. 2–57. 5. At 57. 1, Diodorus twice uses the word *apobasis*, landing, and his language clearly implies that Himilco was going to put his army ashore at Peloris and that the Messanians intended to try to prevent him.

24 Diod. 14. 57. 6–59. 4.

25 Diod. 14. 58. 1–2; Polyaen. 5. 2. 9; Front. *Strat.* 1. 8. 11. If slaves supplied the com-plete crews of the 60 ships and not just the oarsmen, the number liberated would have amounted to some 12,000.

26 Diod. 14. 59. 5–60. 6. For the early sea fights: Hdt. 1. 166; Thuc. 1. 13. 6; Justin 43. 5. 2; Paus. 10. 8. 6, 18. 6.

27 Diod. 14. 60. 7–61. 3.

28 Diod. 14. 61.4–6, 70. 5. Diod.14. 62. 2–5, 63. 4.

29 Diod. 14. 63. 3–4, 62. 1. For the location of Himilco's camp, Stroheker, pp. 208–9 (n. 92).

30 Diod. 14. 63. 4; Polyaen. 2. 11; Beloch, *Rhein. Mus.* 34. 124; Ehrenberg in *RE* XIX. 2. 1816, 4.

31 Diod 14. 63. 1–3; Polyaen. 5. 8. 1. The sea battle and the Assembly (Theodorus' oration): Diod. 14. 64–70. 3. Thuc. 2. 94. 1–2. Stroheker, pp. 77 f., also Berve I. 231.

32 Diod. 14. 70. 4–71. The Athenians had also experienced sickness on very much the same camp site, although to a less serious extent (Thuc. 7. 47. 2, Diod. 13. 12), and another Himilco was to suffer disastrously in 212: Caven, p. 172. Typhus is among the diseases suggested: Mossé, p. 111. Stroheker, p. 210 (n. 98).

33 Diod. 14. 72. 1–2.

34 Diod. 14. 72. 2–74.

35 Diod. 14. 75. 1–3. Stroheker, p. 79, appears to follow Beloch, G. *Gesch.* III. 2. 1. 60 (n. 1), in rejecting the historicity of this agreement.

36 For the hostile interpretation of Dionysius' actions; Diod. 14. 75. 2–3; cf. Diod. 15. 74. 3 and Pl. *Rep.* 566e. Thuc. 4. 62. 4, 17. 3f, 18. 4. The discontent of the mercenaries; see below, n. 38.

37 Diod. 14. 75. 4–5, 75. 5–9.

38 Diod. 14. 78. 1–3; Polyaen. 5. 2. 1.

39 Maurin, pp. 23–9, 34, 37–40, 42. Ar. *Pol.* 1272b 24 ff., 1293b 15. Diod. 14. 76. 3–4; Justin 19. 2. 7–19. 3.

40 Diod. 14. 77; Maurin, pp. 31 f., Harden, pp. 167 f. The Carthaginian and Siculo-Punic coinage: G. K. Jenkins, *Schweiz. Numis. Rundschau* 56 (1977), pp. 5–8. See also Harden, pp. 167–8, and Warmington, p. 113.

CHAPTER 8

1 Diod. 14. 78. 4–7. The Messenians: Diod. 14. 34. 2–3, 78. 5–6. Solus: A. Villa, *I Capitelli di Solunto*, (Sikelika, 1988), Intro., pp. 4–6.

2 Agesilaus' campaigns: Xen. *Hell.* 3. 4. 3–

25; Diod. 14. 79–80. The bribery: Xen. *Hell.* 3. 5. 1–2; cf. Polyaen. 1. 48. 3. The Corinthian War: Xen. *Hell.* 3. 5. 3–4. 2. 8. Diod. 14. 81–83. 2.

3 Xen. *Hell.* 4. 2. 16–23, 4. 3. 16–21; Diod. 14. 83. 1–2. The battle of Cnidus (the date is provided by the solar eclipse of 14/8/394): Xen. *Hell.* 4. 3. 10–13; Diod. 14. 83. 4–7. The collapse of the Spartan empire in the East: Xen. *Hell,* 4. 8. 1–7; Diod. 14. 84. 3–4. Conon in Greece: Xen. *Hell.* 4. 8. 7–11; Diod. 14. 84. 4–5, 85. 2–3; Dem. in *Lept.* 477 (68).

4 Xen. *Hell.* 4. 8. 10; Lys. 19. 20.

5 Conon: Xen. *Hell.* 2. 1. 29; Diod. 13. 106. 6, 14. 39. 1. The decree: Tod II. 108, 24–26. Cinesias: Lys. 21. 20, fr. 73; Arist. e.g. *Birds* 1372 ff., *Frogs* 366, *Eccles.* 330; Schol. Arist. *Frogs* 404; Plut. *De Mus.* 30.

6 Diod. 14. 85. 2; Isoc. 9. 57; Paus. 1. 3. 1; Tod II. 109; Lys. 19. 19.

7 Diod. 14. 40. 1–2, 87. 1–3, 4–88. 6.

8 Diod. 14. 90. 2–3.

9 Diod. 14. 90. 4.

10 Diod. 14. 90. 4–7.

11 Diod. 14. 95. 1–2. Agyris was a good friend to Dionysius: Diod. 14. 9. 3, 78. 7, 95. 4–7.

12 Diod. 14. 95. 3–96. 3.

13 Diod. 14. 96. 3–4, Stroheker, pp. 83 f.

14 Hellenization of the Sicels: Berve I. 247. Tauromenium: Diod. 14. 96. 4. Messana is clearly an ally of Dionysius at the end of 390: Diod. 14. 100. 5. Cf. Polyaen. 5. 2. 18.

15 For the relations between Rhegium and Locri, see above, ch. 7. The Halex frontier: Strabo 6. 260. 9.

16 Dion. Hal. *Ant. Rom.* 20. 19. 4.

17 F. W. Walbank, *A Historical Commentary on Polybius* (Oxford, 1957–), I. 225 f. (nn. 6–7); Diod. 14. 91. 1. Strab. 6. 254. 3.

18 Diod. 14. 100. 1–5. Gales are 'moderately frequent' in winter, in this region, and produce violent squalls in the Straits: *Mediterranean Pilot* I (1963), p. 26, 27 ff.

19 Thuc. 2. 67, 80. 5 f., 6. 88. 6, 8. 18, 37, 58, and nn. 3, 4, above. Xen. *Hell.* 4. 8. 12–16.

20 Diod. 14. 102. 2. Diod. 101. 1–102. 3. Cleandridas' advice: Polyaen. 2. 10. 5.

21 Diod. 14. 103. 1–3; Stroheker, pp. 115, 220 (n. 37). For the Rhegine fleet: Diod. 14. 107. 4, 103. 2–3.

22 Dionysius' supposed aims: Diod. 14. 100. 1. The Italiot army: Diod. 14. 103. 4–6. Heloris' march: Diod. 104. 1. His 'friends': Diod. 104. 3.

23 Diod. 14. 104–105.

24 Diod. 14. 106; Polyaen. 6. 11.

25 Scylletium: Strabo 6. 261. 10. Diod. 14. 107. 2–108. Dionysius' apophthegm: Plut. *Mor.* 330 f.

26 Diod. 14. 108. 3–6.

27 Diod. 14. 109; Lys. 33 (Ol). Evagoras: Diod. 14. 98, 110. 5; Xen. *Hell.* 4. 8. 24.

28 Diod. 14. 111–112.

29 Strabo 6. 258: Theophr. *Hist. of plants,* 4. 56; Pliny *NH* 12. 7; Ar. Pol. 1329b 8; Gellius 4. 1. 1. The Sila forest: Strabo 6. 260 (cf. Diod. 14. 42. 4). The wall: Strabo 6. 261.

30 Xen. *Hell.* 5. 1. 29; Diod. 14. 110. 2. Pollis: Plut. *Dion,* 5. 2. Union of Corinth and Argos: Xen. *Hell.* 4. 4. 6. Plato's misfortunes: Diod. 15. 7. 1; Plut. loc. cit. This matter is touched upon again in ch. 9.

31 *CAH* VI. 53 (M. Cary); Xen. *Hell.* 4. 8. 24, 5. 1. 6, 25, 27, 31; Diod. 14. 110.2–3.

32 Xen. *Hell.* 5. 1. 25–30.

33 Xen. *Hell.* 5. 1. 30–36. Isoc. *Paneg.* 126; Lys. 33.

34 Pl. *Ep.* 7. 326b, *Rep.* 404d. Hdt. 1. 163. 1; Stroheker, pp. 120 ff. Diod. 15. 13. 1–2. Diodorus says that Delphi was Dionysius' objective, but this must be a mistake for Dodona, in Epirus.

35 Diod. 15. 13. 1, 4; Stroheker, pp. 123–4.

36 Xen. *Hell.* 4. 7. 1, Justin 17. 3. 10f., Plut. *Pyrrh.* 1. 4, Thuc. 2. 80. 6, Tod II. 173. 4f., Diod. 14. 34. 2.

37 Diod. 15. 13. 2–3, Tod II. 123. 25, and commentary, *SIG* 154.

38 The Senones: Diod. 14. 113. 3, 115, 117. 7. The Parians: Diod. 15. 14. 1–2. Strabo 7. 315. Ancona: Stroheker, p. 125; Juv. *Sat.* 4. 40; Strabo 5. 241. Adria: Stroheker, p. 125; Theop. fr. 115 (Jacoby IIB); Plin. *NH* 3. 120, Plut. *Dion* 11. 6; Strabo 5. 212. The treaty: Justin 20. 5. 4. The Galatae and Galatea: Stroheker, p. 126; App. *Illy.* 10. 1. 2.

CHAPTER 9

1 Soph. *Ant.* 737; Aes. *Suppl.* 370 f.; Diod. 14. 65. 3. Cicerco (De Rep. 31. 43) says, of Dionysius' Syracuse, that all its greatness and beauty could not make it a *res publica* (= *polis*), 'for nothing belonged to the People and the People itself belonged to an individual'. Cf. Solon fr. 8, 10 (D.). The law as king: Pindar, fr. 169 (Loeb); Hdt. 3. 38. 8, 7. 104. 5, where Herodotus actually de-

scribes the law as *despotēs* (tyrant), since it limits a man's freedom.

2 Berve I. 129–57. Ar. *Pol.* 1310b. 30.

3 Plut. *Mor.* 782c, Dem. *De Cor.* 235. 5. Solon 3 (D.). 32; Ar. *Ath. Pol.* 16. 7.

4 Thuc. 6. 54. 6; Ar. *Ath. Pol.* 14. 3, 16. 1. The Plenipotentiary Generalship: Berve I. 236 f.; Stroheker p. 57; Tod II. 136.

5 Arist. *Knights*, 40 ff. The legitimization of the regime: Stroheker, p. 96. Solon 24. 3 (D.).

6 Diod. 14. 9. 5–9. Cf. Pl. *Ep.* 8. 353b.

7 Polyaen. 5. 2. 14. The mutiny: Diod. 14. 96. 2.

8 Stroheker, pp. 161–7. Ar. *Oec.* 1345b. 30 f. Ar. *Pol.* 1313b 22, *Oec.* 1346a, 30 f.

9 Ar. *Oec.* 1349a. 25, 1349b. 5. Polyaen. 5. 2. 19; Ar. *Oec.* 1349b. 1. *Esphorai* in wartime Athens: Thuc. 3. 19. 1, and A. W. Gomme, *Historical Commentary on Thucydides* (Oxford, 1945–6), II. 278 f. (19). For a levy voted by the Potidaeans: Ar. *Oec.* 1347a. 15. Diod. 13. 106. 3, Justin 21. 1. 5. Pl. *Ep.* 7. 329e. For Dion's remark: Ar. *Oec.* 1344b. 35. Plut. *Mor.* 175e, Ar. *Pol.* 1259a. 23.

10 Two important sources of information about State borrowing from the gods are Tod I. 51A, 3 ff. and Tod I. 64. See also R. E. Meritt, *Athenian Financial Documents of the Fifth Century* (Michigan, 1932), ch. 5, pp. 57 ff. Thuc. 1. 121. 3, 2. 13. 4–5, Plut. *Per.* 31. Ar. *Oec.* 1247a. 25, 1346b. 10. The lawlessness of tyrants: e.g. Eur. *Suppl.* 429 ff.; Hdt. 3. 80. 5; their impiety: Pl. *Rep.* 568d, e. Dionysius' impiety: Ael. *VH* 1. 20; Plut. *Mor.* 379d; Athen. 15. 693e; Polyaen. 5. 2. 19; Ar. *Oec.* 1353b. 20.; Cic. *De Nat. Deor.* 3. 34. 83f. For Dionysius' offerings to Delphi and Olympia: Diod. 16. 57. 2 f. Cf. Paus. 6. 2. 6. Lacinian Hera: Athen. 12. 541b. Eileithyia: see below, ch. 10.

11 Devaluation: Ar. *Oec.* 1349a. 30, 1349b. 25. The women's ornaments: Ar. *Oec.* 1349a. 10.

12 Ar. *Oec.* 1349a. 35, b. 15. Clazomenae etc.: Ar. *Oec.* 1348b. 15, 1350a. 20, 1349a. 5, 1347a. 30. The Segestans: Thuc. 6. 46. 3–4. The coinage: Berve I. 240.

13 Nepos *De Reg.* 2. 2; Plut. *Mor.* 338b. Polyaen. 5. 2. 13; Ar. *Pol.* 1313b. 13; Plut. *Dion* 28, *Mor.* 523a. Polyaen. 5. 2. 1. Polyaenus also describes the discovery of a plot and the execution of the plotters, 5. 2. 15. Diodorus says simply that before 398, Dionysius had been in the habit of banishing people and putting them to death: Diod. 14. 70. 3.

14 Pl. *Rep.* 566e–569b, 579b.

15 Plato at Locri: Cic. *De Fin.* 5. 87. Pl. *Ep.* 7. 326e; Plut. *Dion* 4. 2. Hipparinus: Pl. *Ep.* 8. 353b, 354d; Plut. *Dion* 3. 2. Plato's meeting with Dionysius: Diod. 15. 7; Plut. *Mor.* 471e, *Dion* 5. 1–3; Diog. Laert. 3. 18, Olymp. *Vit. Pl.* 5. The *Vita* would date Plato's sojourn at Syracuse to the summer of 388 (the Olympic year), and this dating is followed by Stroheker, p. 100 and p. 216 (n. 85). However, I find it easier to answer the question, Why did Pollis go to Aegina and not to Gythium, on the completion of his mission? (i.e. he was on his way to the Hellespont), if we suppose that he sailed from Sicily in the late spring or early summer of 387. For the idea of the philosopher king: Pl. *Ep.* 7. 324b–326b.

16 Diod. 15. 7. 3–4. Pl. *Rep.* 567b. For Leptines' popularity: Aen. Tact. 10. 21–2. Plut. *Dion* 11. 3. For the flight of Polyxenus, Plut. *Dion* 21. 4.

17 There may or may not be some significance in the fact that Polyaenus, describing the discovery of a plot (5. 2. 15), actually refers to Dionysius' return *from Italy*. Diod. 15. 7. 4, cf. Plut. *Dion* 11. 3–4.

18 Thuc. 6. 53. 2, 60. The total 11 does not take into account the absurd story of the children of Aristides the Locrian (Plut. *Tim.* 6. 3 f.). Diod. 15. 7. 3. Marsyas: Plut. *Dion* 9. 5; the sentry: ibid. 4; the barber: ibid. 3, also Plut. *Mor.* 508 f., Cic. *Tusc.* 5. 58; the young men: Cic. *Tusc.* 5. 60, *Plut. Mor.* 176a. Antiphon: Ar. *Rhet.* 1385a. 5; Plut. *Mor.* 833b, 1051c; Philostr. *De Vit. Soph.* 500. Leon: Ael. *VH* 13. 34.

19 Plut. *Dion* 5. 4. Philistus' hope of pardon: Paus. 1. 13. 9.

20 Envy: Hdt. 3. 80. 28. Dionysius' mother-in-law: Plut. *Dion* 3. 3. For *pharmaka*: Dem. 23. 22, Ar. *Ath. Pol.* 57. 3. Pl. *Rep.* 567b, f. For Dion's position at Court: Plut. *Dion* 4. 1, 5. 4; Nepos *Dion* 2; Pl. *Ep.* 7. 327.

21 Thrasybulus' advice: Hdt. 5. 92. 23–7; Ar. *Pol.* 1311a. 20 1284a. 26 ff. (roles reversed). For the attitude of the old Athenian aristocracy: Thuc. 6. 89. 4–6. Dionysius' attempts to win over the aristocracy: Diod. 14. 9. 1, 6, 8.

22 Plut. *Dion* 9. 2, 10. 1, Pl. *Ep.* 7. 332d. Dionysius II's bad eyesight: Athen. 6. 249 f., Ael. *VH* 6. 12; Plut. *Mor.* 53 f. His debauchery: Plut. *Dion* 7. 2–4, *Mor.* 175e; Ael. *VH* 2. 41. See also chs. 11 and 12 below.

23 Pl. *Ep.* 7. 331e–332c. The tyrannical nature of the Athenian Empire could not be

gainsaid by anyone who agreed with 'Pericles'' definition of slavery: Thuc. 1. 141. 1, and it is expressly proclaimed at Thuc. 3. 37. 2 and implied at Thuc. 2. 63. 2. That a section of a subject community (the Demos) in many cases found it tolerable for reasons of domestic politics hardly disproves its essentially tyrannical nature. See A. Powell, *Athens and Sparta* (London, 1988), ch. 3. For governors: Pl. *Ep.* 7. 331e f.

24 Berve I. 246f., 258f.; Stroheker, p. 179; Finley, p. 86. The fair treatment of the cities: Diod. 15. 15. 1. Political executions by the Athenians, e.g. at Mytilene: Thuc. 3. 50. 1, and Scione: Thuc. 4. 122. 6, 5. 32. 1. For the political instability of the Sicilians: Thuc. 6. 17. 2, 38. 3; Diod. 11. 86. 3–87. 5. There was fighting between Syracuse and Acrages Prior to 317: Diod. 19. 3. 1. The fall of Thurii: Diod. 16. 15. 2.

25 *Mogis esōthē*: Pl. *Ep.*7. 332c.

26 Plut. *Per.* 7. 5.

27 There are references to Dionysius' judicial activity in, e.g., Plut. *Mor.* 175f, 176e, 56e. The mildness of his rule: Diod. 14. 45. 1, 69. 3. For the *eunoia* of the Syracusans: Diod. 15. 74. 5.

CHAPTER 10

1 Stroheker, pp. 119 f. Plut. *Dion* 11. 4. Jacoby III B. 568 f.

2 The archetype: 'codices – utrosque – ex archetypo iam degenere derivatos,' Teubner, p. xxi (Vogel). Dion. Hal., Thuc. 3. 9.

3 Diod. 15. 14. 4, 15. 1–4; 25. 1–3.

4 Justin 20. 5. 1–7, 10. Polyaen. 6. 16. 1, 5. 10. 5. Ael. *VH* 12. 61. Dion. Hal. 20. 7. 3. Strabo 6. 261. Diod. 15. 46. 2; Beloch III 2. 2. 376 ff.; Stroheker, p. 233 (n. 30). Diod. 15. 37. 3.

5 Harden, pp. 163–4; Hdt. 1. 166. 1–2; Ar. *Pol.* 1280a 36; Polyb. 3. 22. 4f and Welbank, *Commentary* I. 339–45. For Hiero's raid: Diod. 11. 51. 1–2, Pind. *Pyth.* 1. 72 ff. The Syracusan raid: Diod. 11. 88. 4–5. Etruscan aid to Athens: Thuc. 6. 88. 6, 103. 2.

6 Diod. 15. 14. 3; Livy 5. 40, 7. 20; Hdt. 1. 166. 1. Strabo 5. 226 – Strabo speaks of Dionysius sacking the temple 'on his way to Corsica'. Ar. *Oec.* 1349b. 33 f., Polyaen. 5. 2. 21 and Ael. *VH* 1. 20 call the goddess Leucothea. For Pyrgi, see G. Colonna *et al.*, *Le Lamine di Pyrgi* (1970), and *Pyrgi* (1973), Also *Etruscan Cities*, ed. F. Coarelli (London, 1973).

7 Diod. 15. 14. 3; Ar. *Oec.* and Polyaen., loc. cit. (n. 6). Thuc. 6. 43. 2, 2. 56. 1–2.

8 Diod. 15. 14. 4, Strabo, loc. cit.

9 Diod. 15. 15. 1. Himera: Polyaen. 5. 2. 10 (Front. 3. 4. 4); Tim. fr. 29, 24 (Jacoby IIIB. 608), Aen Tact. 10. 21–2.

10 For *syntaxeis*: Isoc. *Peace*, 29, *Antid.* 123, *Areop.* 2. Diod. 15. 15. 2.

11 Strabo 6. 261. Justin 20. 5. 1–7; Pl. *Laws* 638b; Justin 21. 2. 9. Ael. *VH* 12. 61.

12 Hdt. 7. 189, cf. Pl. *Phaedr.* 229c. Ael. *VH* 13. 45; Plut. *Mor.* 338b. Plut. *Dion* 6. 1; Diod. 15. 7. 4.

13 It is to this period that the rebuilding of Selinus' walls may be dated: Stroheker, p. 130. Diod. 15. 15. 2. Diod. 15. 23. 5.

14 Diod. 15. 24. Diod. 14. 107. 2; Dion Hal. 20. 7. 3.

15 Diod. 15. 24. 2.

16 Aen. Tact. 10. 21–2; Stroheker, p. 130. During the early '80s Dionysius was at peace with Carthage (the overlord of Himera) and heavily involved in Italy, and therefore, I believe, unlikely to have wanted to antagonize Carthage by seizing and garrisoning Himera.

17 Dion. Hal. 20. 7. 3; Livy 24. 3. Polyaen. 5. 2. 22; Diog. Laert. 8. 46; Stroheker, pp. 229 f. (n. 139).

18 Polyaen. 6. 16. 1 – the battle was clearly some distance from the coast. Diod. 15. 15. 3.

19 Diod. 15. 15. 4–16. 2; Polyaen. 6. 16. 1.

20 For Masinissa's success: Caven, pp. 269 f.

21 For Himilco: see Polyaen. 5. 10. 5, 6. 16. 3.

22 Polyaen. loc. cit.

23 Diod. 15. 16. 3–17. 4.

24 Diod. 15. 17. 5.

25 Diod. loc. cit. For Heraclea: Diod. 16. 9. 4; Plut. *Dion 25.* 5. Himera belonged to Carthage under Timoleon's 'Halycus line' treaty: Diod. 19. 71. 7, Cf. Stroheker, p. 135. Pl. *Ep.* 7. 333a.

CHAPTER 11

1 For the events of this decade: see S. Hornblower, *The Greek World, 479–323 B. C.* (London, 1983), ch. 15. For Timotheus: Xen. *Hell.* 5. 4. 63 ff.; Diod. 15. 36. 5; Tod II. 126, and p. 67.

2 Diod. 15. 38, 45. 2–4; Tod II. 123, pp. 62, 67; Diod. 15. 46. 2; Xen. *Hell.* 6. 2. 4.

3 Diod. 15. 47. 1–7; Xen. *Hell.* 6. 2. 2–38. Capture of the ships: Diod. 15. 47. 7; Xen. *Hell.* 6. 2. 36; Polyaen. 3. 9. 55. Only Diodorus mentions Cissidas, who, if he did

take part in this ill fated expedition, certainly returned safely to Syracuse. Diod. 16. 57. 2–3.

4 Diod. 15. 50. 4–5; Xen. *Hell.* 6. 3. 12; Plut. *Ages.* 28. For Leuctra: Diod. 15. 51–6; Xen. *Hell.* 6. 4. 2–15; Plut. *Pel.* 20–23. The renewal of peace: Xen. *Hell.* 6. 5. 1.

5 Xen. *Hell.* 6. 5. 6 ff.; Diod. 15. 65–66. 1. Xen. *Hell.* 6. 5. 33 f., 49; Diod. 15. 63. 2, 65. 6, 67. Plut. *Ages.* 32. 8. The alliance: Xen. *Hell.* 7. 1. 14; Diod. 15. 67. 1. Xen. *Hell.* 7.1. 15–19; Diod. 15. 68. 1–69. 4.

6 Xen. *Hell.* 7. 20–22; Diod. 15. 70. 1, Plut. *Mor.* 191e. Tod II. 133, cf. comm. p. 104.

7 Xen. *Hell.* 7. 1. 27; Diod. 15. 70. 2; Tod, loc. cit; *Marm. Par.* 71.

8 Xen. *Hell.* 7. 1. 28–32; Diod. 15. 72. 3; Plut. *Ages.* 33.

9 Diod. 15. 73. 1. Justin 20. 5. 11.

10 Diod. 15. 73. 2 – there were many troops in Lilybaeum. Justin 20. 5. 11–12; Polyaen. 5. 9.

11 Diod. 15. 73. 2–4; Justin 20. 5–12.

12 Diod. loc. cit. Isoc. *Ep. Phil.* 65–Dionysius was master of all the Greek cities of Sicily.

13 Isoc. *Paneg.* 126, *Ep. Dion* 7–8. Stroheker, p. 143.

14 Diod. 15. 74. 1–2; A. Nauck, *Trag. Gr. Fr.* 2. 794.

15 Tod II. 136; Stroheker, p. 235f. (n. 72). For the wording of the treaty, compare Tod I. 72, Thuc. 5. 47. 3, Tod II. 127, 133.

16 Tod II. 127.

17 Xen. *Hell.* 7. 1. 37.

18 Diod. 15. 73. 5, 74. 1–4; Stroheker, p. 237 (n. 83). Cicero, *De Nat. Deor.* 3. 35. 84, in a passage in other respects replete with absurdities, notes that Dionysius died in his bed, an easy death. By 343, Demosthenes, apparently, could compare the threat to Athens' interest posed by his rival, Aeschines, to that posed by Dionysius: Aeschin. *De fals. leg.* 10.

19 Plut. *Dion* 5. 4, 17. 4, 6. 2. cf. Justin 20. 5. 14.

CHAPTER 12

1 Berve I. 260–81. Plut. *Dion* 9. 2, 7. 2–4, 10. 1. Pl. *Ep.* 7 330a, 335d–336d.

2 Plut. *Mor.* 176e; Ael. *VH* 12. 60; Plut. *Mor.* 338b.

3 For Phoibia: Strabo 6. 258.

4 Diod. 15. 74. 5, 16. 6; Plut. *Dion* 1–11. For Damocles: Athen. 6. 250a. f.

5 Plut. *Dion* 6. 3–4, 14. 3.

6 Plut. *Dion* 11. 2–16. 3. Pl. *Ep.* 7. 328c–330a; Plut. *Mor.* 52d. The war: Diod.

16. 5. 2. Timocrates' expedition: Xen. *Hell.* 7. 4. 12. Sellasia: Diod. 15. 64. 1; Xen. *Hell.* 6. 5. 27.

7 Plut. *Dion* 15. 3, 17. 1–5, 18. Pl. *Ep.* 7. 338a–339b.

8 Plut. *Dion* 19–21; Pl. *Ep.* 7. 339b–350b. Diod. 16. 6. 5. For Damocles' embassy: Polyaen. 5. 46.

9 Pl. *Ep.* 7. 350c–d; Plut. *Dion* 22–29. 3; Diod. 16. 9–10; Ar. *Pol.* 1312a 4, 34.

10 Diod. 16. 11–13, 16–20; Plut. *Dion* 29. 4–50. Polyaen. 5. 2. 8; Justin 21. 2. 9–10; Ael. *VH* 9. 8.

11 Diod. 16. 31. 7, 36. 5, 45. 9; Justin 21. 3; Plut. *Dion* 51–58, *Tim.* 1–3; Strabo 6. 259–260; Ael. *VH* 9. 8; Athen. 10. 436a. Athenaeus (11. 508e), states that Callippus *was* a desciple of Plato. For the Brettii: Strabo 6. 255. 4.

12 See Berve II. 760, also p. 651.

13 For Timoleon: Diod. 16. 65–90, passim; Plut. *Tim*; R. J. A. Talbert, *Timoleon and the Revival of Greek Sicily*, 344–317 B. C. (Cambridge, 1974). Dionysius' retirement: Lucian, *The dream*, 23; Plut. *Mor.* 176d, *Tim.* 13. 4–15. 6; Ael. *VH* 12. 60; Diod. 16. 70. 1–3.

CHAPTER 13

1 Stroheker, pp. 12–28, esp. pp. 23 f.

2 Arist. *Plut.* 550; Ephippus: F. Meineke, *Fr. Poet. Com. Med.*, p. 335; Eubulus: ibid. p. 217; Strat. fr. 6 (Kock).

3 Philoxenus: Athen. 1. 6e; Diod. 15. 6; Ael. *VH* 12. 44; Plut. *Mor.* 334c, 471e; Schol. Arist. *Plut.* 290; Paus. 1. 2. 3. According to Aelian, the most beautiful of the caverns was named after Philoxenus. This, I imagine, was the cavern to which Caravaggio gave its present name, The Ear of Dionysius.

4 Thuc. 7. 81. 4, 86. 2. In Cicero's day, the caverns were used by the Syracusans as State prisons (probably for those awaiting trial and for debtors). Cicero attributes their excavation to 'kings and tyrants' in *Verr.* 2. 5. 68), or, sepecifically, to Dionysius (ibid. 143). See also Varro, *L.L.* 5. 151. No doubt it was to the myth of Philoxenus' incarceration that Dionysius owed this attribution. Justin (21. 1. 5) speaks of 3,000 people held in prison, at the end of Dionysius' reign (and released by his son), but the whole passage contains serious errors of fact and this statement is probably quite false.

5 Plut. *Mor.* 855c; Paus. 1. 13. 9; Plut. *Dion* 36. Jacoby III B. 568 (no. 558), 576 (no. 562), 574 (no. 561), 568 (no. 559); Athen.

3. 98d; Diod. 16. 71. 3.

6 Eur. *Suppl.* 429. Peisistratus: Diog. Laert. 1. 108, 122. Hdt. 3. 80–82. Aes. *Suppl.* 365 ff., 397 ff., 942 ff.; Eur. *Suppl.* 399 ff., *Ion* 621 ff. Xen. *Mem.* 4. 6. 12, *Oec.* 21. 12. cf. Isoc. *Nic.*

7 Stroheker, e.g. p. 98.

8 Solon fr. 8 (D), 3–4, 10. 3–4, 23. 8 ff., 21 ff. Hdt. 3. 80; Eur. *Suppl.* 429–444, *Ion* 621 ff. The same themes – that of the suspiciousness, rapacity and envy of tyrants – is echoed by Xenophon, *Hiero* 4–5.

9 Plato's malignity: Athen. 11. 504e–507b. The story of Plato's visit to Syracuse: Sext. Emp. *Pyrrh.* 3. 204; Athen. 11. 507b; Diog. Laert. 3. 18 f. Stroheker, p. 106. Plut. *Dion* 3–8, 11, *passim.*

10 Plut. *Dion* 11–13, *passim.*

11 *Megalopsychia:* Isoc. 9. 3; Ar. *Eth. Nic.* 1123b, 1124b, 1125a; Pl. *Alc.* 2. 140c. 9, 150c. 8; Dem. *De Cor.* 67. Plut. *Dion* 8; cf. also Xen. *Hell.* 5. 2. 28. The attractiveness of tyranny: e.g. Hdt. 3. 5; Eur. *Ion* 622, *Iph. Aul.* 20; *Pel.* 605 (Nauck); Solon fr. 23 (D) 1–7.

12 Plut. *Dion* 17. 22. Dionysius' cowardice: Plut. *Dion* 9. 5; Cic. *De Off.* 2. 25; Philo *De Prov.* 2. 26 ff. His bad conscience: Plut. *Mor.* 1090e. For the lengths to which Cicero could go without reflection, see *De Nat. Deor.* 3. 35. 84. Cic. *Tusc.* 5. 58–63; Plut. *Mor.* 508 f., Diod. 20. 63. 3; Plut. *Mor.* 338b. Dionysius' mother: Ael. *VH.* 13. 45. The Woman of Himera: Schol. Aesch. 2. 10, Val. Max. 1. 7. 6 (Jacoby III B. 608). The high tower: Cic. *Tusc.* 5. 59. For Antiphon, See ch. 9.

13 Plut. *Tim.* 6. 4, Plut. *Mor.* 333 f. Cic. *Tusc.* 5. 63. Aristippus: Athen. 11. 507b, 544a–f, 546e, 565d, 588e, 599b; Sext. Emp. *Pyrrh.* 3. 204; Lucian, *The Parasite,* 32, 33; Stob. *Flor.* 1. 117. The Sword of Damocles: Cic. *Tusc.* 5. 61 f., Timaeus, fr. 32 (Jacoby III B. 610). Damon and Phintias: Cic. *De Off.* 3. 10. 45, *Tusc.* 5. 63; Diod. 10. 4. 3. Stroheker, p. 20; Henry Cecil, *Independent Witness* p. 172.

14 Jacoby III B. 581 ff. Diod. 21. 17. 1, Plut. *Dion* 35. 5–36. 1. Diod. 21. 17. 4; Jos. *Cont. Ap.* 1. 14; Plut. *Nic.* 1; Paus. 1. 13. 9.

15 Diod. 15. 6–7, 74. 1–4. The fourth anecdote – On the familiar 'fear of barbers' theme – is to be found well outside the Dionysiac period, told apropos of Agathocles. But Diodorus specifically rejects Timaeus as a reliable source for Agathocles. Diod. 20. 63. 3, 21. 17. 3. Stroheker, p. 78, also

pp. 16 f.

16 Phaenias: see *RE* XIX. 2. 1565 ff. s.v. Phainias (R. Laqueur). Cic. *Brut.* 42. Pliny *Ep.* 3. 5. 10. Cic. *Ad QF* 2. 11. 4, *Brut.* 66. Criticism of Philistus: Dion. Hal., most conveniently in Jacoby III B. 555 (16); Quint., ibid. (15).

17 Dionysius' appearance: Tim. fr. 29, 1. 7 (Jacoby III B. 608 [29]), Val. Max. 1. 7. 6. Cic. *Tusc.* 5. 57, 60; Polyb. 15. 35. 6. Nepos, *De Reg.* 2. 2. Ael. *VH* 13. 18; Suidas, s.v. Dionysios: it is, of course, not impossible that Suidas has confused the tyrant with the Dionysius of Sinopē mentioned by, e.g., Athenaeus (14. 615e). Athen. 6. 249e, 1. 6ef. His feasts: Diod. 14. 42. 1, 70. 3; Eubul, (Meineke, p. 217). cf. Isoc. *Ep. Dion.* 4 Suidas, loc. cit., cf. Diod. 13. 95. 5; Ael. *VH* 11. 11; Cic. *Tusc.* 5. 63. Plut. *Mor.* 333 f.

18 Philistus' picture of Dionysius: Diod. 15. 18. 6 f. Hom. *Il.* 12. 310–321.

19 Stroheker, p. 177. Tychē: e.g. Archil. fr. 16; Eur. *El.* 890 f., Thuc. 5. 104; Lys. 30. 18; Dem. 2. 22, 18. 208. Dionysius' mother's dream: Cic. *De Div.* 1. 39. Cypselus: Hdt 5. 92. 7 ff. Phalaris: Cic. *De Div.* 1. 23, 2. 66. Peisistratus: Hdt. 1. 59. 1–4. Pericles: Plut. *Per.* 3. 2; Hdt. 6. 131. 2. The Dionysophoroi at Syracuse: Hesych s.v. Ar. *Pol.* 1314b. 39 f.

20 Cic. *Tusc.* 5 58. Definition of Justice: Lys. 9. 20, Pl. *Rep.* 334b; first adumbrated in Solon 1. 5 f (D). See K. J. Dover, *Greek Popular Morality in the Time of Plato and Aristotle* (Oxford, 1974), p. 180. W. W. Jaeger, *Paideia,* 3 vols. (1934–47), I. 296. Hom. *Il.* 9. 443. Jaeger, op.cit., I. 9.

21 Tyrt. 6, 7 (D.), 9 (D.), esp. 23 ff. Aes. *Sept.* 610, *Theog.* 147. Jaeger, op. cit., I. 92–3.

22 Hom. *Il.* 18. 502–8; *politikē technē:* Democr. fr. 157 (H. Diels, Vorsokratiker). Pl. *Prot.* 319a, *Gorg.* 521d; Arist. *Clouds* 889 ff. Thuc. 6. 38. 5.

23 Hom. *Il.* 6. 208. Ar. *Pol.* 1253a 1–20. Plut. *Mor.* 338c.

24 Plut. *Mor.* 782c, 176a, 175e. Ibid., 175d. Ar. *Oec.* 1344b 35. Dion's position at Court: Plut. *Dion* 4. 1, 5. 4. For the synedrion in 367: Plut. *Dion* 6. 3. The 'adamantine bonds': e.g. Plut. *Dion* 10. 3, cf. Ael. *VH* 6. 12.

25 Diod. 15. 6–7, 14. 109. 2. On Dionysius' poetry: Diod. 15. 74. 4; Athen. 11. 482d; Lucian *Adv. indoct.* 15. For the fragments: Nauck, *Trag. Gr. Fr.,* 793–6. Ar. *Poet.* 1449a. Tzetzes, *Chil.* 5. 180.

26 Ar. *Poet.* 1455a 32. Sophocles' generalship;

Plut. *Per.* 8, Strabo 14. 638. Ar. *Poet.* 1450a 25, 1450b7, 1458a 21. Athen. 3. 98d.

27 Diod. 15. 6. 1. Visitors at Court: Berve I. 252; Stroheker, pp. 99 f.

28 Nepos *De Reg.* 2. 2; Cic. *Tusc.* 5. 57. Pl. *Ep.* 7. 332a. Hipparinus: Ar. *Pol.* 1305b 39f. Dion: Plut. *Dion* 6. 4. Dionysius' wives: Ael. *VH* 13. 10. Cic. *Tusc.* 5. 60; Athen. 1. 6e.

29 Dionysius' sons: Diod. 16. 16. 2; Tod II. 133. 19 ff. Athen 6. 249 f., Plut. *Mor.* 53 f., 338b; Ael. *VH* 6. 12.

30 Justin 21. 1; Diod. 16. 36. 5; Plut. *Tim.* 1. 2. The Peisistratids: Thuc. 6. 53. 3, 54. 5 f.; Ar. *Ath. Pol.* 17. 2, 18. 1.

31 Theste: Diod. 13. 96. 3; Plut. *Dion* 21. 4. Arete and Sophrosyne: Plut. *Dion* 6. 1; Dicaeosyne: Diod. 15. 7. 4.

32 Peltasts: Nepos *Iphic.* 1. 2 ff.; Diod. 15. 44, *RE* XIX. 1. 403 ff. (F. Lammert), Pl. *Ep.* 7. 348b, 349c, 350a.

33 Berve I. 256.

34 Criticism of Dionysius' readiness to retreat: Diod. 14. 66, 68, 75. 2–3, 96. 2, 15. 74. 3; cf. Pl. *Rep.* 566e.

35 Remember Archidamus' reaction to Dionysius' 'mechanized warfare'. Plut *Mor.* 191e.

For the Greek attitude to war: Pind. fr. 110 (Loeb); cf. Thuc. 4. 59. 2–4, 1. 141. 1.

36 Isoc. *Ep. Phil.* 65; Plut. *Mor.* 552e, cf. Pl. *Ep.* 7. 333a, 336a; Diod. 14. 66, Pl. *Ep.* 8. 353a, f.

37 Plat. *Ep.* 7. 331e, 332c, 333a. Dion. Hal. *Ant. Rom.* 20. 7. 2. Of Pericles: Thuc. 2. 65. 9. Of Philip: Dem. *Ol.* 2. 3, 15; *De Cor.* 67, 68; *De Fals. Leg.* 67; Plut. *Alex.* 4. 3.

38 Stroheker, p. 183 f., Berve I. 259f.

39 Dionysius' tyranny represented the victory of the political individualism that was the contemporary tendency in Greece: Stroheker, p. 176. Jason of Pherae: Xen. *Hell.* 6. 1. 4–16; Diod. 15. 60. 1.

40 Isoc. *Ep. Phil.* 119, Ep. Dion 7. Plut. *Tim.* 15. 4, *Mor.* 176a.

41 Plut. *Alex.* 8. 3. V. Ehrenberg, *Alexander and the Greeks* (Oxford, 1938), ch. 2. Plut. *Alex.* 5, 6. 5.

42 Polyb. 15. 35. 6. Selinus belonged to the Epicraty after Dionysius II's conclusion of peace with Carthage and in the third century we find Acragas the ally of Carthage; Polyb. 1. 17. 5.

43 Polyb. 12. 23. 7, on the relative unimportance of Sicilian affairs.

INDEX

This index is selective, in that items of very minor or only incidental interest have been omitted from it, and of the items noted some occurrences have been deemed of insufficient importance to be recorded. The spelling of the names of persons and places follows the 'traditional' pattern, Greek words being usually, albeit not wholly consistently, latinized. In the case of towns and cities, the modern equivalent (or approximate equivalent) is given, except where familiarity renders this unnecessary.

INDEX